CONSTITUTIONAL CHALLENGES IN THE ALGORITHMIC SOCIETY

New technologies have always challenged the social, economic, legal, and ideological status quo. Constitutional law is no less impacted by such technologically driven transformations, as the state must formulate a legal response to new technologies and their market applications, as well as the state's own use of new technology. In particular, the development of data collection, data mining, and algorithmic analysis by public and private actors present unique challenges to public law at the doctrinal as well as the theoretical level. This collection, aimed at legal scholars and practitioners, describes the constitutional challenges created by the algorithmic society. It offers an important synthesis of the state of play in law and technology studies, addressing the challenges for fundamental rights and democracy, the role of policy and regulation, and the responsibilities of private actors. This title is also available as Open Access on Cambridge Core.

Hans-W. Micklitz is Professor of Economic Law at the Robert Schuman Centre for Advanced Studies at European University Institute, Florence and Finland Distinguished Professor at the University of Helsinki.

Oreste Pollicino is Full Professor of Constitutional Law at Bocconi University and Member of the Executive Board, European Agency for Fundamental Rights.

Amnon Reichman is Full Professor of Constitutional Law at the University of Haifa.

Andrea Simoncini is Full Professor of Constitutional Law at the University of Florence.

Giovanni Sartor is Professor of Legal Informatics at the University of Bologna and Professor of Legal Informatics and Legal Theory at the European University Institute of Florence.

Giovanni De Gregorio is a Postdoctoral Researcher at the Centre for Socio-Legal Studies at the University of Oxford.

Constitutional Challenges in the Algorithmic Society

Edited by

HANS-W. MICKLITZ
European University Institute

ORESTE POLLICINO
Bocconi University

AMNON REICHMAN
University of Haifa

ANDREA SIMONCINI
University of Florence

GIOVANNI SARTOR
European University Institute

GIOVANNI DE GREGORIO
University of Oxford

CAMBRIDGE
UNIVERSITY PRESS

CAMBRIDGE
UNIVERSITY PRESS

Shaftesbury Road, Cambridge CB2 8EA, United Kingdom

One Liberty Plaza, 20th Floor, New York, NY 10006, USA

477 Williamstown Road, Port Melbourne, VIC 3207, Australia

314–321, 3rd Floor, Plot 3, Splendor Forum, Jasola District Centre, New Delhi – 110025, India

103 Penang Road, #05–06/07, Visioncrest Commercial, Singapore 238467

Cambridge University Press is part of Cambridge University Press & Assessment, a department of the University of Cambridge.

We share the University's mission to contribute to society through the pursuit of education, learning and research at the highest international levels of excellence.

www.cambridge.org
Information on this title: www.cambridge.org/9781108823890

DOI: 10.1017/9781108914857

First published 2022
First paperback edition 2024

A catalogue record for this publication is available from the British Library

Library of Congress Cataloging-in-Publication data
NAMES: Micklitz, Hans-W., editor. | Pollicino, Oreste, editor. | Reichman, Amnon, 1967– editor. | Simoncini, Andrea (Law professor), editor. | Sartor, Giovanni, editor. | De Gregorio, Giovanni, editor.
TITLE: Constitutional challenges in the algorithmic society / edited by Hans Wolfgang Micklitz, European University Institute, Florence; Oreste Pollicino, Bocconi University; Amnon Reichman, University of California, Berkeley; Andrea Simoncini, University of Florence; Giovanni Sartor, European University Institute, Florence; Giovanni De Gregorio, Bocconi University.
DESCRIPTION: Cambridge, United Kingdom ; New York, NY : Cambridge University Press, 2022.
IDENTIFIERS: LCCN 2021017246 (print) | LCCN 2021017247 (ebook) | ISBN 9781108843126 (hardback) | ISBN 9781108823890 (paperback) | ISBN 9781108914857 (ebook)
SUBJECTS: LCSH: Constitutional law – Decision making. | Artificial intelligence – Law and legislation. | Legislation. | Judicial process. | Algorithms – Social aspects.
CLASSIFICATION: LCC K3165 .C5869 2022 (print) | LCC K3165 (ebook) | DDC 342–dc23
LC record available at https://lccn.loc.gov/2021017246
LC ebook record available at https://lccn.loc.gov/2021017247

ISBN 978-1-108-84312-6 Hardback
ISBN 978-1-108-82389-0 Paperback

Contents

Figures

Contributors

Editors

Giovanni De Gregorio, Postdoctoral researcher, Centre for Socio-Legal Studies, University of Oxford

Hans-W. Micklitz, Professor of Economic Law, European University Institute

Oreste Pollicino, Professor of Constitutional Law, Bocconi University

Amnon Reichman, Professor of Constitutional Law, University of Haifa

Giovanni Sartor, Professor of Philosophy of Law, University of Bologna and European University Institute

Andrea Simoncini, Professor of Constitutional Law, University of Florence

Authors

Yaiza Cabedo, Policy Officer, European Security and Markets Authority

Federica Casarosa, Research Fellow, European University Institute

Celine Castest-Renard, Professor of Private Law, University of Ottawa

Mariavittoria Catanzariti, Research Fellow, European University Institute

Damian Clifford, Postdoctoral Researcher in Law, Australian National University

Angela Daly, Professor of Law, University of Strathclyde

Francesca Galli, Research Fellow, European University Institute

Serge Gijrath, Professor of Law, University of Leiden

Thilo Hagendorff, Lecturer in Media and Technology, University of Tübingen

Li Hui, Associate Research Fellow, Shanghai Institute for Science of Science

Jacob Livingston Slosser, Carlsberg Postdoctoral Fellow, University of Copenhagen

Erik Longo, Professor of Constitutional Law, University of Florence

Monique Mann, Senior Lecturer in Criminology, Deakin University

Vidushi Marda, Senior Programme Officer, ARTICLE 19

Henrik Palmer Olsen, Professor of Jurisprudence, University of Copenhagen

Francesco Paolo Patti, Professor of Private Law, Bocconi University

Frank Pasquale, Professor of Law, Brooklyn School of Law

Pietro Sirena, Professor of Private Law, Bocconi University

Viltė Kristina Dessers, Research Associate, KU Leuven

Thomas Troels Hildebrandt, Professor of Computer Science, University of Copenhagen

Peggy Valcke, Professor of Law, KU Leuven

Pieter Van Cleynenbreugel, Professor of European Law, University of Liege

Aurélie Anne Villanueva, European University Institute

Ben Wagner, Assistant Professor in Technology and Policy, Delft University of Technology

Wayne Wei Wang, PhD Candidate in Computational Legal Studies at the University of Hong Kong

Acknowledgements

This project would not have been possible without the authors' contributions and financial support by the European Research Council (ERC) under the European Union's Horizon 2020 research and innovation program (grant agreement no. 833647); the project "SE.CO.R.E TECH: Self- and Co-Regulation for Emerging Technologies: Towards a Technological Rule of Law," funded by the Italian Ministry for University and Research's (MUR's) "Progetti di Ricerca di Rilevante Interesse Nazionale" (PRIN; Bando 2017 – grant prot. no. 2017SW48EB); and the Centre for Cyber Law and Policy at the University of Haifa. The editors wish to thank Costanza Masciotta, Elia Cremona and Pietro Dunn for their help in the revision of the volume.

Introduction

Technologies have always challenged, if not disrupted, the social, economic legal, and to an extent, the ideological status quo. Such transformations impact constitutional law, as the State formulates its legal response to the new technologies being developed and applied by the market, and as it considers its own use of the technologies. The development of data collection, mining, and algorithmic analysis, resulting in predictive profiling – with or without the subsequent potential manipulation of attitudes and behaviors of users – presents unique challenges to constitutional law at the doctrinal as well as theoretical levels.

Historically, liberal constitutionalism has been built on a vertical dimension where the power to limit liberty is only the public one, only in given jurisdictional territory, and therefore should be constrained by the national constitution. Moreover, as of the rise of the bureaucratic state, the technologies for infringing liberty or equality were thought to be containable by the exercise of concrete judicial review (either constitutional or administrative), abstract judicial review, or a combination of the above. In recent years, however, the rise of the algorithmic society has led to a paradigmatic change where the public power is no longer the only source of concern for the respect of fundamental rights and the protection of democracy, where jurisdictional boundaries are in flux, and where doctrines and procedures developed in the pre-cybernetic age do not necessarily capture rights violations in a relevant time frame. This requires either the redrawing of constitutional boundaries so as to subject digital platforms to constitutional law or a revisiting of the relationship between constitutional law and private law, including the duties of the state to regulate the cybernetic complex, within or outside the jurisdictional boundaries of the state.

Within this framework, this book is the result of the biannual work of the IACL Research Group "Algorithmic State, Market and Society" after an inaugural conference at the University of Florence and European University Institute in 2019. This Research Group promotes the debate in the field of law and technology, and primarily regarding the new constitutional challenges raised by the development of algorithmic technologies which assist (if not control) decision-making processes by state agencies or corporations (often large and multinational) that provide key services online. Based on this framework, this book tries to answer the following research questions: How has the relationship among powers changed in the algorithmic society? What are the new substantive and procedural rights protecting individuals and democratic values? How can we balance innovation (and the legal incentives for businesses to pursue innovation) with the need to ensure transparency and accountability? To what extent should new forms of public or private law tools be developed to address the challenges posed by the shift to the algorithmic society?

The answers to these questions have likely changed in the last years due to the evolving landscape of algorithmic technologies and policy. The increasing implementation of algorithmic technologies in the public and private sectors promotes an intertwined framework. The launch of the European proposal for the Artificial Intelligence Act is just an example of the need to provide a framework for mitigating risks while promoting innovation. This book does not aim just to address recent developments and provide answers to evolving dynamics. The goal is to provide a taxonomy of the constitutional challenges of the algorithmic society, with some focuses on specific challenges.

This goal is reflected in the book's structure, which is articulated in three parts. The first part aims to underline the challenges for fundamental rights and democratic values in the algorithmic society. In particular, this part underlines how the fast-growing use of algorithms in various fields like justice, policing, and public welfare could end in biased and erroneous decisions, boosting inequality, discrimination, unfair consequences, and undermining constitutional rights, such as privacy, freedom of expression, and equality. The second part addresses the regulation and policy of the algorithmic society. There are multiple challenges here due to opacity and biases of algorithmic systems, as well as the actors involved in the regulation of these technologies. The third part examines the role and responsibilities of private actors, underlining various constitutional opportunities and threats. In this case, the book aims to underline how the private sector is a relevant player, pursuing functions that reflect public powers.

1

Constitutional Law in the Algorithmic Society

Oreste Pollicino and Giovanni De Gregorio[*]

1.1 INTRODUCTION

Technologies have always led to turning points in society.[1] In the past, technological developments have opened the door to new phases of growth and change, while influencing social values and principles. Algorithmic technologies fit within this framework. These technologies have contributed to introducing new ways to process vast amounts of data.[2] In the digital economy, data and information are fundamental assets which can be considered raw materials the processing of which can generate value.[3] Even simple pieces of data, when processed with a specific purpose and mixed with other information, can provide models and predictive answers. These opportunities have led to the rise of new applications and business models in a new phase of (digital) capitalism,[4] as more recently defined as information capitalism.[5]

Although these technologies have positive effects on the entire society since they increase the capacity of individuals to exercise rights and freedoms, they have also led to new constitutional challenges. The opportunities afforded by algorithmic technologies clash with their troubling opacity and lack of accountability, in what

* Oreste Pollicino is a Full Professor of Constitutional Law at Bocconi University. He authored Sections 1.2, 1.5, and 1.6. Giovanni De Gregorio is Postdoctoral Researcher, Centre for Socio-Legal Studies, University of Oxford. He authored Sections 1.1, 1.3, and 1.4.

1 Roger Brownsword and Karen Yeung (eds), *Regulating Technologies: Legal Futures, Regulatory Frames and Technological Fixes* (Hart 2008).

2 Omer Tene and Jules Polonetsky, 'Big Data for All: Privacy and User Control in the Age of Analytics' (2013) 11 *Northwestern Journal of Technology and Intellectual Property* 239; Sue Newell and Marco Marabelli, 'Strategic Opportunities (and Challenges) of Algorithmic Decision-Making: A Call for Action on the Long-Term Societal Effects of "Datification"' (2015) 24 *Journal of Strategic Information Systems* 3.

3 Viktor Mayer-Schonberger and Kenneth Cukier, *Big Data: A Revolution That Will Transform How We Live, Work, and Think* (Murray 2013).

4 Daniel Schiller, *Digital Capitalism. Networking the Global Market System* (MIT Press 1999).

5 Julie Cohen, *Between Truth and Power. The Legal Construction of Information Capitalism* (Oxford University Press 2020).

has been defined as an 'algocracy'.[6] It is no coincidence that transparency is at the core of the debate about algorithms.[7] There are risks to fundamental rights and democracy inherent in the lack of transparency about the functioning of automated decision-making processes.[8] The implications deriving from the use of algorithms may have consequences on individuals' fundamental rights, such as the right to self-determination, freedom of expression, and privacy. However, fundamental rights do not exhaust the threats which these technologies raise for constitutional democracies. The spread of automated decision-making also challenges democratic systems due to its impact on public discourse and the impossibility of understanding decisions that are made by automated systems affecting individual rights and freedoms.[9] This is evident when focusing on how information flows online and on the characteristics of the public sphere, which is increasingly personalised rather than plural.[10] Likewise, the field of data is even more compelling due to the ability of data controllers to affect users' rights to privacy and data protection by implementing technologies the transparency and accountability of which cannot be ensured.[11] The possibility to obtain financing and insurance or the likelihood of a potential crime are only some examples of the efficient answers which automated decision-making systems can provide and of how such technologies can affect individuals' autonomy.[12]

At a first glance, algorithms seem like neutral technologies processing information which can lead to a new understanding of reality and predict future dynamics. Technically, algorithms, including artificial intelligence technologies, are just methods to express results based on inputs made up of data.[13] This veil of neutrality

[6] John Danaher, 'The Threat of Algocracy: Reality, Resistance and Accommodation' (2016) 29 *Philosophy & Technology* 245.

[7] See, in particular, Daniel Neyland, 'Bearing Accountable Witness to the Ethical Algorithmic System' (2016) 41 *Science, Technology & Human Values* 50; Mariarosaria Taddeo, 'Modelling Trust in Artificial Agents, A First Step toward the Analysis of e-Trust' (2010) 20 *Minds and Machines* 243. Matteo Turilli and Luciano Floridi, 'The Ethics of Information Transparency' (2009) 11 *Ethics and Information Technology* 105.

[8] Jenna Burrell, 'How the Machine "Thinks": Understanding Opacity in Machine Learning Algorithms' (2016) 3 *Big Data & Society*; Christopher Kuner et al., 'Machine Learning with Personal Data: Is Data Protection Law Smart Enough to Meet the Challenge?' (2017) 6 *International Data Privacy Law* 167; Mireille Hildebrandt, 'The Dawn of a Critical Transparency Right for the Profiling Era' in Jacques Bus et al. (eds), *Digital Enlightenment Yearbook* (IOS Press 2012); Meg L. Jones, 'Right to a Human in the Loop: Political Constructions of Computer Automation and Personhood' (2017) 47 *Social Studies of Science* 216.

[9] Paul Nemitz, 'Constitutional Democracy and Technology in the Age of Artificial Intelligence' (2018) *Royal Society Philosophical Transactions A*.

[10] Nicolas Suzor, 'Digital Constitutionalism: Using the Rule of Law to Evaluate the Legitimacy of Governance by Platforms' (2018) 4 *Social Media + Society* 3.

[11] Serge Gutwirth and Paul De Hert, 'Regulating Profiling in a Democratic Constitutional States', in Mireille Hildebrandt and Serge Gutwirth (eds), *Profiling the European Citizen* (2006), 271.

[12] Brent D. Mittlestadt et al., 'The Ethics of Algorithms: Mapping the Debate' (2016) 3 *Big Data & Society*.

[13] Tarleton Gillespie, 'The Relevance of Algorithms' in Tarleton Gillespie et al. (eds), *Media Technologies: Essays on Communication, Materiality, and Society* (MIT Press 2014), 167.

falls before their human fallacy. Processes operated by algorithms are indeed value-laden, since technologies are the result of human activities and determinations.[14] The contribution of humans in the development of data processing standards causes the shift of personal interests and values from the human to the algorithmic realm. If, from a technical perspective, algorithms are instruments that extract value from data, then moving to the social perspective, such technologies constitute automated decision-making processes able to affect society and thus also impacting on constitutional values, precisely fundamental rights and democratic values.

Within this challenging framework between innovation and risk, it is worth wondering about the role of regulation and policy in this field. Leaving the development of algorithmic technologies without safeguards and democratic oversight could lead society towards techno-determinism and the marginalisation of public actors, which would lose their role in ensuring the protection of fundamental rights and democratic values. Technology should not order society but be a means of promoting the evolution of mankind. Otherwise, if the former will order the drive of the latter in the years to come, we could witness the gradual vanishing of democratic constitutional values in the name of innovation.

Since algorithms are becoming more and more pervasive in daily life, individuals will increasingly expect to be aware of the implications deriving from the use of these technologies. Individuals are increasingly surrounded by technical systems influencing their decisions without the possibility of understanding or controlling this phenomenon and, as a result, participating consciously in the democratic debate. This situation is not only the result of algorithmic opacity, but it is firmly linked to the private development of algorithmic technologies in constitutional democracies. Because of the impact of these technologies on our daily lives, the predominance of businesses and private entities in programming and in guiding innovation in the age of artificial intelligence leads one to consider the role and responsibilities of these actors in the algorithmic society. The rise of 'surveillance capitalism' is not only a new business framework but a new system to exercise (private) powers in the algorithmic society.[15]

We believe that constitutional law plays a critical role in addressing the challenges of the algorithmic society. New technologies have always challenged, if not disrupted, the social, economic, legal, and, to a certain extent, ideological *status quo*. Such transformations impact constitutional values, as the state formulates its legal response to new technologies based on constitutional principles which meet market dynamics, and as it considers its own use of technologies in light of the limitation imposed by constitutional safeguards. The development of data collection, mining,

14 Philippe A. E. Brey and Johnny Soraker, *Philosophy of Computing and Information Technology* (Elsevier 2009); Norbert Wiener, *The Human Use of Human Beings: Cybernetics and Society* (Da Capo Press 1988).

15 Shoshana Zuboff, *The Age of Surveillance Capitalism: The Fight for a Human Future at the New Frontier of Power* (Political Affairs 2018).

and algorithmic analysis, resulting in predictive profiling – with or without the subsequent potential manipulation of the attitudes and behaviours of users – present unique challenges to constitutional law at the doctrinal as well as theoretical levels.

Constitutions have been designed to limit public (more precisely governmental) powers and protect individuals against any abuse from the state. The shift of power from public to private hands requires rethinking and, in case, revisiting some well-established assumptions. Moreover, during the rise of the bureaucratic state, the technologies for infringing liberty or equality were thought to be containable by the exercise of concrete judicial review (either constitutional or administrative), abstract judicial review, or a combination of the above. In recent years, however, the rise of the algorithmic society has led to a paradigmatic change where public power is no longer the only source of concern for the respect of fundamental rights and the protection of democracy, where jurisdictional boundaries are in flux, and where doctrines and procedures developed in the pre-cybernetic age do not necessarily capture rights violations in a relevant time frame. This requires either the redrawing of the constitutional boundaries so as to subject digital platforms to constitutional law or to revisit the relationship between constitutional law and private law, including the duties of the state to regulate the cybernetic complex, within or outside the jurisdictional boundaries of the state. Within this framework, the rise of digital private powers challenges the traditional characteristics of constitutional law, thus encouraging to wonder how the latter might evolve to face the challenges brought by the emergence of new forms of powers in the algorithmic society.

The primary goal of this chapter is to introduce the constitutional challenges coming from the rise of the algorithmic society. Section 1.2 examines the challenges for fundamental rights and democratic values, with a specific focus on the right to freedom of expression, privacy, and data protection. Section 1.3 looks at the role of constitutional law in relation to the regulation and policy of the algorithmic society. Section 1.4 examines the role and responsibilities of private actors underlining the role of constitutional law in this field. Section 1.5 deals with the potential remedies which constitutional law can provide to face the challenges of the information society.

1.2 FUNDAMENTAL RIGHTS AND DEMOCRATIC VALUES

Algorithmic technologies seem to promise new answers and an increase of accuracy of decision-making, thus offering new paths to enrich human knowledge.[16] Predictive models can help public administrations provide more efficient public services and spare resources. Likewise, citizens can rely on more sophisticated platforms allowing them to express their identity, build social relationships, and share ideas. Therefore, these technologies can be considered an enabler for the exercise of rights and

[16] Evgeny Morozov, *To Save Everything, Click Here: The Folly of Technological Solutionism* (Public Affairs 2013).

freedoms. Nonetheless, artificial intelligence technologies are far from perfect. Predictive models have already produced biased results and inaccurate outputs, leading to discriminatory results.[17] The implications deriving from the implementation of automated technologies may have consequences for individual fundamental rights, such as the right to self-determination, freedom of expression, and privacy, even at a collective level. It is worth stressing that the relationship between fundamental rights and democracy is intimate, and the case of freedom of expression and data protection underlines this bundle. Without the possibility of expressing opinions and ideas freely, it is not possible to define society as democratic. Likewise, without rules governing the processing of personal data, individuals could be exposed to a regime of private surveillance without a set of accountability and transparency safeguards. Among different examples, the moderation of online information and users' profiling can be taken as two paradigmatic examples of the risks which these technologies raise for fundamental rights and democratic values.

The way in which we express opinions and ideas online has changed in the last twenty years. The Internet has contributed to shaping the public sphere. It would be a mistake to consider the new channels of communication just as threats. The digital environment has indeed been a crucial vehicle to foster democratic values like freedom of expression.[18] However, this does not imply that threats have not appeared on the horizon. Conversely, the implementation of automated decision-making systems is concerning for the protection of the right to freedom of expression online. To understand when automation meets (and influences) free speech, it would be enough to closely look at how information flows online under the moderation of online platforms. Indeed, to organise and moderate countless content each day, platforms also rely on artificial intelligence to decide whether to remove content or signal some expressions to human moderators.[19] The result of this environment is troubling for the rule of law from different perspectives. First, artificial intelligence systems contribute to interpreting legal protection of fundamental rights by de facto setting a private standard of protection in the digital environment.[20] Second, there is also an issue of predictability and legal certainty, since private determinations blur the lines between public and private standards. This leads us to the third point: the lack of transparency and accountability in the decision concerning freedom of expression online.[21] In other words, the challenge in this case is to measure compliance with the principle of the rule of law. Indeed, the implementation of machine

17 Sandra Wachter and Brent Mittelstadt, 'A Right to Reasonable Inferences: Re-Thinking Data Protection Law in the Age of Big Data and AI' (2019) (2) *Columbia Business Law Review*.

18 Yochai Benkler, *The Wealth of Networks* (Yale University Press 2006).

19 Tarleton Gillespie, *Custodians of the Internet. Platforms, Content Moderation, and the Hidden Decisions that Shape Social Media* (Yale University Press 2018).

20 Kate Klonick, 'The New Governors: The People, Rules, and Processes Governing Online Speech' (2018) 131 *Harvard Law Review* 1598.

21 Giovanni De Gregorio, 'Democratising Content Moderation. A Constitutional Framework' (2019) *Computer Law and Security Review*.

learning technologies does not allow to scrutinising decisions over expressions which are still private but involve the public at large. With the lack of regulation of legal safeguards, online platforms will continue to be free to assess and remove speech according to their business purposes.

Within this framework, disinformation deserves special attention.[22] Among the challenges amplified by technology, the spread of false content online has raised concerns for countries around the world. The Brexit referendum and the 'Pizzagate' during the last US elections are just two examples of the power of (false) information in shaping public opinion. The relevance of disinformation for constitutional democracies can be viewed from two angles: the constitutional limits to the regulatory countermeasures and the use of artificial intelligence systems in defining the boundaries of disinformation and moderating this content. While for public actors the decision to intervene to filter falsehood online requires questioning whether and to what extent it is acceptable for liberal democracies to enforce limitations to freedom of expression to falsehood, artificial intelligences catalogue vast amounts of content, deciding whether they deserve to be online according to the policies implemented by unaccountable private actors (i.e., online platforms). This is a multifaceted question since each constitutional system paradigm adopts different paradigms of protection, even when they share the common liberal matrix, like in the case of Europe and the United States. In other words, it is a matter of understanding the limits of freedom of speech to protect legitimate interests or safeguard other constitutional rights.

Besides, the challenges of disinformation are not just directly linked to the governance of online spaces but also to their exploitation. We have experienced in recent years the rise of new (digital) populist narratives manipulating information for political purposes.[23] Indeed, in the political context, technology has proven to be a channel for vehiculating disinformation citizenship, democracy, and democratic values. By exploiting the opportunities of the new social media, populist voices have become a relevant part of the public debate online, as the political situations in some Member States show. Indeed, extreme voices at the margins drive the political debate. It would be enough to mention the electoral successes of Alternative für Deutschland in Germany or the Five Star Movement in Italy to understand how populist narratives are widespread no longer as an answer to the economic crisis but as anti-establishment movements fighting globalised phenomena like migration and proposing a constitutional narrative unbuilding democratic values and the principle of the rule of law.[24]

The threats posed by artificial intelligence technologies to fundamental rights can also be examined by looking at the processing of personal data. Even more evidently,

[22] Giovanni Pitruzzella and Oreste Pollicino, *Disinformation and Hate Speech: A European Constitutional Perspective* (Bocconi University Press 2020).

[23] Maurizio Barberis, *Populismo digitale. Come internet sta uccidendo la democrazia* (Chiareletter 2020).

[24] Giacomo Delle Donne et al., *Italian Populism and Constitutional Law. Strategies, Conflicts and Dilemmas* (Palgrave Macmillan 2020).

automated decision-making systems raise comparable challenges in the field of data protection. The massive processing of personal data from public and private actors leads individuals to be subject to increasingly intrusive interferences in their private lives.[25] Smart applications at home or biometric recognition technologies in public spaces are just two examples of the extensive challenges for individual rights. The logics of digital capitalism and accumulation make surveillance technologies ubiquitous, without leaving any space for individuals to escape. In order to build such a surveillance and profiling framework, automated decision-making systems also rely on personal data to provide output. The use of personal information for this purpose leads one to wonder whether individuals should have the right not to be subjected to a decision based solely on automated processing, including profiling which produces legal effects concerning him or her or similarly significantly affects him or her.[26] These data subjects' rights have been primarily analysed from the perspective of the right to explanation. Scholars have pointed out possible bases for the right to explanation such as those provisions mandating that data subjects receive meaningful information concerning the logic involved, as well as the significance, and the envisaged consequences of the processing.[27]

These threats would suggest looking at these technologies with fear. Nonetheless, new technologies are playing a disruptive role. Society is increasingly digitised, and the way in which values are perceived and interpreted is inevitably shaped by this evolution. New technological development has always led to conflicts between the risks and the opportunities fostered by its newness.[28] Indeed, the uncertainty in the novel situations is a natural challenge for constitutional democracies, precisely for the principle of the rule of law.[29] The increasing degree of uncertainty concerning the applicable legal framework and the exercise of power which can exploit technologies based on legal loopholes also lead one to wonder how to ensure due process in the algorithmic society. Therefore, the challenges at stake broadly involve the principle of the rule of law not only for the troubling legal uncertainty relating to new technologies but also as a limit against the private determination of fundamental rights protection the boundaries of protection of which are increasingly shaped and determined by machines. The rule of law can be seen as an instrument to

[25] David Lyon, *Surveillance Society: Monitoring Everyday Life* (Open University Press 2001).

[26] Ibid., Art 22.

[27] Margot Kaminski, 'The Right to Explanation, Explained' (2019) 34(1) *Berkeley Technology Law Journal* 189; Antoni Roig, 'Safeguards for the Right Not to Be Subject to a Decision Based Solely on Automated Processing (Article 22 GDPR)' (2017) 8(3) *European Journal of Law and Technology* 1; Sandra Wachter et al., 'Why a Right to Explanation of Automated Decision-Making Does Not Exist in the General Data Protection Regulation' (2017) 7 *International Data Privacy Law* 76; Gianclaudio Malgieri and Giovanni Comandé, 'Why a Right to Legibility of Automated Decision-Making Exists in the General Data Protection Regulation' (2017) 7 *International Data Privacy Law* 243; Bryce Goodman and Seth Flaxman, 'European Union Regulations on Algorithmic Decision-Making and a "Right to Explanation"' (2017) 38(3) *AI Magazine* 50.

[28] Monroe E. Price, 'The Newness of Technology' (2001) 22 *Cardozo Law Review* 1885.

[29] Lyria Bennett Moses, 'How to Think about Law, Regulation and Technology: Problems with "Technology" as a Regulatory Target' (2013) 5(1) *Law, Innovation and Technology* 1.

measure the degree of accountability, the fairness of application, and the effectiveness of the law.[30] As Krygier observed, it also has the goal of securing freedom from certain dangers or pathologies.[31] The rule of law is primarily considered as the opposite of arbitrary public power. Therefore, it is a constitutional bastion limiting the exercise of authorities outside any constitutional limit and ensuring that these limits answer to a common constitutional scheme.

Within this framework, the increasing spread and implementation of algorithmic technologies in everyday life lead to wondering about the impact of these technologies on individuals' fundamental rights and freedoms. This process may tend to promote a probabilistic approach to the protection of fundamental rights and democratic values. The rise of probability as the primary dogma of the algorithmic society raises questions about the future of the principle of rule of law. Legal certainty is increasingly under pressure by the non-accountable determination of automated decision-making technologies. Therefore, it is worth focusing on the regulatory framework which could lead to a balance between ensuring the protection of democratic values without overwhelming the private sector with disproportionate obligations suppressing innovation.

1.3 REGULATION AND POLICY

Fundamental rights and democratic values seem to be under pressure in the information society. This threat for constitutional democracies might lead to wondering about the role of regulation and policy within the framework of algorithmic technologies. The debate about regulating digital technologies started with the questioning of consolidated notions such as sovereignty and territory.[32] The case of *Yahoo* v. *Licra* is a paradigmatic example of the constitutional challenges on the horizon in the early 2000s.[33] More precisely, some authors have argued that regulation based on geographical boundaries is unfeasible, so that applying national laws to the Internet is impossible.[34] Precisely, Johnson and Post have held that 'events on the Net occur everywhere but nowhere in particular' and therefore 'no physical jurisdiction has a more compelling claim than any other to subject events

[30] Recent rulings of the European Court of Justice have highlighted the relevance of the rule of law in EU legal order. See Case C-64/16, Associação Sindical dos Juízes Portugueses v. Tribunal de Contas; Case C-216/18 PPU, *LM*; Case C-619/18, Commission v. Poland (2018).

[31] Martin Krygier, 'The Rule of Law: Legality, Teleology, Sociology' in Gianlugi Palomblla and Neil Walker (ed), *Relocating the Rule of Law* (Hart 2009), 45.

[32] John P. Barlow, 'A Declaration of Independence of the Cyberspace' (Electronic Frontier Foundation 1996), www.eff.org/cyberspace-independence.

[33] *Licra et UEJF* v. *Yahoo Inc and Yahoo France TGI Paris* 22 May 2000. See Joel R. Reidenberg, 'Yahoo and Democracy on the Internet' (2001/2002) 42 *Jurimetrics* 261; *Yahoo!, Inc.* v. *La Ligue Contre Le Racisme* 169 F Supp 2d 1181 (ND Cal 2001). See Christine Duh, 'Yahoo Inc. v. LICRA' (2002) 17 *Berkeley Technology Law Journal* 359.

[34] David R. Johnson and David Post, 'Law and Borders: The Rise of Law in Cyberspace' (1996) 48(5) *Stanford Law Review* 1371.

exclusively to its laws'.[35] In the cyber-anarchic view, the rise of internet law would cause the disintegration of state sovereignty over cyberspace,[36] thus potentially making any regulatory attempt irrelevant for the digital environment. This was already problematic for the principle of the rule of law, since self-regulation of cyberspace would have marginalised legal norms, de facto undermining any guarantee.

These positions have partially shown their fallacies, and scholars have underlined how States are instead available to regulate the digital environment through different modalities,[37] along with how to solve the problem of enforcement in the digital space.[38] Nonetheless, this is not the end of the story. Indeed, in recent years, new concerns have arisen as a result of the increasing economic power that some business actors acquired in the digital environment, especially online platforms. This economic power was primarily the result of the potentialities of digital technologies and of the high degree of freedom recognised by constitutional democracies in the private sector.[39] The shift from the world of atoms to that of bits has led to the emergence of new players acting as information gatekeepers that hold significant economic power with primary effects on individuals' everyday lives.[40]

Within this framework, while authoritarian States have been shown to impose their powers online,[41] constitutional democracies have followed another path. In this case, public actors rely on the private sector as a proxy in the digital environment.[42] The role of the private sector in the digitisation of the public administration or the urban environment can be considered a paradigmatic relationship of collaboration between the public and private sectors. Likewise, States usually rely on the algorithmic enforcement of individual rights online, as in the case of the removal of illegal content like terrorism or hate speech.[43] In other words, the intersection between public and private leads one to wonder just how to avoid that public values are subject to the determinations of private business interests. The Snowden revelations have already underlined how much governments rely on

35 Ibid., 1376.

36 John Perry Barlow, 'A Declaration of the Independence of Cyberspace' (1996) https://www.eff.org/it/cyberspace-independence.

37 Lawrence Lessig, *Code 2.0: Code and Other Laws of Cyberspace* (Basic Books 2006); Jack Goldsmith, 'Against Cybernarchy' (1998) 65(4) University of Chicago Law Review 1199.

38 Joel R. Reidenberg, 'States and Internet Enforcement' (2004) 1 *University of Ottawa Law & Techonology Journal* 213.

39 Giovanni De Gregorio, 'From Constitutional Freedoms to Power. Protecting Fundamental Rights Online in the Algorithmic Society' (2019) 11(2) *European Journal of Legal Studies* 65.

40 Emily B. Laidlaw, 'A Framework for Identifying Internet Information Gatekeepers' (2012) 24 *International Review Law, Computers and Technology* 3.

41 Giovanni De Gregorio and Nicole Stremlau, 'Internet Shutdowns and the Limits of the Law' (2020) 14 *International Journal of Communication* 1.

42 Niva Elkin-Koren and Eldar Haber, 'Governance by Proxy: Cyber Challenges to Civil Liberties' (2016) 82 *Brookling Law Review* 105.

43 Kate Klonick, 'The New Governors: The People, Rules, and Processes Governing Online Speech' (2018) 131 *Harvard Law Review* 1598.

Internet companies to extend their surveillance programmes and escape accountability.[44] Even if public actors do not act as participants in the market or a regulator, they operate through an 'invisible handshake' based on the cooperation between market forces and public powers.[45]

This situation leads constitutional democracies to adopt liberal approaches to the digital environment, with the result that self-regulation plays a predominant role. Ordo-liberal thinking considers the market and democracy as two intimate forces. Nonetheless, when market logics and dynamics based on the maximisation of profit and private business purposes prevail over the protection of individuals' fundamental rights and freedoms, it is worth wondering about the role of regulation in mitigating this situation. The challenges raised by the implementation of artificial intelligence technologies compels to define what the proper legal framework for artificial intelligence requires. The creation of a hard law framework rather than of a soft law one is not without consequences. Both options offer a variety of benefits but also suffer from disadvantages, which should be taken into account when developing a framework for artificial intelligence systems.

Technology is also an opportunity, since it can provide better systems of enforcement of legal rules but also a clear and reliable framework compensating the fallacies of certain processes.[46] There is thus no definitive 'recipe' for protecting democratic values, but there are different means to achieve this result, among which there is also technology. Indeed, new technologies like automation should not be considered as a risk per se. The right question to ask instead is whether new technologies can encourage arbitrary public power and challenges for the rule of law.[47] The challenges to fundamental rights raised by these technologies would lead one to avoid approaches based on self-regulation. This strategy may not be sufficient to ensure the protection of fundamental rights in the information society. At the same time, it is well-known that hard law can represent a hurdle to innovation, leading to other drawbacks for the development of the internal market, precisely considering the global development of algorithmic technologies. In the case of the European proposal for the Artificial Intelligence Act,[48] the top-down approach of the Union, which aims to leave small margins to self-regulation, might be an attempt to protect the internal market from algorithmic tools which would not comply with the

44 David Lyon, *Surveillance after Snowden* (Polity Press 2015).

45 Niva Elkin-Koren and Micheal Birnhack, 'The Invisible Handshake: The Reemergence of the State in the Digital Environment' (2003) 8 *Virginia Journal of Law & Technology*.

46 Steven Malby, 'Strengthening the Rule of Law through Technology' (2017) 43 *Commonwealth Law Bulletin* 307.

47 Mireille Hildebrandt, 'The Artificial Intelligence of European Union Law' (2020) 21 *German Law Journal* 74.

48 Proposal for Regulation of the European Parliament and of the Council laying down Harmonised Rules on Artificial Intelligence (Artificial Intelligence Act) and Amending certain Union Legislative Acts COM (2021) 206 final.

European standard of protection. Rather than making operators accountable for developing and implementing artificial intelligence systems, the regulation aims to prevent the consolidation of external standards.

Therefore, a fully harmonised approach would constitute a sound solution to provide a common framework and avoid fragmentation, which could undermine the aim of ensuring the same level of protection of fundamental rights. Besides, co-regulation in specific domains could ensure that public actors are involved in determining the values and principles underpinning the development of algorithmic technologies while leaving the private sector room to implement these technologies under the guidance of constitutional principles. The principle of the rule of law constitutes a clear guide for public actors which intend to implement technologies for public tasks and services. To avoid any effect on the trust and accountability of the public sector, consistency between the implementation of technology and the law is critical for legal certainty. Nonetheless, it is worth stressing that this is not an easy task. Even when legislation is well designed, limiting public power within the principle of legality could be difficult to achieve from different perspectives, like the lack of expertise or the limited budget to deal with the new technological scenario.[49] Besides, with the lack of any regulation, private actors are not required to comply with constitutional safeguards. In this case, the threats for the principle of the rule of law are different and linked to the possibility that private actors develop a set of private standards clashing with public values, precisely when their economic freedoms turn into forms of power.

The COVID-19 pandemic has highlighted the relevance of online platforms in the information society. For instance, Amazon provided deliveries during the lockdown phase, while Google and Apple offered their technology for contact-tracing apps.[50] These actors have played a critical role in providing services which other businesses or even the State had failed to deliver promptly. The COVID-19 crisis has led these actors to become increasingly involved in our daily lives, becoming part of our social structure.

Nonetheless, commentary has not been exclusively positive. The model of the contact-tracing app proposed by these tech giants has raised various privacy and data protection concerns.[51] The pandemic has also shown how artificial intelligence can affect fundamental rights online without human oversight. Once Facebook and Google sent their moderators home, the effects of these measures extended to the process of content moderation, resulting in the suspension of various accounts and the removal of some content, even though there was no

49 Roger Brownsword, 'Technological Management and the Rule of Law' (2016) 8(1) *Law Innovation and Technology* 100.

50 'Privacy-Preserving Contact Tracing' *Apple.com* (accessed 30 July 2020) at www.apple.com/covid19/contacttracing.

51 Jennifer Daskal and Matt Perault, 'The Apple-Google Contact Tracing System Won't Work. It Still Deserves Praise' *Slate* (22 May 2020) at https://slate.com/technology/2020/05/apple-google-contact-tracing-app-privacy.html.

specific reason for it.[52] This situation not only affected users' right to freedom of expression but also led to discriminatory results and to the spread of disinformation, thus pushing one to wonder about the roles and responsibilities of private actors in the information society.

1.4 THE ROLE AND RESPONSIBILITIES OF PRIVATE ACTORS

At the advent of the digital era, the rise of new private actors could be seen merely as a matter of freedom. The primary legal (but also economic) issue thus was that of protecting such freedom while, at the same time, preventing any possible abuse thereof. This is the reason why competition law turned out to be a privileged tool in this respect,[53] sometimes in combination with ex ante regulation. Constitutional democracies have adopted a liberal approach – for instance, exempting online intermediaries from liability and providing a minimum regulation to ensure a common legal environment for circulating personal data.[54] Such an approach was aimed at preserving a new environment, which, at the end of the last century, seemed to promise a new phase of opportunities.

Thanks to minimum intervention in the digital environment, the technological factor played a crucial role. The mix of market and automated decision-making technologies has led to the transformation of economic freedoms into something that resembles the exercise of powers as vested in public authorities. The implementation of algorithmic technologies to process vast amounts of information and data is not exclusively a matter of profits any longer. Such a power can be observed from many different perspectives, like in the field of competition law, as economic and data power.[55] For the purposes of constitutional law, the concerns are instead about forms of freedoms which resemble the exercise of authority. The development of new digital and algorithmic technologies has led to the rise of new opportunities to foster freedom but also to the consolidation of powers proposing a private model of protection and governance of users. The freedom to conduct business has now turned into a new dimension, namely that of private power, which – it goes without saying – brings significant challenges to the role and tools of constitutional law.

One may actually wonder where the connection between algorithms and powers lies, apparently so far, but in fact, so close. To explain why these two expressions are connected, we argue that the implementation of the former on a large scale has the

52 Elizabeth Dwoskin and Nitasha Tiku, 'Facebook Sent Home Thousands of Human Moderators due to the Coronavirus. Now the Algorithms Are in Charge' *The Washington Post* (24 March 2020) at www.washingtonpost.com/technology/2020/03/23/facebook-moderators-coronavirus.

53 Angela Daly, *Private Power, Online Information Flows and EU Law: Mind the Gap* (Hart 2016).

54 Directive 2000/31/EC of the European Parliament and of the Council of 8 June 2000 on certain legal aspects of information society services, in particular, electronic commerce, in the Internal Market ('Directive on electronic commerce') (2000) OJ L 178/1.

55 Inge Graef, *EU Competition Law, Data Protection and Online Platforms: Data as Essential Facility* (Wolter Kluwer 2016).

potential to give rise to a further transmutation of the classic role of constitutionalism and constitutional theory, in addition to that already caused by the shift from the world of atoms to the world of bits,[56] where constitutionalism becomes 'digital constitutionalism' and power is relocated between different actors in the information society.[57] This statement needs an attempt to clarification. As is well-known, constitutional theory frames powers as historically vested in public authorities, which *by default* hold the monopoly on violence under the social contract.[58] It is no coincidence that constitutional law was built around the functioning of public authorities. The goal of constitutions (and thus of constitutional law) is to allocate powers between institutions and to make sure that proper limits are set to constrain their action, with a view to preventing any abuse.[59] In other words, the original mission of constitutionalism was to set some mechanisms to restrict government power through self-binding principles, including by providing different forms of separation of powers and constitutional review. To reach this goal, it is crucial to focus on the exploration of the most disruptive challenges which the emergence of private powers has posed to the modern constitutional state and the various policy options for facing said transformations. This requires questioning the role that constitutions play in the information society and leads one to investigate whether constitutions can and should do something in light of the emergence of new powers other than those exercised by public authorities. Our claim is that if constitutions are meant as binding on public authorities, something new has to be developed to create constraints on private actors.

Therefore, focusing on the reasons behind the shift from freedom to conduct business to private power becomes crucial to understanding the challenges for constitutional law in the algorithmic society. Private actors other than traditional public authorities are now vested with some forms of power that are no longer economic in nature. The apparently strange couple 'power and algorithms' does actually make sense and triggers new challenges in the specific context of democratic constitutionalism. Algorithms, as a matter of fact, allow to carry out activities of various nature that may significantly affect individuals' rights and freedoms. Individuals may not notice that many decisions are carried out in an automated manner without, at least prima facie, any chance of control for them. A broad range of decision-making activities are increasingly delegated to algorithms which can advise and in some cases make decisions based on the data they process. As scholars have observed, 'how we perceive and understand our environments and interact with them and each other is increasingly mediated by algorithms'.[60] In other words, algorithms are not necessarily driven by the pursuit of public interests but are instead

56 Nicholas Negroponte, *Being Digital* (Alfred A. Knopf 1995).
57 Giovanni De Gregorio, 'The Rise of Digital Constitutionalism in the European Union' (2021) International Journal of Constitutional Law.
58 Thomas Hobbes, *The Leviathan* (1651).
59 Andras Sajo and Renata Uitz, *The Constitution of Freedom: An Introduction to Legal Constitutionalism* (Oxford University Press 2017).
60 Mittlestadt et al. (n 11), 1.

sensitive to business needs. Said concerns are even more serious in light of the learning capabilities of algorithms, which – by introducing a degree of autonomy and thus unpredictability – are likely to undermine 'accountability' and the human understanding of the decision-making process. For instance, the opacity of algorithms is seen by scholars as a possible cause of discrimination or differentiation between individuals when it comes to activities such as profiling and scoring.[61]

In the lack of any regulation, the global activity of online platforms contributes to producing a para-legal environment on a global scale competing with States' authorities. The consolidation of these areas of private power is a troubling process for democracy. Indeed, even if, at a first glance, democratic States are open environments for pluralism flourishing through fundamental rights and freedoms, at the same time their stability can be undermined when those freedoms transform into new founding powers overcoming basic principles such as the respect of the rule of law. In this situation, there is no effective form of participation or representation of citizens in determining the rules governing their community. In other words, the creation of a private legal framework outside any representative mechanism is a threat to democracy due to the marginalisation of citizens and their representatives from law-making and enforcement. This situation shows why it is important to focus on the constitutional remedies to solve the imbalances of powers in the algorithmic society.

1.5 CONSTITUTIONAL REMEDIES

Within this troubling framework for the protection of fundamental rights and democracies, constitutional law could provide two paths. The first concerns the possible horizontal application of fundamental rights vis-à-vis private parties. The second focuses instead on the path that could be followed in the new season of digital constitutionalism and on a constellation of new rights that could be identified to deal with the new challenges posed by algorithms.

A good starting point is Alexy's assumption that the issue of the horizontal effect of fundamental rights protected by constitutions (and bills of rights) cannot be detached in theoretical terms from the more general issue of the direct effect of those rights.[62] In other words, according to the German legal theorist, once it is recognised that a fundamental right has a direct effect, that recognition must be characterised by a dual dimension. The first vertical dimension concerns the classic relationship of 'public authority vs individual freedom', while the second horizontal dimension focuses on the relationship between privates but also, as mentioned previously, the much less classic relationship between new private powers and individuals/users.

[61] Danielle K. Citron and F. Pasquale, 'The Scored Society: Due Process for Automated Predictions' (2014) 89 *Washington Law Review* 1; Tal Zarsky, 'Transparent Predictions' (2013) 4 *University of Illinois Law Review* 1507.

[62] Robert Alexy, A *Theory of Constitutional Rights* (Oxford University Press 2002), 570.

The problem with Alexy's assumption, which is quite convincing from a theoretical point of view, is that the shift from the Olympus of the legal theorist to the arena of the law in action risks neglecting the fact that the approach of courts from different jurisdictions might be quite different, as far as the concrete recognition of the horizontal effect of fundamental rights is concerned. This should not come as any surprise because the forms and limits of that recognition depend on the cultural and historical crucible in which a specific constitutional order is cultivated.

As far as the United States is concerned, the state action doctrine apparently precludes any possibility to apply the US Federal Bill of Rights between private parties and consequently any ability for individuals to rely on such horizontal effects, and accordingly to enforce fundamental rights vis-à-vis private actors.[63] The reason for this resistance to accepting any general horizontal effect to the rights protected by the US Federal Bill of Rights is obviously that the cultural and historical basis for US constitutionalism is rooted in the values of liberty, individual freedom, and private autonomy. The state action doctrine is critical to understanding the scope of the rights enshrined in the US Constitution. Indeed, were the fundamental rights protected by the US Constitution to be extended to non-public actors, this would result in an inevitable compression of the sphere of freedom of individuals and, more generally, private actors. For instance, such friction is evident when focusing on the right to free speech, which can only be directly enforced vis-à-vis public actors. Historically, the state action doctrine owes its origins to the civil rights cases, a series of rulings dating back to 1883 in which the US Supreme Court recognised the power of the US Congress to prohibit racially based discrimination by private individuals in the light of the Thirteenth and Fourteenth Amendments. Even in the area of freedom of expression, the US Supreme Court extended the scope of the First Amendment to include private actors on the grounds where they are substantially equivalent to a state actor.

In *Marsh* v. *Alabama*,[64] the US Supreme Court held that the State of Alabama had violated the First Amendment by prohibiting the distribution of religious material by members of the Jehovah's Witness community within a corporate town which, although privately owned, could be considered to perform a substantially recognisable 'public function' in spite of the fact that, formally speaking, it was privately owned. In *Amalgamated Food Emps. Union Local 590* v. *Logan Valley Plaza*,[65] the US Supreme Court considered a shopping centre similar to the corporate town in *Marsh*. In *Jackson* v. *Metropolitan Edison*,[66] the US Supreme Court held that equivalence should be assessed in the exercise of powers traditionally reserved exclusively to the state. Nonetheless, in *Manhattan*

63 Stephen Gardbaum, 'The "Horizontal Effect" of Constitutional Rights' (2003) 102 *Michigan Law Review*, 388; Mark Tushnet, 'The Issue of State Action/Horizontal Effect in Comparative Constitutional Law' (2003) 1 *International Journal of Constitutional Law* 79; Wilson R. Huhn, 'The State Action Doctrine and the Principle of Democratic Choice' (2006) 84 *Hofstra Law Review* 1380.

64 *Marsh* v. *Alabama* 326 U.S. 501 (1946).

65 *Amalgamated Food Emps Union Local 590* v. *Logan Valley Plaza* 391 U.S. 308 (1968).

66 *Jackson* v. *Metropolitan Edison Co* 419 U.S. 345 (1974).

Community Access Corp. v. *Halleck*,[67] the US Supreme Court more recently adopted a narrow approach to the state action doctrine, recalling in particular, its precedent in *Hudgens* v. *NLRB*.[68]

This narrow approach is also the standard for protecting fundamental rights in the digital domain, and consequently, the US Supreme Court seemingly restricts the possibility of enforcing the free speech protections enshrined in the First Amendment against digital platforms, as new private powers.[69] More specifically, and more convincingly, it has been observed by Berman that the need to call into question the implications of a radical state action doctrine[70] can lead, in the digital age, to the transformation of cyberspace into a totally private 'constitution free zone'.[71] Balkin has recently highlighted a shift in the well-established paradigm of free speech, described as a triangle involving nation-states, private infrastructure, and speakers.[72] In particular, digital infrastructure companies must be regarded as governors of social spaces instead of mere conduit providers or platforms. This new scenario, in Balkin's view, leads to a new school of speech regulation triggered by the dangers of abuse by the privatised bureaucracies that govern end-users arbitrarily and without due process and transparency; it also entails the danger of digital surveillance which facilitates manipulation.[73]

Despite the proposal that a 'functional approach' be adopted[74] and partial attempts to reveal the limits on fully embracing the state action doctrine in the digital age, the US Supreme Court recently confirmed in its case law the classic view of the intangibility of the state action doctrine.[75] However, even one of the US scholars who is more keenly aware of the de facto public functions carried out by the digital platforms concedes that

> however important Facebook or Google may be to our speech environment, it seems much harder to say that they are acting like the government all but in name. It is true that one's life may be heavily influenced by these and other large companies, but influence alone cannot be the criterion for what makes something a state actor; in that case, every employer would be a state actor, and perhaps so would nearly every family.[76]

67 *Manhattan Community Access Corp* v. *Halleck* 587 U.S. ___ (2019).
68 *Hudgens* v. *NLRB* 424 U.S. 507 (1976).
69 Jonathan Peters, 'The "Sovereigns of Cyberspace" and State Action: The First Amendment's Application (or Lack Thereof) to Third-Party Platforms' (2017) 32 *Berkeley Technology Law Journal* 989.
70 Paul S. Berman, 'Cyberspace and the State Action Debate: The Cultural Value of Applying Constitutional Norms to 'Private' Regulation' (2000) 71 *University of Colorado Law Review* 1263.
71 Bassini (n 42) 182.
72 Jack M. Balkin, 'Free Speech Is a Triangle' (2012) 118 *Columbia Law Review*.
73 Balkin (n 44).
74 Peters (n 81) 1022–24.
75 *Manhattan Community Access Corp* v. *Halleck* (n 79).
76 Tim Wu, 'Is first Amendment Obsolete?' in Lee C. Bollinger and Geoffrey R. Stone (eds), *Free Speech Century* (Oxford University Press, 2019) 272.

Shifting from the United States to Europe, the relevant historical, cultural, and consequently constitutional milieu is clearly very different. The constitutional keyword is *Drittwirkung*, a legal concept originally developed in the 1950s by the German Constitutional Court,[77] presuming that an individual plaintiff can rely on a national bill of rights to sue another private individual alleging the violation of those rights. In other words, it can be defined as a form of horizontality in action or a total constitution.[78] It is a legal concept that, as mentioned, has its roots in Germany and then subsequently migrated to many other constitutional jurisdictions, exerting a strong influence even on the case law of the CJEU and ECtHR.[79]

It should not come as any surprise that a difference emerged between the US and European constitutional practices in regard to the recognition of horizontal effects on fundamental rights. As previously noted, individual freedom and private autonomy are not constitutionally compatible with such recognition. On the other hand, however, human dignity as a super-constitutional principle supports such recognition, at least in theory.[80] The very concept of the abuse of rights, which is not recognised under US constitutional law, while instead being explicitly codified in the ECHR and the EUCFR,[81] seems to reflect the same Euro-centric approach.

In the light of this scenario, it is no coincidence that, as early as 1976, the CJEU decided in *Defrenne II* to acknowledge and enforce the obligation for private employers (and the corresponding right of employees) to ensure equal pay for equal work, in relation to a provision of the former Treaty establishing the European Economic Community.[82] Article 119 of the EC Treaty was unequivocally and exclusively addressed to Member States. It provided that 'each Member State shall ensure that the principle of *equal pay* for male and female workers for work of *equal value* is applied'. When compared to the wording of that provision, it could be observed that each provision of the EUCFR is more detailed and, therefore, more amenable to potential horizontal direct effect. It is no coincidence that, in 2014, while in *AMS* the CJEU adopted a minimalist approach to the possible horizontal direct effect only of those provisions of the EU Charter of Fundamental Rights from

77 The Lüth case concerned a *querelle* about the distribution of the anti-Semitic movie "Jüd Jüss" in a private location. Following the conviction, Lüth appealed to the German Constitutional Court complaining about the violation of her freedom of expression. The German Constitutional Court, therefore, addressed a question relating to the extension of constitutional rights in a private relationship. In this case, for the first time, the German court argued that constitutional rights not only constitute individual claims against the state but also constitute a set of values that apply in all areas of law by providing axiological indications to the legislative power, executive, and judicial. In the present case, the protection of freedom of expression does not only develop vertically towards the state but also horizontally since civil law rules must be interpreted according to the spirit of the German Constitution. German Constitutional Court, judgment of 15 January 1958, BVerfGE 7, 198.

78 Mattias Kumm, 'Who Is Afraid of the Total Constitution? Constitutional Rights as Principles and the Constitutionalization of Private Law' (2006) 7(4) *German Law Journal* 341.

79 *X e Y* v. *The Netherlands*, App no 8978/80, judgment of 26 March 1985.

80 Catherine Dupré, *The Age of Dignity. Human Rights and Constitutionalism in Europe* (Hart 2016).

81 Art 17 ECHR; Art 54 EUCFR.

82 Case C-43/75 *Defrenne* v. *Sabena* [1976] ECR 455.

which it could derive a legal right for individuals and not simply a principle, it also applied Articles 7 and 8 EUCFR in relation to the enforcement of digital privacy rights, specifically against search engines in *Google Spain*.[83]

Several years later, the CJEU had the opportunity to further develop the horizontal application of the EUCFR. More specifically, in four judgments from 2018 – *Egenberger*,[84] *IR* v. *JQ*,[85] *Bauer*,[86] and *Max Planck*[87] – the CJEU definitively clarified the horizontal scope of Articles 21, 31(2), and 47 of the EUCFR within disputes between private parties.[88] In the light of the emerging scenario, it seems clear that a potential initial answer to the new challenges of constitutional law in the age of new private powers could be found in the brave horizontal enforcement of fundamental rights, especially in the field of freedom of expression and privacy and data protection.

However, as mentioned previously, it is also worth reaching beyond the debate about the horizontal/vertical effects of fundamental rights in the digital age in order to suggest an alternative weapon for the challenges that will need to be faced during the new round of digital constitutionalism. Most notably, it is necessary to design a frame that describes the relationship between the three parties that Balkin puts at the heart of the information society: platforms, states, and individuals.[89] In other words, a digital *habeas corpus* of substantive and procedural rights should be identified, which can be enforced by the courts as they are inferred from existing rights protected under current digital constitutionalism.[90] Therefore, a new set of rights can be derived by such revisited understanding of individuals in the new digital context – among others, the right that decisions impacting the legal and political sphere of individuals are undertaken by human beings, and not exclusively by machines, even the most advanced and efficient ones.

The significant shift of paradigm that individuals are witnessing in their relationship with power thus requires to revisit their traditional status and to focus on a set of rights that can be enforced vis-à-vis not only governmental powers but also private actors. In particular, hard law could certainly play a role in order to remedy the lack

83 *Google Spain* (n 41).

84 Case C-414/16 *Vera Egenberger* v. *Evangelisches Werk für Diakonie und Entwicklung eV*. ECLI:EU:C:2018:257.

85 Case C-68/17 *IR* v. *JQ*, ECLI:EU:C:2018:696.

86 Joined Cases C-569/16 and C-570/16 *Stadt Wuppertal* v. *Maria Elisabeth Bauer and Volker Willmeroth* v. *Martina Broßonn*, ECLI:EU:C:2018:871.

87 Case C-684/16 *Max-Planck-Gesellschaft zur Förderung der Wissenschaften eV* v. *Tetsuji Shimizu*, ECLI:EU:C:2018:874.

88 Aurelia Colombi Ciacchi, 'The Direct Horizontal Effect of EU Fundamental Rights: ECJ 17 April 2018, Case C-414/16, Vera Egenberger v. Evangelisches Werk für Diakonie und Entwicklung e.V. and ECJ 11 September 2018, Case C-68/17, IR v. JQ' (2019) 15(2) *European Constitutional Law Review* 294; Eleni Frantziou, *The Horizontal Effect of Fundamental Rights in the European Union: A Constitutional Analysis* (Oxford University Press 2019); Sonya Walkila, *Horizontal Effect of Fundamental Rights in EU Law* (Europa Law Publishing 2016).

89 Jack Balkin, 'Free Speech in the Algorithmic Society: Big Data, Private Governance, and New School Speech Regulation' (2018) 51 *University of California Davis* 1151.

90 De Gregorio (n 56).

of fairness, transparency, and accountability which appears as the most important challenge to face in respect of the implementation of algorithmic systems. Although ensuring transparency could be complex, for multiple reasons such as trade secrets, it is possible to mitigate this issue by granting different forms of transparency and defining some procedural safeguards, which online platforms should abide by when making decisions which, otherwise, would be deprived of any public guarantee. While substantive rights concern the status of individuals as subjects of a kind of sovereign power that is no longer exclusively vested in public authorities, procedural rights stem from the expectation that individuals have of claiming and enforcing their rights before bodies other than traditional jurisdictional bodies, which employ methods different from judicial discretion, such as technological and horizontal due process. As a result of this call for algorithmic accountability, a new set of substantive and procedural rights would constitute an attempt to remedy the weakness and the transparency gap that individuals suffer from their technologically biased relationship with private actors and the lack of any bargaining power.

The right to explanation is only just one of the new rights that could contribute to mitigating the lack of fairness, transparency, and accountability in automated decision-making. Indeed, together with the right to obtain information on the way their data are being processed, individuals should also rely on a right to easy access (right to accessibility) and on a right to obtain translation from the language of technology to the language of human beings. While the former is meant as the right to be provided with the possibility to interact with algorithms and digital platforms implementing the use thereof, the latter requires the use of simple, clear, and understandable information and allows users not only to rely on, for example, the reasons for the removal of online content, but also to better exercise their rights before a judicial or administrative body.

These substantive rights find their justification in the 'hidden price' that individual users pay to digital platforms, while enjoying their services apparently free of charge – a cost that is not limited to personal data. Human behaviours, feelings, emotions, and political choices as well have a value for algorithms, most notably to the extent that they help machines learn something about individual reactions based on certain inputs. The new set of rights seems to respond to Pasquale's questions about the transparency gap between users and digital platforms:

> Without knowing what Google actually does when it ranks sites, we cannot assess when it is acting in good faith to help users, and when it is biasing results to favour its own commercial interests. The same goes for status updates on Facebook, trending topics on Twitter, and even network management practices at telephone and cable companies. All these are protected by laws of secrecy and technologies of obfuscation.[91]

[91] Frank Pasquale, *The Black Box Society. The Secret Algorithms That Control Money and Information* (Harvard University Press 2015).

If, on the one hand, this new digital *pactum subjectionis* requires new rights being recognised and protected, it is also necessary to understand how their enforcement can be effective and how they can actually be put into place. This new set of substantive rights is associated with the need for certain procedural guarantees that allow individuals to ensure that these expectations can actually be met. Therefore, it is necessary to investigate also the 'procedural counterweight' of the creation of new substantive rights, focusing on the fairness of the process through which individuals may enforce them. Indeed, since within existing literature the focus up to date has been on the exercise of powers, there is no reason to exclude from the scope of application of procedural guarantees those situations where powers are conferred upon private bodies charged with the performance of public functions.[92]

Digital platforms can be said to exercise administrative powers which are normally vested in public authorities. However, looking at the way rights can be exercised vis-à-vis these new actors, vagueness and opacity can still be noticed in the relevant procedures. Among others, the right to be forgotten shows in a clear way the lack of appropriate procedural safeguards, since steps such as the evaluation of the requests of delisting and the adoption of the relevant measures (whether consisting of the removal of a link or of the confirmation of its lawfulness) entirely rely on a discretionary assessment supported by the use of algorithms. Therefore, the mere horizontal application of the fundamental right to protection of personal data enshrined in Article 8 of the Charter of Fundamental Rights of the European Union does not prove to be satisfactory. Also, the notice and takedown mechanisms implemented by platforms hosting user-generated content and social networks do not entirely meet the requirements of transparency and fairness that make the status of users/individuals enforcing their rights vis-à-vis them comparable to the status of citizens exercising their rights against public authorities.

In order for these new substantive rights to be actually protected, and made enforceable vis-à-vis the emerging private actors, procedural rights play a pivotal role. Crawford and Schultz have explored the need to frame a 'procedural data due process'.[93] The application of such a technological due process would also impact the substantive rights, as they should preserve, in accordance with the Redish and Marshall model of due process, values such as accuracy; appearance of fairness; equality of inputs; predictability, transparency, and rationality; participation; revelation; and privacy-dignity.[94] The due process traditional function of keeping powers separate has to be fine-tuned with the specific context of algorithms, where interactions occur between various actors (algorithm designers, adjudicators, and individuals). Citron has pointed out some requirements that automated systems

92 Giacinto della Cananea, *Due Process of Law Beyond the State* (Oxford University Press 2016).

93 Kate Crawford and Jason Schultz, 'Big Data and Due Process: Toward a Framework to Redress Predictive Privacy Harms' (2014) 55 *Boston College Law Review* 93.

94 Martin Redish and Lawrence Marshall, 'Adjudicatory Independence and the Values of Procedural Due Process' (1986) 95(3) *Yale Law Journal* 455.

should meet in order to fulfil the procedural due process, including (a) adequate notice to be given to individuals affected by the decision-making process; (b) opportunity for individuals of being heard before the decision is released; (c) and record, audits, or judicial review.[95] According to Crawford and Schultz's model of procedural data due process, the notice requirement can be fulfilled by providing individuals with 'an opportunity to intervene in the predictive process' and to know (i.e., to obtain an explanation about) the type of predictions and the sources of data. Besides, the right to being heard is seen as a tool for ensuring that once data are disclosed, individuals have a chance to challenge the fairness of the predictive process. The right to being heard thus implies having access to a computer program's source code, or to the logic of a computer program's decision. Lastly, this model requires guarantees of impartiality of the 'adjudicator', including judicial review, to ensure that individuals do not suffer from any bias while being subject to predictive decisions.

The proposal for the Digital Services Act provides an example of these procedural safeguards limiting platforms' powers.[96] With the goal of defining a path towards the digital age, the proposal maintains the rules of liability for online intermediaries, now established as the foundation of the digital economy and instrumental to the protection of fundamental rights. In fact, based on the proposal, there will no changes in the liability system but rather some additions which aim to increase the level of transparency and accountability of online platforms. It is no coincidence that, among the proposed measures, the DSA introduces new obligations of due diligence and transparency with particular reference to the procedure of notice and takedown and redress mechanisms.

1.6 CONCLUSIONS

Algorithmic systems have contributed to the introduction of new paths for innovation, thus producing positive effects for society as a whole, including fundamental rights and freedoms. Technology is also an opportunity for constitutional democracies. Artificial intelligence can provide better systems of enforcement of legal rules or improve the performance of public services. Nonetheless, the domain of inscrutable algorithms characterising contemporary society challenges the protection of fundamental rights and democratic values while encouraging lawmakers to find a regulatory framework balancing risk and innovation, considering the role and responsibilities of private actors in the algorithmic society.

The challenges raised by artificial intelligence technologies are not limited to freedom of expression, privacy, and data protection. Constitutional democracies

95 Danielle K. Citron, 'Technological Due Process' (2008) 85(6) *Washington University Law Review* 1249.

96 Proposal for a Regulation of the European Parliament and of the Council on Contestable and Fair Markets in the Digital Sector (Digital Markets Act) COM (2020) 842 final.

are under pressure to ensure legal certainty and predictability of automated decision-making processes which can collectively affect democratic values. Individuals are increasingly surrounded by ubiquitous systems that do not always ensure the possibility of understanding and controlling their underlying technologies. Leaving algorithms without any safeguards would mean opening the way towards techno-determinism, allowing the actors who govern these automated systems to arbitrarily determine the standard of protection of rights and freedoms at a transnational level under the logics of digital capitalism. This is why it is critical to understand the role of regulation in the field of artificial intelligence, where cooperative efforts between the public and private sector could lead to a balanced approach between risk and innovation. Constitutional democracies cannot leave private actors to acquire areas of power outside constitutional limits.

Within this framework, both the horizontal effect doctrines and new substantive and procedural rights seem to be promising candidates among the available remedies. In the face of these challenges, it is likely that *ius dicere* will by no means lose its predominant role over political power acquired in recent years. The challenges raised by new automated technologies are likely to operate as a call for courts to protect fundamental rights in the information society while increasing pressures on lawmakers to adopt new rights and safeguards.[97] It is conceivable that, despite the codification of new safeguards, the role of courts in interpreting the challenges raised by new technologies is far from being exhausted, also due to the role of online platforms. Indeed, artificial intelligence technologies have raised different questions concerning the protection of fundamental rights, which still have not been answered through the political process. We have seen how constitutional law can provide some solutions to these new challenges. Nonetheless, in the absence of any form of regulation, the role of courts is likely to be predominant. The COVID-19 pandemic has only amplified this dynamic. It has confirmed the role of legislative inertia in the face of the new challenges associated with the implementation of technology and the increasing role of online platforms in providing services and new solutions to combat the global pandemic.

Therefore, the primary challenge for constitutional democracies in the algorithmic society might be to limit the rise of global private powers replacing democratic values with private determinations. This does not entail intervening in the market or adopting a liberal approach, but involves defining a constitutional framework where public and private powers are bound by safeguards and procedures.

97 Oreste Pollicino, *Judicial Protection of Fundamental Rights on the Internet. A Road Towards Digital Constitutionalism?* (Hart 2021).

PART I

Algorithms, Freedom, and Fundamental Rights

2

Fundamental Rights and the Rule of Law in the Algorithmic Society

Andrea Simoncini and Erik Longo

2.1 NEW TECHNOLOGIES AND THE RISE OF THE ALGORITHMIC SOCIETY

New technologies offer human agents entirely new ways of doing things.[1] However, as history shows, 'practical' innovations always bring with them more significant changes. Each new option introduced by technological evolution allowing new forms affects the substance, eventually changing the way humans think and relate to each other.[2] The transformation is especially true when we consider information and communication technologies (so-called ICT); as indicated by Marshall McLuhan, 'the media is the message'.[3] Furthermore, this scenario has been accelerated by the appearance of artificial intelligence systems (AIS), based on the application of machine learning (ML).

These new technologies not only allow people to find information at an incredible speed; they also recast decision-making processes once in the exclusive remit of human beings.[4] By learning from vast amounts of data – the so-called Big Data – AIS offer predictions, evaluations, and hypotheses that go beyond the mere application of pre-existing rules or programs. They instead 'induce' their own rules of action from data analysis; in a word, they make autonomous decisions.[5]

1 Pedro Domingos, *The Master Algorithm: How the Quest for the Ultimate Learning Machine Will Remake Our World* (Basic Books 2015).

2 One of the most prominent prophets of the idea of a new kind of progress generated through the use of technologies is surely Jeremy Rifkin. See his book *The Zero Marginal Cost Society: The Internet of Things, the Collaborative Commons, and the Eclipse of Capitalism* (St. Martin's Press 2014).

3 Marshall McLuhan and Quentin Fiore, *The Medium Is the Massage* (Ginko Press 1967).

4 Committee of Experts on Internet Intermediaries of the Council of Europe (MSI-NET), 'Algorithms and Human Rights. Study on the Human Rights Dimensions of Automated Data Processing Techniques and Possible Regulatory Implications' (2016) DGI(2017)12.

5 According to the European Parliament, 'Resolution of 16 February 2017 with recommendations to the Commission on Civil Law Rules on Robotics (2015/2103(INL))' (P8_TA(2017)0051, Bruxelles), 'a robot's autonomy can be defined as the ability to take decisions and implement them in the outside world, independently of external control or influence.'

We have entered a new era, where big multinational firms (called 'platforms') use algorithms and artificial intelligence to govern vast communities of people.[6] Conversely, data generated by those platforms fuel the engine of the 'Algorithmic Society'.[7]

From this point of view, the Algorithmic Society is a distinctive evolution of the 'Information Society',[8] where a new kind of 'mass-surveillance' becomes possible.[9]

This progress generates a mixture of excitement and anxiety.[10] The development of algorithms and artificial intelligence technologies is becoming ubiquitous, omnipresent, and seemingly omnipotent. They promise to eliminate our errors and make our decisions better suited for any purpose.[11]

In this perspective, a relatively old prophecy, predicted by Herbert Marcuse in one of the 'red books' of that massive socio-political movement usually known as '1968', *The One-Dimensional Man*, becomes reality. Marcuse starts the first page of that seminal book as follows:

> A comfortable, smooth, reasonable, democratic unfreedom prevails in advanced industrial civilization, a token of technical progress.
>
> Indeed, what could be more rational than the suppression of individuality in the mechanization of socially necessary but painful performances; . . . That this technological order also involves a political and intellectual coordination may be a regrettable and yet promising development. The rights and liberties which were such vital factors in the origins and earlier stages of industrial society yield to a higher stage of this society: they are losing their traditional rationale and content. . . .
>
> To the degree to which freedom from want, the concrete substance of all freedom, is becoming a real possibility. The liberties that pertain to a state of lower productivity are losing their former content. . . . In this respect, it seems to

6 According to Statista, Facebook is the biggest social network platform worldwide, with more than 2.7 billion monthly active users in the second quarter of 2020. During the last reported quarter, the company stated that 3.14 billion people were using at least one of the company's core products (Facebook, WhatsApp, Instagram, or Messenger) each month. To the contrary, as of the end of 2019, Twitter had 152 million monetizable daily active users worldwide.

7 Jack M. Balkin, 'Free Speech in the Algorithmic Society: Big Data, Private Governance, and New School Speech Regulation' (2017) 51 *UCDL Rev* 1149; Agnieszka M. Walorska, 'The Algorithmic Society' in Denise Feldner (ed), *Redesigning Organizations Concepts for the Connected Society* (Springer 2020); Giovanni De Gregorio, 'From Constitutional Freedoms to the Power of the Platforms: Protecting Fundamental Rights Online in the Algorithmic Society' (2018) 11 *Eur J Legal Stud* 65.

8 Frank Webster, *Theories of the Information Society*, 4th ed. (Routledge 2014).

9 Neil M. Richards, 'The Dangers of Surveillance' (2012) 126 *Harv L Rev* 1934;

10 Jonathan Zittrain, *The Future of the Internet – And How to Stop It* (Yale University Press 2008); Cary Coglianese and David Lehr, 'Regulating by Robot: Administrative Decision Making in the Machine-Learning Era' (2016) 105 *Geo LJ* 1147. Responsibility for the production of recent anxiety in large part can be attributed to Nick Bostrom, *Superintelligence* (Oxford University Press 2014).

11 E. Morozov uses the expression 'digital solutionism' to name the idea that technological innovation should solve every social problem. Evgeny Morozov, *To Save Everything, Click Here: The Folly of Technological Solutionism* (Public Affairs 2013).

> make little difference whether the increasing satisfaction of needs is accomplished by an authoritarian or a non-authoritarian system.[12]

If technology replaces all 'socially necessary but painful performances' – work included – personal freedom reaches its final fulfilment (that is, its very end). In Marcuse's eyes, this is how technological power will take over our freedom and political system: not through a bloody 'coup' but by inducing people – practically and happily – to give up all their responsibilities.

However, this dystopic perspective – a future of 'digital slavery', where men and women will lose their liberty and quietly reject all democratic principles[13] – produces a reaction. It is not by chance that the European Commission's strategically endorsing the transformation of the EU into an AI-led economy, at the same time, requires great attention to people's trust and a high level of fundamental rights protection.[14]

One of the most common areas where we experience the rise of these concerns is public and private security.[15] For a large part of the 2010s onward, technological innovations have focused on safety and control; the consequence has been an alarming increase in public and private surveillance, coupled with growing threats to political and civil liberties.[16] In addition to this, the global 'COVID-19' pandemic has doubtlessly boosted the already fast-growing 'surveillance capitalism'.[17]

While at the beginning of the twenty-first century, there was an increasing awareness of the risks of the new pervasive surveillance technologies, today, hit by the pandemic and searching for practical tools to enforce social distancing or controlling policies, the general institutional and academic debate seems to be less worried by liberty-killing effects and more allured by health-preserving results.[18]

Regardless, the most worrying challenges stem from the increasing power of algorithms, created through Big Data analytics such as machine learning and used

12 Herbert Marcuse, *One-Dimensional Man: Studies in the Ideology of Advanced Industrial Society*, 2nd ed. (Beacon Press 2019) 1.

13 Michael Veale and Lilian Edwards, 'Clarity, Surprises, and Further Questions in the Article 29 Working Party Draft Guidance on Automated Decision-Making and Profiling' (2018) 34 *Computer Law Security Review* 398.

14 European Commission, 'White Paper on Artificial Intelligence: A European Approach to Excellence and Trust' (COM (2020) 65 final, Bruxelles).

15 Inga Kroener and Daniel Neyland, 'New Technologies, Security and Surveillance' in Kirstie Ball, Kevin Haggerty, and David Lyon (eds), *Routledge Handbook of Surveillance Studies* (Routledge 2012) 141.

16 Radha D'Souza, *The Surveillance State: A Composition in Four Movements*, (Pluto 2019); Cathy O'Neil, *Weapons of Math Destruction: How Big Data Increases Inequality and Threatens Democracy* (Broadway Books 2016).

17 Shoshana Zuboff, *The Age of Surveillance Capitalism: The Fight for a Human Future at the New Frontier of Power* (PublicAffairs 2019).

18 Natalie Ram and David Gray, 'Mass Surveillance in the Age of COVID-19' (2020) 7 *Journal of Law and the Biosciences* 1.

to automate decision-making processes.[19] Their explicability,[20] liability, and culpability are still far from being clearly defined.[21] As a consequence, several scholars and policymakers are arguing, on the one hand, to aggressively regulate tech firms[22] (since classic antitrust law is unfit for this purpose) or, on the other, to require procedural safeguards, allowing people to challenge the decisions of algorithms which can have significant consequences on their lives (such as credit score systems).[23]

2.2 THE IMPACT OF THE ALGORITHMIC SOCIETY ON CONSTITUTIONAL LAW

As we know, at its very origin, constitutional theory wrestles with the problem of power control.[24] Scholars commonly consider constitutional law that part of the legal system whose function is to legally[25] delimit power.[26] In the 'modern sense',[27] this discipline establishes rules or builds institutions capable of shielding personal freedoms from external constraints.[28] According to this idea, constitutionalism

19 In the broadest sense, algorithms are encoded procedures for solving a problem by transforming input data into a desired output. As we know the excitement surrounding Big Data is largely attributable to machine learning. Paul Dourish, 'Algorithms and Their Others: Algorithmic Culture in Context' (2016) 3 *Big Data & Society* 1; Tarleton Gillespie, 'The Relevance of Algorithms' in Tarleton Gillespie, Pablo J. Boczkowski. and Kirsten A. Foot (eds), *Media Technologies: Essays on Communication, Materiality, and Society* (MIT Press 2014); Viktor Mayer-Schoenberger and Kenneth Cukier, *Big Data: A Revolution That Will Transform How We Live, Work, and Think* (Houghton Mifflin Harcourt 2013).

20 This idea – sometimes abbreviated as XAI (explainable artificial intelligence) – means that machines could give access to data about their own deliberative processes, simply by recording them and making them available as data structures. See Wojciech Samek and Klaus-Robert Müller, 'Towards Explainable Artificial Intelligence' in Wojciech Samek et al. (eds), *Explainable AI: Interpreting, Explaining and Visualizing Deep Learning* (Springer 2019); Tim Miller, 'Explanation in Artificial Intelligence: Insights from the Social Sciences' (2019) 267 *Artificial Intelligence* 1 Brent Mittelstadt, Chris Russell, and Sandra Wachter, *Explaining Explanations in AI* (ACM 2019).

21 Frank Pasquale, *The Black Box Society: The Secret Algorithms That Control Money and Information* (Harvard University Press 2015); Tal Z. Zarsky, 'Understanding Discrimination in the Scored Society' (2014) 89 *Wash L Rev* 1375.

22 See, for example, the 'Proposal for a Regulation of the European Parliament and of the Council on a Single Market for Digital Services (Digital Services Act)' and amending Directive 2000/31/EC, COM (2020) 825 final, 15.12.2020, and the proposals for a Digital Services Act (DSA), COM/2020/842 final, 15.12.2020, and for an Artificial Intelligence Act, COM (2017) 85 final, 21.4.2021.

23 Danielle Keats Citron and Frank Pasquale, 'The Scored Society: Due Process for Automated Predictions' (2014) 89 *Wash L Rev* 1.

24 Giovanni Sartori, 'Constitutionalism: A Preliminary Discussion' (1962) 56 *American Political Science Review* 853.

25 Being that constitutional theory is part of the legal system, this feature distinctively differentiates constitutional law from political philosophy or political sociology.

26 Giorgio Pino, *Il costituzionalismo dei diritti struttura e limiti del costituzionalismo contemporaneo* (il Mulino 2017).

27 Benjamin Constant, 'De la liberté des anciens comparée à celle des modernes' in *Collection complète des ouvrages: publiés sur le gouvernement représentatif et la constitution actuelle ou Cours de politique constitutionelle* (Plancher 1820).

28 Richard Bellamy, 'Constitutionalism' in Bertrand Badie, Dirk Berg-Schlosser, and Leonardo Morlino (eds), *International Encyclopedia of Political Science*, vol. 2 (SAGE 2011).

historically always 'adapted' itself to power's features; that is to say, the protection of freedoms in constitutions has been shaped following the evolving character of the threats to those same freedoms.[29]

At the beginning of the modern era, the power to be feared was the king's private force.[30] The idea of 'sovereignty', which appeared at the end of the Middle Ages, had its roots in the physical and military strength of the very person of the 'Sovereign'.[31] Sovereignty evoked an 'external power'[32] grounded on the monopoly (actual or potential) of the physical 'force'[33] used against individuals or communities (e.g., 'military force' or the 'force of law').[34] Consequently, liberties were those dimensions of human life not subjected to that power (e.g., habeas corpus). As the offspring of the French and American Revolutions, the 'rule of law' doctrine was the main legal tool 'invented' by constitutional theory to delimit the king's power and protect personal freedom and rights. To be 'legitimate', any power has to be subjected to the rule of law.

The other decisive turning point in the history of constitutionalism was World War II and the end of twentieth-century European totalitarian regimes. It may sound like a paradox, but those regimes showed that the 'legislative state', built on the supremacy of law and therefore exercising a 'legitimate power', can become another terrible threat to human freedom and dignity.

If the law itself has no limits, whenever it 'gives' a right, it can 'withdraw' it. This practice is the inhuman history of some European twentieth-century states that cancelled human dignity 'through the law'.

With the end of World War II, a demolition process of those regimes began, and learning from the American constitutional experience, Europe transformed 'flexible' constitutions – until then, mere ordinary laws – into 'rigid' constitutions,[35] which are effectively the 'supreme law' of the land.[36]

29 Andrea Buratti, *Western Constitutionalism: History, Institutions, Comparative Law* (Springer-Giappichelli 2019).

30 Martin Loughlin, *Foundations of Public Law* (Oxford University Press 2010).

31 Jean Bodin, *On Sovereignty: Four Chapters from the Six Books of the Commonwealth* (Cambridge University Press 1992).

32 Carl Schmitt, *Political Theology: Four Chapters on the Concept of Sovereignty* (University of Chicago Press 1985).

33 Absolutism was the crucible in which this modern concept of sovereignty was forged. As J. Bodin expressed, 'sovereignty' is 'the greatest power of command' and is 'not limited either in power, charge, or time certain'. Jean Bodin, *Les six livres de la république* (Jacques du Puis 1576).

34 As Hart asserted: 'In any society where there is law, there actually is a sovereign, characterized affirmatively and negatively by reference to the habit of obedience: a person or body of persons whose orders the great majority of the society habitually obey and who does not habitually obey any other person or persons.' Herbert L. A. Hart, *The Concept of Law*, 1st ed. (Oxford University Press 1961).

35 Regarding this distinction, see James Bryce, 'Flexible and Rigid Constitutions' (1901) 1 *Studies in History and Jurisprudence* 145, 124.

36 In *Marbury v. Madison*, 5 U.S. (1 Cr.) 137, 173–180 (1803), Chief Justice Marshall gave the Constitution precedence over laws and treaties, providing that only laws 'which shall be made in pursuance of the constitution' shall be 'the supreme law of the land'. For further information on

In this new scenario, the power that instils fear is no longer the king's private prerogative; the new limitless force is the public power of state laws, and the constitutional tool intended to effectively regulate that power is vested in the new 'rigid' constitution: a superior law, 'stronger' than ordinary statutes and thus truly able to protect freedoms, at least apparently, even against legal acts.

With the turn of the twenty-first century, we witness the rise of a new kind of power. The advent of new digital technologies, as discussed previously, provides an unprecedented means of limiting and directing human freedom that has appeared on the global stage; a way based on not an 'external' force (as in the two previous constitutional scenarios, the private force of the king or the public 'force of the law') but rather an 'internal' force, able to affect and eventually substitute our self-determination 'from inside'.[37]

This technological power is at the origin of 'platform capitalism',[38] which is a vast economic transformation induced by the exponentially fast-growing markets of Internet-related goods and services – for example, smart devices (Apple, Samsung, Huawei, Xiaomi), web-search engines (Google), social media corporations (Facebook, Instagram, Twitter), cloud service providers (Amazon, Microsoft, Google), e-commerce companies (Amazon, Netflix), and social platforms (Zoom, Cisco Webex).

Consider that today,[39] the combined value of the S&P 500's five most prominent companies[40] now stands at more than $7 trillion, accounting for almost 25 per cent of the market capitalization of the index, drawing a picture of what a recent doctrine accurately defined as a 'moligopoly'.[41]

this topic, see generally Bruce Ackerman, 'The Rise of World Constitutionalism' (1997) *Virginia Law Review* 771; Alec Stone Sweet, *Governing with Judges: Constitutional Politics in Europe* (Oxford University Press 2000); Ronald Dworkin, *Freedom's Law: The Moral Reading of the American Constitution* (Oxford University Press 1999); Michaela Hailbronner, 'Transformative Constitutionalism: Not Only in the Global South' (2017) 65 *The American Journal of Comparative Law* 527; and Mark Tushnet, *Advanced Introduction to Comparative Constitutional Law* (Edward Elgar 2018). For a specific insight into the Italian experience, see Vittoria Barsotti et al., *Italian Constitutional Justice in Global Context* (Oxford University Press 2016), 263; Maurizio Fioravanti, 'Constitutionalism' in Damiano Canale, Paolo Grossi, and Basso Hofmann (eds), *A Treatise of Legal Philosophy and General Jurisprudence*, vol. 9 (Springer 2009).

37 In the view of Bodei, from 'algorithmic capitalism' (which will use artificial intelligence and robotics to increasingly link economics and politics to certain forms of knowledge) originates a new 'occult' power in which 'the human logos will be more and more subject to an impersonal logos'. See Remo Bodei, *Dominio e sottomissione. Schiavi, animali, macchine, Intelligenza Artificiale* (il Mulino 2019).

38 Frank Pasquale, 'Two Narratives of Platform Capitalism' (2016) 35 *Yale L & Pol'y Rev* 309.

39 Lawrence Delevingne, 'U.S. Big Tech Dominates Stock Market after Monster Rally, Leaving Investors on Edge', Reuters (28 August 2020) www.reuters.com/article/us-usa-markets-faangs-analysis-idUSKBN25O0FV.

40 Apple Inc, AAPL.O; Amazon.com Inc., AMZN.O; Microsoft Corp, MSFT.O; Facebook Inc., FB.O; and Google parent Alphabet Inc., GOOGL.O.

41 Nicolas Petit, *Big Tech and the Digital Economy: The Moligopoly Scenario* (Oxford University Press 2020).

These 'moligopolists'[42] are not only creating communities and benefitting from network effects generated by users' transactions, but they also develop a *de facto* political authority and influence once reserved for legal and political institutions. More importantly, they are taking on configurations that are increasingly similar to the state and other public authorities.[43] Their structure reflects a fundamental shift in the political and legal systems of Western democracies – what has been called a new type of 'functional sovereignty'.[44] Elsewhere we used the term 'cybernetic power',[45] which perhaps sounds like an old-fashioned expression. Still, it is more accurate in its etymology ('cyber', from its original ancient Greek meaning,[46] shares the same linguistic root as 'govern' and 'governance') to identify how automation and ICT have radically transformed our lives.

As algorithms begin to play a dominant role in the contemporary exercise of power,[47] it becomes increasingly important to examine the 'phenomenology' of this new sovereign power and its unique challenges to constitutional freedoms.

2.3 THE 'ALGORITHMIC STATE' VERSUS FUNDAMENTAL RIGHTS: SOME CRITICAL ISSUES

As already stated, the main force of algorithms is their practical convenience, so their interference with our freedom is not perceived as an 'external' constraint or a disturbing power. Instead, it is felt as evidence-based support for our decisions, capturing our autonomy by lifting our deliberation burden.

Who would like to switch back to searching for information in volumes of an encyclopaedia? Who would want to filter their email for spam manually anymore? Who would like to use manual calculators instead of a spreadsheet when doing complex

42 Ibid.

43 Airbnb, for example, has developed market power to shape urban planning in smaller cities in the United States. Amazon has received offers from democratically elected mayors to assume political power when the company moves its headquarters to these cities. More importantly, Facebook has become one of the most important actors in political campaigns all over the world, not to mention the famous and controversial case of Cambridge Analytica, when we experienced the disruptive force of the social network for people's lives in terms of political participation, data protection, and privacy. See Emma Graham-Harrison and Carole Cadwalladr, 'Data Firm Bragged of Role in Trump Victory' The Guardian (21 March 2018) https://www.theguardian.com/uk-news/2018/mar/20/cambridge-analytica-execs-boast-of-role-in-getting-trump-elected.

44 Frank Pasquale, 'From Territorial to Functional Sovereignty: The Case of Amazon' (accessed 6 December 2020) http://lpeblog.org/2017/12/06/from-territorial-to-functional-sovereignty-the-case-of-amazon/; Denise Feldner, 'Designing a Future Europe' in Denise Feldner (ed), *Redesigning Organizations: Concepts for the Connected Society* (Springer 2020).

45 Andrea Simoncini, 'Sovranità e potere nell'era digitale' in Tommaso Edoardo Frosini et al. (eds), *Diritti e libertà in internet* (Le Monnier Università 2017) 19.

46 Wiener decided to call 'the entire field of control and communication theory, whether in the machine or in the animal, by the name Cybernetics, which we form from the Greek χυβερνήτης or steersman'. See Norbert Wiener, *Cybernetics or Control and Communication in the Animal and the Machine* (2nd reissued edn, MIT Press 2019) 18.

47 Ugo Pagallo, 'Algo-Rhythms and the Beat of the Legal Drum' (2018) 31 *Philosophy & Technology* 507.

calculations? We are not just living in an increasingly automated world; we are increasingly enjoying the many advantages that come with it. Public administrations are using more and more algorithms to help public-sector functions, such as welfare, the labour market, tax administration, justice, crime prevention, and more. The use of algorithms in decision-making and adjudications promises more objectivity and fewer costs.

However, as we said, algorithms have a darker side, and the following chapters of this section of the book illustrate some of the facets of the Algorithmic State phenomenology.

The fast-growing use of algorithms in the fields of justice, policing, public welfare, and the like could end in biased and erroneous decisions, boosting inequality, discrimination, unfair consequences, and undermining constitutional rights, such as privacy, freedom of expression, and equality.[48]

And these uses raise considerable concerns not only for the specific policy area in which they are operated but also for our society as a whole.[49] There is an increasing perception that humans do not have complete control over Algorithmic State decision-making processes.[50] Despite their predictive outperformance over analogue tools, algorithmic decisions are difficult to understand and explain (the so-called black box effect).[51] While producing highly effective practical outcomes, algorithmic decisions could undermine procedural and substantive guarantees related to democracy and the rule of law.

Issues related to the use of algorithms as part of the decision-making process are numerous and complex, but at the same time, the debate is at an early stage. However, efforts towards a deeper understanding of how algorithms work when applied to legally tricky decisions will be addressed soon.

In this section, we will examine four profiles of the use of algorithmic decisions: the relation between automation and due process, the so-called 'emotional' AI, the algorithmic bureaucracy, and predictive policing.

Due Process in the Age of AI

In Chapter 3, entitled 'Inalienable Due Process in an Age of AI: Limiting the Contractual Creep toward Automated Adjudication', Frank Pasquale argues that

48 Nicol Turner Lee, 'Detecting Racial Bias in Algorithms and Machine Learning' (2018) 16 *Journal of Information, Communication and Ethics in Society* 252; Jack M. Balkin, 'Free Speech in the Algorithmic Society: Big Data, Private Governance, and New School Speech Regulation' (2017) 51 *UCDL Rev* 1149; Ryan Calo, 'Privacy, Vulnerability, and Affordance' (2016) 66 *DePaul L Rev* 591; Oreste Pollicino and Laura Somaini, 'Online Disinformation and Freedom of Expression in the Democratic Context' in Sandrine Boillet Baume, Véronique Martenet Vincent (eds), *Misinformation in Referenda* (Routledge 2021).

49 O'Neil, *Weapons of Math Destruction.*

50 'Robotics Ethics' (SHS/YES/COMEST-10/17/2 REV, Paris); Jon Kleinberg et al., 'Discrimination in the Age of Algorithms' (2018) 10 *Journal of Legal Analysis* 113; McKenzie Raub, 'Bots, Bias and Big Data: Artificial Intelligence, Algorithmic Bias and Disparate Impact Liability in Hiring Practices' (2018) 71 *Ark L Rev* 529.

51 Pasquale, *The Black Box Society.*

robust legal values must inspire the current efforts to 'fast track' cases by judges and agencies, via statistical methods, machine learning, or artificial intelligence. First, he identifies four core features to be included in due process rights when algorithmic decisions are under consideration. They are related to the 'ability to explain one's case', the 'necessity of a judgment by a human decision-maker', an 'explanation for that judgment', and an 'ability to appeal'. As a second step, he argues that given that legal automation threatens due process rights, we need proper countermeasures, such as explainability and algorithmic accountability. Courts should not accept legal automation because it could be a hazard for vulnerable and marginalized persons, despite all good intentions. In the last part of his article, Pasquale traces a way to stem the tide of automation in the field of justice and administration, recalling the doctrine of Daniel Farber concerning 'unconstitutional conditions', which sets principles and procedures to block governments from requiring waiver of a constitutional right as a condition of receiving some governmental benefit.[52]

Far from a solution that brings us back to an 'analogic' world, we agree with Frank Pasquale. In his article, he calls for a more robust and durable theory of constitutionalism to pre-empt the problems that may arise from using automation. However, this is not sufficient, since we need a parallel theory and practice of computer science to consider ethical values and constitutional rights involved in the algorithmic reasoning and to empower officials with the ability to understand when and how to develop and deploy the technology.[53] Besides, it is necessary to maintain a 'human-centric' process in judging for the sake of courts and citizens, who could be destroyed, as Pasquale warns, by the temptation of the acceleration, abbreviation, and automation of decisional processes.

Constitutional Challenges from 'Emphatic' Media

Chapter 4, by Peggy Valcke, Damian Clifford, and Viltė Kristina Steponėnaitė, focuses on 'Constitutional Challenges in the Emotional AI Era'. The emergence of 'emotional AI', meaning technologies capable of using computing and artificial intelligence techniques to sense, learn about, and interact with human emotional life (so-called 'emphatic media')[54] raises concerns and challenges for constitutional rights and values from the point of view of its use in the business to consumer context.[55]

These technologies rely on various methods, including facial recognition, physiological measuring, voice analysis, body movement monitoring, and eye-tracking.

[52] Daniel A. Farber, 'Another View of the Quagmire: Unconstitutional Conditions and Contract Theory' (2005) 33 *Fla St UL Rev* 913 914.

[53] Coglianese and Lehr, 'Regulating by Robot'.

[54] Andrew McStay, *Emotional AI: The Rise of Empathic Media* (SAGE 2018).

[55] Vian Bakir and Andrew McStay, 'Empathic Media, Emotional AI, and the Optimization of Disinformation' in Megan Boler and Elizabeth Davis (eds), *Affective Politics of Digital Media* (Routledge 2020) 263.

The social media business gauges several of these techniques to quantify, track, and manipulate emotions to increase their business profits.

In addition to technical issues about 'accuracy', these technologies pose several concerns related to protecting consumers' fundamental rights and the rights of many other individuals, such as voters and ordinary people. As Peggy Valcke, Damian Clifford, and Viltė Kristina Steponėnaitė claim, emotional AI generates a growing pressure on the whole range of fundamental rights involved with the protection against the misuse of AI, such as privacy, data protection, respect for private and family life, non-discrimination, freedom of thought, conscience, and religion.

Although the authors argue for the necessity of constitutional protection against the possible impacts of emotional AI on existing constitutional freedoms, they ask themselves whether we need new rights in Europe in the light of growing practices of manipulation by algorithms and emotional AI. By highlighting the legal and ethical challenges of manipulating emotional AI tools, the three authors suggest a new research agenda that harnesses the academic scholarship and literature on dignity, individual autonomy, and self-determination to inquiring into the need for further constitutional rights capable of preventing or deterring emotional manipulation.

Algorithmic Surveillance as a New Bureaucracy

Chapter 5 is entitled 'Algorithmic Surveillance as a New Bureaucracy: Law Production by Data or Data Production by Law?', in which Mariavittoria Catanzariti explores the vast topic of algorithmic administration. Her argument deals with the legitimation of administrative power, questioning the rise of a 'new bureaucracy' in Weberian terms. Like bureaucracy, algorithms have a rational power requiring obedience and excluding non-predictable choices. Whereas many aspects of public administration could undoubtedly benefit from applying machine learning algorithms, their substitution for human decisions would 'create a serious threat to democratic governance, conjuring images of unaccountable, computerized overlords'.[56]

Catanzariti points out that with private sectors increasingly relying on machine learning power, even administration and public authorities, in general, keep pace and make use of the same rationale, giving birth to an automated form of technological rationality. The massive use of classification and measurement techniques affect human activity, generating new forms of power that standardize behaviours for inducing specific conduct. The social power of algorithms is currently visible in the business of many governmental agencies in the United States.

While producing a faster administration, decision-making with algorithms is likely to generate multiple disputes. The effects of algorithmic administration are far from being compliant with the same rationality as law and administrative

[56] Coglianese and Lehr, 'Regulating by Robot', 1152.

procedures. Indeed, the use of algorithms determines results that are not totally 'explainable', a fact that is often accused of being 'obscure, crazy, wrong, in short, incomprehensible'.[57]

As Catanzariti explains, algorithms are not neutral, and technology is not merely a 'proxy' for human decisions. Whenever an automated decision-making technology is included in a deliberative or administrative procedure, it tends to 'capture' the process of deciding or make it extremely difficult to ignore it. Consequently, the author argues that law production by data 'is not compatible with Weberian legal rationality', or as we have claimed, automation, far from appearing a mere 'slave', unveils its true nature of being the 'master' of decision-making when employed, due to its 'practical appeal'.[58] Indeed, algorithms put a subtle but potent spell on administrations: by using them, you can save work, time, and above all, you are relieved of your burden of motivating. Yet is this type of algorithmic administration really accountable? Coming back to Frank Pasquale's question, are 'due process' principles effectively applicable to this kind of decision?

Predictive Policing

Finally, Chapters 6 and 7, 'Human Rights and Algorithmic Impact Assessment for Predictive Policing' by Céline Castets-Renard and 'Law Enforcement and Data-Driven Predictions at the National and EU Level: A Challenge to the Presumption of Innocence and Reasonable Suspicion?' by Francesca Galli, touch upon the issue of law enforcement and technology.[59] The first addresses the dilemma of human rights challenged by 'predictive policing' and the use of new tools such as the 'Algorithmic Impact Assessment' to mitigate the risks of such systems. The second explores the potential transformation of core principles of criminal law and whether the techniques of a data-driven society may hamper the substance of legal protection. Both the authors argue for the necessity to protect fundamental rights against the possible increase of coercive control of individuals and the development of a regulatory framework that adds new layers of fundamental rights protection based on ethical principles and other practical tools.

In some countries, police authorities have been granted sophisticated surveillance technologies and much more intrusive investigative powers to reduce crime by

57 Andrea Simoncini, 'Amministrazione digitale algoritmica. Il quadro costituzionale' in Roberto Cavallo Perin and Diana-Urania Galletta (eds), *Il diritto dell'amministrazione pubblica digitale* (Giappichelli 2020) 1.

58 Andrea Simoncini, 'Profili costituzionali dell'amministrazione algoritmica' (2019) Riv trim dir pubbl 1149.

59 Andrew Guthrie Ferguson, *The Rise of Big Data: Surveillance, Race and the Future of Law Enforcement* (New York University Press 2017).

mapping the likely locations of future unlawful conduct so that the deployment of police resources can be more effective.[60]

Here again, the problem regards the ability and sustainability of decisions by intelligent machines and their consequences for the rights of individuals and groups.[61] Machine learning and other algorithmic tools can now correlate multiple variables in a data set and then predict behaviours. Such technologies open new scenarios for information gathering, monitoring, surveilling, and profiling criminal behaviour. The risk here is that predictive policing represents more than a simple shift in tools and could result in less effective and maybe even discriminatory police interventions.[62]

2.4 THE EFFECTS OF THE 'ALGORITHMIC STATE' ON THE PRACTICE OF LIBERTY

Trying to synthetize some of the most critical issues brought about by the advent of what we call the Algorithmic State on the practice of constitutional liberties, there appear to be two main sensitive areas: surveillance and freedom.

Surveillance

As we have already seen, the rise of the algorithmic state has produced the change foreseen more than forty years ago by Herbert Marcuse. In general, technology is improving people's lives. However, we know that this improvement comes at a 'price'. We are increasingly dependent on big-tech-platform services, even if it is clear that they make huge profits with our data. They promise to unchain humans from needs and necessities, but they themselves are becoming indispensable.

Therefore, we are taking for granted that the cost of gaining such benefits – security, efficiency, protection, rewards, and convenience – is to consent to our personal data being recorded, stored, recovered, crossed, traded, and exchanged through surveillance systems. Arguing that people usually have no reason to question surveillance (the 'nothing to hide' misconception)[63] strengthens the

[60] Lyria Bennett Moses and Janet Chan, 'Algorithmic Prediction in Policing: Assumptions, Evaluation, and Accountability' (2018) 28 *Policing and Society* 806; Gavin J. D. Smith, Lyria Bennett Moses, and Janet Chan, 'The Challenges of Doing Criminology in the Big Data Era: Towards a Digital and Data-Driven Approach' (2017) 57 *British Journal of Criminology* 259; Wim Hardyns and Anneleen Rummens, 'Predictive Policing as a New Tool for Law Enforcement? Recent Developments and Challenges' (2018) 24 *European Journal on Criminal Policy and Research* 201.

[61] Karen Yeung, 'Algorithmic Regulation: A Critical Interrogation' (2018) 12 *Regulation & Governance* 505.

[62] Albert Meijer and Martijn Wessels, 'Predictive Policing: Review of Benefits and Drawbacks' (2019) 42 *International Journal of Public Administration* 1031.

[63] Bruce Schneier, *Data and Goliath: The Hidden Battles to Collect Your Data and Control Your World* (W. W. Norton & Company 2015).

order built by the system, and people become 'normalized' (as Foucault would have said).[64]

Because of this massive use of technology, we are now subject to a new form of surveillance, which profoundly impacts individual freedom, as it is both intrusive and invasive in private life.[65] Both explicit and non-explicit forms of surveillance extend to virtually all forms of human interaction.[66]

As the EU Court of Justice pointed out, mass surveillance can be produced by both governments and private companies. This is likely to create 'in the minds of the persons concerned the feeling that their private lives are the subject of constant surveillance'.[67] In both cases, we have a kind of intrusive surveillance on people's lives, and this is evidence of individuals' loss of control over their personal data.

Freedom

This process also affects the very idea of the causal link between individual or collective actions and their consequences, therefore, the core notion of our freedom. Replacing causation with correlation profoundly affects the fundamental distinction embedded in our moral and legal theory between instruments and ends.[68] Today's cybernetic power is no longer just an *instrument* to achieve ends decided by human agents. Machines make decisions autonomously on behalf of the person, thus interfering with human freedom.

As it is very clearly described in the following chapters, human agents (individual or collective) explicitly delegate the power to make decisions or express assessments on their behalf to automated systems (judicial support systems, algorithmic administration, emotional assessments, policing decisions). But we must be aware of another crucial dimension of that *substitution*.

There are two ways to capture human freedom: the first, as we saw in the previously noted cases, occurs whenever we ask a technological system to decide directly on our behalf (we reduce our self-determination to choose our proxy) and the second is when we ask automated machinery to provide the information upon which we take a course of action. Knowledge always shapes our freedom. One key factor (although not the only one) influencing our decisions is the information

64 David Lyon, *Surveillance after September 11* (Polity 2003).

65 Surveillance consists of the 'collection and processing of personal data, identifiable or not, for the purpose of influencing or controlling those to whom they belong'. Surveillance is a necessary correlative of a risk-based new idea of state power. See David Lyon, *Surveillance Society: Monitoring Everyday Life* (Open University Press 2001).

66 J. Guelke et al., 'SURVEILLE Deliverable 2.6: Matrix of Surveillance Technologies' (2013) Seventh Framework Programme Surveillance: Ethical Issues, Legal Limitations, and Efficiency, FP7-SEC -2011-284725.

67 Joined cases C-293/12 and C-594/12, *Digital Rights Ireland* (C-293/12) and *Seitlinger* (C-594/12), EU: C:2014:238, at 37.

68 Andrea Simoncini and Samir Suweis, 'Il cambio di paradigma nell'intelligenza artificiale e il suo impatto sul diritto costituzionale' (2019) 8 *Rivista di filosofia del diritto* 87.

background we have. Deciding to drive a specific route rather than another to reach our destination is usually affected by information we have either on traffic or roadworks; the choice to vote for one political candidate instead of another depends on the information we get about his or her campaign or ideas. If we ask ourselves which channel we will use today to get information about the world beyond our direct experience, the answer will be more than 80 per cent from the Internet.[69]

Automated technological systems increasingly provide knowledge.[70] Simultaneously, 'individual and collective identities become conceivable as fluid, hybrid and constantly evolving' as the result of 'continuous processes bringing together humans, objects, energy flows, and technologies'.[71] This substitution profoundly impacts the very idea of autonomy as it emerged in the last two centuries and basically alters the way people come to make decisions, have beliefs, or take action.

In this way, two distinctive elements of our idea of freedoms' violations seem to change or disappear in the Algorithmic Society. In the first case – when we explicitly ask technology to decide on our behalf – we cannot say that the restriction of our freedom is unwanted or unvoluntary because we ourselves consented to it. We expressly ask those technologies to decide, assuming they are 'evidence-based', more effective, more neutral, science-oriented, and so forth. Therefore, we cannot say that our freedom has been violated against our will or self-determination, given that we expressly asked those systems to make our decisions.

On the other hand, when our decisions are taken on the informative basis provided by technology, we can no longer say that such threats to our liberty are 'external'; as a matter of fact, when we trust information taken from the Internet (from web search engines, like Google, or from social media, like Facebook or Twitter), there is no apparent coercion, no violence. That information is simply welcomed as a sound and valid basis for our deliberations. Yet there is a critical point here. We trust web-sourced information provided by platforms, assuming they are scientifically accurate or at least trustworthy. However, this trust has nothing to do with science or education. Platforms simply use powerful algorithms that learn behavioural patterns from previous preferences to reinforce individuals or groups in filtering overwhelming alternatives in our daily life. The accuracy of these algorithms in predicting and giving us helpful information with their results only occurs because they confirm – feeding a 'confirmation bias'[72] – our beliefs or, worst, our ideological positions ('bubble effect').[73]

69 According to Statista in 2019, around the 50 per cent of the Italian population accesses information from the Internet.

70 Brent Daniel Mittelstadt et al., 'The Ethics of Algorithms: Mapping the Debate' (2016) 3 *Big Data & Society* 1.

71 Holger Pötzsch, 'Archives and Identity in the Context of Social Media and Algorithmic Analytics: Towards an Understanding of iArchive and Predictive Retention' (2018) 20 *New Media & Society* 3304.

72 Andreas Kappes et al., 'Confirmation Bias in the Utilization of Others' Opinion Strength' (2020) 23 *Nature Neuroscience* 130.

73 Users tend to aggregate in communities of interest causing reinforcements and support of conformation bias, segregation, and polarization. Erik Longo, 'Dai big data alle "bolle filtro": nuovi rischi per i sistemi democratici' (2019) XII *Percorsi costituzionali* 29.

There is something deeply philosophically and legally problematic about restricting people's freedom based on predictions about their conduct. For example, as an essential requirement for a just society, liberal and communitarian doctrines share not only the absence of coercion but also independence and capacity when acting; from this point of view, new algorithmic decision-making affects the very basis of both liberal and communitarian theories. As Lawrence Lessig wrote, we have experienced, through cyberspace, a 'displacement of a certain architecture of control and the substitution with an apparent freedom.'[74]

Towards the Algorithmic State Constitution: A 'hybrid' Constitutionalism

Surveillance capitalism and the new algorithmic threats to liberty share a common feature: when a new technology has already appeared, it is often too late for the legal system to intervene. The gradual anticipation in the field of privacy rights, from subsequent to preventive (from protection by regulation, to protection 'by design' and finally 'by default'), exactly traces this sort of 'backwards' trajectory. This is the main feature of the Algorithmic State constitutionalism.

It is necessary to incorporate the values of constitutional rights within the 'design stage' of the machines; for this, we need what we would define as a 'hybrid' constitutional law – that is, a constitutional law that still aims to protect fundamental human rights and at the same time knows how to express this goal in the language of technology.[75] Here the space for effective dialogue is still abundantly unexplored, and consequently, the rate of 'hybridization' is still extraordinarily low.

We argue that after the season of protection by design and by default, a new season ought to be opened – that of protection *'by education'*, in the sense that it is necessary to act when scientists and technologists are still studying and training, to communicate the fundamental reasons for general principles such as personal data protection, human dignity, and freedom protection, but also for more specific values as the explainability of decision-making algorithms or the 'human in the loop' principle.

Technology is increasingly integrated with the life of the person, and this integration cannot realistically be stopped, nor it would be desirable, given the huge importance for human progress that some new technologies have had.

The only possible way, therefore, is to ensure that the value (i.e., the meaning) of protecting the dignity of the person and his or her freedom becomes an integral part of the training of those who will then become technicians. Hence the decisive role of school, university, and other training agencies, professional or academic associations, as well as the role of soft law.

74 Lawrence Lessig, *Code. Version 2.0* (Basic Books 2006) 2.

75 This is the reason we use the 'hybrid' image, coming from the world of the automotive industry: a 'hybrid' vehicle means it uses both classical combustion engines and electric power.

3

Inalienable Due Process in an Age of AI: Limiting the Contractual Creep toward Automated Adjudication

Frank Pasquale

3.1 INTRODUCTION

Automation is influencing ever more fields of law. The dream of disruption has permeated the US and British legal academies and is making inroads in Australia and Canada, as well as in civil law jurisdictions. The ideal here is law as a product, simultaneously mass producible and customizable, accessible to all and personalized, openly deprofessionalized.[1] This is the language of idealism, so common in discussions of legal technology – the Dr. Jekyll of legal automation.

But the shadow side of legal tech also lurks behind many initiatives. Legal disruption's Mr. Hyde advances the cold economic imperative to shrink the state and its aid to the vulnerable. In Australia, the Robodebt system of automated benefit overpayment adjudication clawed back funds from beneficiaries on the basis of flawed data, false factual assumptions, and misguided assumptions about the law. In Michigan, in the United States, a similar program (aptly named "MIDAS," for Michigan Integrated Data Automated System) "charged more than 40,000 people, billing them about five times the original benefits" – and it was later discovered that 93 percent of the charges were erroneous.[2] Meanwhile, global corporations are finding the automation of dispute settlement a convenient way to cut labor costs. This strategy is particularly tempting on platforms, which may facilitate millions of transactions each day.

When long-standing appeals to austerity and business necessity are behind "access to justice" initiatives to promote online dispute resolution, some skepticism is in order. At the limit, jurisdictions may be able to sell off their downtown real estate, setting up trusts to support a rump judicial system.[3] To be sure, even online courts

[1] Frank Pasquale, "A Rule of Persons, Not Machines: The Limits of Legal Automation" (2019) 87 *Geo Wash LR* 1, 28–29.

[2] Stephanie Wykstra, "Government's Use of Algorithm Serves Up False Fraud Charges" Undark (2020) https://undark.org/2020/06/01/michigan-unemployment-fraud-algorithm.

[3] Owen Bowcott, "Court Closures: Sale of 126 Premises Raised Just £34m, Figures Show" *The Guardian* (London, Mar 8 2018) www.theguardian.com/law/2018/mar/08/court-closures-people-facing-days-travel-to-attend-hearings.

require some staffing. But perhaps an avant-garde of legal cost cutters will find some inspiration from US corporations, which routinely decide buyer versus seller disputes in entirely opaque fashion.[4] In China, a large platform has charged "citizen juries" (who do not even earn money for their labor but, rather, reputation points) to decide such disputes. Build up a large enough catalog of such encounters, and a machine learning system may even be entrusted with deciding disputes based on past markers of success.[5] A complainant may lose credibility points for nervous behavior, for example, or gain points on the basis of long-standing status as someone who buys a great deal of merchandise or pays a taxes in a timely manner.

As these informal mechanisms become more common, they will test the limits of due process law. As anyone familiar with the diversity of administrative processes will realize, there is an enormous variation at present in how much opportunity a person is entitled to state their case, to demand a written explanation for a final (or intermediate) result, and to appeal. A black lung benefits case differs from a traffic violation, which in term differs from an immigration case. Courts permit agencies a fair amount of flexibility to structure their own affairs. Agencies will, in all likelihood, continue to pursue an agenda of what Julie Cohen has called "neoliberal managerialism" as they reorder their processes of investigation, case development, and decision-making.[6] That will, in turn, bring in more automated and "streamlined" processes, which courts will be called upon to accommodate.

While judicial accommodations of new agency forms are common, they are not automatic. At some point, agencies will adopt automated processes that courts can only recognize as simulacra of justice. Think, for instance, of an anti-trespassing robot equipped with facial recognition, which could instantly identify and "adjudicate" a person overstepping a boundary and text that person a notice of a fine. Or a rail ticket monitoring system that would instantly convert notice of a judgment against a person into a yearlong ban on the person buying train tickets. Other examples might be less dramatic but also worrisome. For example, consider the possibility of "mass claims rejection" for private health care providers seeking government payment for services rendered to persons with government-sponsored health insurance. Such claims processing programs may simply compare a set of claims to a corpus of past denied claims, sort new claimants' documents into categories, and then reject them without human review.

In past work, I have explained why legislators and courts should reject most of these systems, and should always be wary of claims that justice can be automated.[7]

4 Rory van Loo, "Corporation as Courthouse" (2016) 33 *Yale J on Reg* 547.

5 Frank Pasquale and Glyn Cashwell, "Prediction, Persuasion, and the Jurisprudence of Behaviorism" (2018) 68 *U Toronto LJ* 63.

6 Julie Cohen, *Between Truth and Power* (Oxford University Press 2019).

7 Jathan Sadowski and Frank Pasquale, "The Spectrum of Control: A Social Theory of the Smart City" (2015) 20(7) *First Monday* https://firstmonday.org/ojs/index.php/fm/article/view/5903/4660; Pasquale (n 1).

And some initial jurisprudential stirrings are confirming that normative recommendation. For example, there has been a backlash against red-light cameras, which automatically cite drivers for failing to obey traffic laws. And even some of those who have developed natural language processing for legal settings have cautioned that they are not to be used in anything like a trial setting. These concessions are encouraging.

And yet there is another danger lurking on the horizon. Imagine a disability payment scheme that offered something like the following "contractual addendum" to beneficiaries immediately before they began receiving benefits:

> The state has a duty to husband resources and to avoid inappropriate payments. By signing below, you agree to the following exchange. You will receive $20 per month extra in benefits, in addition to what you are statutorily eligible for. In exchange, you agree to permit the state (and any contractor it may choose to employ) to review all your social media accounts, in order to detect behavior indicating you are fit for work. If you are determined to be fit for work, your benefits will cease. This determination will be made by a machine learning program, and there will be no appeal.[8]

There are two diametrically opposed ways of parsing such a contract. For many libertarians, the right to give up one's rights (here, to a certain level of privacy and appeals) is effectively the most important right, since it enables contracting parties to eliminate certain forms of interference from their relationship. By contrast, for those who value legal regularity and due process, this "addendum" is anathema. Even if it is possible for the claimant to re-apply after a machine learning system has stripped her of benefits, the process offends the dignity of the claimant. A person must pass on whether such a grave step is to be taken.

These divergent approaches are mirrored in two lines of US Supreme Court jurisprudence. On the libertarian side, the Court has handed down a number of rulings affirming the "right" of workers to sign away certain rights at work, or at least the ability to contest their denial in court.[9] Partisans of "disruptive innovation" may argue that startups need to be able to impose one-sided terms of service on customers, so that investors will not be deterred from financing them. Exculpatory clauses have spread like kudzu, beckoning employers with the jurisprudential equivalent of

[8] For one aspect of the factual foundations of this hypothetical, see Social Security Administration, *Fiscal Year 2019 Budget Overview* (2018) 17–18: "We will study and design successful strategies of our private sector counterparts to determine if a disability adjudicator should access and use social media networks to evaluate disability allegations. Currently, agency adjudicators may use social media information to evaluate a beneficiary's symptoms only when there is an OIG CDI unit's Report of Investigation that contains social media data corroborating the investigative findings. Our study will determine whether the further expansion of social media networks in disability determinations will increase program integrity and expedite the identification of fraud."

[9] Frank Pasquale, "Six Horsemen of Irresponsibility" (2019) 79 *Maryland LR* 105 (discussing exculpatory clauses).

a neutron bomb: the ability to leave laws and regulations standing, without any person capable of enforcing them.

On the other side, the Supreme Court has also made clear that the state must be limited in the degree to which it can structure entitlements when it is seeking to avoid due process obligations. A state cannot simply define an entitlement to, say, disability benefits, by folding into the entitlement itself an understanding that it can be revoked for any reason, or no reason at all. On this dignity-centered approach, the "contractual addendum" posited above is not merely one innocuous add-on, a bit of a risk the claimant must endure in order to engage in an arms' length exchange for $20. Rather, it undoes the basic structure of the entitlement, which included the ability to make one's case to another person and to appeal an adverse decision.

If states begin to impose such contractual bargains for automated administrative determinations, the "immoveable object" of inalienable due process rights will clash with the "irresistible force" of legal automation and libertarian conceptions of contractual "freedom." This chapter explains why legal values must cabin (and often trump) efforts to "fast track" cases via statistical methods, machine learning (ML), or artificial intelligence. Section 3.2 explains how due process rights, while flexible, should include four core features in all but the most trivial or routine cases: the ability to explain one's case, a judgment by a human decision maker, an explanation for that judgment, and the ability to appeal. Section 3.3 demonstrates why legal automation often threatens those rights. Section 3.4 critiques potential bargains for legal automation and concludes that the courts should not accept them. Vulnerable and marginalized persons should not be induced to give up basic human rights, even if some capacious and abstract versions of utilitarianism project they would be "better off" by doing so.

3.2 FOUR CORE FEATURES OF DUE PROCESS

Like the rule of law, "due process" is a multifaceted, complex, and perhaps even essentially contested concept.[10] As J. Roland Pennock has observed, the "roots of due process grow out of a blend of history and philosophy."[11] While the term itself is a cornerstone of the US and UK legal systems, it has analogs in both public law and civil law systems around the world.

While many rights and immunities have been evoked as part of due process, it is important to identify a "core" conception of it that should be inalienable in all significant disputes between persons and governments. We can see this grasping for

[10] For rival definitions of the rule of law, see Pasquale, "A Rule of Persons" (n 1). The academic discussion of "due process" remains at least as complex as it was in 1977, when the Nomos volume on the topic was published. See, e.g., Charles A. Miller, "The Forest of Due Process Law" in J. Roland Pennock and John W. Chapman (eds), *Nomos XVII: Due Process* (NYU Press 1977).

[11] Pennock, "Introduction" in Pennock and Chapman, *Nomos XVII: Due Process* (n 10).

a "core" of due process in some US cases, where the interest at stake was relatively insignificant but the court still decided that the person affected by government action had to have some opportunity to explain him or herself and the contest the imposition of a punishment. For example, in *Goss* v. *Lopez*, students who were accused of misbehavior were suspended from school for ten days. The students claimed they were due some kind of hearing before suspension, and the Supreme Court agreed:

> We do not believe that school authorities must be totally free from notice and hearing requirements if their schools are to operate with acceptable efficiency. Students facing temporary suspension have interests qualifying for protection of the Due Process Clause, and due process requires, in connection with a suspension of 10 days or less, that the student be given oral or written notice of the charges against him and, if he denies them, an explanation of the evidence the authorities have and an opportunity to present his side of the story.[12]

This is a fair encapsulation of some core practices of due process, which may (as the stakes rise) become supplemented by all manner of additional procedures.[13]

One of the great questions raised by the current age of artificial intelligence (AI) is whether the notice and explanation of the charges (as well as the opportunity to be heard) must be discharged by a human being. So far as I can discern, no ultimate judicial authority has addressed this particular issue in the due process context. However, given that the entire line of case law arises in the context of humans confronting other humans, it does not take a stretch of the imagination to imagine such a requirement immanent in the enterprise of due process.

Moreover, legal scholars Kiel Brennan-Marquez and Henderson argue that "in a liberal democracy, there must be an aspect of 'role-reversibility' to judgment. Those who exercise judgment should be vulnerable, reciprocally, to its processes and effects."[14] The problem with robot or AI judges is that they cannot experience punishment the way that a human being would. Role-reversibility is necessary for "decision-makers to take the process seriously, respecting the gravity of decision-making from the perspective of affected parties." Brennan-Marquez and Henderson derive this principle from basic principles of self-governance:

> In a democracy, citizens do not stand outside the process of judgment, as if responding, in awe or trepidation, to the proclamations of an oracle. Rather, we

[12] 419 US 565, 581 (1975). In rare cases, the hearing may wait until the threat posed by the student is contained: "Since the hearing may occur almost immediately following the misconduct, it follows that as a general rule notice and hearing should precede removal of the student from school. We agree with the District Court, however, that there are recurring situations in which prior notice and hearing cannot be insisted upon. Students whose presence poses a continuing danger to persons or property or an ongoing threat of disrupting the academic process may be immediately removed from school. In such cases, the necessary notice and rudimentary hearing should follow."

[13] Henry J. Friendly, "Some Kind of Hearing" (1975) 123 *U Pa LR* 1267 (listing 11 potential requirements of due process).

[14] Kiel Brennan-Marquez and Stephen E. Henderson, "Artificial Intelligence and Role-Reversible Judgment" (2019) 109 *J Crim L and Criminology* 137.

> are collectively responsible for judgment. Thus, the party charged with exercising judgment – who could, after all, have been any of us – ought to be able to say: *This decision reflects constraints that we have decided to impose on ourselves, and in this case, it just so happens that another person, rather than I, must answer to them.* And the judged party – who could likewise have been any of us – ought to be able to say: *This decision-making process is one that we exercise ourselves, and in this case, it just so happens that another person, rather than I, is executing it.*

Thus, for Brennan-Marquez and Henderson, "even assuming role-reversibility will not improve the accuracy of decision-making; it still has intrinsic value."

Brennan-Marquez and Henderson are building on a long tradition of scholarship that focuses on the intrinsic value of legal and deliberative processes, rather than their instrumental value. For example, applications of the US Supreme Court's famous *Mathews* v. *Eldridge* calculus have frequently failed to take into account the effects of abbreviated procedures on claimants' dignity.[15] Bureaucracies, including the judiciary, have enormous power. They owe litigants a chance to plead their case to someone who can understand and experience, on a visceral level, the boredom and violence portended by a prison stay, the "brutal need" resulting from the loss of benefits (as put in *Goldberg* v. *Kelly*), the sense of shame that liability for drunk driving or pollution can give rise to. And as the classic *Morgan* v. *United States* held, even in complex administrative processes, the one who hears must be the one who decides. It is not adequate for persons to play mere functionary roles in an automated judiciary, gathering data for more authoritative machines. Rather, humans must take responsibility for critical decisions made by the legal system.

This argument is consistent with other important research on the dangers of giving robots legal powers and responsibilities. For example, Joanna Bryson, Mihailis Diamantis, and Thomas D. Grant have warned that granting robots legal personality raises the disturbing possibility of corporations deploying "robots as liability shields."[16] A "responsible robot" may deflect blame or liability from the business that set it into the world. This is dangerous because the robot cannot truly be punished: it lacks human sensations of regret or dismay at loss of liberty or assets. It may be programmed

15 Under the *Mathews* balancing test, "Identification of the specific dictates of due process generally requires consideration of three distinct factors: First, the private interest that will be affected by the official action; second, the risk of an erroneous deprivation of such interest through the procedures used, and the probable value, if any, of additional or substitute procedural safeguards; and finally, the Government's interest, including the function involved and the fiscal and administrative burdens that the additional or substitute procedural requirement would entail." *Mathews* v. *Eldridge* 424 US 319, 335 (1976). For an early critique, see Jerry L Mashaw, "The Supreme Court's Due Process Calculus for Administrative Adjudication in *Mathews* v. *Eldridge*: Three Factors in Search of a Theory of Value" (1976) 44 *U Chi LR* 28.

16 Joanna J. Bryson, Mihailis E. Diamantis, and Thomas D. Grant, "Of, for and by the People: The Legal Lacuna of Synthetic Persons" (2017) 25 *Artificial Intelligence and Law* 273. For a recent suggestion on how to deal with this problem, by one of the co-authors, see Mihailis Diamantis, "Algorithms Acting Badly: A Solution from Corporate Law" SSRN (accessed 5 Mar 2020) https://papers.ssrn.com/sol3/papers.cfm?abstract_id=3545436.

to look as if it is remorseful upon being hauled into jail, or to frown when any assets under its control are seized. But these are simulations of human emotion, not the thing itself. Emotional response is one of many fundamental aspects of human experience that is embodied. And what is true of the robot as an object of legal judgment is also true of robots or AI as potential producers of such judgments.

3.3 HOW LEGAL AUTOMATION AND CONTRACTUAL SURRENDER OF RIGHTS THREATEN CORE DUE PROCESS VALUES

There is increasing evidence that many functions of the legal system, as it exists now, are very difficult to automate.[17] However, as Cashwell and I warned in 2015, the legal system is far from a stable and defined set of tasks to complete. As various interest groups jostle to "reform" legal systems the range of procedures needed to finalize legal determinations may shrink or expand.[18] There are many ways to limit existing legal processes, or simplify them, in order to make it easier for computation to replace or simulate them. The clauses mentioned previously – forswearing appeals of judgments generated or informed by machine learning or AI – would make non-explainable AI far easier to implement in legal systems.

This type of "moving the goalposts" may be accelerated by extant trends toward neoliberal managerialism in public administration.[19] This approach to public administration is focused on throughput, speed, case management, and efficiency. Neoliberal managerialists urge the public sector to learn from the successes of the private sector in limiting spending on disputes. One potential here is simply to outsource determinations to private actors – a move widely criticized elsewhere.[20] I am more concerned here with a contractual option: to offer to beneficiaries of government programs an opportunity for more or quicker benefits, in exchange for an agreement not to pursue appeals of termination decisions, or to thereby accepting their automated resolution.

17 Dana Remus and Frank S. Levy, "Can Robots Be Lawyers? Computers, Lawyers, and the Practice of Law" SSRN (Nov 30 2016) https://papers.ssrn.com/sol3/papers.cfm?abstract_id=2701092; Brian S. Haney, "Applied Natural Language Processing for Law Practice" SSRN (Feb 14 2020) https://papers.ssrn.com/sol3/papers.cfm?abstract_id=3476351 ("The state-of-the-art in legal question answering technology is far from providing any more valuable insight than a simple Google search ... [and] legal Q&A is not a promising application of NLP in law practice.").

18 Frank A. Pasquale and Glyn Cashwell, "Four Futures of Legal Automation" (2015) 63 *UCLA LR Discourse* 26.

19 See Cohen (n 6). See also Karen Yeung, "Algorithmic Regulation: A Critical Interrogation" (2018) 12 *Regulation and Governance* 505.

20 Ellen Dannin, "Red Tape or Accountability: Privatization, Public-ization, and Public Values" (2005) 15 *Cornell JL & Pub Pol'y* 111, 143 ("If due process requirements governing eligibility determinations for government-delivered services appear to produce inefficiencies, lifting them entirely through reliance on private service delivery may produce unacceptable inequities."); Jon D. Michaels, *Constitutional Coup: Privatization's Threat to the American Republic* (Harvard University Press 2017).

I focus on the inducement of quicker or more benefits, because it appears to be settled law (at least in the US) that such restrictions of due process cannot be embedded into benefits themselves. A failed line of US Supreme Court decisions once attempted to restrict claimants' due process rights by insisting that the government can create property entitlements with no due process rights attached. On this reasoning, a county might grant someone benefits with the explicit understanding that they could be terminated at any time without explanation: the "sweet" of the benefits could include the "bitter" of sudden, unreasoned denial of them. In *Cleveland Board of Education* v. *Loudermill* (1985), the Court finally discarded this line of reasoning, forcing some modicum of reasoned explanation and process for termination of property rights.

What is less clear now is whether side deals might undermine the delicate balance of rights struck by *Loudermill*. In the private sector, companies have successfully routed disputes with employees out of process-rich Article III courts, and into stripped-down arbitral forums, where one might even be skeptical of the impartiality of decision-makers.[21] Will the public sector follow suit? Given some current trends in the foreshortening of procedure and judgment occasioned by public sector automation, the temptation will be great.

These concerns are a logical outgrowth of a venerable literature critiquing rushed, shoddy, and otherwise improper automation of legal decision-making. In 2008, Danielle Keats Citron warned that states were cutting corners by deciding certain benefits (and other) claims automatically, on the basis of computer code that did not adequately reflect the complexity of the legal code it claimed to have reduced to computation.[22] Virginia Eubanks's *Automating Inequality* has identified profound problems in governmental use of algorithmic sorting systems. Eubanks tells the stories of individuals who lose benefits, opportunities, and even custody of their children, thanks to algorithmic assessments that are inaccurate or biased. Eubanks argues that complex benefits determinations are not something well-meaning tech experts can "fix." Instead, the system itself is deeply problematic, constantly shifting the goal line (in all too many states) to throw up barriers to access to care.

A growing movement for algorithmic accountability is both exposing and responding to these problems. For example, Citron and I coauthored work setting forth some basic procedural protections for those affected by governmental scoring systems.[23] The AI Now Institute has analyzed cases of improper algorithmic

21 Frank Blechschmidt, "All Alone in Arbitration: *AT&T Mobility* v. *Concepcion* and the Substantive Impact of Class Action Waivers" (2012) 160 *U Pa LR* 541.

22 Danielle Keats Citron, "Technological Due Process" (2008) 85 *Wash U LR* 1249.

23 Danielle Keats Citron and Frank Pasquale, "The Scored Society: Due Process for Automated Predictions" (2014) 89 *Wash LR* 1; Frank Pasquale and Danielle Keats Citron, "Promoting Innovation While Preventing Discrimination: Policy Goals for the Scored Society" (2015) 89 *Wash LR* 1413. See also Kate Crawford and Jason Schultz, "Big Data and Due Process: Toward a Framework

determinations of rights and opportunities.[24] And there is a growing body of scholarship internationally exploring the ramifications of computational dispute resolution.[25] As this work influences more agencies around the world, it is increasingly likely that responsible leadership will ensure that a certain baseline of due process values applies to automated decision-making.

Though they are generally optimistic about the role of automation and algorithms in agency decision-making, Coglianese and Lehr concede that one "due process question presented by automated adjudication stems from how such a system would affect an aggrieved party's right to cross-examination. … Probably the only meaningful way to identify errors would be to conduct a proceeding in which an algorithm and its data are fully explored."[26] This type of examination is at the core of Keats Citron's concept of technological due process. It would require something like a right to an explanation of the automated profiling at the core of decision.[27]

3.4 DUE PROCESS, DEALS, AND UNRAVELING

However, all such protections could be undone. The ability to explain oneself, and to hear reasoned explanations in turn, is often framed as being needlessly expensive. This expense of legal process (or administrative determinations) has helped fuel

to Redress Predictive Privacy Harms" (2014) 55 *Boston Coll LR* 93; Kate Crawford and Jason Schultz, "AI Systems as State Actors" (2019) 119 *Colum LR* 1941.

24 Rashida Richardson, Jason M. Schultz, and Vincent M. Southerland, "Litigating Algorithms 2019 US Report: New Challenges to Government Use of Algorithmic Decision Systems" AI Now Institute (September 2019) https://ainowinstitute.org/litigatingalgorithms-2019-us.html.

25 Monika Zalnieriute, Lyria Bennett Moses and George Williams, "The Rule of Law and Automation of Government Decision-Making" (2019) 82 *Modern Law Review* 425 (report on automated decision-making). In the UK, see Simon Deakin and Christopher Markou (eds), *Is Law Computable? Critical Perspectives on Law and Artificial Intelligence* (Bloomsbury Professional, forthcoming); Jennifer Cobbe, "The Ethical and Governance Challenges of AI" (Aug 1 2019) www.youtube.com/watch?v=ujZUCSQ1_e8. In continental Europe, see the work of COHUBICOL and scholars at Bocconi and Florence, among many other institutions.

26 Cary Coglianese and David Lehr, "Regulating by Robot: Administrative Decision Making in the Machine-Learning Era" (2017) 105 *Geo LJ* 1147, 1189–90. Note that such inspections may need to be in-depth, lest automation bias lead to undue reassurance. Hramanpreet Kaur et al., "Interpreting Interpretability: Understanding Data Scientists' Use of Interpretability Tools for Machine Learning" CHI 2020 Paper (accessed Mar 9 2020) www-personal.umich.edu/~harmank/Papers/CHI2020_Interpretability.pdf (finding "the existence of visualizations and publicly available nature of interpretability tools often leads to over-trust and misuse of these tools").

27 Andrew D. Selbst and Julia Powles, "Meaningful Information and the Right to Explanation" (2017) 7 (4) *International Data Privacy Law* 233; Gianclaudio Malgieri and Giovanni Comandé, "Why a Right to Legibility of Automated Decision-Making Exists in the General Data Protection Regulation" (2017) 7(4) *International Data Privacy Law* 243. But see *State* v. *Loomis* 881 NW2d 749 (Wis 2016), *cert denied*, 137 S Ct 2290 (2017) ("[W]e conclude that if used properly, observing the limitations and cautions set forth herein, a circuit court's consideration of a COMPAS risk assessment at sentencing does not violate a defendant's right to due process," even when aspects of the risk assessment were secret and proprietary.)

a turn to quantification, scoring, and algorithmic decision procedures.[28] A written evaluation of a person (or comprehensive analysis of future scenarios) often requires subtle judgment, exactitude in wording, and ongoing revision in response to challenges and evolving situations. A pre-set formula based on limited, easily observable variables, is far easier to calculate.[29] Moreover, even if individuals are due certain explanations and hearings as part of law, they may forego them in some contexts.

This type of rights waiver has already been deployed in some contexts. Several states in the United States allow unions to waive the due process rights of public employees.[30] We can also interpret some Employee Retirement Income Security Act (ERISA) jurisprudence as an endorsement and approval of a relatively common situation in the United States: employees effectively signing away a right to a more substantive and searching review of adverse benefit scope and insurance coverage determinations via an agreement to participate in an employer-sponsored benefit plan. The US Supreme Court has gradually interpreted ERISA to require federal courts to defer to plan administrators, echoing the deference due to agency administrators, and sometimes going beyond it.[31]

True, *Loudermill* casts doubt on arrangements for government benefits premised on the beneficiary's sacrificing due process protections. However, a particularly innovative and disruptive state may decide that the opinion is silent as to the *baseline* of what constitutes the benefit in question, and leverage that ambiguity. Consider a state that guaranteed health care to a certain category of individuals, as a "health care benefit." Enlightened legislators further propose that the disabled, or those without robust transport options, should also receive assistance with respect to transportation to care. Austerity-minded legislators counter with a proviso: to receive transport assistance in addition to health assistance, beneficiaries need to agree to automatic adjudication of a broad class of disputes that might arise out of their beneficiary status.

The automation "deal" may also arise out of long-standing delays in receiving benefits. For example, in the United States, there have been many complaints by disability rights groups about the delays encountered by applicants for Social

28 Electronic Privacy Information Center (EPIC), "Algorithms in the Criminal Justice System: Pre-Trial Risk Assessment Tools" (accessed Mar 6 2020) https://epic.org/algorithmic-transparency/crim-justice/ ("Since the specific formula to determine 'risk assessment' is proprietary, defendants are unable to challenge the validity of the results. This may violate a defendant's right to due process.").

29 For intellectual history of shifts toward preferring the convenience and reliability of numerical forms of evaluation, see Theodore Porter, *Trust in Numbers: The Pursuit of Objectivity in Science and Public Life* (Princeton University Press 1995); William Deringer, *Calculated Values: Finance, Politics, and the Quantitative Age* (Harvard University Press 2018).

30 *Antinore* v. *State*, 371 NYS2d 213 (NY App Div 1975); *Gorham* v. *City of Kansas City*, 590 P2d 1051 (Kan 1979); Richard Wallace, Comment, "Union Waiver of Public Employees' Due Process Rights" (1986) 8 *Indus Rel LJ* 583; Ann C. Hodges, "The Interplay of Civil Service Law and Collective Bargaining Law in Public Sector Employee Discipline Cases" (1990) 32 *Boston Coll LR* 95.

31 The problem of "rights sacrifice" is not limited to the examples in this paragraph. See also Dionne L. Koller, "How the United States Government Sacrifices Athletes' Constitutional Rights in the Pursuit of National Prestige" 2008 *BYU LR* 1465, for an example of outsourcing decision-making to venues without the robustness of traditional due process protections.

Security Disability Benefits, even when they are clearly entitled to them. On the other side of the political spectrum, some complain that persons who are adjudicated as disabled, and then regain capacities to work, are able to keep benefits for too long after they regain the capacity to work. This concern (and perhaps some mix of cruelty and indifference) motivated British policy makers who promoted "fit for work" reviews by private contractors.[32]

It is not hard to see how the "baseline" of benefits might be defined narrowly, and all future benefits would be conditioned in this way. Nor are procedures the only constitution-level interest that may be "traded away" for faster access to more benefits. Privacy rights may be on the chopping block as well. In the United States, the Trump administration proposed reviews of the social media of persons receiving benefits.[33] The presumption of such review is that a picture of, say, a self-proclaimed depressed person smiling, or a self-proclaimed wheelchair-bound person walking, could alert authorities to potential benefits fraud. And such invasive surveillance could again feed into automated review, which could be flagged by such "suspicious activity" in a way similar to the activation of investigation at US fusion centers by "suspicious activity reports."

What is even more troubling about these dynamics is the way in which "preferences" to avoid surveillance or preserve procedural rights might themselves become new data points for suspicion or investigation. A policymaker may wonder about the persons who refuse to accept the new due-process-lite "deal" offered by the state: What have they got to hide? Why are they so eager to preserve access to a judge and the lengthy process that may entail? Do they know some discrediting fact about their own status that we do not, and are they acting accordingly? Reflected in the economics of information as an "adverse selection problem," this kind of speculative suspicion may become widespread. It may also arise as a byproduct of machine learning: those who refuse to relinquish privacy or procedural rights may, empirically, turn out to be more likely to pose problems for the system, or non-renewal of benefits, than those who trade away those rights. Black-boxed flagging systems may silently incorporate such data points into their own calculations.

The "what have you got to hide" rationale leads to a phenomenon deemed "unraveling" by economists of information. This dynamic has been extensively analyzed by the legal scholar Scott Peppet. The bottom line of Peppet's analysis is that every individual decision to reveal something about himself or herself may also create social circumstances that pressure others to also disclose. For example, if only

[32] Peter J. Walker, "Private Firms Earn £500m from Disability Benefit Assessments" *The Guardian* (Dec 27 2016) www.theguardian.com/society/2016/dec/27/private-firms-500m-governments-fit-to-work-scheme; Dan Bloom, "Privately-Run DWP Disability Benefit Tests Will Temporarily Stop in New 'Integrated' Trial" The Mirror (Mar 2 2020) www.mirror.co.uk/news/politics/privately-run-dwp-disability-benefit-21617594.

[33] Robert Pear, "On Disability and on Facebook? Uncle Sam Wants to Watch What You Post" *New York Times* (2019 Mar 10) www.nytimes.com/2019/03/10/us/politics/social-security-disability-trump-facebook.html; see also n 8.

a few persons tout their grade point average (GPA) on their resumes, that disclosure may merely be an advantage for them in the job-seeking process. However, once 30 percent, 40 percent, 50 percent, or more of job-seekers include their GPAs, human resources personnel reviewing the applications may wonder about the motives of those who do not. If they assume the worst about non-revealers, it becomes a rationale for all but the very lowest GPA holders to reveal their GPA. Those at, say, the thirtieth percentile, reveal their GPA to avoid being confused with those in the twentieth or tenth percentile, and so on.

This model of unraveling parallels similar theorizing in feminist theorizing. For example, Catharine Mackinnon insisted that the "personal is political," in part because any particular family's division of labor helped either reinforce or challenge dominant patterns.[34] A mother may choose to quit work and stay home to raise her children, while her husband works fifty hours a week, and that may be an entirely ethical choice for her family. However, it also helps reinforce patterns of caregiving and expectations in that society which track women into unpaid work and men into paid work. It is not merely accommodating but also promoting gendered patterns of labor.[35] Like a path through a forest trod ever clearer of debris, it becomes the natural default.

This inevitably social dimension of personal choice also highlights the limits of liberalism in addressing due process trade-offs. Civil libertarians may fight the direct imposition of limitations of procedural or privacy rights by the state. However, "freedom of contract" may itself be framed as a civil liberties issue. If a person in great need wants immediate access to benefits, in exchange for letting the state monitor his social network feed (and automatically terminate benefits if suspect pictures are posted), the bare rhetoric of "freedom" also pulls in favor of permitting this deal. We need a more robust and durable theory of constitutionalism to preempt the problems that may arise here.

3.5 BACKSTOPPING THE SLIPPERY SLOPE TOWARD AUTOMATED JUSTICE

As the spread of plea bargaining in the United States shows, there is a clear and present danger of the state using its power to make an end-run around protections established in the constitution and guarded by courts. When a prosecutor threatens a defendant with a potential hundred-year sentence in a trial, or a plea for five to eight years, the coercion is obvious. By comparison, given the sclerotic slowness of much of the US administrative state, giving up rights in order to accelerate receipt of benefits is likely to seem to many liberals a humane (if tough) compromise.

34 Catharine A. Mackinnon, *Toward a Feminist Theory of the State* (Harvard University Press 1989).

35 G. A. Cohen, "Where the Action Is: On the Site of Distributive Justice" (1997) 26(1) *Philosophy & Public Affairs* 3–30.

Nevertheless, scholars should resist this "deal" by further developing and expanding the "unconstitutional conditions" doctrine. Daniel Farber deftly explicates the basis and purpose of the doctrine:

> [One] recondite area of legal doctrine [concerns] the constitutionality of requiring waiver of a constitutional right as a condition of receiving some governmental benefit. Under the unconstitutional conditions doctrine, the government is sometimes, but by no means always, blocked from imposing such conditions on grants. This doctrine has long been considered an intellectual and doctrinal swamp. As one recent author has said, "[t]he Supreme Court's failure to provide coherent guidance on the subject is, alas, legendary."[36]

Farber gives several concrete examples of the types of waivers that have been allowed over time. "[I]n return for government funding, family planning clinics may lose their right to engage in abortion referrals"; a criminal defendant can trade away the right to a jury trial for a lighter sentence. Farber is generally open to the exercise of this right to trade one's rights away.[37] However, even he acknowledges that courts need to block particularly oppressive or manipulative exchanges of rights for other benefits. He offers several rationales for such blockages, including one internal to contract theory and another based on public law grounds.[38] Each is applicable to many instances of "automated justice."

Farber's first normative ground for unconstitutional conditions challenges to waivers of constitutional rights is the classic behavioral economics concern about situations "where asymmetrical information, imperfect rationality, or other flaws make it likely that the bargain will not be in the interests of both parties."[39] This rationale applies particularly well to scenarios where black-box algorithms (or secret data) are used.[40] No one should be permitted to accede to an abbreviated process when the foundations of its decision-making are not available for inspection. The problem of hyperbolic discounting also looms large. A benefits applicant in brutal need of help may not be capable of fully thinking through the implications of trading away due process rights. Bare concern for survival occludes such calculations.

The second normative foundation concerns the larger social impact of the rights-waiver bargain. For example, Farber observes, "when the agreement would adversely affect the interests of third parties in some tangible way," courts should

36 Daniel A. Farber, "Another View of the Quagmire: Unconstitutional Conditions and Contract Theory" (2006) 33 *Fla St LR* 913, 914–15.

37 Ibid., 915 ("Most, if not all, constitutional rights can be bartered away in at least some circumstances. This may seem paradoxical, but it should not be: having a right often means being free to decide on what terms to exercise it or not.").

38 Ibid., 916.

39 Ibid.

40 Frank Pasquale, "Secret Algorithms Threaten the Rule of Law" *MIT Tech Review* (June 1 2017) www.technologyreview.com/s/608011/secret-algorithms-threaten-the-rule-of-law/; Frank Pasquale, *Black Box Society: The Secret Algorithms That Control Money and Information* (Harvard University Press 2015).

be wary of it. The unraveling dynamic described above offers one example of this type of adverse impact on third parties from rights sacrifices. Though it may not be immediately "tangible," it has happened in so many other scenarios that it is critical for courts to consider whether particular bargains may pave the way to a future where the "choice" to trade away a right is effectively no choice at all, because the cost of retaining it is a high level of suspicion generated by exercising (or merely retaining the right to exercise) the right.

Under this second ground, Farber also mentions that we may "block exchanges that adversely affect the social meaning of constitutional rights, degrading society's sense of its connection with personhood." Here again, a drift toward automated determination of legal rights and duties seems particularly apt for targeting. The right of due process at its core means something more than a bare redetermination by automated systems. Rather, it requires some ability to identify a true human face of the state, as Henderson and Brennan-Marquez's work (discussed previously) suggests. Soldiers at war may hide their faces, but police do not. We are not at war with the state; rather, it is supposed to be serving us in a humanly recognizable way. The same is true *a fortiori* of agencies dispending benefits and other forms of support.

3.6 CONCLUSION: WRITING, THINKING, AND AUTOMATION IN ADMINISTRATIVE PROCESSES

Claimants worried about the pressure to sign away rights to due process may have an ally within the administrative state: persons who now hear and decide cases. AI and ML may ease their workload, but could also be a prelude to full automation. Two contrasting cases help illuminate this possibility. In *Albathani* v. *INS* (2003), the First Circuit affirmed the Board of Immigration Appeals' policy of "affirmance without opinion" (AWO) of certain rulings by immigration judges.[41] Though "the record of the hearing itself could not be reviewed" in the ten minutes which the Board member, on average, took to review each of more than fifty cases on the day in question, the court found it imperative to recognize "workload management devices that acknowledge the reality of high caseloads." However, in a similar Australian administrative context, a judge ruled against a Minister in part due to the rapid disposition of two cases involving more than seven hundred pages of material. According to the judge, "43 minutes represents an insufficient time for the Minister to have engaged in the active intellectual process which the law required of him."[42]

In the short run, decision-makers at an agency may prefer the *Albathani* approach. As Chad Oldfather has observed in his article "Writing, Cognition, and the Nature of the Judicial Function," unwritten, and even visceral, snap decisions have a place

41 318 F3d 365 (1st Cir 2003).

42 *Carrascalao* v. *Minister for Immigration* [2017] FCAFC 107; (2017) 347 ALR 173. For an incisive analysis of this case and the larger issues here, see Will Bateman, "Algorithmic Decision-Making and Legality: Public Law Dimensions" (2019) 93 *Australian LJ*.

in our legal system.[43] They are far less tiring to generate than a written record and reasoned elaboration of how the decision-maker applied the law to the facts. However, in the long run, when the reduction of thought and responsibility for review reduces to a certain vanishing point, it is difficult for decision-makers to justify their own interposition in the legal process. A "cyberdelegation" to cheaper software may be proper then.[44]

We must connect current debates on the proper role of automation in agencies to requirements for reasoned decision-making. It is probably in administrators' best interests for courts to actively ensure thoughtful decisions by responsible persons. Otherwise, administrators may ultimately be replaced by the types of software and AI now poised to take over so many other roles now performed by humans. The temptation to accelerate, abbreviate, and automate human processes is, all too often, a prelude to destroying them.[45]

[43] Chad M. Oldfather, "Writing, Cognition, and the Nature of the Judicial Function" (2008) 96 *Geo LJ* 1283.

[44] Cary Coglianese and David Lehr, "Regulating by Robot: Administrative Decision: Making in the Machine-Learning Era" 105 *Geo LJ* 1147 (2017).

[45] Mark Andrejevic, *Automated Media* (Routledge 2020).

4

Constitutional Challenges in the Emotional AI Era

Peggy Valcke, Damian Clifford, and Viltė Kristina Dessers[*]

4.1 INTRODUCTION

Is a future in which our emotions are being detected in real time and tracked, both in private and public spaces, dawning? Looking at recent technological developments, studies, patents, and ongoing experimentations, this may well be the case.[1] In its Declaration on the manipulative capabilities of algorithmic processes of February 2019, the Council of Europe's Committee of Ministers alerts us for the growing capacity of contemporary machine learning tools not only to predict choices but also to influence emotions, thoughts, and even actions, sometimes subliminally.[2] This certainly adds a new dimension to existing computational means, which increasingly make it possible to infer intimate and detailed information about individuals from readily available data, facilitating the micro-targeting of individuals based on profiles in a way that may profoundly affect

[*] The chapter is based on the keynote delivered by P. Valcke at the inaugural conference 'Constitutional Challenges in the Algorithmic Society' of the IACL Research Group on Algorithmic State Market & Society – Constitutional Dimensions', which was held from 9 to 11 May 2019 in Florence (Italy). It draws heavily from the PhD thesis of D. Clifford, entitled 'The Legal Limits to the Monetisation of Online Emotions' and defended at KU Leuven – Faculty of Law on July 3, 2019, to which the reader is referred for a more in-depth discussion.

[1] For some illustrations, see B. Doerrfeld, '20+ Emotion Recognition APIs That Will Leave You Impressed, and Concerned' (Article 2015) https://nordicapis.com/20-emotion-recognition-apis-that-will-leave-you-impressed-and-concerned/ accessed 11 June 2020; M. Zhao, F. Adib and D. Katabi, 'EQ-Radio: Emotion Recognition using Wireless Signals' (Paper 2016) http://eqradio.csail.mit.edu/ accessed 11 June 2020; CB Insights, 'Facebook's Emotion Tech: Patents Show New Ways for Detecting and Responding to Users' Feelings' (Article 2017) www.cbinsights.com/research/facebook-emotion-patents-analysis/ accessed 11 June 2020; R. Murdoch et al., 'How to Build a Responsible Future for Emotional AI' (Research Report 2020) www.accenture.com/fi-en/insights/software-platforms/emotional-ai accessed 11 June 2020. Gartner predicts that by 2022, 10 per cent of personal devices will have emotion AI capabilities, either on-device or via cloud services, up from less than 1% in 2018: Gartner, 'Gartner Highlights 10 Uses for AI-Powered Smartphones' (Press Release 2018) www.gartner.com/en/newsroom/press-releases/2018-03-20-gartner-highlights-10-uses-for-ai-powered-smartphones accessed 11 June 2020.

[2] Committee of Ministers, 'Declaration by the Committee of Ministers on the Manipulative Capabilities of Algorithmic Processes' (Declaration 2019) https://search.coe.int/cm/pages/result_details.aspx?ObjectId=090000168092dd4b accessed 11 June 2020, para. 8.

their lives.[3] *Emotional artificial intelligence* (further 'emotional AI') and *empathic media* are new buzzwords used to refer to the affective computing sub-discipline and, specifically, to the technologies that are claimed to be capable of detecting, classifying, and responding appropriately to users' emotional lives, thereby appearing to understand their audience.[4] These technologies rely on a variety of methods, including the analysis of facial expressions, physiological measuring, analyzing voice, monitoring body movements, and eye tracking.[5]

Although there have been important debates as to their accuracy, the adoption of emotional AI technologies is increasingly widespread, in many areas and for various purposes, both in the public and private sectors.[6] It is well-known that advertising and marketing go hand in hand with an attempt to exploit emotions for commercial gain.[7] Emotional AI facilitates the systematic gathering of insights[8] and allows for the further personalization of commercial communications and the optimization of marketing campaigns in real time.[9] Quantifying, tracking, and manipulating emotions is a growing part of the social media business model.[10] For example, Facebook is now infamous in this regard due to its emotional contagion[11] experiment where users' newsfeeds were manipulated to assess changes in emotion (to assess whether Facebook posts with emotional content were more engaging).[12] A similar trend has been witnessed in the political sphere – think of the Cambridge

3 Ibid, para, 6.

4 A. McStay, *Emotional AI: The Rise of Empathic Media* (SAGE 2018) 3.

5 For more details, see, e.g., J. Stanley, 'The Dawn of Robot Surveillance' (Report 2019) www.aclu.org/sites/default/files/field_document/061119-robot_surveillance.pdf accessed 11 June 2020 21–25.

6 Particular employment examples include uses for health care or pseudo-health care (e.g., to detect mood for the purposes of improving mental well-being), road safety (e.g., to detect drowsiness and inattentiveness), employee safety, uses to assess job applicants and people suspected of crimes. See more e.g., A. Fernández-Caballero et al., 'Smart Environment Architecture for Emotion Detection and Regulation' [2016] 64 J Biomed Inform 55; Gartner, '13 Surprising Uses For Emotion AI Technology' (Article 2018) www.gartner.com/smarterwithgartner/13-surprising-uses-for-emotion-ai-technology accessed 11 June 2020; C. Jee, 'Emotion Recognition Technology Should Be Banned, Says an AI Research Institute' (Article 2019) www.technologyreview.com/2019/12/13/131585/emotion-recognition-technology-should-be-banned-says-ai-research-institute/ accessed 11 June 2020; J. Jolly, 'Volvo to Install Cameras in New Cars to Reduce Road Deaths' (Article 2019) www.theguardian.com/business/2019/mar/20/volvo-to-install-cameras-in-new-cars-to-reduce-road-deaths accessed 11 June 2020; Stanley (n 6) 21–24; D. Clifford, 'The Legal Limits to the Monetisation of Online Emotions' (PhD thesis, KU Leuven, Faculty of Law 2019) 12.

7 Clifford (n 7) 10.

8 Clifford (n 7) 103.

9 See, e.g., C. Burr, N. Cristianini, and J. Ladyman, 'An Analysis of the Interaction between Intelligent Software Agents and Human Users' [2018] MIND MACH 735; C. Burr and N. Cristianini, 'Can Machines Read Our Minds?' [2019] 29 MIND MACH 461.

10 L. Stark and K. Crawford, 'The Conservatism of Emoji: Work, Affect, and Communication' [2015] 1 SM+S, 1, 8.

11 E. Hatfield, J. Cacioppo, and R. Rapson, 'Emotional Contagion' [1993] Curr Dir Psychol Sci 96.

12 See, e.g., A. Kramer, J. Guillory, and J. Hancock, 'Experimental Evidence of Massive-Scale Emotional Contagion through Social Networks' (Research Article 2014) https://doi.org/10.1073/pnas.1320040111 accessed 11 June 2020. There are also data to suggest that Facebook had offered advertisers the ability to target advertisements to teenagers based on real-time extrapolation of their mood:

Analytica scandal[13] (where data analytics was used to gauge the personalities of potential Trump voters).[14] The aforementioned Declaration of the Council of Europe, among others, points to the dangers for democratic societies that emanate from the possibility to employ algorithmic tools capable of manipulating and controlling not only economic choices but also social and political behaviours.[15]

Do we need new (constitutional) rights, as suggested by some, in light of growing practices of manipulation by algorithms, in general, and the emergence of emotional AI, in particular? Or, is the current law capable of accommodating such developments adequately? This is undoubtedly one of the most fascinating debates for legal scholars in the coming years. It is also on the radar of CAHAI, the Council of Europe's Ad Hoc Committee on Artificial Intelligence, set up on 11 September 2019, with the mission to examine the feasibility and potential elements of a legal framework for the development, design, and application of AI, based on the Council of Europe's standards on human rights, democracy, and the rule of law.[16]

In the light of these ongoing policy discussions, the ambition of this chapter is twofold. First, it will discuss certain legal-ethical challenges posed by the emergence of emotional AI and its manipulative capabilities. Second, it will present a number of responses, specifically those suggesting the introduction of new (constitutional) rights to mitigate the potential negative effects of such developments. Given the limited scope of the chapter, it does not seek to evaluate the appropriateness of the identified suggestions, but rather to provide the foundation for a future research agenda in that direction. The focus of the chapter lies on the *European* legal framework and on the use of emotions for *commercial business-to-consumer purposes*, although some observations are also valid in the context of other highly relevant uses of emotional AI,[17] such as implementations by the public sector, or for the purpose of political micro-targeting, or fake news. The chapter is based on a literature review, including recent academic scholarship and grey literature. Its methodology relies on a legal analysis of how the emergence of emotional AI raises concerns and challenges for 'constitutional' rights and values through the lens of its use in the business to consumer context. With constitutional rights, we do not refer to national

N. Tiku, 'Facebook's Ability to Target Insecure Teens Could Prompt Backlash' (Article 2017) www.wired.com/2017/05/welcome-next-phase-facebook-backlash/ accessed 11 June 2020.

13 See, e.g., L. Stark, 'Algorithmic Psychometrics and the Scalable Subject' (2018) https://static1.squarespace.com/static/59a34512c534a5fe6721d2b1/t/5cb0bdbc4192024cf8e7e587/1555086781059/Stark+-+Algorithmic+Psychometrics+%28pre-print%29.pdf accessed 11 June 2020; Guardian, 'Cambridge Analytica Files' www.theguardian.com/news/series/cambridge-analytica-files accessed 11 June 2020.

14 Stark (n 14).

15 Declaration by the Committee of Ministers on the Manipulative Capabilities of Algorithmic Processes (n 3), para. 8.

16 For more information, see www.coe.int/en/web/artificial-intelligence/cahai. Transparency declaration: one of the co-authors serves as CAHAI's vice-chair.

17 For example, political micro-targeting, fake news. See more Clifford (n 7) 13.

constitutions, but given the chapter's focus on the European level, to the fundamental rights and values as enshrined in the European Convention for the Protection of Human Rights and Fundamental Freedoms ('ECHR'), on the one hand, and the EU Charter of Fundamental Rights ('CFREU') and Article 2 of the Treaty on European Union ('TEU'), on the other.

4.2 CHALLENGES TO CONSTITUTIONAL RIGHTS AND UNDERLYING VALUES

Protecting the Citizen-Consumer

Emotion has always been at the core of advertising and marketing, and emotion detection has been used in market research for several decades.[18] Consequently, in various areas of EU and national law, rules have been adopted to protect consumers and constrain forms of manipulative practices in business-to-consumer relations. Media and advertising laws have introduced prohibitions on false, misleading, deceptive, and surreptitious advertising, including an explicit ban on subliminal advertising.[19] Consumer protection law instruments shield consumers from aggressive, unfair, and deceptive trade practices.[20] Competition law prohibits exploitative abuses of market power.[21] Data protection law has set strict conditions under which consumers' personal data can be collected and processed.[22] Under contract law, typical grounds for a contract being voidable include coercion, undue influence, misrepresentation, or fraud. The latter, fraud (i.e., the intentional deception to secure an unfair or unlawful gain, or deprive a victim of her legal right) is considered a criminal offence. In the remainder of the text, these rules are referred to as

18 A well-known video fragment illustrating this (and described by Sunstein in his article , C. Sunstein, 'Fifty Shades of Manipulation' [2016] 1 J. Behavioral Marketing 213) is Mad Men's Don Draper delivering his Kodak Pitch (see at www.youtube.com/watch?v=UrkGsur75Uc). See, e.g., T. Brader, *Campaigning for Hearts and Minds: How Emotional Appeals in Political Ads Work* (University of Chicago Press 2006); E. Mogaji, *Emotional Appeals in Advertising Banking Services* (Emerald Publishing Ltd 2018).

19 See, e.g., Article 9 of the Parliament and Council Directive 2010/13/EU on the coordination of certain provisions laid down by law, regulation, or administrative action in Member States concerning the provision of audiovisual media services (Audiovisual Media Services Directive) [2010] OJ L 95.

20 See, e.g., Parliament and Council Directive 2019/2161 amending Council Directive 93/13/EEC and Directives 98/6/EC, 2005/29/EC and 2011/83/EU of the European Parliament and of the Council as regards the better enforcement and modernisation of Union consumer protection rules [2019] OJ L 328.

21 Article 102 of the Treaty on the Functioning of the European Union. See Consolidated Version of the Treaty on the Functioning of the European Union [2012] OJ C 326.

22 In particular, Parliament and Council Regulation 2016/679 on the protection of natural persons with regard to the processing of personal data and on the free movement of such data, and repealing Directive 95/46/EC (General Data Protection Regulation) [2016] OJ L 119. Also see Parliament and Council Directive 2002/58/EC concerning the processing of personal data and the protection of privacy in the electronic communications sector (Directive on Privacy and Electronic Communications) [2002] OJ L 201.

'consumer protection law in the broad sense', as they protect citizens as economic actors.

Nevertheless, the employment of emotional AI may justify additional layers of protection. The growing effectiveness of the technology drew public attention following Facebook's aforementioned emotional contagion[23] experiment, where users' newsfeeds were manipulated to assess changes in emotion (to assess whether Facebook posts with emotional content were more engaging),[24] as well as the Cambridge Analytica scandal[25] (where it was used to gauge the personalities of potential Trump voters).[26] There are also data to suggest that Facebook had offered advertisers the ability to target advertisements to teenagers based on real-time extrapolation of their mood.[27] Yet Facebook is obviously not alone in exploiting emotional AI (and emotions) in similar ways.[28] As noted by Stark and Crawford, commenting on the fallout from the emotional contagion experiment, it is clear that quantifying, tracking, and 'manipulating emotions' is a growing part of the social media business model.[29] Researchers are documenting the emergence of what Zuboff calls 'surveillance capitalism'[30] and, in particular, its reliance on behavioural tracking and manipulation.[31] Forms of 'dark patterns' are increasingly detected, exposed, and – to some extent – legally constrained. Dark patterns can be described as exploitative design choices, 'features of interface design crafted to trick users into doing things that they might not want to do, but which benefit the business in question'.[32] In its report from 2018, the Norwegian Consumer Authority called the use by large digital service providers (in particular Facebook, Google, and Microsoft) of such dark patterns an 'unethical' attempt to push consumers towards the least privacy friendly options of their services.[33] Moreover, it questioned whether such practices are in accordance with the principles of data protection by default and data protection by design, and whether consent given under these circumstances can be said to be explicit, informed, and freely given. It stated that '[w]hen digital services employ dark patterns to nudge users towards sharing more personal data, the financial incentive has taken precedence over respecting users' right to choose. The practice of misleading consumers into making certain choices, which may put their privacy at risk, is unethical and exploitative.' In 2019, the French data

23 Hatfield (n 12).
24 See, e.g., Kramer (n 13).
25 Guardian, 'Cambridge Analytica Files' (n 14); Stark (n 14).
26 Stark (n 14).
27 Tiku (n 13).
28 Clifford (n 7) 112.
29 Stark and Crawford (n 11) 1, 8.
30 S. Zuboff, *The Age of Surveillance Capitalism: The Fight for a Human Future at the New Frontier of Power* (PublicAffairs 2019).
31 Stark (n 14).
32 The Norwegian Consumer Council, 'Deceived by Design' (Report 2018) www.forbrukerradet.no /undersokelse/no-undersokelsekategori/deceived-by-design/ accessed 11 June 2020 7.
33 Ibid.

protection authority, CNIL, effectively fined Google for the violation of transparency and information obligations and lack of (valid) consent for advertisements personalization. In essence, the users were not aware of the extent of personalization.[34] Notably, the Deceptive Experiences to Online Users Reduction Act, as introduced by senators Deb Fischer and Mark Warner in the United States (the so-called DETOUR Act), explicitly provided protection against 'manipulation of user interfaces' and offered prohibiting dark patterns when seeking consent to use personal information.[35]

It is unlikely, though, that existing consumer protection law (in the broad sense) will be capable of providing a conclusive and exhaustive answer to the question of where to draw the line between forms of permissible persuasion and unacceptable manipulation in the case of emotional AI. On the one hand, there may be situations in which dubious practices escape the scope of application of existing laws. Think of the cameras installed at Piccadilly Lights in London which are able to detect faces in the crowd around the Eros statue in Piccadilly Circus, and 'when they identify a face the technology works out an approximate age, sex, mood (based on whether think you are frowning or laughing) and notes some characteristics such as whether you wear glasses or whether you have a beard'.[36] The cameras have been used during a certain period with the purpose of optimizing the advertising displayed on Piccadilly Lights.[37] Even if such practices of emotional AI in public spaces are not considered in violation of the EU General Data Protection Regulation (given the claimed immediate anonymization of the faces detected), they raise serious question marks from an ethical perspective.[38] On the other hand, the massive scale with which certain practices are deployed may surpass the enforcement of individual rights. The Council of Europe's Parliamentary Assembly expressed concerns that persuasive technologies enable 'massive psychological experimentation and persuasion on the internet'.[39] Such practices seem to

34 In accordance with the General Data Protection Regulation (n 23): CNIL, 'Deliberation of the Restricted Committee SAN-2019-001 of 21 January 2019 Pronouncing a Financial Sanction against GOOGLE LLC' (Decision 2019) www.cnil.fr/sites/default/files/atoms/files/san-2019-001.pdf accessed 11 June 2020.

35 Deceptive Experiences to Online Users Reduction Act 2019 www.congress.gov/bill/116th-congress/senate-bill/1084/text accessed 11 June 2020; M. Kelly, 'Big Tech's 'Dark Patterns' Could Be Outlawed under New Senate Bill' (Article 2019) www.theverge.com/2019/4/9/18302199/big-tech-dark-patterns-senate-bill-detour-act-facebook-google-amazon-twitter accessed 11 June 2020.

36 Landsec, 'Archived Privacy Policy Piccadilly Lights' https://landsec.com/policies/privacy-policy/piccadilly-lights-english accessed 11 June 2020.

37 According to the Archived Privacy Policy Piccadilly Lights (n 37), the data collection ended in September 2018.

38 A. McStay and L. Urquhart, '"This Time with Feeling?" Assessing EU Data Governance Implications of Out of Home Appraisal Based Emotional AI'. [2019] 24 First Monday 10 https://doi.org/10.5210/fm.v24i10.9457 accessed 11 June 2020.

39 Council of Europe, Committee on Culture, Science, Education and Media, Rapporteur Mr Jean-Yves LE DÉAUT, 'Technological Convergence, Artificial Intelligence and Human Rights' (Report 2017) www.assembly.coe.int/nw/xml/XRef/XRef-DocDetails-EN.asp?FileId=23531 accessed 11 June 2020 para. 26.

require a collective answer (e.g., by including them in the blacklist of commercial practices),[40] since enforcement in individual cases risks being ineffective in remedying harmful effects on society as a whole.

Moreover, emotional AI is arguably challenging the very underlying rationality-based paradigm imbued in (especially, but not limited to) consumer protection law. Modern legality is characterized by a separation of rational thinking (or reason) from emotion and consumer protection essentially rely on rationality.[41] As noted by Maloney, the law works from the perspective that rational thinking and emotion 'belong to separate spheres of human existence; the sphere of law admits only of reason; and vigilant policing is required to keep emotion from creeping in where it does not belong'.[42] The law is traditionally weighted towards the protection of the verifiable propositional content of commercial communications; however, interdisciplinary research is increasingly recognizing the persuasive effect of the unverifiable content (i.e., images, music)[43] and has long recognized that people interact with computers as social agents and not just tools.[44] It may be reasonably argued that the separation of rationality from affect in the law fails to take interdisciplinary insights into account.[45] In relation to this, the capacity of the current legal framework to cope with the advancements is in doubt. In particular, since the development of emotion detection technology facilitates the creation of emotion-evolved consumer-facing interactions, it poses challenges to the framework which relies on rationality.[46] The developments arguably raise concerns regarding the continuing reliance on the rationality paradigm within consumer protections, and hence consumer self-determination and individual autonomy, as core underlying principles of the legal protections.

Motivating a Constitutional Debate

The need for guidance about how to apply and, where relevant, complement existing consumer protection laws (in the broad sense) in light of the rise of

40 European Parliament and Council Directive 2005/29/EC concerning unfair business-to-consumer commercial practices in the internal market [2005] OJ L 149, Annex I. D. Clifford, 'Citizen-Consumers in a Personalised Galaxy: Emotion Influenced Decision-Making, a True Path to the Dark Side?', in L. Edwards, E. Harbinja, and B. Shaffer (eds) *Future Law: Emerging Technology, Regulation and Ethics* (Edinburgh University Press 2020).

41 D. Clifford, 'The Emergence of Emotional AI Emotion Monetisation and Profiling Risk, Nothing New?', *Ethics of Data Science Conference* (Paper 2020, forthcoming).

42 T. Maroney, 'Law and Emotion: A Proposed Taxonomy of an Emerging Field' [2019] 30 Law Hum Behav 119.

43 M. Hütter and S. Sweldens, 'Dissociating Controllable and Uncontrollable Effects of Affective Stimuli on Attitudes and Consumption' [2018] 45 J Consum Res 320, 344.

44 M. Lee, 'Understanding Perception of Algorithmic Decisions: Fairness, Trust, and Emotion in Response to Algorithmic Management' [2018] 5 BD&S 1, 2.

45 Clifford (n 7) 82.

46 In particular, such technologies allow for the development of inter alia content, formats, and products, or indeed entire campaigns that are optimized (i.e., at least at face value) and tailored by emotion insights. Clifford (n 7).

emotional AI motivates the need for a debate at a more fundamental level, looking at constitutional and ethical frameworks. The following paragraphs – revolving around three main observations – focus on the former of these frameworks, and will highlight how emotion detection and manipulation may pose threats to the effective enjoyment of constitutional rights and freedoms.

What's in a Name?

By way of preliminary observation, it should be stressed that, as noted by Sunstein, manipulation has 'many shades' and is extremely difficult to define.[47] Is an advertising campaign by an automobile company showing a sleek, attractive couple exiting from a fancy car before going to a glamorous party 'manipulation'? Do governments – in an effort to discourage smoking – engage in 'manipulation' when they require cigarette packages to contain graphic, frightening health warnings, depicting people with life-threatening illnesses? Is showing unflattering photographs of your opponent during a political campaign 'manipulation'? Is setting an opt-out consent system for deceased organ donation as the legislative default 'manipulation'? Ever since Nobel Prize winner Richard Thaler and Cass Sunstein published their influential book *Nudge*, a rich debate has ensued on the permissibility of deploying choice architectures for behavioural change.[48] The debate, albeit extremely relevant in the emotional AI context, exceeds the scope of this chapter, and is inherently linked to political-philosophical discussions. A key takeaway from Sunstein's writing is that, in a social order that values free markets and is committed to freedom of expression, it is 'exceptionally difficult to regulate manipulation as such'.[49] He suggests to consider a statement or action as manipulative to the extent that it does not sufficiently engage or appeal to people's capacity for reflective and deliberative choice. This reminds us of the notions of consumer self-determination and individual autonomy, which we mentioned previously and which will also be discussed further in this section.

From Manipulation over Surveillance to Profiling Errors

Second, it is important to understand that, in addition to the concerns over its manipulative capabilities, on which the chapter focused so far, emotional AI and

47 Sunstein (n 19).

48 See, e.g., H. Micklitz, L. Reisch and K. Hagen, 'An Introduction to the Special Issue on "Behavioural Economics, Consumer Policy, and Consumer Law"' [2011] 34 J Consum Policy 271 https://doi.org/10.1007/s10603-011-9166-5 accessed 11 June 2020; R. Calo, 'Digital Market Manipulation' [2014] 82 Geo Wash L Rev 995; D. Citron and F. Pasquale, 'The Scored Society: Due Process for Automated Predictions' [2014] 89 Wash L Rev 1 https://papers.ssrn.com/sol3/papers.cfm?abstract_id=2376209 accessed 11 June 2020; H. Micklitz, A. Sibony, and F. Esposito (eds), *Research Methods in Consumer Law* (Edward Elgar 2018).

49 Sunstein (n 19).

its employment equally require to take into consideration potential *harmful affective impacts*, on the one hand, and potential *profiling errors*, on the other. In relation to the former (the latter are discussed later), it is well-known that surveillance may cause a chilling effect on behaviour[50] and, in this way, encroach on our rights to freedom of expression (Article 10 ECHR; Article 10 CFREU), freedom of assembly and association (Article 11 ECRH; Article 12 CFREU), and – to the extent that our moral integrity is at stake – our right to private life and personal identity (Article 8 ECHR; Article 7 CFREU).[51] Significantly, as noted by Calo, '[e]ven where we know intellectually that we are interacting with an image or a machine, our brains are hardwired to respond as though a person were actually there'.[52] The mere observation or perception of surveillance can have a chilling effect on behaviour.[53] As argued by Stanley (in the context of video analytics), one of the most worrisome concerns is 'the possibility of widespread chilling effects as we all become highly aware that our actions are being not just recorded and stored, but scrutinized and evaluated on a second-by-second' basis.[54] Moreover, such monitoring can also have an impact on an individual's ability to 'self-present'.[55] This refers to the ability of individuals to present multifaceted versions of themselves,[56] and thus behave differently depending on the circumstances.[57] Emotion detection arguably adds a layer of intimacy-invasion via the capacity to not only detect emotions as *expressed* but also detect underlying emotions that are being deliberately *disguised*. This is of particular significance, as it not only limits the capacity to self-present but potentially erodes this capacity entirely. This could become problematic if such technologies and the outlined technological capacity become commonplace.[58] In that regard, it is

50 Clifford (n 42).

51 See, e.g., the case of *Antović and Mirković* v. *Montenegro* concerning the installation of video surveillance equipment in auditoriums at a university, in which the ECtHR emphasized that video surveillance of employees at their workplace, whether covert or not, constituted a considerable intrusion into their 'private life' (*Antović and Mirković* v. *Montenegro* App no 70838/13 (ECtHR, 28 February 2018) para. 44). See also, e.g., *Liberty and Others* v. *the United Kingdom* App no 58243/00 (ECtHR, 1 July 2008); *Vukota-Bojić* v. *Switzerland* App no 61838/10 (ECtHR, 18 October 2016; *Bărbulescu* v. *Romania* App no 61496/08 (ECtHR, 5 September 2017).

52 R. Calo, 'The Boundaries of Privacy Harm' (2011) 86 Indiana Law J 1131, 1147.

53 One should also note surveillance can have a chilling effect even if it is private or public; see N. Richards, 'The Dangers of Surveillance' [2013] 126 Harv Law Rev 1934, 1935: '[W]e must recognize that surveillance transcends the public/private divide. Public and private surveillance are simply related parts of the same problem, rather than wholly discrete. Even if we are ultimately more concerned with government surveillance, any solution must grapple with the complex relationships between government and corporate watchers.'

54 Stanley (n 6) 35–36.

55 O. Lynskey, *The Foundations of EU Data Protection Law* (First, OUP 2016) 202, 218.

56 R. Warner and R. Sloan, 'Self, Privacy, and Power: Is It All Over?' [2014] 17 Tul J Tech & Intell Prop 8.

57 J. Rachels, 'Why Privacy Is Important' [1975] 4 Philos Public Aff 323, 323–333, 323-333. The author goes on to discuss how we behave differently depending on who we are talking to, and this has been argued as dishonest or a mask by certain authors; but the author disagrees, saying that these 'masks' are, in fact, a crucial part of the various relationships and are therefore not dishonest. See also H. Nissenbaum, 'Privacy as Contextual Integrity' [2004] 79 Wash L Rev 119.

58 Clifford (n 7) 124; Clifford (n 42).

important to understand that emotional AI can have an impact on an individual's capacity to self-present irrespective of its accuracy (i.e., what is important is that the individual's belief or the mere observation or perception of surveillance can have a chilling effect on behaviour).[59]

The lack of accuracy of emotional AI, resulting in profiling errors and incorrect inferences, presents additional risks of harm,[60] including inconvenience, embarrassment, or even material or physical harm.[61] In this context, it is particularly important that a frequently adopted approach[62] for emotion detection relies on the six basic emotions as indicated by Ekman (i.e., happiness, sadness, surprise, fear, anger, and disgust). However, this classification is heavily criticized as not accurately reflecting the complex nature of an affective state.[63] The other major approaches for detecting emotions, namely the dimensional and appraisal-based approach, also present challenges of their own.[64] As Stanley puts it, emotion detection is an area where there is a special reason to be sceptical, since many such efforts spiral into 'a rabbit hole of naïve technocratic simplification based on dubious beliefs about emotions'.[65] The AI Now Institute at New York University alerts (in the light of facial recognition) that new technologies reactivate 'a long tradition of physiognomy – a pseudoscience that claims facial features can reveal innate aspects of our character and personality' – and emphasizes that contextual, social, and cultural factors play a larger role in emotional expression than was believed by Ekman and his peers.[66] Leaving the point that emotion detection through facial expressions is a pseudoscience to one side, improving the accuracy of emotion detection more generally may arguably require more invasive surveillance to gather more contextual insights and signals, paradoxically creating additional difficulties from a privacy perspective. Building on the revealed circumstances, the risks associated with profiling are strongly related to the fact that the databases being mined for inferences are often 'out-of-context, incomplete or partially polluted', resulting in the risk of

59 Calo (n 53) 1142–1143.

60 For example, practical use cases such as the ones in health care or pseudo-health care shed light on the potential for inaccuracy to have damaging effects on the physical and mental well-being of the individual concerned. For details, see, e.g., Clifford (n 42).

61 Ibid.

62 AI Now Institute, New York University, 'AI Now Report 20184; (Report 2018), https://ainowinstitute.org/AI_Now_2018_Report.pdf 14.

63 In this regard, it is interesting to refer to the work of Barret, who views the focus on basic emotions as misguided, as such categories fail to capture the richness of emotional experiences. L. Barrett, 'Are Emotions Natural Kinds?' [2006] 1 Perspectives on Psychological Science 28, as cited by R. Markwica, *Emotional Choices: How the Logic of Affect Shapes Coercive Diplomacy* (Oxford University Press 2018) 18, 72.

64 Clifford (n 42).

65 For more details, see Stanley (n 6) 38–39.

66 AI Now Report 2018 (n 63) 14. For a discussion in the context of emotion detection, see also A. McStay, 'Empathic Media and Advertising: Industry, Policy, Legal and Citizen Perspectives (the Case for Intimacy)' [2016] 3 BD&S 1, 3–6.

false positives and false negatives.[67] This risk remains unaddressed by the individual participation rights approach in the EU data protection framework. Indeed, while the rights of access, correction, and erasure as evident in the EU General Data Protection Regulation may have theoretical significance, the practical operation of these rights requires significant effort and is becoming increasingly difficult.[68] This in turn may have a significant impact on the enjoyment of key fundamental rights and freedoms, such as inter alia the right to respect for private and family life and protection of personal data (Article 8 ECHR; Articles 7–8 CFREU); equality and non-discrimination (Article 14 ECHR; Articles 20–21 CFREU); and freedom of thought, conscience, and religion (Article 9 ECHR; Article 10 CFREU); but also – and this brings us to our third observation – the underlying key notions of *autonomy* and *human dignity*.

Getting to the Core Values: Autonomy and Human Dignity

Both at the EU and Council of Europe level, institutions have stressed that new technologies should be designed in such a way that they preserve human dignity and autonomy – both physical and psychological: 'the design and use of persuasion software and of ICT or AI algorithms … must fully respect the dignity and human rights of all users'.[69] Manipulation of choice can inherently interfere with autonomy.[70] Although the notion of autonomy takes various meanings and conceptions, based on different philosophical, ethical, legal, and other theories,[71] for the purposes of this chapter, the Razian interpretation of autonomy is adopted, as it recognizes the need to facilitate an environment in which individuals can act autonomously.[72] According to Razian legal philosophy, rights are derivatives of autonomy[73] and, in contrast with the traditional liberal approach, autonomy

67 B. Koops, 'On Decision Transparency, or How to Enhance Data Protection after the Computational Turn' in M. Hildebrandt and K. de Vries (eds), *Privacy, Due Process and the Computational Turn: The Philosophy of Law Meets the Philosophy of Technology* (Routledge 2013) 199.

68 Koops (n 68) 199.

69 Parliamentary Assembly, 'Technological Convergence, Artificial Intelligence and Human Rights' (Recommendation 2102 2017) https://assembly.coe.int/nw/xml/XRef/Xref-XML2HTML-en.asp?fileid=23726&lang=en accessed 11 June 2020 para. 9.1.5. In relation to bio-medicine, reference can be made to the 1997 Convention for the Protection of Human Rights and Dignity of the Human Being with regard to the Application of Biology and Medicine: Convention on Human Rights and Biomedicine (also known as 'Oviedo Convention'). At EU level, see, for example, in the area of robotics and AI the European Parliament resolution on civil law rules on robotics: Parliament resolution with recommendations to the Commission 2015/2103(INL) on Civil Law Rules on Robotics [2015] OJ C 252.

70 P. Bernal, *Internet Privacy Rights: Rights to Protect Autonomy* (1st ed., Cambridge University Press 2014).

71 E. Harbinja, 'Post-Mortem Privacy 2.0: Theory, Law, and Technology' [2017] 31 Int Rev Law Comput Tech 26, 29.

72 Clifford (n 7) 277.

73 J. Raz, The Morality of Freedom (Clarendon Press, 1986) 247.

requires more than simple non-interference. Raz's conception of autonomy does not preclude the potential for positive regulatory intervention to protect individuals and enhance their freedom. In fact, such positive action is at the core of this conception of autonomy, as a correct interpretation must allow effective choice in reality, thus at times requiring regulatory intervention.[74] Raz argues that certain regulatory interventions which support certain activities and discourage those which are undesirable 'are required to provide the conditions of autonomy'.[75] According to Raz, '[a]utonomy is opposed to a life of coerced choices. It contrasts with a life of no choices, or of drifting through life without ever exercising one's capacity to choose. Evidently the autonomous life calls for a certain degree of self-awareness. To choose one must be aware of one's options.'[76] Raz further asserts: 'Manipulating people, for example, interferes with their autonomy, and does so in much the same way and to the same degree, as coercing them. Resort to manipulation should be subject to the same conditions as resort to coercion.'[77] Hence the manipulation of choice can inherently interfere with autonomy, and one can conclude that through this lens, excessive persuasion also runs afoul of autonomy.[78]

Autonomy is inherent in the operation of the democratic values, which are protected at the foundational level by fundamental rights and freedoms. However, there is no express reference to a *right to autonomy* or *self-determination* in either the ECHR or the CFREU. Despite not being expressly recognized in a distinct ECHR provision, the European Court of Human Rights (further 'ECtHR') has ruled on several occasions that the protection of autonomy comes within the scope of Article 8 ECHR,[79] which specifies the right to respect for private and family life. This connection has been repeatedly illustrated in the ECtHR jurisprudence dealing with individuals' fundamental life choices, including inter alia in relation to sexual preferences/orientation, and personal and social life (i.e., including a person's interpersonal relationships). Such cases illustrate the role played by the right to privacy in the development of one's personality through self-realization and autonomy (construed broadly).[80] The link between the right to privacy and autonomy is thus strong, and therefore, although privacy and autonomy are not synonyms,[81] it may be reasonably argued that the right to privacy currently offers an avenue for

74 P. Bernal, *Internet Privacy Rights: Rights to Protect Autonomy* (1st ed., Cambridge University Press 2014) 25–27; Raz (n 73) 382.

75 Raz (n 74) 420; Clifford (n 7).

76 Raz (n 74) 371; Clifford (n 7).

77 Raz (n 74).

78 Bernal (n 74) 26; Clifford (n 7).

79 For example, in *Pretty* v. *United Kingdom*, the ECtHR found that Article 8 ECHR included the ability to refuse medical treatment and that the imposition of treatment on a patient who has not consented 'would quite clearly interfere with a person's physical integrity in a manner capable of engaging the rights protected under art 8(1) of the Convention'. *Pretty* v. *United Kingdom* App no 2346/02 (ECtHR, 29 April 2002) para. 63.

80 Clifford (n 7) 104.

81 See more, e.g., Clifford (n 7) 104–105.

protection of autonomy (as evidenced by the ECtHR case law).[82] The emergence of emotional AI and the detection of emotions in real time through emotion surveillance challenges the two strands of the right simultaneously, namely (1) privacy as seclusion or intimacy through the detection of emotions and (2) privacy as freedom of action, self-determination, and autonomy via their monetization.[83]

Dignity, similar to autonomy, cannot be defined easily. The meaning of the word is by no means straightforward, and its relationship with fundamental rights is unclear.[84] The Rathenau Institute has touched upon this issue, noting that technologies are likely to interfere with other rights if the use of technologies interferes with human dignity.[85] However, there is little or no consensus as to what the concept of human dignity demands of lawmakers and adjudicators, and as noted by O'Mahony, as a result, many commentators argue that it is at best meaningless or unhelpful, and at worst potentially damaging to the protection of human rights.[86] Whereas a full examination of the substantive content of the concept is outside the scope of this chapter, it can be noted that human dignity, despite being interpreted differently due to cultural differences,[87] is considered to be a *central value* underpinning the entirety of international human rights law,[88] one of the core principles of fundamental rights,[89] and the basis of most of the values emphasized in the ECHR.[90] Although the ECHR itself does not explicitly mention *human dignity*,[91] its importance has been highlighted in several legal sources related to the ECHR,

82 Ibid, 110.

83 K. Ziegler, 'Introduction: Human Rights and Private Law – Privacy as Autonomy' in K. Ziegler (ed), *Human Rights and Private Law: Privacy as Autonomy* (1st ed., Hart Publishing 2007). This view is shared by Yeung in her discussion of population-wide manipulation; see K. Yeung, 'A Study of the Implications of Advanced Digital Technologies (Including AI Systems) for the Concept of Responsibility within a Human Rights Framework (DRAFT)' (Council of Europe 2018) https://rm.coe.int/draft-study-of-the-implications-of-advanced-digital-technologies-inclu/16808ef255 accessed 11 June 2020 29.

84 See, e.g., D. Feldman, 4;Human Dignity as a Legal Value: Part 14; [1999] Public Law 682, 690.

85 For details, see R. van Est and J. Gerritsen, 'Human Rights in the Robot Age: Challenges Arising from the Use of Robotics, Artificial Intelligence, and Virtual and Augmented Reality' (Rathenau Instituut Expert report written for the Committee on Culture, Science, Education and Media of the Parliamentary Assembly of the Council of Europe 2017) www.rathenau.nl/sites/default/files/2018-02/Human%20Rights%20in%20the%20Robot%20Age-Rathenau%20Instituut-2017.pdf accessed 11 June 2020 27–28.

86 C. O'Mahony, 'There Is No Such Thing as a Right to Dignity' [2012] 10 Int J Const Law 551.

87 O'Mahony (n 87) 557–558.

88 O'Mahony (n 87) 552.

89 Its value is emphasized in a number of international treaties and national constitutional documents. For details, see, e.g., O'Mahony (n 87) 552–553.

90 See, for instance, *Pretty* v. *United Kingdom (2346/02) [2002] ECHR 423 (29 April 2002)*, where the ECtHR held that the 'very essence of the Convention is respect for human dignity and human freedom' (para. 65). The Universal Declaration of Human Rights – on which the ECHR is based – provides that '[a]ll human beings are born free and equal in dignity and rights' (Article 1). For details, see R. van Est and J. Gerritsen (n 86) 27–28.

91 Except Protocol No. 13 to the Convention for the Protection of Human Rights and Fundamental Freedoms concerning the abolition of the death penalty in all circumstances.

including the case law of ECtHR and various documents of the CoE.[92] Human dignity is also explicitly recognized as the foundation of all fundamental rights guaranteed by the CFREU,[93] and its role was affirmed by the Court of Justice of the EU (further 'CJEU').[94]

With regard to its substantive content, it can be noted that as O'Mahony argues, perhaps the most universally recognized aspects of human dignity are equal treatment and respect.[95] In the context of emotional AI, it is particularly relevant that although human dignity shall not be considered as a right itself,[96] it is the source of the right to personal autonomy and self-determination (i.e., the latter are derived from the underlying principle of human dignity).[97] As noted by Feldman, there is arguably no human right which is unconnected to human dignity; however, 'some rights seem to have a particularly prominent role in upholding human dignity', and these include the right to be free of inhuman or degrading treatment, the right to respect for private and family life, the right to freedom of conscience and belief, the right to freedom of association, the right to marry and found a family, and the right to be free of discriminatory treatment.[98] Feldman argues that, apart from freedom from inhuman and degrading treatment, these rights are 'not principally directed to protecting dignity and they are more directly geared to protecting the interests in autonomy, equality and respect'.[99] However, it is argued that these interests – autonomy, equality, and respect – are important in providing circumstances in which 'dignity can flourish', whereas rights which protect them usefully serve as a cornerstone of dignity.[100] In relation to this, since the employment of emotional AI may pose threats to these rights (e.g., to the right to respect for private and family life, as illustrated above, or to the right to be free of discriminatory treatment),[101] in essence it may pose threats to human dignity, respectively. To illustrate, one may refer to the analysis of live facial recognition technologies by the EU Agency for Fundamental Rights (further 'FRA'),[102] emphasizing that the processing of facial

92 R. van Est and J. Gerritsen (n 86) 27–28.

93 Article 1 of the Charter provides that human dignity is inviolable and shall be respected and protected. See also, e.g., A. Barak, 'Human Dignity as a Framework Right (Motherright)', in A. Barak, *Human Dignity: The Constitutional Value and the Constitutional Right* (Cambridge University Press, 2015) 156–169.

94 Case C-377/98 *Netherlands* v. *European Parliament and Council of the European Union* [2001] ECR I-7079 paras 70–77.

95 O'Mahony (n 87) 560.

96 See, e.g., O'Mahony (n 87); Feldman (n 85).

97 O'Mahony (n 87) 574.

98 Feldman (n 85) 688.

99 Ibid.

100 Ibid.

101 For details about interaction between discrimination and dignity, see, e.g., AI Now Report 2018 (n 63) 14; Feldman (n 85) 688.

102 Although this report focuses on the employment of technologies in the context of law enforcement, certain insights are relevant both for private and public sectors. European Union Agency for Fundamental Rights, 'Facial Recognition Technology: Fundamental Rights Considerations in the

images may affect human dignity in different ways.[103] According to FRA, human dignity may be affected, for example, when people feel uncomfortable going to certain places or events, change their behaviours, or withdraw from social life. The 'impact on what people may perceive as surveillance technologies on their lives may be so significant as to affect their capacity to live a dignified life'.[104] FRA argues that the use of facial recognition can have a negative impact on people's dignity and, relatedly, may pose threats to (rights to) privacy and data protection.[105]

To summarize, the deployment of emotional AI in a business-to-consumer context necessitates a debate at a fundamental, constitutional level. Although it may benefit both businesses and consumers (e.g., by providing revenues and consumer satisfaction respectively), it has functional weaknesses[106] and also begs for the revealed legal considerations. Aside from the obvious privacy and data protection concerns, from the consumer's perspective, individual autonomy and human dignity as overarching values may be at risk. Influencing activities evidently interfere not only with an individual's autonomy and self-determination, but also with the individual's freedom of thought, conscience, and religion.[107] It may be clear, as the CoE's Committee of Ministers has noted, that also in other contexts (e.g., political campaigning), fine-grained, subconscious, and personalized levels of algorithmic

Context of Law Enforcement' (Paper 2019) https://fra.europa.eu/sites/default/files/fra_uploads/fra-2019-facial-recognition-technology-focus-paper-1_en.pdf accessed 11 June 2020.

103 Ibid, 20.

104 Ibid.

105 Ibid, 33. Academic researchers have also argued that facial recognition technologies are to be treated as 'the Plutonium of AI', 'nuclear-level threats', 'a menace disguised as a gift', and an 'irresistible tool for oppression', which shall be banned entirely and without further delay both in public and private sectors . L. Stark, 'Facial Recognition Is the Plutonium of AI' (Article 2019) https://xrds.acm.org/article.cfm?aid=3313129 accessed 11 June 2020; E. Selinger and W. Hartzog, 'What Happens When Employers Can Read Your Facial Expressions?' (Article 2019) www.nytimes.com/2019/10/17/opinion/facial-recognition-ban.html accessed 11 June 2020; W. Hartzog, 'Facial Recognition Is the Perfect Tool for Oppression' (Article 2018) https://medium.com/s/story/facial-recognition-is-the-perfect-tool-for-oppression-bc2a08f0fe66 accessed 11 June 2020; E. Selinger, 'Amazon Needs to Stop Providing Facial Recognition Tech for the Government' (Article 2018) https://medium.com/s/story/amazon-needs-to-stop-providing-facial-recognition-tech-for-the-government-795741a016a6 accessed 11 June 2020; E. Selinger, 'Why You Can't Really Consent to Facebook's Facial Recognition' (Article 2019) https://onezero.medium.com/why-you-cant-really-consent-to-facebook-s-facial-recognition-6bb94ea1dc8f accessed 11 June 2020. It remains to be seen whether legislators will adopt specific rules on face recognition technologies. Although the European Commission apparently contemplated a temporary five-year ban on facial recognition, the final version of its White Paper on Artificial Intelligence of 19 February 2020 no longer draws such a hard line (COM (2020) 65 final); see J. Espinoza, 'EU Backs Away from Call for Blanket Ban on Facial Recognition Tech' (Article 2020) www.irishtimes.com/business/innovation/eu-backs-away-from-call-for-blanket-ban-on-facial-recognition-tech-1.4171470 accessed 15 June 2020. California recently adopted a Bill, referred to as the Body Camera Accountability Act, which (if signed into law) would ban the use of facial recognition software in police body cameras. See R. Metz, 'California Lawmakers Ban Facial-Recognition Software from Police Body Cams' (Article 2019) https://edition.cnn.com/2019/09/12/tech/california-body-cam-facial-recognition-ban/index.html accessed 11 June 2020.

106 See, e.g., Stanley (n 6); Barrett (n 64); Feldman (n 85).

107 R. van Est and J. Gerritsen (n 86) 23.

persuasion may have significant effects on the cognitive autonomy of individuals and their right to form opinions and take independent decisions.[108] As a result, not only the exercise and enjoyment of individual human rights may be weakened, but also democracy and the rule of law may be threatened, as they are equally grounded on the fundamental belief in the equality and *dignity* of all humans as *independent* moral agents.[109]

4.3 SUGGESTIONS TO INTRODUCE NEW (CONSTITUTIONAL) RIGHTS

In the light of the previously noted factors, it comes as no surprise that some authors have discussed or suggested the introduction of some novel rights, in order to reinforce the existing legal arsenal.[110] Although both autonomy and dignity as relevant underlying values and some relevant rights such as right to privacy, freedom of thought, and freedom of expression are protected by the ECHR, some scholars argue that the ECHR does not offer sufficient protection in the light of the manipulative capabilities of emotional AI.[111] The subsequent paragraphs portray, in a non-exhaustive manner, such responses that concern the introduction of some new (constitutional) rights.

A first notable (American) scholar is Shoshana Zuboff, who has argued (in a broader context of *surveillance capitalism*)[112] for the 'right to the future tense'. As noted by Zuboff, 'we now face the moment in history when the elemental right to future tense is endangered' by digital architecture of behavioural modification owned and operated by 'surveillance capital'.[113] According to Zuboff, current legal frameworks as mostly centred on privacy and antitrust have not been sufficient to prevent undesirable practices,[114] including the exploitation of technologies for manipulative purposes. The author argues for the laws that reject the fundamental legitimacy of certain practices,

> including the illegitimate rendition of human experience as behavioral data; the use of behavioural surplus as free raw material; extreme concentrations of the new means of production; the manufacture of prediction products; trading in behavioral futures; the use of prediction products for third-party operations of modification, influence and control; the operations of the means of behavioural modification; the

108 Declaration by the Committee of Ministers on the Manipulative Capabilities of Algorithmic Processes (n 3), para. 9.
109 Ibid.
110 See, e.g., Yeung (n 84); Zuboff (n 31); J. Bublitz, 'My Mind Is Mine!? Cognitive Liberty as a Legal Concept' in E. Hildt and A. Franke (eds), *Cognitive Enhancement: An Interdisciplinary Perspective* (Springer Netherlands 2013).
111 Yeung (n 84) 79–80.
112 Zuboff (n 31).
113 Ibid., 332.
114 Ibid., 344.

accumulation of private exclusive concentrations of knowledge (the shadow text); and the power that such concentrations confer.[115]

While arguing about the rationale of the so-called right to the future tense, the author relies on the importance of free will (i.e., Zuboff argues that in essence manipulation eliminates the freedom to will). Consequently, there is no future without the freedom to will, and there are no subjects but only 'objects'.[116] As the author puts it, 'the assertion of freedom of will also asserts the right to the future tense as a condition of a fully human life'.[117] While arguing for the recognition of such a right as a human right, Zuboff relies on Searle, who argues that elemental rights are crystallized as formal human rights only at that moment in history when they come under systematic threat. Hence, given the development of surveillance capitalism, it is necessary to recognize it as a human right. To illustrate, Zuboff argues that no one is recognizing, for example, a right to breathe because it is not under attack, which cannot be said about the right to the future tense.[118]

German scholar Jan Christoph Bublitz argues for the 'right to cognitive liberty' (phrased alternatively a 'right to mental self-determination'), relying in essence on the fact that the right to freedom of thought has been insignificant in practice, despite its theoretical importance.[119] Bublitz calls for the law to redefine the right to freedom of thought in terms of its theoretical significance in light of technological developments capable of altering thoughts.[120] The author argues that such technological developments require the setting of normative boundaries 'to secure the freedom of the *forum internum*'.[121]

In their report for the Council of Europe analyzing human rights in the robot age, Dutch scholars Rinie van Est and Joost Gerritsen from the Rathenau Institute suggest reflecting on two novel human rights, namely, the right to not be measured, analyzed or coached and the right to meaningful human contact.[122] They argue that such rights are indirectly related to and aim to elaborate on existing human rights, in particular, the classic privacy right to be let alone and the right to respect for family life (i.e., the right to establish and develop relationships with other human beings).[123] While discussing the rationale of a potential right not to be measured, analyzed, or coached, they rely on scholarly work revealing detrimental effects of ubiquitous monitoring, profiling or scoring, and

115 Ibid.
116 Ibid, 332, 336–337.
117 Ibid.
118 Ibid, 332; J. Searle, *Making the Social World: The Structure of Human Civilization* (Oxford University Press 2010).
119 Bublitz (n 111).
120 J. Bublitz, 'Freedom of Thought in the Age of Neuroscience' [2014] 100 Archives for Philosophy of Law and Social Philosophy 1; Clifford (n 7) 286.
121 Ibid, 25.
122 R. van Est and J. Gerritsen (n 86) 43–45; Clifford (n 7) 287.
123 R. van Est and J. Gerritsen (n 86) 43.

persuasion.[124] They argue that what is at stake given the technological development is not only the risk of abuse but the right to remain anonymous and/or the right to be let alone, 'which in the robot age could be phrased as the right to not be electronically measured, analyzed or coached'.[125] However, their report ultimately leaves it unclear whether they assume it is necessary to introduce the proposed rights as new formal human rights. Rather, it calls for the CoE to clarify how these rights – the right to not be measured, analyzed, or coached, and the right to meaningful human contact – could be included within the right to privacy and the right to family life respectively.[126] In addition to considering potential novel rights, the Rathenau report calls for developing fair persuasion principles, 'such as enabling people to monitor the way in which information reaches them, and demanding that firms must be transparent about the persuasive methods they apply'.[127]

According to UK scholar Karen Yeung, manipulation may threaten individual autonomy and the 'right to cognitive sovereignty'.[128] While arguing about the rationale of such a right, Yeung relies on the importance of individual autonomy and on the Razian approach comparing manipulation to coercion,[129] as discussed previously. In addition, Yeung relies on Nissenbaum, who observes that the risks of manipulation are even more acute in a digital world involving 'pervasive monitoring, data aggregation, unconstrained publication, profiling, and segregation', because the manipulation that deprives us of autonomy is more subtle than the world in which lifestyle choices are punished and explicitly blocked.[130] When it comes to arguing about the need to introduce a new formal human right, Yeung notes that human dignity and individual autonomy are not sufficiently protected by Articles 8, 9, and 10 of the ECHR; however, the study in question does not provide detailed arguments in that regard. The author also refrains from elaborating on the content of such a right.[131]

Some novel rights are discussed at the institutional level as well. For example, the CoE's Parliamentary Assembly has proposed working on guidelines which would cover, among other things, the recognition of some new rights, including the right not to be manipulated.[132]

Further research is undoubtedly necessary to assess whether the current legal framework is not already capable of accommodating the developments properly.

124 For reference see R. van Est and J. Gerritsen (n 86) 43–44.
125 Ibid, 44.
126 Ibid, 43–45.
127 Rathenau Institute argues that such principles could be developed by the Council of Europe. R. van Est and J. Gerritsen (n 86) 26.
128 Yeung (n 84) 79.
129 Ibid, 79.
130 Yeung (n 84); H. Nissenbaum, *Privacy in Context: Technology, Policy and the Integrity of Social Life* (Stanford Law Books 2010) 83.
131 Yeung (n 84) 79–80.
132 Parliamentary Assembly (n 70).

While the introduction of novel constitutional rights may indeed contribute to defining normative beacons, we should at the same time be cautious not to dilute the significance of constitutional rights by introducing new ones that could, in fact, be considered as manifestations of existing constitutional rights.[133] Hence, it is particularly important to delineate, as noted by Clifford, between primary and secondary law, and to assess the capabilities of the latter in particular.[134] In other words, it is necessary to exercise restraint and consider what already exists and also to delineate between rights and the specific manifestation of these rights in their operation and/or in secondary law protections (i.e., derived sub-rights). For example, key data subject rights like the right to erasure, object, access, and portability are all manifestations of the aim of respecting the right to data protection as balanced with other rights and interests. Admittedly, while the right to data protection has been explicitly recognized as a distinct fundamental right in the CFREU, this is not the case in the context of the ECHR, where the ECtHR has interpreted the right to privacy in Article 8 ECHR as encompassing informational privacy.[135] The rich debate on the relation between the right to privacy and the right to data protection, and how this impacts secondary law like the GDPR and Convention 108+, clearly exceeds the scope of this chapter.[136]

4.4 BLUEPRINT FOR A FUTURE RESEARCH AGENDA

The field of affective computing, and more specifically the technologies capable of detecting, classifying, and responding to emotions – in this chapter referred to as

133 Clifford (n 7) 287. This reminds us of the discussion about the positioning of consumer rights as fundamental rights; see, e.g., S. Deutch, 'Are Consumer Rights Human Rights? (Includes Discussion of 1985 United Nations Guidelines for Consumer Protection)' [1994] 32 Osgoode Hall Law Journal. For a general criticism of the creation of new human rights, see Ph. Alston, 'Conjuring up New Human Rights: A Proposal for Quality Control' [1984] 78 The American Journal of International Law 607.

134 Clifford (n 7) 287.

135 See, for instance, *Satakunnan Markkinapörssi OY and Satamedia OY* v. *Finland [2017] ECHR 607*, para. 137, in which the ECtHR derived a (limited form of) right to informational self-determination from Article 8 ECHR.

136 For further reference, see Clifford (n 7) 124–133, and references there to M. Brkan, 'The Essence of the Fundamental Rights to Privacy and Data Protection: Finding the Way through the Maze of the CJEU's Constitutional Reasoning' [2019] 20 German Law Journal; O. Lynskey, 'Deconstructing Data Protection: The "Added-Value" of a Right to Data Protection in the EU Legal Order' [2014] 63 International & Comparative Law Quarterly 569; H. Hijmans, *The European Union as Guardian of Internet Privacy* (Springer International Publishing 2016); G. González Fuster, *The Emergence of Personal Data Protection as a Fundamental Right of the EU* (Springer International Publishing 2014); G. González Fuster and R. Gellert, 'The Fundamental Right of Data Protection in the European Union: In Search of an Uncharted Right' [2012] 26 *International Review of Law, Computers & Technology* 73; J. Kokott and C. Sobotta, 'The Distinction between Privacy and Data Protection in the Jurisprudence of the CJEU and the ECtHR' [2013] International Data Privacy Law; S. Gutwirth, Y. Poullet, P. De Hert, C. de Terwangne, and S. Nouwt (eds) *Reinventing Data Protection?* (Springer 2009).

emotional AI – hold promises in many application sectors, for instance, for patient well-being in the health sector, for road safety, consumer satisfaction in retail sectors, and so forth. But, just like most (if not all) other forms of artificial intelligence, emotional AI brings with it a number of challenges and calls for assessing whether the existing legal frameworks are capable of accommodating the developments properly. Due to its manipulative capabilities, its potential harmful affective impact and potential profiling errors, emotional AI puts pressure on a whole range of constitutional rights, such as the right to respect for private and family life, non-discrimination, and freedom of thought, conscience, and religion. Moreover, the deployment of emotional AI poses challenges to individual autonomy and human dignity as underlying values underpinning the entirety of international human rights law, as well as to the underlying rationality-based paradigm imbued in law.

Despite the constitutional protection already offered at the European level, some scholars argue, in particular in the context of the ECHR, that this framework does not offer sufficient protection in light of the manipulative capabilities of emotional AI. They suggest (contemplating or introducing) novel rights such as the right to the future tense; the right to cognitive liberty (or, alternatively, the right to mental self-determination); the right to not be measured, analyzed, or coached; the right to cognitive sovereignty; and the right not to be manipulated.

At the same time, it should be noted that the field of constitutional law (in this chapter meant to cover the field of European human rights law) is a very dynamic area that is further shaped through case law, along with societal, economic, and technological developments. The way in which the ECtHR has given a multifaceted interpretation of the right to privacy in Article 8 ECHR is a good example of this.

This motivates the relevance of further research into the scope of existing constitutional rights and secondary sub-rights, in order to understand whether there is effectively a need to introduce new constitutional rights. A possible blueprint for IACL's Research Group 'Algorithmic State, Society and Market – Constitutional Dimensions' could include

- empirical research into the effects of fine-grained, subconscious, and personalised levels of algorithmic persuasion based on affective computing (in general or for specific categories of vulnerable groups, like children[137]);
- interdisciplinary research into the rise of new practices, such as the trading or renting of machine learning models for emotion classification, which may escape the traditional legal protection frameworks;[138]

[137] See, in this regard, for instance, V. Verdoodt, 'Children's Rights and Commercial Communication in the Digital Era', KU Leuven Centre for IT & IP Law Series, n 10, 2020.

[138] See, for instance, M. Veale, R. Binns, and L. Edwards, 'Algorithms That Remember: Model Inversion Attacks and Data Protection Law' [2018] 376 Philosophical Transactions of the Royal Society A3.

- doctrinal research into the scope and limits of existing constitutional rights at European level in light of affective computing; Article 9 ECHR and Article 8 CFREU seem particularly interesting from that perspective;
- comparative research, on the one hand, within the European context into constitutional law traditions and interpretations at the national level (think of Germany, where the right to human dignity is explicitly recognised in Article 1 Grundgesetz, versus Belgium or France, where this is not the case), and on the other hand, within the global context (comparing, for instance, the fundamental rights orientated approach to data protection in the EU and the more market-driven approach in other jurisdiction such as the US and Australia[139]); and
- policy research into the level of jurisdiction, and type of instrument, best suited to tackle the various challenges that emotional AI brings with it. (Is there, for instance, a need for a type of 'Oviedo Convention' in relation to (emotional) AI?)

At the beginning of this chapter, reference was made to the CoE's Declaration on the Manipulative Capabilities of Algorithmic Processes of February 2019.[140] In that Declaration, the Committee of Ministers invites member States to

> initiat[e], within appropriate institutional frameworks, open-ended, informed and inclusive public debates with a view to providing guidance on where to draw the line between forms of permissible persuasion and unacceptable manipulation. The latter may take the form of influence that is subliminal, exploits existing vulnerabilities or cognitive biases, and/or encroaches on the independence and authenticity of individual decision-making.

Aspiring to deliver a modest contribution to this much-needed debate, this chapter has set the scene and hopefully offers plenty of food for thought for future activities of the IACL Research Group on Algorithmic State Market & Society – Constitutional Dimensions.

[139] Clifford (n 7) 331.
[140] Declaration by the Committee of Ministers on the Manipulative Capabilities of Algorithmic Processes (n 3), para. 9.

5

Algorithmic Law: Law Production by Data or Data Production by Law?

Mariavittoria Catanzariti

5.1 INTRODUCTION

Online human interactions are a continuous matching of data that affects both our physical and virtual life. How data are coupled and aggregated is the result of what algorithms constantly do through a sequence of computational steps that transform the input into the output. In particular, machine learning techniques are based on algorithms that identify patterns in datasets. The paper explores how algorithmic rationality may fit into Weber's conceptualization of legal rationality. It questions the idea that technical disintermediation may achieve the goal of algorithmic neutrality and objective decision-making.[1] It argues that such rationality is represented by surveillance purposes in the broadest meaning. Algorithmic surveillance reduces the complexity of reality calculating the probability that certain facts happen on the basis of repeated actions. Algorithms shape human behaviour, codifying situations and facts, stigmatizing groups rather than individuals, and learning from the past: predictions may lead to static patterns that recall the idea of caste societies, in which the individual potential of change and development is far from being preserved. The persuasive power of algorithms (the so-called nudging) largely consists of small changes aimed at predicting social behaviours that are expected to be repeated in time. This boost in the long run builds a model of anti-social mutation, where actions are oriented. Against such a backdrop, the role of law and legal culture is relevant for individual emancipation and social change in order to frame a model of data production by law. This chapter is divided into four sections: the first part describes commonalities and differences between legal bureaucracy and algorithms, the second part examines the linkage between a data-driven model of law production and algorithmic rationality, the third part shows the different perspective of the socio-legal approach to algorithmic regulation, and the fourth section questions the idea of law production by data as a product of legal culture.

[1] Massimo Airoldi and Daniele Gambetta, 'Sul mito della neutralità algoritmica', (2018) 4 *The Lab's Quarterly*, 29.

5.2 BUREAUCRATIC ALGORITHMS

'On-life' dimensions represent the threshold for a sustainable data-driven rationality.[2] As stated in the White Paper on AI, 'today 80% of data processing and analysis that takes place in the cloud occurs in data centres and centralized computing facilities, and 20% in smart connected objects, such as cars, home appliances or manufacturing robots, and in computing facilities close to the user ("edge computing")'. By means of unceasing growth of categorizations and classifications, algorithms develop mechanisms of social control connecting the dots. This entails that our actions mostly depend or are somehow affected by the usable form in which the algorithm code is rendered. In order to enhance their rational capability in calculating every possible action, algorithms aim at reducing human discretion and at structuring behaviours and decisions similarly to bureaucratic organizations. Algorithms act as normative systems that formalize certain patterns. As pointed out by Max Weber, modern capitalist enterprise is mainly based on calculation. For its existence, it requires justice and an administration whose operation can at least in principle be rationally calculated on the basis of general rules – in the same way in which the foreseeable performance of a machine is calculated.[3] This entails that, on the one hand, like bureaucracy, algorithms, in fact, use impersonal laws requiring obedience that impede free not predictable choices.[4] In fact, according to the Weberian bureaucratic ideal types, the separation between the administrative body and the material means of the bureaucratic enterprise is quintessential to the most perfect form of bureaucratic administration: political expropriation towards specialized civil servants.[5] Nonetheless, impersonality of legal rules does not entail in any case lack of responsibility by virtue of the principle of the division of labour and the hierarchical order on which modern bureaucracy is based:[6] civil servants' responsibility is indeed to obey impersonal rules or pretend they are impersonal, whereas the exclusive and personal responsibility belongs to the political boss for his actions.[7] Bureaucracy is characterized by the objective fulfilment of duties, 'regardless of the person' and based on foreseeable rules and independent from human considerations.[8]

On the contrary, the risk of algorithmic decision-making is that no human actor is to take responsibility for the decision.[9] The supervision and the attribution of specialized competences from the highest bureaucratic levels towards the lowest

[2] Luciano Floridi, *The Onlife Manifesto. Being Human in a Hyperconnected Era* (Springer, 2015).

[3] Max Weber, *Economia e società*, (Edizioni di Comunità, 1st ed., 1974), 687.

[4] Chiara Visentin, 'Il potere razionale degli algoritmi tra burocrazia e nuovi idealtipi', *The Lab's Quarterly*, 47–72, 57, 58.

[5] Max Weber, 'Politics as a Vocation', in Hans Gehrt (ed.) and C. Wright Mills (trans.), *From Max Weber: Essays in Sociology* (Oxford University Press, 1946), 77; *Economia e società*, 685.

[6] Max Weber, *Economia e società*, 260, 262.

[7] Max Weber, 'Politics as a vocation', 88.

[8] Max Weber, *Economia e società*, 278.

[9] Karen Yeung, 'Why Worry about Decision-Making by Machine?', in Karen Yeung and Martin Lodge (eds.), *Algorithmic Regulation* (Oxford University Press, 2019), 24. However, there is a big debate on

ones (Weber uses the example of 'procurement')[10] assures that the exercise of authority is compliant to precise competences and technical qualities.[11] Standardization, rationalization, and formalization are common aspects both for bureaucratic organizations and algorithms. Bureaucratic administration can be considered economic as far as it is fast, precise, continuous, specialized, and avoids possible conflicts.[12] Testing algorithms as legal rational means imposes a double question: (1) whether through artificial intelligence and isocratic forms of administration the explainability of algorithmic processes improves the institutional processes and in what respect towards staff competence and individual participation, and (2) whether algorithms take on some of the role of processing institutional and policy complexity much more effectively than humans.[13]

According to Aneesh, 'bureaucracy represents an "efficient" ideal-typical apparatus characterized by an abstract regularity of the exercise of authority centred on formal rationality'.[14] In fact, algorithms 'are trained to infer certain patterns based on a set of data. In such a way actions are determined in order to achieve a given goal'.[15] The socio-technical nature of public administration consists in the ability to share data: this is the enabler of artificial intelligence for rationalization. Like bureaucracy, algorithms would be apparently compatible with three Weberian rationales: the *Zweckverein* (purpose union), as an ideal type of the voluntary associated action; the *Anstalt* (institution), as an ideal type of institutions, rational systems achieved throughout coercive measures; the *Verband* (social group), as an ideal type of common action that aims to an agreement for a common purpose.[16] According to the first rationale, algorithms are used to smoothly guide a predictable type of social behaviour through

digital personhood and responsibility; see G. Teubner, 'Digital Personhood: The Status of Autonomous Software Agents in Private Law', (2018) *Ancilla Iuris*, 35. According to the Robotic Charter of the EU Parliament, in the event that a robot can make autonomous decisions, the traditional rules are not sufficient to activate liability for damages caused by a robot, as they would not allow to determine which is the person responsible for the compensation or to demand from this person to repair the damage caused.

10 Max Weber, *Economia e società*, 269.

11 Ibid., 260.

12 Ibid., 277.

13 Thomas Vogl, Cathrine Seidelin, Bharath Ganesh, and Jonathan Bright, 'Algorithmic Bureaucracy. Managing Competence, Complexity, and Problem Solving in the Age of Artificial Intelligence' (2019), https://papers.ssrn.com/sol3/papers.cfm?abstract_id=3327804.

14 A. Aneesh, 'Technologically Coded Authority: The Post-Industrial Decline in Bureaucratic Hierarchies' (2002) Stanford University Papers, http://web.stanford.edu/class/sts175/NewFiles/AlgocraticGovernance.pdf.

15 European Commission, White Paper on Artificial Intelligence – A European Approach to Excellence and Trust, 'The output of the AI system does not become effective unless it has been previously reviewed and validated by a human', https://ec.europa.eu/info/sites/info/files/commission-white-paper-artificial-intelligence-feb2020_en.pdf, 21.

16 Furio Ferraresi, 'Genealogie della legittimità. Città e stato in Max Weber', (2014) 5 *Società Mutamento Politica*, 143, 146.

data extraction on an 'induced' and mostly accepted voluntary basis;[17] as for the second, the induction of needs is achieved through forms of 'nudging', such as the customization of contractual forms and services based on profiling techniques and without meaningful mechanisms of consent; finally, the legitimacy is based on the social agreement on their utility to hasten and cheapen services (automation theory) or also improve them (augmentation system).[18]

However, unlike bureaucracy, technology directly legitimizes action enabling users with the bare option 'can/cannot'. Legitimacy is embedded within the internal rationality of technology. As Pasquale observes, 'authority is increasingly expressed algorithmically'.[19] Moreover, similar to the rise of bureaucratic action, technologies have been thought to be controlled by the exercise of judicial review not to undermine civil liberties and equality. As a matter of fact, algorithmic systems are increasingly being used as part of the continuous process of *Entzauberung der Welt* (disenchantment of the world) – the achievement of rational goals through organizational measures – with potentially significant consequences for individuals, organizations and societies as a whole.

There are essentially four algorithmic rational models of machine learning that are relevant for law-making: the Neural Networks that are algorithms learning from examples through neurons organized in layers; the Tree Ensemble methods that combine more than one learning algorithm to improve the predictive power of any of the single learning algorithms that they combine; the Support Vector Machines that utilize a subset of the training data, called support vectors, to represent the decision boundary; the Deep Neural Network that can model complex non-linear relationship with multiple hidden layers.[20]

Opaqueness and automation are their main common features, consisting of the secrecy of the algorithmic code and the very limited human input.[21] This typical rationality is blind, as algorithms – Zuboff notes – inform operations given the interaction of these two aspects. Nonetheless, explainability and interpretability are also linked to the potential of algorithmic legal design as rational means.[22]

17 On the concept of data extraction, see Deborah De Felice, Giovanni Giuffrida, Giuseppe Giura, Vilhelm Verendel, and Calogero G. Zarba, 'Information Extraction and Social Network Analysis of Criminal Sentences. A Sociological and Computational Approach', (2013) *Law and Computational Social Science*, 243–262, 251.

18 Michael Veale and Irina Brass, 'Administration by Algorithm?', in Karen Yeung and Martin Lodge (eds.), *Algorithmic Regulation* (Oxford University Press, 2019), 123–125; Anthony J Casey and Anthony Niblett, 'A Framework for the New Personalization of Law' (2019) 86 *University of Chicago Law Review* 333, 335.

19 Frank Pasquale, *The Black Box Society: The Secret Algorithms That Control Money and Society* (Harvard University Press, 2015), 8.

20 Riccardo Guidotti et al., 'A Survey of Methods for Explaining Black Box Models' (2018), *ACM Computing Surveys*, February, 1, 18.

21 T. Zarsky, 'The Trouble with Algorithmic Decisions: An Analytic Road Map to Examine Efficiency and Fairness in Automated and Opaque Decision Making', (2016) 41 *Science, Technology, & Human Values*, 119.

22 Riccardo Guidotti et al. at n. 19, 5.

Rational algorithmic capability is linked to the most efficient use of data and inferences based on them. However, the development of data-driven techniques in the algorithmic architecture determines a triangulation among market, law, and technology. To unleash the full potential of data, rational means deployed to create wider data accessibility and sharing for private and public actors are now being devised in many areas of our lives. However, it should be borne in mind that the use of algorithms as a tool for speeding up the efficiency of the public sector cannot be separately examined from the risk of algorithmic surveillance based on indiscriminate access to private-sector data.[23] This is due to the fact that the entire chain of services depends upon more or less overarching access to private sector data. Access to those data requires a strong interaction between public actors' political power and private actors' economic and technological capability. This dynamic is pervasive as much as it entirely dominates our daily life from market strategy to economic supply. Furthermore, once the 'sovereigns' of the nation-states and their borders have been trumped, data flows re-articulate space in an endless way. The paradox of creating space without having a territory is one of the rationales of the new computational culture that is building promises for the future.

5.3 LAW PRODUCTION BY DATA

Law production is increasingly subjected to a specialized rationality.[24] Quantitative knowledge feeds the aspiration of the state bureaucracy's 'rationality', since it helps dress the exercise of public powers of an aura of technical neutrality and impersonality, apparently leaving no room to the discretion of the individual power.[25] Behind the appearance of the Weberian bureaucratic principle *sine ira et studio* – which refers to the exclusion of affective personal, non-calculable, and non-rational factors in the fulfilment of civil servants' duties[26] – the use of classification and measurement techniques affecting human activities generate new forms of power that standardize behaviours for forecasting expectations, performances and conducts of agents.[27] As correctly highlighted by Zuboff, 'instrumentarian power reduces the human experience to measurable observable behaviour while remaining steadfastly indifferent to the meaning of that experience'.[28] However, even though the production of the law through customized and tailored solutions can be a legitimate goal of computational law, it is not all. Social context may change while the law is ruling,

[23] Ira Rubinstein, 'Big Data: The End of Privacy or a New Beginning?', (2013) 3 *International Data Privacy Law*, 74.

[24] Marta Infantino, *Numera et impera. Gli indicatori giuridici globali e il diritto comparato* (Franco Angeli, 2019), 29.

[25] Enrico Campo, Antonio Martella, and Luca Ciccarese, 'Gli algoritmi come costruzione sociale. Neutralità, potere e opacità', (2018) 4 *The Lab's Quarterly*, 7.

[26] Max Weber, *Economia e società*, 278.

[27] David Beer 'The Social Power of Algorithms', (2017) 20 *Information, Communication & Society*, 1–13.

[28] Shoshana Zuboff, *The Age of Surveillance Capitalism. The Fight for a Human Future at the New Frontier of Power* (Public Affairs, 2019), 376–377.

but technology reflects changing social needs in a more visible way than the law and apparently provides swifter answers.[29] On the contrary, the law should filter daily changes, including technological ones, into its own language, while it is regulating a mutable framework. To be competing with other prescriptive systems, the law may be used either as an element of computational rationality or a tool to be computable itself for achieving specific results. In the first case, the law guides and shrinks the action of rational agents through the legal design of algorithms, as an external constraint. In the second case, regulatory patterns are conveyed by different boosts that use the law in a predetermined way for achieving a given goal. Depending on which of those models is chosen, there could be a potential risk for the autonomy of the law in respect to algorithmic rationality. Both the autonomy of the law and the principle of certainty applicable to individuals are at stake. This is an increasingly relevant challenge since the whole human existence is fragmented through data.

Against these two drawbacks, the law may develop its internal rationality even in a third way: as the product of the legal culture that copes with social challenges and needs. Essentially, legal culture is a tough way in which society reflects upon itself, through doctrinal and conceptual systems elaborated by lawyers; through interpretation; and through models of reasoning.[30] This entails the law being a rational means not only due to its technical linguistic potential[31] but also due to its technical task aimed at producing social order.[32] As Weber notes, the superiority of bureaucratic legal rationality over other rational systems is technical.

Nonetheless, not all times reflect a good legal culture, as this can be strongly affected by political and social turmoil. In the age of datification, all fragments of daily life are translated into data, and it is technically possible to shape different realities *on demand*, including information politics and market. The creation of propensities and assumptions through algorithms as a basis of a pre-packaged concept of the law – driven by colonizing factors – breaks off a spontaneous process through which legal culture surrounds the law. As a result, the effects of algorithmic legal predictions contrast with the goal of legal rationality, which is to establish certain hypotheses and to cluster factual situations into them. The production of the legal culture entails the law being the outcome of a specific knowledge and normative meanings as the result of a contextual Weltanschauung. This aspect has nothing to do either with the legitimacy or with the effectiveness, rather with the way in which the law relies on society. In particular, the capability to produce social consequences that are not directly addressed by the law, by suggesting certain social behaviours and by activating standardized decisions on a large scale, represents such a powerful tool that has been considered the core of

[29] Karen Yeung and Martin Lodge, 'Introduction', in Karen Yeung and Martin Lodge (eds.), *Algorithmic Regulation* (Oxford University Press, 2019), 5.

[30] Giovanni Tarello, *Cultura giuridica e politica del diritto* (Il Mulino, 1988), p. 24, 25.

[31] Ibid., 162.

[32] Ibid., 176.

algorithmic exception states.[33] The idea of exception is explained by the continuous confusion between the rule of causality and the rule of correlation.[34] Such a blurring between cause and effects, evidences and probabilities, causal inferences and variables, affects database structures, administrative measures that are showed under the form of the algorithmic code, and ultimately rules.[35] Algorithms lack adaptability because they are based on a casual model that cannot replicate the inferential process of humans to which the general character of the law refers. Human causal intuitions dominate uncertainty differently from machine learning techniques.[36]

Data is disruptive for its capability to blur the threshold between what is inside and what is outside the law. The transformation of the human existence into data is at the crossroad of the most relevant challenges for law and society. Data informs the functioning of legal patterns, but it can be also a component of law production. A reflection on the social function of the law in the context of algorithmic rationality is useful in order to understand what type of data connections are created for regulatory purposes within an 'architecture of assumptions', to quote McQuillan. Decoding algorithms sometimes allows one to interpret such results, even though the plurality and complexity of societal patterns cannot be reduced to the findings of data analysis or inferential interpretation generated by automated decision-making processes. The growing amount of data, despite being increasingly the engine of law production, does reflect the complexity of the social reality, which instead refers to possible causal interactions between technology, reality and regulatory patterns, and alternative compositions of them, depending upon uncertain variables. Datification, on which advanced technologies are generally based, has profoundly altered the mechanisms of production of legal culture, which cannot be easily reduced to what data aggregation or data analysis is. Relevant behaviours and social changes nourish inferences that can be made from data streams: despite the fact that they can be the *output* of the law, they will never be the *input* of the legal culture. Between the dry facts and the causal explanation, there is a very dense texture for the elaboration of specialized jurists, legal scholars, and judges. Furthermore, globalization strongly shapes common characters across different legal traditions no longer identifiable with an archetypal idea of state sovereignty. This depends upon at least two factors: on the one hand, the increasing cooperation between private and public actors in data access and information management beyond national borders; on the other hand, the increasing production of data from different sources. Nonetheless, not

[33] According to Dan McQuillan, 'Algorithmic States of Exception, European Journal of Cultural Studies', (2015) 18 *European Journal of Cultural Studies*, 564, 569: 'While tied to clearly constituted organisational and technical systems, the new operations have the potential to create social consequences that are unaddressed in law.'

[34] Ibid., 576.

[35] Ibid., 566.

[36] For a deep analysis of causality and correlation, see Judea Pearl and Dana Mackenzie, *The Book of Why: The New Science of Cause and Effect* (Penguin Books, 2018), 27.

much attention has been paid to the necessity of safeguarding the space of the legal culture in respect to law overproduction by data. Regulation of technology combined with the legal design of technology tends to create a misleading overlap between both, because technological feasibility is becoming the natural substitution of legal rationales. Instead, I argue that the autonomous function of the legal culture should be revenged and preserved as the theoretical grid for data accumulation. What legal culture calls into question is the reflexive social function of the law that data-driven law erases immediately by producing a computational output. In addition, the plurality of interconnected legal systems cannot be reduced to data. The increasing production of the law resulting from data does not reflect the complexity of social reality. How data and technologies based on them affect the rise of legal culture and the production of data-driven laws has not only to do with data. According to a simple definition of legal culture as 'one way of describing relatively stable patterns of legally oriented social behaviour and attitudes',[37] one may think of data-driven law as a technologically oriented legal conduct.

'Commodification of "reality" and its transformation into behavioural data for analysis and sales',[38] defined by Zuboff as surveillance capitalism, has made the private human experience a 'free raw material'[39] that can be elaborated and transformed into behavioural predictions feeding production chain and business. Data extraction allows the capitalistic system to know all about all. It is a 'one-way process, not a relationship', which produces identity fragmentation and attributes an exchange value to single fragments of the identity itself.[40] Algorithmic surveillance indeed produces a twofold phenomenon: on the one hand, it forges the extraction process itself, which is predetermined to be predictive; on the other hand, it determines effects that are not totally explainable, despite all accurate proxies input into the system. Those qualities are defined operational variables that are processed at a very high speed so that it is hard for humans to monitor them.[41]

In the light of an unprecedented transformation that is radically shaping the development of personality as well as common values, the role of the law should be not only to guarantee *ex post* legal remedies but also to reconfigure the dimension of human beings, technology, and social action within integrated projects of coexistence with regulatory models. When an individual is subject to automation – the decision-making process, which determines the best or worst chances of well-being, the easiest or least opportunities to find a good job, or in the case of the predictive

[37] David Nelken, 'Using the Concept of Legal Culture', p. 1.

[38] Lionel Ching Kang Teo, 'Are All Pawns in a Simulated Reality? Ethical Conundrums in Surveillance Capitalism', 10 June 2019, https://anthrozine.home.blog/tag/capitalism/.

[39] Shoshana Zuboff, *The Age of Surveillance Capitalism, The Definition* (Penguin Books, 2015).

[40] Shoshana Zuboff, 'Big Other: Surveillance Capitalism and the Prospects of an Information Civilization', (2015) 30 *Journal of Information Technology*, 75–89.

[41] Frederik Z. Borgesius, *Discrimination, Artificial Intelligence, and Algorithmic Decision-Making* (Council of Europe, Strasbourg, 2018), https://rm.coe.int/discrimination-artificial-intelligence-and-algorithmic-decision-making/1680925d73, 10; Karen Yeung, at n. 8, 25.

police, a threat to the presumption of innocence – the social function of the law is necessary to cope with the increasing complexity of relevant variables and to safeguard freedom. Power relationships striving to impose subjugation vertically along command and obedience relationships are replaced by a new 'axiomatic' one: the ability to continuously un-code and re-code the lines along which information, communication, and production intertwine, combining differences rather than forcing unity.

5.4 THE SOCIO-LEGAL APPROACH

The current socio-legal debate on algorithmic application on legal frameworks is very much focused on issues related to data-driven innovation. Whereas the internal approach is still dominant in many regulatory areas, the relationship between law and technology requires an external perspective that takes into account different possibilities. As the impact of artificial intelligence on the law produces social and cultural patterns, a purely internal legal approach cannot contribute to a comprehensive understanding. However, whereas the law produces bindings effects depending on if certain facts may or not happen, algorithms are performative in the sense that the effect that they aim to produce is encompassed in the algorithmic code. The analysis of both the benefits and the risks of algorithmic rationality have societal relevance for the substantial well-being of individuals. On one hand, the lack of an adequate sectoral regulatory framework requires a cross-cutting analysis to highlight potential shortcomings in the existing legal tools and their inter-relationships. In addition, operational solutions should be proactive in outlining concrete joined-up policy actions, which also consider the role of soft-law solutions. On the other hand, the potential negative impact of biased algorithms on rights protection and non-discrimination risks establishing a legal regime for algorithmic rationality that does not meet societal needs. In order to address the interplay between societal needs, rights, and algorithmic decision-making, it is relevant to pinpoint several filters on the use of AI technology in daily life.

For example, a *social filter* sets a limits for the manner in which technology is applied on the basis of the activities of people and organizations. A well-known recent example of a social filter is how taxi drivers and their backing organizations have opposed transport platforms and services. An *institutional filter* sets institutionally determined limits on the ways in which technology can be applied. This type of institutional system includes the corporate governance model, the education system, and the labour market system. A *normative filter* sets regulatory and statute-based limitations on the manner in which technology can be applied. For example, the adoption of self-steering vehicles in road traffic will be slow until the related issues regarding responsibilities have been conclusively determined in legislation. Last but not least, an *ethical filter* sets restrictions on the ways in which technology is applied.

A further step requires identifying a changing legal paradigm that progressively shifts attention from the idea of a right to a reasonable explanation of the algorithm as a form of transparency to the right to reasonable inferences (through the extensive interpretation of the notion of personal data that it includes the notion of decisional inference) or towards an evolutionary interpretation of the principle of good administration.[42] The evolutionary interpretation of the principle of good administration has hinged on the algorithmic 'black box' within a more fruitful path, oriented towards the legality and responsibility of the decision maker in the algorithmic decision-making process. This is particularly relevant in the field of preventive surveillance, for example, as it is mainly a public service whose technological methods can be interpreted in the light of the principle of good administration.

More broadly, the rationale of AI in the digital single market should inter alia guarantee: (1) better services that are cost-efficient; (2) unifying cross-border public services, increasing efficiency and improving transparency; (3) promoting the participation of individuals in the decision-making process; and (4) improving the use of AI in the private sector as a potential to improve business and competitiveness.[43]

In order to achieve these objectives, it is necessary to evaluate the social impact, as well as the risks and opportunities, that the interaction between public and private actors in accessing data through the use of algorithmic rationality combined with legal rationality entails. However, the optimization of organizational processes in terms of efficiency, on the one hand, and the degree of users' satisfaction, on the other hand, are not relevant factors to face the impact of algorithms on rights. The law preserving individual chances of emancipation is at the centre of this interaction, constituting the beginning and the end of the causal chain, since both the production of law for protecting rights and the violation of rights significantly alter this relationship. This aspect is significant, for instance, in the field of machine learning carried out on the basis of the mass collection of data flows, from which algorithms are able to learn. The ability of machine learning techniques to model human behaviour, to codify reality and to stigmatize groups, increases the risk of couching static social situations, undermining the free and self-determined development of personality. Such a risk is real, irrespective of the fact that algorithms are used to align a legal system to a predetermined market model or to reach a precise outcome of economic policy. In both cases, algorithms exceed the primary function of the law, which is to match the provision of general and abstract rules with concrete situations through adaptive solutions. Such an adaptation process is missing in the algorithmic logic, because the algorithmic code is unchangeable.

Law as a social construction is able to address specific situations and change at the same time in its interpretation or according to social needs. Indeed, law should advocate an emancipatory function for human beings who are not subject to

42 Riccardo Guidotti, Anna Monreale, Salvatore Ruggieri, Franco Turini, Dino Pedreschi, and Fosca Giannotti, 'A Survey of Methods for Explaining Black Box Models', ACM *Computing Surveys*, February 2018, 1 ff.

43 European Commission, A European Strategy for Data, 66 final, 19 February 2020, https://ec.europa.eu/info/sites/info/files/communication-european-strategy-data-19feb2020_en.pdf.

personal powers. If applied to algorithmic decision-making in the broadest context, the personality of laws may result in tailored and fragmented pictures corresponding to 'social types' on the basis of profiling techniques. This is the reason why law production by data processed through algorithms cannot be the outcome of any legal culture, as it would be a pre-packaged solution regardless of the institutional and political context surrounding causes and effects. Nonetheless, the increasing tailored production of *data-driven* law through algorithmic rationality cannot overcome such a threshold in a way that enables a decision-making process – at every level of daily life – being irrespective of autonomy, case-by-case evaluation, and freedom.

The alignment of legal requirements and algorithmic operational rules must always be demonstrated ex post both at a technical level and at a legal level in relation to the concrete case.

5.5 DATA PRODUCTION BY LAW

Against the backdrop of data-driven law, legal rationality should be able to frame a model rather based on data production by law. However, a real challenge that should be borne in mind is that algorithmic bureaucracy does not need a territory as legal bureaucracy.[44] Algorithmic systems are ubiquitous, along with data that feed machine learning techniques. Whereas a bureaucratic state is a way to organize and manage the distribution of power over and within a territory, algorithms are not limited by territory. Sovereignty's fragmentation operated by data flows shows that virtual reality is a radical alternative form to territorial sovereignty and cannot be understood as a mere assignment of sovereign powers upon portions of data. The ubiquity of data requires a new description of regulatory patterns in the field of cross-border data governance as data location that would create under certain conditions the context of the application of legal regime, and the exclusion of another is not necessarily a criterion which is meaningfully associated with the data flow. Data is borderless, as it can be scattered everywhere across different countries.[45] Although data can be accessed everywhere irrespective of where it is located, its regulation and legal effects are still anchored to the territoriality principle. Access to data does not depend on physical proximity; nor are regulatory schemes arising from data flows intrinsically or necessarily connected to any particular territory. Connection with territory must justify jurisdictional concerns but does not have much to do with physical proximity. Such disconnection between information and its un-territorial nature potentially generates conflicts of law and may produce contrasting claims of sovereign powers.[46] This is magnified by algorithmic systems that do not have a *forum loci* because they are valid formulations regardless of the geographical

[44] Max Weber, *Economia e società*, 253.

[45] Jennifer Daskal, 'Data Un-territoriality', (2015) 125 *The Yale Law Journal*, 326.

[46] Andrew Keane Woods, 'Litigating Data Sovereignty', (2018) 128 *The Yale Law Journal*, 328.

space where they are applied. Furthermore, they gather data sets irrespective of borders or jurisdictions. Bureaucracy's functioning much depends upon borders, as it works only within a limited territory.[47] On the contrary, algorithms are unleashed from territories but can affect multiple jurisdictions, as the algorithmic code is territorially neutral. This may be potentially dangerous for two reasons: on the one hand, algorithms can transversally impact different jurisdictions, regardless of the legal systems and regulatory regimes involved; on the other hand, the disconnection of the algorithmic code from territory and implies a law production that does not emerge from legal culture. Even though legal culture is not necessarily bound to the concept of state sovereignty,[48] it is inherent to a territory as a political and social space. Weber rejects the vision of the modern judge as a machine in which 'documents are input together with expenses' and which spits out the sentence together with the motives mechanically inferred from the paragraphs. Indeed, there is the space for the individualizing assessment in respect of which the general norms have a negative function in that they limit the official's positive and creative activity.[49] This massive difference between legal rationality and algorithmic rationality imposes rethinking the relationship between law, technology, and legal culture. Data production by law can be a balanced response to reconnect algorithmic codes to the boundaries of jurisdictions. Of course, many means of data production by law exist. A simple legal design of data production is not the optimal option. Matching algorithmic production of data and legal compliance can be mechanically ensured through the application of certain patterns that are inserted in the algorithmic process. Instead, the impact of legal culture over the algorithmic production of data shape a socio-legal context inspiring the legal application of rules on data production.

The experience of the Italian Administrative Supreme Court (Council of State) is noteworthy. After the leading case of 8 April 2019 n. 2270 that opened the path to administrative algorithmic decision-making, the Council of State confirmed its case law.[50] It holds the lawfulness of automated decision-making in administrative law, providing limits and criteria.[51] It extended for the first time the automated decision-making both to public administration's discretionary and binding activities. The use of algorithmic administrative decision-making is encompassed by the principle of good performance of administration pursuant to article 97 of the Italian Constitution. The Council stated that the fundamental need for protection posed

47 Ibid., 203, 204, 205.

48 David Nelken, 'Using the Concept of Legal Culture', (2004) 29 *Australian Journal of Legal Philosophy*, 4: 'Given the extent of past and present transfer of legal institutions and ideas, it is often misleading to try and relate legal culture only to its current national context.'

49 Max Weber, *Economia e società*, 281–282.

50 See Nicolò Muciaccia, 'Algoritmi e procedimento decisionale: alcuni recenti arresti della giustizia amministrativa', (2020) 10 *Federalismi.it*, 344, www.sipotra.it/wp-content/uploads/2020/04/Algoritmi-e-procedimento-decisionale-alcuni-recenti-arresti-della-giustizia-amministrativa.pdf.

51 Consiglio di Stato, sec VI, 13 December 2019, n. 8472, n. 8473, n. 8474. Against the application of algorithmic decision-making to administrative proceedings, see T.A.R. Lazio Roma, sec. III bis, 27 May 2019, n. 6606 and T.A.R. Lazio Roma, sec. III bis, 13 September 2019, n. 10964.

by the use of the so-called IT tool algorithmic is transparency due to the principle of motivation of the decision.[52] It expressly denied algorithmic neutrality, holding that predictive models and criteria are the result of precise choices and values. Conversely, the issue of the dangers associated with the instrument is not overcome by the rigid and mechanical application of all detailed procedural rules of Law no. 241 of 1990 (such as, for example, the notice of initiation of the proceeding).

The underlying innovative rationale is that the 'multidisciplinary character' of the algorithm requires not only legal but technical, IT, statistical, and administrative skills, and does not exempt from the need to explain and translate the 'technical formulation' of the algorithm into the 'legal rule' in order to make it legible and understandable.

Since algorithm becomes a modality of the authoritative decision, it is necessary to determine specific criteria for their use. Surprisingly, the Council made an operation of legal blurring, affirming that knowability and transparency must be interpreted according to articles 13, 14, and 15 GDPR. In particular, the interested party must be informed of the possible execution of an automated decision-making process; in addition, the owner of algorithms must provide significant information on the logic used, as well as the importance and expected consequences of this treatment for the interested party.

Additionally, the Council adopted three supranational principles: (1) the full knowability of the algorithm used and the criteria applied pursuant to article 42 of the EU Charter ('Right to a good administration'), according to which everyone has the right to know the existence of automated decision-making processes concerning him or her and, in this case, to receive significant information on the logic used; (2) the non-exclusivity of automated decision-making, according to which everyone has the right not to be subjected to solely automated decision-making (similarly to article 22 GDPR); and (3) the non-discrimination principle, as a result of the application of the principle of non-exclusivity, plus data accuracy, minimization of risks of errors, and data security.[53] In particular, the data controller must use appropriate mathematical or statistical procedures for profiling, implementing adequate technical and organizational measures in order to ensure correction of the factors that involve data inaccuracy, thus minimizing the risk of errors.[54] Input data should be corrected to avoid discriminatory effects in decision-making output. This operation requires the necessary cooperation of those who instruct the machines that produce these decisions. The goal of a legal design approach is to filter data production through the production of potential algorithmic harms and the protection of individual rights,

[52] Consiglio di Stato, sec. VI, 8 April 2019, n. 2270. See Gianluca Fasano, 'Le decisioni automatizzate nella pubblica amministrazione: tra esigenze di semplificazione e trasparenza algoritmica', (2019) 3 *Medialaws*, www.medialaws.eu/rivista/le-decisioni-automatizzate-nella-pubblica-amministrazione-tra-esigenze-di-semplificazione-e-trasparenza-algoritmica/.

[53] See Enrico Carloni, 'AI, algoritmi e pubblica amministrazione in Italia', (2020) 30 *Revista de los Estudios de Derecho y Ciencia Política*, www.uoc.edu/idp.

[54] Consiglio di Stato recalls recital 71 GDPR.

and figure out which kind of legal remedies are available and also useful to individuals. The first shortcoming of such endeavour is that – given for granted the logic of *garbage in/garbage out*, according to which inaccurate inputs produce wrong outputs – it is noteworthy that a legal input is not a sufficient condition to produce a lawful output. Instead, an integrated approach such as the one adopted by the Council of State is based on more complex criteria to consider the lawfulness of algorithmic decision-making, also in respect of actors involved. First, it is necessary to ensure the traceability of the final decision to the competent body pursuant to the law conferring the power of the authoritative decision to the civil servants in charge.[55] Second, the comprehensibility of algorithms must involve all aspects but cannot result in harm for IP rights. In fact, pursuant to art. 22, let. c, Law 241/90 holders of an IP right on software are considered counter-interested,[56] but Consiglio di Stato does not specifically address the issue of holders of trade secrets.

5.6 CONCLUSIONS: TOWARDS DATA PROTECTION OF LAW

While discussing similarities between bureaucratic and algorithmic rationality, I voluntarily did not address the issue of secrecy. According to Weber, each power that aims to its preservation is a secret power in one of its features. Secrecy is functional for all bureaucracies to the superiority of their technical tasks towards other rational systems.[57] Secrecy is also the fuel of algorithmic reasoning, as its causal explanation is mostly secret. This common aspect, if taken for granted as a requirement of efficient rational decision-making, should be weighted in a very precise way in order to render algorithms compliant with the principle of legality.

This chapter has explored how algorithmic bureaucracy proves to be a valuable form of rationality as far as it does not totally eliminate human intermediation under the form of imputability, responsibility, and control.[58] To be sure, this may happen only under certain conditions that are summarized as follows: (1) Technological neutrality for law production cannot be a space 'where legal determinations are deactivated'[59] in such a way that externalizes control. (2) Law production by data is not compatible with Weberian's legal rationality. (3) Translation of technical rules into legal rules needs to be filtered through legal culture. (4) Data production by law is the big challenge of algorithmic rationality. (5) Algorithmic disconnection from territory cannot be replaced by algorithmic global surveillance. (6) Legal design of algorithmic functioning is not an exhaustive solution. (7) The linkage of automated decision-making to the principle of good administration is a promising trajectory

55 Similarly, see T.A.R. Lazio Roma, sec. III bis, 28 May 2019, n. 6686; Consiglio di Stato, sec VI, 4 February 2020, n. 881.

56 Consiglio di Stato, sec. VI, 2 January 2020, n. 30.

57 Max Weber, *Economia e società*, 257, 276; Massimo Cacciari, *Il lavoro dello spirito*, (Adelphi, 2020).

58 On the idea of adapting technology, see Luciano Gallino, *Tecnologia e democrazia. Conoscenze tecniche e scientifiche come beni pubblici* (Einaudi, 2007), 132, 195.

59 Dan McQuillan at n. 32, 570.

along which concepts such as traceability, knowability, accessibility, readability, imputability, responsibility, and non-exclusivity of the automated decision have been developed in the public interest.

All these conditions underlie a regulatory idea that draws the role of lawyers from what Max Weber defined as *die geistige Arbeit als Beruf* (the spiritual work as profession). In this respect, algorithmic rationality may be compatible with a legal creative activity as long as a society is well equipped with good lawyers.[60] The transformation of law production by data into data production by law is a complex challenge that lawyers can drive if they do not give up being humanists for being only specialized experts.[61] From this perspective, algorithmic bureaucratic power has a good chance of becoming an 'intelligent humanism'.[62] To accomplish this task, the law should re-appropriate its own instruments of knowledge's production. This does not mean to develop a simplistic categorization of legal compliance requirements for machine-learning techniques. Nor it only relies on the formal application of legal rationality to the algorithmic process. In the long run, it shall bring towards increasing forms of data production of law. Data production of law defines the capability of the law to pick and choose those data that are relevant to elaborate new forms of legal culture. How the law autonomously creates knowledge from experiences that impact on society is a reflexive process that needs institutions as well as individuals. As much as this process is enshrined in a composite legal culture, the law has more chances to recentre its own role in the development of democratic societies.

[60] Anthony T. Kronman, *Education's End Why Our Colleges and Universities Have Given Up on the Meaning of Life* (Yale University Press, 2007), 205; Margerita Ramajoli, 'Quale cultura per l'amministrazione pubblica?', in Beatrice Pasciuta and Luca Loschiavo (eds.), *La formazione del giurista. Contributi a una riflessione* (Roma Tre-press, 2018), 103.

[61] According to Roderick A. Macdonald and Thomas B. McMorrow, 'Decolonizing Law School', (2014) 51 *Alberta Law Review*, 717: 'The process of decolonizing law school identified by the authors is fundamentally a process of moving the role of human agency to the foreground in designing, building, and renovating institutional orders that foster human flourishing.'

[62] David Howarth, 'Is Law a Humanity (Or Is It More Like Engineering)?', (2004) 3 *Arts & Humanities in Higher Education*, 9.

6

Human Rights and Algorithmic Impact Assessment for Predictive Policing

Céline Castets-Renard[*]

6.1 INTRODUCTION

Artificial intelligence (AI) constitutes a major form of scientific and technological progress. For the first time in human history, it is possible to create autonomous systems capable of performing complex tasks, such as processing large quantities of information, calculating and predicting, learning and adapting responses to changing situations, and recognizing and classifying objects.[1] For instance, algorithms, or so-called Algorithmic Decision Systems (ADS),[2] are increasingly involved in systems used to support decision-making in many fields,[3] such as child welfare, criminal justice, school assignment, teacher evaluation, fire risk assessment, homelessness prioritization, Medicaid benefit, immigration decision systems or risk assessment, and predictive policing, among other things.

An Automated Decision(-making/-support) System (ADS) is a system that uses automated reasoning to facilitate or replace a decision-making process that would otherwise be performed by humans.[4] These systems rely on the analysis of large amounts of data from which they derive useful information to make

[*] Support from the Artificial and Natural Intelligence Toulouse Institute (ANITI), ANR-3IA, and the Civil Law Faculty of the University of Ottawa is gratefully acknowledged. I also thank law student Roxane Fraser and the attendees at the Conference on *Constitutional Challenges in the Algorithmic Society* for their helpful comments, and especially Professor Ryan Calo, Chair of the Panel. This text has been written in 2019 and does not take into account the EC proposal on AI published in April 2021.

[1] Preamble section of the Montréal Declaration, www.montrealdeclaration-responsibleai.com/the-declaration accessed 23 May 2019.

[2] Guido Noto La Diega, 'Against Algorithmic Decision-Making' (2018) https://papers.ssrn.com/abstract=3135357 accessed 23 May 2019.

[3] AINow Institute, 'Government Use Cases' https://ainowinstitute.org/nycadschart.pdf accessed on 22 December 2019.

[4] AINow Institute, 'Algorithmic Accountability Policy Toolkit' (October 2018) https://ainowinstitute.org/aap-toolkit.pdf accessed 23 May 2019 [Toolkit].

decisions and to infer[5] correlations,[6] with or without artificial intelligence techniques.[7]

Law enforcement agencies are increasingly using algorithmic predictive policing systems to forecast criminal activity and allocate police resources. For instance, New York, Chicago, and Los Angeles use predictive policing systems built by private actors, such as PredPol, Palantir, and Hunchlab,[8] to assess crime risk and forecast its occurrence, in hope of mitigating it. More often, such systems predict the places *where* crimes are most likely to happen in a given time window (place-based) based on input data, such as the location and timing of previously reported crimes.[9] Other systems analyze *who* will be involved in a crime as either victim or perpetrator (person-based). Predictions can focus on variables such as places, people, groups, or incidents. The goal is also to better deploy officers in a time of declining budgets and staffing.[10] Such tools are mainly used in the United States, but European police forces have expressed an interest in using them to protect the largest cities.[11] Predictive policing systems and pilot projects have already been deployed,[12] such as PredPol, used by the Kent Police in the United Kingdom.

However, these predictive systems challenge fundamental rights and guarantees of the criminal procedure (Section 6.2). I will address these issues by taking into account the enactment of ethical norms to reinforce constitutional rights (Section 6.3),[13] as well as the use of a practical tool, namely Algorithmic Impact Assessment, to mitigate the risks of such systems (Section 6.4).

5 Sandra Wachter and Brent Mittelstadt, A *Right to Reasonable Inferences: Re-Thinking Data Protection Law in the Age of Big Data and AI* (2018) Columbia Business Law Review https://papers.ssrn.com/abstract=3248829 accessed 11 March 2019.

6 European Parliamentary Research Service (EPRS) Study, 'Panel for the Future of Science and Technology, Understanding Algorithmic Decision-Making: Opportunities and Challenges, March 2019' (PE 624.261), 21 [PE 624.261].

7 See, for instance, Florian Saurwein, Natascha Just and Michael Latzer, 'Governance of Algorithms: Options and Limitations' (2015) vol. 17 (6) info 35–49 https://ssrn.com/abstract=2710400 accessed 21 January 2020.

8 Toolkit, supra note 4.

9 PE 624.261, supra note 6.

10 Walter L. Perry et al., 'Predictive Policing: The Role of Crime Forecasting in Law Enforcement Operations' (2013) www.rand.org/pubs/research_reports/RR233.html accessed 29 November 2018.

11 Lubor Hruska et al., 'Maps of the Future, Research Project of the Czeck Republic' (2015) www.mvcr.cz/mvcren/file/maps-of-the-future-pdf.aspx accessed 23 May 2019 [Maps].

12 Don Casey, Phillip Burrell, and Nick Sumner, 'Decision Support Systems in Policing' (2018 (4 SCE)) *European Law Enforcement Research Bulletin* https://bulletin.cepol.europa.eu/index.php/bulletin/article/view/345 accessed 23 May 2019.

13 James Harrison, 'Measuring Human Rights: Reflections on the Practice of Human Rights Impact Assessment and Lessons for the Future' (2010) Warwick School of Law Research Paper 2010/26 https://papers.ssrn.com/abstract=1706742 accessed 23 May 2019.

6.2 HUMAN RIGHTS CHALLENGED BY PREDICTIVE POLICING SYSTEMS

In proactive policing, law enforcement uses data and analyzes patterns to understand the nature of a problem. Officers attempt to prevent crime and mitigate the risk of future harm. They refer to the power of information, geospatial technologies, and evidence-based intervention models to predict what and where something is likely to happen, and then deploy resources accordingly.[14]

6.2.1 *Reasons for Predictive Policing in the United States*

There are many reasons why predictive policing systems have been specifically deployed in the United States. First, the high level of urban gun violence pushed the police departments of Chicago,[15] New York, Los Angeles, and Miami, among others, to take preventative action.

Second, it is an opportunity for American tech companies to deploy, within the national territory, products that have previously been developed and put into practice within the framework of international US military operations.

Third, beginning in 2007, within the context of the financial and economic crisis and ensuing budget cuts in police departments, predictive policing tools have been seen as a way 'to do more with less'.[16] Concomitantly, the National Institute of Justice (NIJ), an agency of the US Department of Justice, granted several police departments permission to conduct research and try these new technologies.[17]

Fourth, the emergence of predictive policing tools has been incited by the crisis of weakened public trust in law enforcement in numerous cities. Police violence, particularly towards young African Americans, has led to the research on more 'objective' methods to improve the social climate and conditions of law enforcement. Public outcry against the discrimination risks inherent to traditional methods has come from citizens, social movements such as 'Black Lives Matter', and even in an official capacity from the US Department of Justice (DOJ) investigations surrounding the actions of the Ferguson Police Department after the death of Michael Brown.[18] Following this incident, the goal was to find new and modern methods which are unbiased toward African Americans as much as possible. The unconstitutionality of methods,[19] such as Stop-and-Frisk in New York and Terry

[14] National Institute of Justice, 'Overview of Predictive Policing' (9 June 2014) www.nij.gov/topics/law-enforcement/strategies/predictive-policing/Pages/research.aspx accessed 23 May 2019 [NIJ].

[15] 'Tracking Chicago Shooting Victims' *Chicago Tribune* (16 December 2019) www.chicagotribune.com/news/data/ct-shooting-victims-map-charts-htmlstory.html accessed 16 December 2019.

[16] Andrew Fergurson, *The Rise of Big Data Policing: Surveillance, Race, and the Future of the Law Enforcement* (2017), 21.

[17] NIJ, supra note 14.

[18] US Department of Justice, 'Investigation of the Ferguson Police Department' (2015) www.justice.gov/sites/default/files/opa/press-releases/attachments/2015/03/04/ferguson_police_department_report.pdf accessed 23 May 2019 [US DJ].

[19] *Floyd* v. *City of New York* (2013) 739 F Supp 2d 376.

Stop,[20] based on the US Supreme Court's decision in the *Terry* v. *Ohio* case, converged with the rise of new, seemingly perfect technologies. The Fourth Amendment of the US Constitution prohibits 'unreasonable searches and seizures', and states, 'no warrants shall issue, but upon probable cause, supported by oath or affirmation, and particularly describing the place to be searched, and the persons or things to be seized'.

Fifth, the privacy laws are less stringent in the United States than in the European Union, due to a sectorial approach to protection within the United States. Such normative difference can explain why the deployment of predicting policing systems was easier in the United States.

6.2.2 *Cases Studies: PredPol and Palantir*

When working to predict crime, multiple methods and tools are available for use. I propose a closer analysis of two tools offered by the PredPol and Palantir companies.

6.2.2.1 PredPol

PredPol is a commercial software offered by the American company PredPol Inc. and was initially used in tests by the LAPD[21] and eventually used in Chicago and in Kent County in the United Kingdom. The tool's primary purpose is to predict, both accurately and in real time, the locations and times where crimes have the highest risk of occurring.[22] In other words, this tool identifies risk zones (*hotspots*) based on the same types of statistical models used in seismology. The input data include city and territorial police archives (reports, ensuing arrests, emergency calls), all applied in order to identify the locations where crimes occur most frequently, so as to 'predict' which locations should be prioritized. Here, the target is based on places, not people. The types of offenses can include robberies, automobile thefts, and thefts in public places. A US patent regarding the invention of an 'Event Forecasting System'[23] was approved on 3 February 2015 by the US Patent and Trademark Office (USPTO). The PredPol company claims that its product assists in improving the allocation of resources in patrol deployment. Finally, the tool also incorporates the position of all patrols in real time, which allows departments to not only know where patrols are located but also control their positions. Providing information on a variety of mobile tools such as tablets, smartphones, and laptops, in addition to desktop computers, was also a disruption from previously used methods.

20 *Terry* v. *Ohio* (1968) 392 US 1.

21 Issie Lapowsky, 'How the LAPD Uses Data to Predict Crime' (22 May 2018) www.wired.com/story/los-angeles-police-department-predictive-policing accessed 23 May 2019.

22 'PredPol Predicts Gun Violence' (2013) www.predpol.com/wp-content/uploads/2013/06/predpol_gun-violence.pdf accessed 23 May 2019.

23 US Patent No. 8,949,164 (Application filed on 6 September 2012) https://patents.justia.com/patent/8949164 accessed 23 May 2019.

The patent's claims do not specify the manner in which data are used, calculated, or applied. The explanation provided in the patent is essentially based on the processes used by the predictive policing systems, particularly the organizational method used (the three types of data (place, time, offense), geographic division into cells, the transfer of information by a telecommunications system, the reception procedure of historic data, access to GPS data, the link with legal information from penal codes, etc.), rather than on any explanation of the technical aspects. The patent focuses more particularly on the various graphic interfaces and features available to users, such as hotspot maps (heatmaps), which display spatial-temporal smoothing models of historical crime data. It also allows for the use of the method in its entirety but does not relate to the predictive algorithm. The technical aspects are therefore not subject to ownership rights but are instead covered by trade secrets. Even if PredPol claims to provide transparency of its approach, the focus is on the procedure, rather than on the algorithm and mathematical methods used, despite the publication of several articles by the inventors.[24] Some technical studies[25] have been carried out by using publicly available data in cities, such as Chicago, and applying the data to models similar to that of PredPol. However, this tool remains opaque.

It is difficult to estimate the value that these forecasts add in comparison to historic hotspot maps. The few works evaluating this approach that have been published do not concern the quality of the forecasting, but the crime statistics. Contrary to PredPol's claims,[26] the difference in efficiency is ultimately modest, depending on both the quantity of data available on a timescale and on the type of offense committed. The studies most often demonstrate that the prediction of crimes occurred most frequently in the historically most criminogenic areas within the city. Consequently, the software does not teach anything to the most experienced police officers who may be using it. While the Kent Police Department was the first to introduce 'predictive policing' in Europe in 2013, it has been officially recognized that it is difficult to prove whether the system has truly reduced crime. It was finally stopped in 2018[27] and replaced by a new internal tool, the NDAS (National Data Analytics Solution) project, to reduce costs and achieve a higher efficiency. It is likely that a tool developed in one context will not necessarily be relevant in another criminogenic context, as the populations, geographic configurations of cities, and the organization of criminal groups are different.

24 George O. Mohler, 'Marked Point Process Hotspot Maps for Homicide and Gun Crime Prediction in Chicago' 2014 30(3) *International Journal of Forecasting*, 491–497; 'Does Predictive Policing Lead to Biased Arrests? Results from a Randomized Controlled Trial, Statistics and Public Policy' 5:1 1–6 10.1080/2330443X.2018.1438940 accessed 23 May 2019 [Mohler].

25 Ismael Benslimane, 'Étude critique d'un système d'analyse prédictive appliqué à la criminalité: PredPol®' *CorteX Journal* https://cortecs.org/wp-content/uploads/2014/10/rapport_stage_Ismael_Benslimane.pdf accessed 23 May 2019.

26 Mohler, supra note 24.

27 BBC News, 'Kent Police Stop Using Crime Predicting Software' (28 November 2018) www.bbc.com/news/uk-england-kent-46345717 accessed 23 May 2019.

Moreover, the software tends to systematically send patrols into neighbourhoods that are considered as more criminogenic, which are mainly inhabited in the United States by African American and Latino/a populations.[28] Historical data certainly show high risk in these neighbourhoods, but most of the data were collected in the age of policies such as Terry Stop and Stop-and-Frisk, and were biased, discriminatory, and ultimately unconstitutional. The system, however, does not examine or question the trustworthiness of these types of data. Furthermore, the choice of the type of offense, primarily related to property crime (burglaries, car thefts), constitutes a type of crime that is more likely to be practiced by the poorest and most vulnerable populations, which are frequently composed of the aforementioned minority groups. The results would naturally be different if white-collar crimes were considered. These crimes are excluded from today's predictive policing due to the difficulties of modelling and the absence of significant data. The fact that law enforcement wants to prevent certain types of offenses rather than others, via the use of automated tools is not socially neutral and carries out discrimination against a part of the population. The founders of PredPol and its developers responded to these critiques of bias in several articles published in 2017 and 2018, in which they largely emphasize the auditing of learning data.[29] High-quality learning data are essential to avoid and reduce bias. But if the data used by PredPol are biased, this demonstrates that society itself is biased as a whole. PredPol simply emphasizes this fact, without actually being a point of origin of discrimination. Consequently, the bias present in the tool is no greater than the bias previously generated by the data collected by police officers on the ground.

6.2.2.2 Palantir

Crime Risk Forecasting is the patent held by the company Palantir Technologies Inc., based in California. This device has been deployed in Los Angeles, New York, and New Orleans, but the contracts are often kept secret.[30] Crime Risk Forecasting is an ensemble of software and material that constitutes an 'invention' outlined in US patent and obtained on 8 September 2015.[31] The patent combines several

[28] See the problem of algorithmic biases with COMPAS: Jeff Larson et al., 'How We Analyzed the COMPAS Recidivism Algorithm ProPublica' (2016) www.propublica.org/article/how-we-analyzed-the-compas-recidivism-algorithm accessed 12 August 2018.

[29] P. Jeffrey Brantingham, 'The Logic of Data Bias and Its Impact on Place-Based Predictive Policing' (2017) 15(2) *Ohio State Journal of Criminal Law* 473.

[30] For instance, Ali Winston, 'Palantir Has Secretly Been Using New Orleans to Test Its Predictive Policing Technology' (27 February 2018) www.theverge.com/2018/2/27/17054740/palantir-predictive-policing-tool-new-orleans-nopd accessed 23 May 2019. However, New Orleans ended its Palantir predictive policing program in 2018, after the public's opposition regarding the secret nature of the agreement: Ali Winston, 'New Orleans Ends Its Palantir Predictive Policing Program' (15 March 2018) www.theverge.com/2018/3/15/17126174/new-orleans-palantir-predictive-policing-program-end accessed 23 May 2019.

[31] Crime Risk Forecasting, US Patent 9,129,219 (8 September 2015) https://patentimages.storage.googleapis.com/60/94/95/5dbde28fe6eea2/US9129219.pdf accessed 23 May 2019.

components and features, including a database manager, visualization tools (notably interactive geographic cartography), and criminal forecasts. The goal is to assist police in predicting when and where crime will take place in the future. The forecasts of criminal risk are established within a geographic and temporal grid, for example, of 250 square meters, during an eight-hour police patrol.

The data include:

- Crime history, classified by date, type, location, and more. The forecast can provide either a precise date and time, or a period of time over which risk is uniformly distributed. Similarly, the location can be more or less precise, either by address, GPS coordinates, or geographic zone. The offenses can be, for example, robberies, vehicle thefts (or thefts of belongings from within vehicles), and violence.
- Historical information which is not directly connected to crime: weather, presence of patrols within the grid or in proximity, distribution of emergency service personnel.
- Custody data indicating individuals who have been apprehended or who are in custody for certain types of crimes. These data can be used to decrease crime risk within a zone or to increase risk after the release of accused or convicted criminal.

Complex algorithms can be developed by aggregating methods associating hot-spotting, histograms, criminology models, and learning algorithms. The combination possibilities and the aggregation of multiple models and algorithms, as well as the large numbers of variables, result in a highly complex system, with a considerable number of parameters to estimate and hyperparameters to optimize. The patent does not specify how these parameters are optimized, nor does it define the expected quality of the forecasts. It is difficult to imagine that any police force could actually use this tool regularly, without constant assistance from Palantir. Moreover, one can wonder: what are the risks of possible re-identification of victims from the historical data? What precautions are taken to anonymize and prevent re-identification? How about custody data, which are not only personal data, but are, in principle, only subject to treatment by law enforcement and government criminal justice services? Consequently, the features of these ADS remain opaque while the processed data are also unclear.

In this context, it would be a mistake to take predictive policing as a panacea to eradicate crime. Many concerns focus on inefficiency, risk of discrimination, as well as lack of transparency.

6.2.3 *Fundamental Rights Issues*

Algorithms are fallible human creations, and they are embedded with errors and bias, similar to human processes. More precisely, an algorithm is not neutral and depends notably on the data used. Many legal scholars have revealed bias and racial discrimination in algorithmic systems,[32] as well as their opacity.[33] When algorithmic tools are adopted by governmental agencies without adequate transparency, accountability, and oversight, their use can threaten civil liberties and exacerbate existing issues within government agencies. Most often, the data used to train automated decision-making systems will come from the agency's own databases, and existing bias in an agency's decisions will be carried over into new systems trained on biased agency data.[34] For instance, many data used by predictive policing systems come from the Stop-and-Frisk program in New York City and the Terry Stop policy. This historical data ('dirty data')[35] create a discriminatory pattern because data from 2004 to 2012 showed that 83 per cent of the stops were of black and Hispanic individuals and 33 per cent white. The overrepresentation of black and Hispanic people who were stopped may lead an algorithm to associate typically black and Hispanic traits with stops that lead to crime prevention.[36] Despite its over-inclusivity, inaccuracy, and disparate impact,[37] such data continue to be processed.[38] Consequently, the algorithms will consider African Americans as a high-risk population (resulting in a 'feedback loop' or a self-fulfilling prophecy),[39] as greater rates of police inspection lead to a higher rate of reported crimes, therefore reinforcing disproportionate and discriminatory policing practices.[40] Obviously, these tools may violate human rights protections in the United States, as well as in the European Union, both before or after their deployment.

A *priori*, predictive policing activities can violate the fundamental rights of individuals if certain precautions are not taken. Though predictive policing tools are useful for the prevention of offenses and the management of police forces, they should not be accepted as sufficient motive for stopping and/or questioning individuals. Several fundamental rights can be violated in case of abusive, disproportionate, or unjustified use of predictive policing tools: the right to physical and mental integrity (Charter of Fundamental Rights of the European Union, art. 3); the right to liberty and security (CFREU, art. 6); the right to respect for private and family life,

32 Anupam Chander, 'The Racist Algorithm?' (2017)115 *Michigan Law Review* 1023–1045.

33 Frank Pasquale, *The Black Box Society: The Secret Algorithms That Control Money and Information* (Harvard University Press 2015).

34 Kristian Lum and William Isaac, 'To Predict and Serve?' (7 October 2016) 13(5) *Significance* 14–19 https://doi.org/10.1111/j.1740-9713.2016.00960.x accessed 23 May 2019.

35 Rashida Richardson, Jason Schultz, and Kate Crawford, 'Dirty Data, Bad Predictions: How Civil Rights Violations Impact Police Data, Predictive Policing Systems, and Justice' (2019) https://papers.ssrn.com/abstract=3333423 accessed 15 February 2019.

36 Solon Barocas and Andrew D. Selbst, 'Big Data's Disparate Impact' (2016) 104 *California Law Review* 671–732; Joshua Kroll et al., 'Accountable Algorithms' (2017) 165 *U Pa L Rev* 633.

37 Solon Barocas and Andrew D. Selbst, 'Big Data's Disparate Impact' (2016) 104 *California Law Review* 671–732; Alexandra Chouldechova, 'Fair Prediction with Disparate Impact: A Study of Bias in Recidivism Prediction Instruments' (2016) http://arxiv.org/abs/1610.07524 accessed 12 August 2018.

38 NYCLU, 'Stop and Frisk Data' (14 March 2019) www.nyclu.org/en/publications/stop-and-frisk-de-blasio-era-2019 accessed 23 May 2019.

39 US DJ, supra note 18.

40 PE 624.261, supra note 6.

home, and communications; the right to freedom of assembly and of association (CFREU, art. 12); the right to equality before the law (CFREU, art. 20); and the right to non-discrimination (CFREU, art. 21). The risks of infringing on these rights are greater if predictive policing tools target people, as opposed to places. The fact remains that the mere identification of a high-risk zone does not naturally lead to more rights for the police, who, in principle, must continue to operate within the framework of crime prevention and the maintenance of order.

In the United States, due process (the Fifth and Fourteenth Amendments)[41] and equal treatment clauses (the Fourteenth Amendment) could be infringed. Moreover, predictive policing could constitute a breach of privacy or infringe on citizens' rights to be secure in their persons, houses, papers, and effects against unreasonable searches and seizures without a warrant based on a 'probable cause' (the Fourth Amendment). Similar provisions have been enacted in the State Constitutions. Despite the presence of these *theoretical* precautions, some infringements of fundamental rights have been revealed *in practice*.[42]

A posteriori, these risks are higher when algorithms are involved in systems used to support decision-making by police departments. Law enforcement may find it needs to answer to the conditions of use of these tools on a case-by-case basis when decisions are reached involving individuals. To provide an example, the NYPD was taken to court for the use of the Palantir Gotham tool and its technical features.[43] The lack of information on the existence and use of predictive tools, the nature of the data in question, and the conditions of application of algorithmic results based on automated treatment were all contested on the basis of a lack of transparency and the resulting impossibility to enforce the defence's right to due process (the Fifth and Fourteenth Amendments).[44] Additionally, the media,[45] academics,[46] and civil rights defence organizations[47] have called out against the issues of bias and discrimination within these tools, which violate the Fourteenth Amendment principle of Equal Protection for all citizens under the law. In EU law, the Charter of Fundamental Rights also guarantees the right to an effective remedy and access to a fair trial (CFREU, art. 47), as well as the right to presumption of innocence and right of defence (CFREU, art.

41 Danielle Keats Citron, 'Technological Due Process' (2008) 85 *Washington University Law Review*.

42 David Robinson and Logan Koepke, 'Stuck in a Pattern: Early Evidence on "Predictive Policing" and Civil Rights' *Upturn* (August 2016) www.stuckinapattern.org accessed 23 May 2019.

43 *Brennan Center for Justice at New York University, School of Law* v. *NYPD*, Case n. 160541/2016, December 22nd, 2017 (FOIA request (Freedom of Information Law Act)). The judge approved the request and granted access to the *Palantir Gotham* system used by the NYPD: https://law.justia.com/cases/new-york/other-courts/2017/2017-ny-slip-op-32716-u.html.

44 *State of Wisconsin* v. *Loomis*, 371 Wis 2d 235, 2016 WI 68, 881 N W 2d 749 (13 July 2016).

45 For example, Ben Dickson, 'What Is Algorithmic Bias?' (26 March 2018) https://bdtechtalks.com/2018/03/26/racist-sexist-ai-deep-learning-algorithms accessed 23 May 2019.

46 For example, AINow Institute https://ainowinstitute.org.

47 For example, Vera Eidelman, 'Secret Algorithms Are Deciding Criminal Trials and We're Not Even Allowed to Test Their Accuracy' (ACLU 15 September 2017) www.aclu.org/blog/privacy-technology/surveillance-technologies/secret-algorithms-are-deciding-criminal-trials-and accessed 23 May 2019.

48). All of these rights can be threatened if the implementation of predictive policing tools is not coupled with sufficient legal and technical requirements.

The necessity of protecting fundamental rights has to be reiterated in the algorithmic society. To achieve this, adapted tools must be deployed to ensure proper enforcement of fundamental rights. Some ethical principles need to be put in place in order to effectively protect fundamental rights and reinforce them. The goal is not substituting human rights with ethical principles but adding new ethical considerations focused on risks generated by ADS. These ethical principles must be accompanied by practical tools that will make it possible to provide designers and users with concrete information regarding what is expected when making or using automated decision-making tools. Algorithmic Impact Assessment (AIA) constitutes an interesting way to provide a concrete governance of ADS. I argue that while the European constitutional and ethical framework is *theoretically* sufficient, other tools must be adopted to guarantee the enforcement of Fundamental Rights and Ethical Principles *in practice* to provide a robust *framework* for putting human rights at the centre.

6.3 HUMAN RIGHTS REINFORCED BY ETHICAL PRINCIPLES TO GOVERN AI

Before considering the enactment of ethical principles to reinforce fundamental rights in the use of ADS, one needs to identify whether or not efficient legal provisions are already enacted.

6.3.1 *Statutory Provisions in the European Law*

At this time, very few statutory provisions in European Law are capable of reinforcing the respect and protection of fundamental rights with the use of ADS. ADS are algorithmic processes which require data in order to perform. Predictive policing systems do not automatically use personal data, but some of them do. In this case, if the processed personal data concerns some data subjects within the European Union, the General Data Protection Regulation (GDPR) may be applied by the private companies. Moreover, police services are subject to the Data Protection Law Enforcement Directive. It provides for several rights in favour of the data subject, especially the 'right to receive a meaningful information concerning the logic involved' (art. 13–15) and the right 'not to be subject to a decision based solely on automated processing, including profiling, which produces legal effects concerning one or similarly significantly affects one' (art. 22),[48] in addition to a Data Protection Impact Assessment (DPIA) tool (art. 35).[49]

[48] Margot E. Kaminski, 'The Right to Explanation, Explained' (2018) *Berkeley Technology Law Journal* 34(1).

[49] Margot E. Kaminski and Malgieri, Gianclaudio, 'Algorithmic Impact Assessments under the GDPR: Producing Multi-layered Explanations' (2019). U of Colorado Law Legal Studies Research Paper No. 19–28. Available at SSRN: https://ssrn.com/abstract=3456224.

However, these provisions fail to provide adequate protection against the violation of human rights. First, several exceptions restrict the impact of these rights. Article 22 paragraph 1 is limited by paragraph 2, according to which the right 'not to be subject to an automated decision' is excluded, when consent has been given or a contract concluded. This right is also excluded if exceptions have been enacted by the member states.[50] For instance, French Law[51] provides an exception in favour of the governmental use of ADS. Consequently, Article 22 is insufficient per se to protect data subjects. Second, ADS can produce biased decisions without processing personal data, especially when a group is targeted in the decision-making process. Even if the GDPR attempts to consider the profiling of data subjects and decisions that affect groups of people, for instance, through collective representation, such provisions are insufficient to prevent group discrimination.[52] Third, other risks against fundamental rights have to be considered, such as procedural guarantees related to the presumption of innocence and due process. The protection of such rights is not, or at least not directly, within the scope of the GDPR. The personal data protection regulations cannot address all the social and ethical risks associated with ADS. Consequently, such provisions are insufficient, and because other specific statutory provisions have not yet been enacted,[53] ethical guidelines could be helpful as a first step.[54]

6.3.2 *European Ethics Guidelines for Trustworthy AI*

In the EU, the *Ethics Guidelines for Trustworthy Artificial Intelligence (AI)* is a document prepared by the High-Level Experts Group on Artificial Intelligence (AI HLEG). This group was set up by the European Commission in June 2018 as part of the AI strategy announced earlier that year. The AI HLEG presented a first draft of the *Guidelines* in December 2018. Following further deliberations, the *Guidelines*

50 Céline Castets-Renard, 'Accountability of Algorithms: A European Legal Framework on Automated Decision-Making' (2019) *Fordham Intell. Prop., Media & Ent. Law Journal* 30(1). Available at https://ir.lawnet.fordham.edu/iplj/vol30/iss1/3.

51 Loi n 78–66 'Informatique et Libertés' enacted on 6 January 1978 and modified by the Law n 2018–493, enacted on 20 June 2018: www.legifrance.gouv.fr/eli/loi/2018/6/20/JUSC1732261L/jo/texte.

52 However, we also have to consider antidiscrimination directives: Directive 2000/43/EC against discrimination on grounds of race and ethnic origin; Directive 2000/78/EC against discrimination at work on grounds of religion or belief, disability, age, or sexual orientation; Directive 2006/54/EC equal treatment for men and women in matters of employment and occupation; Directive 2004/113/EC equal treatment for men and women in the access to and supply of goods and services.

53 The situation is similar in the United States, except the adoption of the NYC Local Law n 2018/049 concerning automated decision systems used by the local agencies. In the state of Idaho, the Bill n 118 concerning the pretrial risk assessment algorithms and the risk to civil rights of automated pretrial tools in criminal justice was enacted on 4 March 2019: www.muckrock.com/news/archives/2019/mar/05/algorithms-idaho-legislation.

54 See Luciano Floridi et al., 'AI4People – An Ethical Framework for a Good AI Society: Opportunities, Risks, Principles, and Recommendations' (2018) 28 *Minds & Machines* 689–707.

were revised and published in April 2019, the same day as a European Commission Communication on *Building Trust in Human-Centric Artificial Intelligence*.[55]

Guidelines are based on the fundamental rights enshrined in the EU Treaties, with reference to dignity, freedoms, equality and solidarity, citizens' rights, and justice, such as the right to a fair trial and the presumption of innocence. These fundamental rights are at the top of the hierarchy of norms of many States and international texts. Consequently, they are non-negotiable and even less optional. However, the concept of 'fundamental rights' is integrated with the concept of 'ethical purpose' in these *Guidelines*, which creates a normative confusion.[56] According to the Experts Group, while fundamental human rights legislation is binding, it still does not provide comprehensive legal protection in the use of ADS. Therefore, the *AI Ethics Principles* have to be understood both within and beyond these fundamental rights. Consequently, trustworthy AI should be (1) lawful – respecting all applicable laws and regulations; (2) ethical – respecting ethical principles and values; and (3) robust – both from a technical perspective while taking into account its social environment.

The key principles are the principle of respect for human autonomy, the principle of prevention of harm, the principle of fairness, and the principle of explicability.[57] However, an explanation as to why a model has generated a particular output or decision (and what combination of input factors contributed to that) is not always possible.[58] These cases are referred to as 'black box' algorithms and require special attention. In those circumstances, other explicability measures (e.g., traceability, auditability, and transparent communication on system capabilities) may be required, provided that the system as a whole respects fundamental rights.

In addition to the four principles, the Expert Group established a set of seven key requirements that AI systems should meet in order to be deemed trustworthy: (1) Human Agency and Oversight; (2) Technical Robustness and Safety; (3) Privacy and Data Governance; (4) Transparency; (5) Diversity, Non-Discrimination, and Fairness; (6) Societal and Environmental Well-Being; and (7) Accountability.

Such principles and requirements certainly push us in the right direction, but they are not concrete enough to indicate to ADS designers and users how they can ensure the respect of fundamental rights and ethical principles. Back to the predictive policing activity, the risks against fundamental rights have been identified but

55 European Commission, 'Communication to the European Parliament, the Council, the European Economic and Social Committee and the Committee of the Regions, Building Trust in Human-Centric Artificial Intelligence' COM (2019) 168 final.

56 B. Wagner and S. Delacroix, 'Constructing a Mutually Supportive Interface between Ethics and Regulation' (14 June 2019): https://ssrn.com/abstract=3404179.

57 Lilian Edwards and Michael Veale, 'Enslaving the Algorithm: From a "Right to an Explanation" to a "Right to Better Decisions"?' (2018) *IEEE Security & Privacy* 16(3) https://papers.ssrn.com/abstract=3052831 accessed 5 December 2018.

58 Paul B. de Laat, 'Algorithmic Decision-Making Based on Machine Learning from Big Data: Can Transparency Restore Accountability?' (2017) *Philos Technol* 1–17.

not yet addressed. The recognition of ethical principles adapted to ADS is useful for highlighting specific risks but nothing more. It is insufficient to protect human rights, and they must be accompanied by practical tools to guarantee their respect on the ground.

6.4 HUMAN RIGHTS REINFORCED BY PRACTICAL TOOLS TO GOVERN ADS

In order to identify solutions and practical tools, excluding the instruments of self-regulation,[59] the 'Trustworthy AI Assessment List' proposed by the Group of Experts can first be considered. Aiming to operationalize the ethical principles and requirements, the Guidelines present an assessment list that offers guidance on the practical implementation of each requirement. This assessment list will undergo a piloting process in which all interested stakeholders can participate, in order to gather feedback for its improvement. In addition, a forum to exchange best practices for the implementation of Trustworthy AI has been created. However, the goal of these Guidelines and the List is to regulate the activities linked with AI technologies via a general approach. Consequently, the measures proposed are broad enough to cover many situations and different applications of AI, such as climate action and sustainable infrastructure, health and well-being, quality education and digital transformation, tracking and scoring individuals, and lethal autonomous weapon systems (LAWS). But while our study concerns predictive policing activities, it is more relevant to consider specific, practical tools which regulate the governmental activities and ADS.[60] In this sense, the Canadian government enacted in February 2019 a Directive on Automated Decision-Making[61] and a method on AIA.[62] These tools pursue the goal of offering governmental institutions a practical method to comply with fundamental rights, laws, and ethical principles. I argue that these methods are relevant to assess the activity of predictive policing in theory.

59 European Parliamentary Research Service (EPRS), 'Panel for the Future of Science and Technology, A Governance Framework of Algorithmic Accountability and Transparency' April 2019 (PE 624.262) [PE 624.262]. I exclude the self-regulation solutions, such as ethics committees, because they may, in fact, be a way to manage public image and avoid government regulation. See Ben Wagner, *Ethics as an Escape from Regulation: From Ethics-Washing to Ethics-Shopping?* (Amsterdam University Press, 2018); Yeung Karen et al., *AI Governance by Human Rights-Centred Design, Deliberation and Oversight: An End to Ethics Washing* (Oxford University Press, 2019). Luciano Floridi, 'Translating Principles into Practices of Digital Ethics: Five Risks of Being Unethical' (2019) *Philosophy & Technology* 32(2).

60 For instance , Marion Oswald et al., 'Algorithmic Risk Assessment Policing Models: Lessons from the Durham HART Model and "Experimental" Proportionality' (2017) *Information & Communications Technology Law* https://papers.ssrn.com/abstract=3029345 accessed 23 May 2019.

61 Directive on Automated Decision-Making (2019) www.tbs-sct.gc.ca/pol/doc-eng.aspx?id=32592.

62 Government of Canada, Algorithmic Impact Assessment (8 March 2019) https://open.canada.ca/data/en/dataset/748a97fb-6714-41ef-9fb8-637a0b8e0da1 accessed 23 May 2019.

6.4.1 *Methods: Canadian Directive on Algorithmic Decision-Making and the Algorithmic Impact Assessment Tool*

The Canadian Government announced its intention to increasingly look to utilize artificial intelligence to make, or assist in making, administrative decisions to improve the delivery of social and governmental services. This government is committed to doing so in a manner that is compatible with core administrative legal principles such as transparency, accountability, legality, and procedural fairness, as based on the directive, and an AIA. An AIA is a framework to help institutions better understand and reduce the risks associated with ADS and to provide the appropriate governance, oversight, and reporting/audit requirements that best match the type of application being designed. The Canadian AIA is a questionnaire designed to assist the administration in assessing and mitigating the risks associated with deploying an ADS. The AIA also helps identify the impact level of the ADS under the proposed Directive on Automated Decision-Making. The questions are focused on the business processes, the data, and the systems to make decisions.

The Directive took effect on 1 April 2019, with compliance required by no later than 1 April 2020. It applies to any ADS developed or procured after 1 April 2020 and to any system, tool, or statistical model used to recommend or make an administrative decision about a client (the recipient of a service). Consequently, this provision does not apply in the criminal justice system or criminal proceedings. This Directive is divided into eleven parts and three appendices on Purpose, Authorities, Definitions, Objectives and Expected Results, Scope, Requirements, Consequences, Roles and Responsibilities of Treasury Board of Canada Secretariat, Application, References, and Enquiries. The three appendices concern the Definitions (appendix A), the Impact Assessment Levels (appendix B), and the Impact Level Requirements (appendix C).

The objective of this Directive is to ensure that ADS are deployed in a manner that reduces risks to Canadians and federal institutions, leading to more efficient, accurate, consistent, and interpretable decisions made pursuant to Canadian law. The expected results of this Directive are as follows:

- Decisions made by federal government departments are data-driven, responsible, and comply with procedural fairness and due process requirements.
- Impacts of algorithms on administrative decisions are assessed, and negative outcomes are reduced, when encountered.
- Data and information on the use of ADS in federal institutions are made available to the public, where appropriate.

Concerning the requirements, the Assistant Deputy Minister responsible for the program using the ADS, or any other person named by the Deputy Head, is responsible for AIA, transparency, quality assurance, recourse, and reporting. He has to provide with any applicable recourse options that are available to them to challenge the administrative decision, and to complete an AIA prior to the production of any ADS. He can use the AIA tool to assess and mitigate the risks associated with deploying an ADS based on a questionnaire.

6.4.2 *Application of These Methods to Predictive Policing Activities*

Though such measures specifically concern the Government of Canada and do not apply to criminal proceedings, I propose to use this method both abroad and more extensively. It can be relevant for any governmental decision-making, especially for predictive policing activities. I will consider the requirements that should be respected by people responsible for predictive policing programs. Those responsible should be appointed to perform their work on the ground, for each predictive tool used. This would be done using a case-by-case approach.

The first step is to assess the impact in consideration of the 'impact assessment levels' provided by appendix B of the Canadian Directive.

Appendix B: Impact Assessment Levels

Level	Description
I	The decision will likely have little to no impact on: • the rights of individuals or communities, • the health or well-being of individuals or communities, • the economic interests of individuals, entities, or communities, • the ongoing sustainability of an ecosystem. Level I decisions will often lead to impacts that are reversible and brief.
II	The decision will likely have moderate impacts on: • the rights of individuals or communities, • the health or well-being of individuals or communities, • the economic interests of individuals, entities, or communities, • the ongoing sustainability of an ecosystem. Level II decisions will often lead to impacts that are likely reversible and short-term.
III	The decision will likely have high impacts on: • the rights of individuals or communities, • the health or well-being of individuals or communities, • the economic interests of individuals, entities, or communities, • the ongoing sustainability of an ecosystem. Level III decisions will often lead to impacts that can be difficult to reverse, and are ongoing.
IV	The decision will likely have very high impacts on: • the rights of individuals or communities, • the health or well-being of individuals or communities, • the economic interests of individuals, entities, or communities, • the ongoing sustainability of an ecosystem. Level IV decisions will often lead to impacts that are irreversible, and are perpetual.

At least level III would be probably reached for predictive policing activities in consideration of the high impact on the freedoms and rights of individuals and communities previously highlighted.

Keeping these levels III and IV in mind, they reveal in a second step the level of risks and requirements. Defined in appendix C, it indicates the 'requirements', concerning especially the notice, the explanation, and the human-in-loop process. The 'notice requirements' are focus on more transparency, which is particularly relevant to address the opacity problem of predictive policing systems.

Appendix C: Impact level requirements

Requirement	Level I	Level II	Level III	Level IV
Notice	None	Plain language notice posted on the program or service website.	Publish documentation on relevant websites about the automated decision system, in plain language, describing: • How the components work; • How it supports the administrative decision; and • Results of any reviews or audits; and • A description of the training data, or a link to the anonymized training data if these data are publicly available.	

These provisions allow one to know if the algorithmic system makes or supports the decision at levels III and IV. They also inform the public about the data used, especially from the start of the training process. This point is particularly relevant, in consideration of the historical and biased data mainly used in predictive policing systems. These requirements could help solve the discriminatory problem.

Moreover, AIAs usually provide a pre-procurement step that gives the public authority the opportunity to engage in a public debate and proactively identify concerns, establish expectations, and draw on expertise and understanding from relevant stakeholders. This is also when the public and elected officials can push back against deployment before potential harms occur. In implementing AIAs, authorities should consider incorporating them into the consultation procedures that they already use for procuring algorithmic systems or for assessing their pre-acquisition.[63] It would be a way to address the lack of transparency of predictive policing systems which should be addressed at levels III and IV.

Besides, other requirements concern the 'explanation'.

63 PE 624.262, supra note 60.

Requirement	Level I	Level II	Level III	Level IV
Explanation	In addition to any applicable legislative requirement, ensuring that a meaningful explanation is provided for common decision results. This can include providing the explanation via a Frequently Asked Questions section on a website.	In addition to any applicable legislative requirement, ensuring that a meaningful explanation is provided upon request for any decision that resulted in the denial of a benefit, a service, or other regulatory action.	In addition to any applicable legislative requirement, ensuring that a meaningful explanation is provided with any decision that resulted in the denial of a benefit, a service, or other regulatory action.	

At levels III and IV, each regulatory action that impacts a person or a group requires the provision of a meaningful explanation. Concretely, if these provisions were made applicable to police services, the police departments who use some predictive policing tools should be able to give an explanation of the decisions made and the way of reasoning, especially in the case of using personal data. The place or a person targeted by predictive policing should also be explained.

Concerning the 'human-in-loop for decisions' requirement, levels III and IV impose a human intervention during the decision-making process. That is also relevant for predictive policing activities which require that the police officers keep their free will and self-judgment. Moreover, the human decision has to prevail over the machine-decision. That is crucial to preserve the legitimacy and autonomy of the law enforcement authorities, as well as their responsibility.

Requirement	**Level I**	**Level II**	**Level III**	**Level IV**
Human-in-the-loop for decisions	Decisions may be rendered without direct human involvement.		Decisions cannot be made without having specific human intervention points during the decision-making process, and the final decision must be made by a human.	

Furthermore, if infringement on human rights has to be prevented, additional requirements on testing, monitoring, and training have to be respected at all levels. Before going into production, the person in charge of the program has to develop the appropriate processes to ensure that training data are tested for unintended data biases and other factors that may unfairly impact the outcomes. Moreover, he has to ensure that data being used by the ADS are routinely tested to verify that it is still relevant, accurate, and up-to-date. He also has to monitor the outcomes of ADS on an ongoing basis to safeguard against unintentional outcomes and to ensure compliance with legislations.

Finally, the 'training' requirement for level III concerns the documentation on the design and functionality of the system. Training courses must be completed, but contrary to level IV, there is surprisingly no obligation to verify that it has been done.

The sum of these requirements is relevant to mitigate the risks of opacity and discrimination. However, alternately, it does not address the problem of efficiency. Such criteria should also be considered in the future, as the example of predictive policing activities reveals a weakness regarding the efficiency and social utility of this kind of algorithmic tool at this step. It is important not to consider that an ADS is necessarily efficient *by principle*. Public authorities should provide evidence of it.

6.5 CONCLUSION

Human rights are a representation of the fundamental values of a society and are universal. However, in an algorithmic society, even if a European lawmaker pretends to reinforce the protection of these rights through ethical principles, I have demonstrated that the current system is not good enough when it comes to guaranteeing their respect *in practice*. Constitutional rights must be reinforced not only by ethical principles but even more by specific practical tools taking into account the risks involved in ADS, especially when the decision-making concerns sensitive issues such as predictive policing. Beyond the *Ethics Guidelines for Trustworthy AI*, I argue that the European lawmaker should consider enacting similar tools as the *Canadian Directive on Automated Decision Making* and AIAs policies that must be made applicable to police services to make them accountable.[64] AIAs will not solve all of the problems that algorithmic systems might raise, but they do provide an important mechanism to inform the public and to engage policymakers and researchers in productive conversation.[65] Even if this tool is certainly not perfect, it constitutes a good starting point. Moreover, I argue this policy should come from the European Union and not its member states. The protection of human rights in an algorithmic society may be considered globally as a whole system integrating human rights. The final result is providing a robust theoretical and practical framework, while human rights keep a central place within this broad system.

64 See a similar recommendation in EPRS Study PE 624.262, supra note 60.
65 Ibid.

7

Law Enforcement and Data-Driven Predictions at the National and EU Level

A Challenge to the Presumption of Innocence and Reasonable Suspicion?

Francesca Galli

7.1 INTRODUCTION

Technological progress could constitute a huge benefit for law enforcement and criminal justice more broadly.[1] In the security context,[2] alleged opportunities and benefits of applying big data analytics are greater efficiency, effectiveness, and speed of law enforcement operations, as well as more precise risk analyses, including the discovery of unexpected correlations,[3] which could nourish profiles.[4]

The concept of 'big data' refers to the growing ability of technology to capture, aggregate, and process an ever-greater volume and variety of data.[5] The combination of mass digitisation of information and the exponential growth of computational power allows for their increasing exploitation.[6]

[1] See, e.g., H Fenwick (ed), *Development in Counterterrorist Measures and Uses of Technology* (Routledge 2012). See also, on policing more specifically, National Institute of Justice, *Research on the Impact of Technology on Policing Strategy in the 21st Century. Final Report*, May 2016, www.ncjrs.gov/pdffiles1/nij/grants/251140.pdf, accessed 27 July 2020; J Byrne and G Marx, 'Technological Innovations in Crime Prevention and Policing. A Review of the Research on Implementation and Impact' (2011) 20(3) *Cahiers Politiestudies* 17–40.

[2] B Hoogenboom, *The Governance of Policing and Security: Ironies, Myths and Paradoxes* (Palgrave Macmillan 2010).

[3] J Chan, 'The Technology Game: How Information Technology Is Transforming Police Practice' (2001) 1 *Journal of Criminal Justice* 139.

[4] D Broeders et al., 'Big Data and Security Policies: Serving Security, Protecting Freedom' (2017) *WRR-Policy Brief* 6.

[5] For instance, data acquisition is a kind of data processing architecture for big data, which has been understood as the process of gathering, filtering, and cleaning data before the data are put in a data warehouse or any other storage solution. See K Lyko, M Nitzschke, and A-C Ngonga Ngomo, 'Big Data Acquisition' in JM Cavanillas et al. (eds), *New Horizons for a Data-Driven Economy. A Roadmap for Usage and Exploitation of Big Data in Europe* (Springer 2015).

[6] S Brayne, 'The Criminal Law and Law Enforcement Implications of Big Data' (2018) 14 *Annual Review of Law and Social Science* 293.

A number of new tools have been developed. Algorithms are merely an abstract and formal description of a computational procedure.[7] Besides, law enforcement can rely on artificial intelligence (i.e., the theory and development of computer systems capable of performing tasks which would normally require human intelligence), such as visual perception, speech recognition, decision-making, and translation between languages.[8] For the purpose of this contribution, these systems are relevant because they do not simply imitate the intelligence of human beings; they are meant to formulate and often execute decisions. The notion of an allegedly clever agent, capable of taking relatively autonomous decisions, on the basis of its perception of the environment, is in fact, pivotal to the current concept of artificial intelligence.[9] With machine learning, or 'self-teaching' algorithms, the knowledge in the system is the result of 'data-driven predictions', the automated discovery of correlations between variables in a data set, often to make estimates of some outcome.[10] Correlations are relationships or patterns, thus more closely related to the concept of 'suspicion' rather than the concept of 'evidence' in criminal law.[11] Data mining, or 'knowledge discovery from data', refers to the process of discovery of remarkable patterns from massive amounts of data.

Such tools entail new scenarios for information gathering, as well as the monitoring, profiling, and prediction of individual behaviours, thus allegedly facilitating

7 RK Hill, 'What an Algorithm Is' (2016) 29 *Philosophy and Technology* 35–59; TH Cormen et al., *Introduction to Algorithms* (3rd ed., The MIT Press 2009).

8 K Yeung for the Expert Committee on human rights dimensions of automated data processing and different forms of artificial intelligence (MSI-AUT), *A Study of the Implications of Advanced Digital Technologies (Including AI Systems) for the Concept of Responsibility within a Human Rights Framework*, Council of Europe study DGI(2019)05, September 2019, https://rm.coe.int/responsability-and-ai-en/168097d9c5, accessed 27 July 2020.

9 On the role of algorithms and automated decisions in security governance, as well as numerous concerns associated with the notion of 'algorithmic regulation', see L Amoore and R Raley, 'Securing with Algorithms: Knowledge, Decision, Sovereignty' (2017) 48(1) *Security Dialogue* 3; C Aradau and T Blancke, 'Governing Others: Anomaly and the Algorithmic Subject of Security' (2018) 3(1) *European Journal of International Security* 1.

10 See M Oswald et al., 'Algorithmic Risk Assessment Policing Models: Lessons from the Durham HART Model and "Experimental" Proportionality' (2018) 27(2) *Information & Communications Technology Law* 223; P MacFarlane, 'Why the Police Should Use Machine Learning – But Very Carefully', *The Conversation*, 21 August 2019, https://theconversation.com/why-the-police-should-use-machine-learning-but-very-carefully-121524, accessed 27 July 2020; D Lehr and P Ohm, 'Playing with the Data: What Legal Scholars Should Learn about Machine Learning' (2017) 51 *UCDL Rev* 653; 'Reinventing Society in the Wake of Big Data. A Conversation with Alex "Sandy" Pentland', *The Edge*, www.edge.org/conversation/reinventing-society-in-the-wake-of-big-data, accessed 27 July 2020.

11 Although crime prevention should be rational and based on the best possible evidence. See BC Welsh and DP Farrington, 'Evidence-Based Crime Prevention' in BC Welsh and DP Farrington (eds), *Preventing Crime* (Springer 2007).

crime prevention.[12] The underlying assumption is that data could change public policy, addressing biases and fostering a data-driven approach in policy-making. Clearer evidence could support both evaluations of existing policies and impact assessments of new proposals.[13]

Law enforcement authorities have already embraced the assumed benefits of big data, irrespective of criticism questioning the validity of crucial assumptions underlying criminal profiling.[14] In a range of daily operations and surveillance activities, such as patrol, investigation, as well as crime analysis, the outcomes of computational risk assessment are increasingly the underlying foundation of criminal justice policies.[15] Existing research on the implications of 'big data' has mostly focused on privacy and data protection concerns.[16] However, potential gains in security come also at the expenses of accountability[17] and could lead to the erosion of fundamental rights, emphasising coercive control.[18]

This contribution first addresses the so-called rise of the algorithmic society and the use of automated technologies in criminal justice to assess whether and how the gathering, analysis, and deployment of big data are changing law enforcement activities. It then examines the actual or potential transformation

12 See BJ Koops, 'Technology and the Crime Society. Rethinking Legal Protection' (2009) 1(1) *Law, Innovation and Technology* 93.

13 M Leese, 'The New Profiling' (204) 45(5) *Security Dialogue* 494.

14 For an in-depth study, see GG Fuster, *Artificial Intelligence and Law Enforcement. Impact on Fundamental Rights*. Study Requested by the LIBE Committee. Policy Department for Citizens' Rights and Constitutional Affairs, PE 656.295, July 2020.

15 A Završnik, 'Criminal Justice, Artificial Intelligence Systems, and Human Rights' (2020) 20 *ERA Forum* 567; P Hayes et al., 'Algorithms and Values in Justice and Security' (2020) 35 *Artificial Intelligence and Society* 533.

16 C Kuner, F Cate, O Lynskey, C Millard, N Ni Loideain, and D Svantesson, 'An Unstoppable Force and an Immoveable Object? EU Data Protection Law and National Security' (2018) 8 *International Data Privacy Law* 1; O Lynskey, 'Criminal Justice Profiling and EU Data Protection Law' (2019) 15 *International Journal of Law in Context* 162; R Bellanova, 'Digital, Politics and Algorithms. Governing Digital Data through the Lens of Data Protection' (2017) 20(3) *European Journal of Social Theory* 329; J Hernandez Ramos et al., 'Towards a Data-Driven Society: A Technological Perspective on the Development of Cybersecurity and Data Protection Policies' (2020) 18(1) *IEEE Security and Privacy* 28.

17 F Doshi-Velez and M Kortz, 'Accountability of AI Under the Law: The Role of Explanation' (2017) Berkman Klein Center Working Group on Explanation and the Law, Berkman Klein Center for Internet & Society working paper, https://dash.harvard.edu/bitstream/handle/1/34372584/2017-11_aiexplainability-1.pdf, accessed 25 August 2020.

18 A Braga et al., 'Moving the Work of Criminal Investigators Towards Crime Control' in *New Perspectives in Policing*, (Harvard Kennedy School 2011); The European Commission for the Efficiency of justice (CEPEJ, Council of Europe), *European Ethical Charter on the Use of Artificial Intelligence in Judicial Systems and Their Environment*, adopted at the 31st plenary meeting of the CEPEJ (Strasbourg, 3–4 December 2018), https://rm.coe.int/ethical-charter-en-for-publication-4-december-2018/16808f699c, accessed 20 July 2020; Council of Europe's MIS-NET, 'Study on the Human Rights Dimensions of Automated Data Processing Techniques and Possible Regulatory Implications', https://edoc.coe.int/en/internet/7589-algorithms-and-human-rights-study-on-the-human-rights-dimensions-of-automated-data-processing-techniques-and-possible-regulatory-implications.html, accessed 2 August 2020.

of core principles of criminal law and whether the substance of legal protection[19] may be weakened in a 'data-driven society'.[20]

7.2 THE RISE OF THE ALGORITHMIC SOCIETY AND THE USE OF AUTOMATED TECHNOLOGIES IN CRIMINAL JUSTICE

7.2.1 *A Shift in Tools Rather than Strategy?*

One could argue that the development of predictive policing is more a shift in tools than strategy. Prediction has always been part of policing, as law enforcement authorities attempt to predict where criminal activities could take place and the individuals involved in order to deter such patterns.[21]

Law enforcement has over time moved towards wide-ranging monitoring and even more preventative approaches. Surveillance technologies introduced in relation to serious crimes (e.g., interception of telecommunications) are increasingly used for the purpose of preventing and investigating 'minor' offences; at the same time, surveillance technologies originally used for public order purposes in relation to minor offences (e.g., CCTV cameras) are gradually employed for the prevention and investigation of serious crime.[22] On the one side, serious crime including terrorism has had a catalysing effect on the criminal justice system, prompting increased use of surveillance techniques and technologies. The subsequent introduction of exceptional provisions has been first regarded as exceptional and limited in scope first to terrorism and then to organised crime. However, through a long-lasting normalisation process at the initiative of the legislator, specific measures have become institutionalised as part of the ordinary criminal justice system and have a tendency to be applied beyond their original

[19] The fundamental right to effective judicial protection has been one of the pillars of European integration, codified by the Treaty of Lisbon in Article 47 of the EU Charter of Fundamental Rights and Article 19(1) TEU. The CJEU has been insisting on the access for individuals to the domestic judicial review of any acts that may affect the interests of these individuals. Thus the CJEU sought to ensure not only the subjective legal protection of these individuals but also the objective legality of domestic administrative action implementing EU law, as well as ensuing unity and consistency in the application of EU law across different jurisdictions. However, specific requirements stemming from the right to effective judicial protection are not always clear. Effective judicial protection is largely a judge-made concept. There has been no comprehensive legislative harmonisation of domestic procedural provisions applied to implement EU law. See M Safjan and D Dusterhaus, 'A Union of Effective Judicial Protection: Addressing a Multi-level Challenge through the Lens of Article 47 CFREU' (2014) 33 *Yearbook of European Law* 3; R Barents, 'EU Procedural Law and Effective Judicial Protection' (2014) 51 *Common Market Law Review* 1437, 1445 ff.

[20] S Lohr, 'The Promise and Peril of the "Data-Driven Society"', *New York Times*, 25 February 2013, https://bits.blogs.nytimes.com/2013/02/25/the-promise-and-peril-of-the-data-driven-society/, accessed 27 July 2020.

[21] AG Ferguson, 'Policing Predictive Policing' (2017) 94(5) *Washington University Law Review* 1115, 1128–1130.

[22] C Cocq and F Galli, 'The Catalysing Effect of Serious Crime on the Use of Surveillance Technologies for Prevention and Investigation Purposes' (2013) 4(3) *NJECL* 256.

scope.[23] On the other side, a parallel shift has occurred in the opposite direction. Video surveillance technologies, which are one of the most obvious and widespread signs of the development of surveillance, were originally conceived by the private sector for security purposes. They have been subsequently employed for public order purposes and finally in the prevention of minor offences and/or petty crimes (such as street crimes or small drug dealers), without any significant change in the level of judicial scrutiny and on the basis of a simple administrative authorisation. In such contexts, they were rather a tool to deter would-be criminals than an investigative means.[24] The terrorist threat has become an argument to justify an even more extensive deployment and use of video surveillance, as well as a broader use of the information gathered for the purposes of investigation.

Anticipative criminal investigations have a primary preventive function, combined with evidence gathering for the purpose of eventual prosecution.[25] The extensive gathering, processing, and storage of data for criminal law purposes imply a significant departure from existing law enforcement strategies. The relentless storage combined with an amplified memory capacity make a quantitative and qualitative jump as compared to traditional law enforcement activities. The growth of available data over the last two centuries has been substantial, but the present explosion in data size and variety is unprecedented.[26]

First, the amount of data that are generated, processed, and stored has increased enormously (e.g., internet data) because of the direct and intentional seizure of information on people or objects; the automated collection of data by devices or systems; and the volunteered collection of data via the voluntary use of systems, devices, and platforms. Automated and volunteered collection have exponentially increased due to the widespread use of smart devices, social media, and digital transactions.[27] The 'datafication'[28] of everyday activities, which is furthered driven by the 'Internet of Things',[29] leads to the virtually

[23] O Gross, 'Chaos and Rules' (2003) 112 *Yale Law Journal* 1011, 1090; D Dyzenhaus, 'The Permanence of the Temporary' in RJ Daniels et al. (eds), *The Security of Freedom* (University of Toronto Press 2001).

[24] For example, A Bauer and F Freynet, *Vidéosurveillance et vidéoprotection* (PUF 2008); EFUS, *Citizens, Cities and Video Surveillance, towards a Democratic and Responsible Use of CCTV* (EFUS 2010), 183–184; *Vidéo-surveillance Infos, 'Dispositif de sécurité au stade de France: ergonomie et évolutivité'* (14 October 2011).

[25] See, e.g., MFH Hirsch Ballin, *Anticipative Criminal Investigations. Theory and Counter-terrorism Practice in the Netherlands and the United States* (TMC Asser Press 2012).

[26] R Van Brakel and P De Hert, 'Policing, Surveillance and Law in a Pre-crime Society: Understanding the Consequences of Technology-Based Strategies' (2011) 3(20) *Cahiers Politiestudies Jaargang* 163.

[27] G González Fuster and A Scherrer, 'Big Data and Smart Devices and Their Impact on Privacy', Study for the European Parliament, Directorate General for Internal Policies, Policy Department C: Citizens' Rights and Constitutional Affairs, Civil Liberties, Justice and Home Affairs, PE 536.455, Sept 2015.

[28] 'Datafication' indicates the increasing on data-driven technologies.

[29] The Internet of Things is the interconnection via the Internet of computing devices embedded in everyday objects, enabling them to send and receive data. See J Davies and C Fortuna (eds), *The Internet of Things: From Data to Insight* (Wiley 2020).

unnoticed gathering of data, often without the consent or even the awareness of the individual.

Second, new types of data have become available (e.g., location data). Irrespective of whether law enforcement authorities will eventually use these forms of data, much of the electronically available data reveal information about individuals which were not available in the past. Plus, there is a vast amount of data available nowadays on people's behaviour.[30] Moreover, because of the combination of digitisation and automated recognition, data has become increasingly accessible, and persons can be easily monitored at distance.

Third, the growing availability of real-time data fosters real-time analyses. Thus the increased use of predictive data analytics is a major development. Their underlying rationale is the idea of predicting a possible future with a certain degree of probability.

7.2.2 *Interoperable Databases: A New Challenge to Legal Protection?*

Although police have always gathered information about suspects, now data can be stored in interoperable databases,[31] furthering the surveillance potential.[32] The possibility to link data systems and networks fosters the systematic analysis of computer processors as well as increased data storage capacity.

Interoperability challenges existing modes of cooperation and integration in the EU AFSJ and also the existing distribution of competences between the EU and Member States, between law enforcement authorities and intelligence services, and between public and private actors, which are increasingly involved in information-management activities. Moreover, large-scale information exchanges via interoperable information systems have progressively eroded the boundaries between law enforcement and intelligence services. Besides, they have facilitated a reshuffling of responsibilities and tasks within the law enforcement community, such as security and migration actors. Furthermore, competent authorities have access to huge amounts of data in all types of public and private databases. Interoperable information systems function not only across national boundaries but also across the traditional public-private divide.

30 S Lohr (n 20).

31 See J Ballaschk, *Interoperability of Intelligence Networks in the European Union: An Analysis of the Policy of Interoperability in the EU's Area of Freedom, Security and Justice and Its Compatibility with the Right to Data Protection*, PhD thesis, University of Copenhagen 2015 (still unpublished); F Galli, 'Interoperable Databases: New Cooperation Dynamics in the EU AFSJ?' in Special Issue a cura di D Curtin e FB Bastos (eds) (2020) 26(1) *European Public Law* 109–130.

32 KF Aas et al. (eds), *Technologies of Insecurity. The Surveillance of Everyday Life* (Routledge 2009); see P De Hert and S Gutwirth, 'Interoperability of Police Databases within the EU: An Accountable Political Choice' (2006) 20 (1–2) *International Review of Law, Computers and Technology* 21–35; V Mitsilegas, 'The Borders Paradox' in H Lindahl (ed), *A Right to Inclusion and Exclusion?* (Hart 2009), at 56.

If, on the one hand, the so-called big data policing partially constitutes a restatement of existing police practices, then on the other hand, big data analytics bring along fundamental transformations in police activities. There has been also an evolution of the share of roles, competences, and technological capabilities of intelligence services and law enforcement authorities. The means at the disposal of each actor for the prevention and investigation of serious crime are evolving so that the share of tasks and competences have become blurred. Nowadays the distinction is not always clear, and this leads to problematic coordination and overlap.[33] Intelligence has also been given operational tasks. Law enforcement authorities have resorted to ever more sophisticated surveillance technologies and have been granted much more intrusive investigative powers to use them. Faith in technological solutions and the inherent expansionary tendency of surveillance tools partially explains this phenomenon. Surveillance technologies, in fact, are used in areas or for purposes for which they were not originally intended.[34]

Information sharing and exchange do not in itself blur the institutional barriers between different law enforcement authorities, but the nature of large-scale information-sharing activities does provide a new standing to intelligence activities in the law enforcement domain. The resources spent on and the knowledge developed by such large-scale information gathering and analysis are de facto changing police officers into intelligence actors or intelligence material users.

In addition, EU initiatives enhancing access to information by law enforcement authorities have a direct impact on the functional borders in the security domain. With the much-debated interoperability regulations,[35] the intention of the Commission has been to improve information exchanges not only between police authorities but also between customs authorities and financial intelligence units and in interactions with the judiciary, public prosecution services, and all other public bodies that participate in a process that ranges from the early detection of security threats and criminal offences to the conviction and punishment of suspects. The Commission has portrayed obstacles to the functional sharing of tasks as follows: 'Compartmentalization of information and lack of a clear policy on information channels hinder information exchange',[36] whereas there is, allegedly, a need to

33 See J Vervaele, 'Terrorism and Information Sharing between the Intelligence and Law Enforcement Communities in the US and the Netherlands: Emergency Criminal Law?' (2005) 1(1) *Utrecht Law Review* 1.

34 C Cocq and F Galli (n 22).

35 *Regulation (EU) 2019/817 of the European Parliament and of the Council of 20 May 2019 on establishing a framework for interoperability between EU information systems in the field of borders and visa*, OJ L 135/27, 22.5.2019; *Regulation (EU) 2019/818 of the European Parliament and of the Council of 20 May 2019 on establishing a framework for interoperability between EU information systems in the field of police and judicial cooperation, asylum and migration*, OJ L 135/85, 22.5.2019.

36 In May 2004, the European Commission issued a Communication to the Council of Europe and the European Parliament aiming at enhancing law enforcement access to information by law enforcement agencies.

facilitate the free movement of information between competent authorities within Member States and across borders.

In this context, a controversial aspect of interoperability is that systems and processes are linked with information systems that do not serve law enforcement purposes, including other state-held databases and ones held by private actors. With reference to the first category, the issue to address concerns the blurring of tasks between different law enforcement actors. In fact, a key aspect of the EU strategy on databases and their interoperability is an aim to maximise access to personal data, including access by police authorities to immigration databases, and to personal data related to identification. This blurring has an impact on the applicable legal regime (in terms of jurisdiction) and also in terms of legal procedure (e.g., administrative/criminal). In fact, the purpose for which data are gathered, processed, and accessed is crucial, not only because of data protection rules but because it links the information/data with a different stage of a procedure (either administrative or criminal) to which a set of guarantees are (or are not) attached, and thus has serious consequences for the rights of individuals (including access, appeal, and correction rights). Neither legal systems nor legal provisions are fully compatible either because they belong to administrative or criminal law or because of a lack of approximation between Member State systems. Such differences also have an impact on the potential use of information: information used for identification purposes (the focus of customs officers at Frontex), or only for investigation purposes with no need to reach trial (the focus of intelligence actors), or for prosecution purposes (the focus of police authorities). Eventually, of course, the actors involved in the process have different impacts on the potential secret use of data, with consequent transparency concerns.[37]

7.2.3 A '*Public-Private Partnership*'

The information society has substantially changed the ways in which law enforcement authorities can obtain information and evidence. Beyond their own specialised databases, competent authorities have access to huge amounts of data in all types of public and private databases.[38]

Nowadays the legal systems in most Western countries thus face relevant changes in the politics of information control. The rise of advanced technologies has magnified the capability of new players to control both the means of communication and data flows. To an increasing extent, public authorities are sharing their regulatory competences with an indefinite number of actors by imposing preventive duties on the private sector, such as information-gathering and sharing (e.g., on telecommunication

[37] M Ananny and K Crawford, 'Seeing without Knowing: Limitations of the Transparency Ideal and Its Application to Algorithmic Accountability' (2018) 20 *New Media and Society* 973; Eleni Kosta and Magda Brewczyńska, 'Government Access to User Data' in RM Ballardini, P Kuoppamäki, and O Pitkänen (eds), *Regulating Industrial Internet through IPR, Data Protection and Competition Law* (Kluwer Law Intl 2019), ch 13.

[38] See FH Cate and JX Dempsey (eds), *Bulk Collection: Systematic Government Access to Private-Sector Data* (Oxford University Press 2017).

companies for data retention purposes).[39] This trend is leading to a growing privatisation of surveillance practises. In this move, key players in private information society (producers, service providers, key consumers) are given law enforcement obligations.

Private actors are not just in charge of the operational enforcement of public authority decisions in security matters. They are often the only ones with the necessary expertise, and therefore they profoundly shape decision-making and policy implementation. Their choices are nevertheless guided by reasons such as commercial interest, and they are often unaccountable.

In the context of information sharing, and particularly in the area of interoperable information systems, technical platform integration (information hubs) functions across national boundaries and across the traditional public–private divide. Most of the web giants are established overseas, so that often private actors – voluntarily or compulsorily – transfer data to third countries. Companies do not just cooperate with public authorities but effectively and actively come to play a part in bulk collection and security practices. They identify, select, search, and interpret suspicious elements by means of 'data selectors'. Private actors, in this sense, have become 'security professionals' in their own right.

Systematic government access to private sector data is carried out not only directly via access to private sector databases and networks but also through the cooperation of third parties, such as financial institutions, mobile phone operators, communication providers, and the companies that maintain the available databases or networks.

Personal data originally circulated in the EU for commercial purposes may be transferred by private intermediaries to public authorities, often also overseas, for other purposes, including detection, investigation, and prosecution. The significant blurring of purposes among the different layers of data-gathering – for instance, commercial profiling techniques and security – aims to exploit the 'exchange value' of individuals' fragmented identities, as consumers, suspects of certain crimes, 'good citizens', or 'others'.

In this context, some have argued that the most important shortcoming of the 2016 data protection reform is that it resulted in the adoption of two different instruments, a Regulation and a Directive.[40] This separation is a step backwards regarding the objective envisaged by Article 16 TFEU – which instead promotes a cross-sectoral approach potentially leading to a comprehensive instrument embracing different policy areas (including the AFSJ) in the same way. This is a weakness because the level of protection envisaged by the 2016 Police Data Protection Directive is de facto lower than in the Regulation, as data gathering for law enforcement and national security purposes is mostly exempted from general data protection laws or constitutes an exemption under

[39] V Mitsilegas, 'The Transformation of Privacy in an Era of Pre-emptive Surveillance' (2015) 20 *Tilburg Law Review* 35–57; HE De Busser, 'Privatisation of Information and the Data Protection Reform' in S Gutwirth et al. (eds), *Reloading Data Protection: Multidisciplinary Insights and Contemporary Challenges* (Springer 2013).

[40] P Hustinx, 'EU Data Protection Law: The Review of Directive 95/46/EC and the Proposed General Data Protection Regulation' in M Cremona (ed), *New Technologies and EU Law* (Oxford University Press 2017).

those provisions even at the EU level.[41] Furthermore, what happens in practice mostly depends on terms and conditions in contractual clauses signed by individuals every time they subscribe as clients of service providers and media companies.

A further element of novelty is thus the linkage of separate databases, which increased their separate utility since law enforcement authorities and private companies partially aggregated their data.[42] Such a link between criminal justice data with private data potentially provides numerous insights about individuals. Law enforcement and private companies have therefore embraced the idea of networking and sharing personal information. Law enforcement thus benefits from the growth of private surveillance gathering of information.

The nature and origins of data that are available for security purposes are thus further changing. Public and private data are increasingly mixed. Private data gathering tools play a broader role in security analyses, complementing data from law enforcement authorities' sources.[43] An example is the use of social media analyses tools by the police together with intelligence (e.g., in counter-terrorism matters). It is often not merely the data itself which is valuable but the fact of linking large amounts of data.

Having examined the use of surveillance technologies for preventive and investigative purposes, it would be interesting to focus on the next phase of criminal procedure – that is, the retention and use of information gathered via surveillance technologies for the prosecution during trials for serious crimes, including terrorism. In fact, a huge amount of information is nowadays retained by private companies such as network and service providers, but also by different CCTV operators. The question is under which circumstances such information can be accessed and used by different actors of criminal procedures (police officers, intelligence services, prosecutors, and judges) for the purposes of investigating and prosecuting serious crimes. The retention of data for investigation and prosecution purposes poses the question of the collaboration between public authorities and private companies and what kind of obligations one may impose upon the latter.

7.3 THE TRANSFORMATION OF CORE PRINCIPLES OF CRIMINAL LAW

7.3.1 *Control People to Minimise Risk*

Technology is pivotal in the development of regulatory legislation that seeks to control more and more areas of life.[44]

[41] See Recital no. 19 and art. 2(d), GDPR.

[42] An interesting example are the data sets of the EU-US Passenger Name Records and Terrorism Financing Programs. See R Bellanova and M De Goede, 'The Algorithmic Regulation of Security: An Infrastructural Perspective' (2020) *Regulation and Governance*.

[43] AG Ferguson, *The Rise of Big Data Policing* (NYU Press 2017).

[44] K Brennan-Marquez, 'Big Data Policing and the Redistribution of Anxiety' (2018) 15 *Ohio State Journal of Criminal Law* 487; J Byrne and D Rebovich (2007), *The New Technology of Crime, Law and Social Control* (Criminal Justice Press 2007).

In fact, predictive policing is grounded and further supports a social growing desire to control people to minimise risk.[45] Sociologists such as Ulrich Beck have described the emergence of a 'risk society': industrial society produces a number of serious risks and conflicts – including those connected with terrorism and organised crime – and has thus modified the means and legitimisation of state intervention, putting risks and damage control at the centre of society as a response to the erosion of trust among people.[46]

Along similar lines, Feeley and Simon have described a 'new penology' paradigm (or 'actuarial justice'[47]): a risk management strategy for the administration of criminal justice, aiming at securing at the lowest possible cost a dangerous class of individuals whose rehabilitation is deemed futile and impossible.[48] The focus is on targeting and classifying a suspect group of individuals and making assessments of their likelihood to offend in particular circumstances or when exposed to certain opportunities.

According to David Garland, the economic, technological, and social changes in our society during the past thirty years have reconfigured the response to crime and the sense of criminal justice leading to a 'culture of control' counterbalancing the expansion of personal freedom.[49] In his view, criminal justice policies thus develop from political actors' desire to 'do something' – not necessarily something effective – to assuage public fear, shaped and mobilised as an electoral strategy.

The culture of control together with risk aversion sees technological developments as key enabling factors and is intimately linked to the rise of a surveillance society and the growth of surveillance technologies and infrastructures.

Koops has built upon pre-existing concepts of the culture of control and depicts the current emergence of what he calls 'crime society', which combines risk aversion and surveillance tools, with the preventative and architectural approaches to crime prevention and investigation.[50] Technology supports and facilitates the crucial elements at the basis of a crime society, pushing a further shift towards prevention in the fight against crime.

Finally, the prediction of criminal behaviours is supposed to enable law enforcement authorities to reorganise and manage their presence more efficiently and effectively. However, there is very little evidence as to whether police have, in fact, increased efficiency and improved fairness in daily tasks, and it seems to be very much related to the type of predictive policing under evaluation.

[45] S Leman-Langlois, *Technocrime: Technology, Crime, and Social Control* (Willan Publishing 2008).

[46] U Beck, *Risk Society: Towards a New Modernity* (Sage 1992), 21.

[47] O Gandy, *Race and Cumulative Disadvantage: Engaging the Actuarial Assumption*, The B. Aubrey Fisher Memorial Lecture, University of Utah, 18 October 2007.

[48] MM Feeley and J Simon, 'The New Penology' (1992) 30(4) *Criminology* 449.

[49] D Garland, *The Culture of Control* (Oxford University Press 2001).

[50] Koops (n 12).

7.3.2 *Would Crime-Related Patterns Question Reasonable Suspicion and the Presumption of Innocence?*

The emergence of the 'data-driven society'[51] allows for the mining of both content and metadata, allegedly inferring crime-related patterns and thus enable pre-emption, prevention, or investigation of offences. In the view of law enforcement authorities and policymakers, by running algorithms on a massive amount of data, it is allegedly possible to predict the occurrence of criminal behaviours.[52] In fact, data-driven analysis is different from the traditional statistical method because its aim is not merely testing hypotheses but also to find relevant and unexpected correlations and patterns, which may be relevant for public order and security purposes.[53]

For instance, a computer algorithm can be applied to data from past crimes, including crime types and locations, to forecast in which city areas criminal activities are most likely to develop.

The underlying assumption of predictive policing is that certain aspects of the physical and social environment would encourage acts of wrongdoing. Patters emerging from the data could allow individuals to be identified predictively as suspects because past actions create suspicions about future criminal involvement. Moreover, there seems to be the belief that automated measured could provide better insight than traditional police practices, because of a general faith in predictive accuracy.

Yet a number of limits are inherent in predictive policing. It could be hard to obtain usable and accurate data to integrate into predictive systems of policing.[54] As a consequence, notwithstanding big data perceived objectivity, there is a risk of increased bias in the sampling process. Law enforcement authorities' focus on a certain ethnic group or neighbourhood could instead take to the systematic overrepresentation of those groups and neighbourhoods in data sets, so that the use of a biased sample to train an artificial intelligence system could be misleading. The predictive model could reproduce the same bias which poisoned the original data set.[55] Artificial intelligence predictions could even amplify biases, thus fostering profiling and discrimination patterns. The same could happen with reference to the linkage between law enforcement databases and private companies' data, which could increase errors exponentially, as the gathering of data for commercial purposes is surrounded by less procedural safeguards, thus leading to a diminished

[51] A Pentland, 'The Data-Driven Society', ScientificAmerican.com, October 2013, 79, https://connection.mit.edu/sites/default/files/publication-pdfs/data%20driven%20society%20sci%20amer_0.pdf, accessed 27 July 2020.

[52] H-B Kang, 'Prediction of Crime Occurrence from Multi-modal Data Using Deep Learning' (2017) 12 (4) *PLoS ONE*.

[53] M Hildebrandt, 'Criminal Law and Technology in a Data-Driven Society' in *Oxford Handbook of Criminal Law* (Oxford University Press 2018).

[54] AG Ferguson, *The Rise of Big Data Policing. Surveillance, Race, and the Future of Law Enforcement* (NYU Press 2017).

[55] K Lum and W Isaac, 'To Predict and Serve?' (2016) 13(5) *Significance* 14.

quality of such data.[56] Existing data could be of limited value for predictive policing, possibly resulting in a sort of technology-led version of racial profiling.

Could big data analyses strengthen social stratifications, reproducing and reinforcing the bias that is already present in data sets? Data are often extracted through observations, computations, experiments, and record-keeping. Thus the criteria used for gathering purposes could distort the results of data analyses because of their inherent partiality and selectivity. The bias may over time translate into discrimination and unfair treatment of particular ethnic or societal groups. The link between different data sets and the combined result of big data analyses may then well feed on each other.

Datafication and the interconnection of computing systems which grounds hyper-connectivity is transforming the concept of law, further interlinking it with other disciplines.[57] Moreover, the regulatory framework surrounding the use of big data analytics is underdeveloped if compared with criminal law. Under extreme circumstances, big data analysis could unfortunately lead to judging individuals on the basis of correlations and inferences of what they might do, rather than what they actually have done.[58] The gathering, analysis, and deployment of big data are transforming not only law enforcement activities but also core principles of criminal law, such as reasonable suspicion and the presumption of innocence.

A reasonable suspicion of guilt is a precondition for processing information, which would eventually be used as evidence in court. Reasonable suspicion is, however, not relevant in big data analytics. Instead, in a 'data-driven surveillance society', criminal intent is somehow pre-empted, and this could, at least to a certain extent, erode the preconditions of criminal law in a constitutional democracy – especially when there is little transparency with reference to profiles inferred and matched with subjects' data.[59]

Such major change goes even beyond the notorious 'shift towards prevention' in the fight against crime witnessed during the last decades.[60] First, the boundaries of what is a dangerous behaviour are highly contentious, and problems arise with the assessment of future harm.[61] Second, 'suspicion' has replaced an objective 'reasonable belief' in most cases in order to justify police intervention at an early stage

56 AG Ferguson, 'Big Data and Predictive Reasonable Suspicion' (2015) 163(2) *University of Pennsylvania Law Review* 327.

57 M Hildebrandt, *Smart Technologies and the End(s) of Law: Novel Entanglements of Law and Technology* (Elgar 2015).

58 Yet individuals also make discriminatory choices, and there is no evidence that artificial intelligence systems would necessarily do worse.

59 P Nemitz, 'Constitutional Democracy and Technology in the Age of AI' (2018) 376 *Philosophical Transactions of the Royal Society*.

60 See F Galli, *The Law on Terrorism. The United Kingdom, France and Italy Compared* (Bruylant 2015).

61 See K Sugman Stubbs and F Galli, 'Inchoate Offences. The Sanctioning of an Act Prior to and Irrespective of the Commission of Any Harm' in F Galli and A Weyembergh (eds), *EU Counter-terrorism Offences* (Ed de l'Université Libre de Bruxelles 2011), 291. Child and Hunt concisely point out the lack of justification for the existence of the special part inchoate offences. See J Child and

without the need to envisage evidence-gathering with a view to prosecution.[62] Traditionally, 'reasonable grounds for suspicion' depend on the circumstances in each case. There must be an objective basis for that suspicion based on facts, evidence, and/or intelligence which are relevant to the likelihood of finding an article of a certain kind. Reasonable suspicion should never be supported on the basis of personal factors. It must rely on intelligence or information about an individual or his/her particular behaviour. Facts on which suspicion is based must be specific, articulated, and objective. Suspicion must be related to a criminal activity and not simply to a supposed criminal or group of criminals.[63] The mere description of a suspect, his/her physical appearance, or the fact that the person is known to have a previous conviction cannot alone, or in combination with each other, become factors for searching such individual. In its traditional conception, reasonable suspicion cannot be based on generalisations or stereotypical images of certain groups or categories of people as more likely to be involved in criminal activity. This has, at least partially, changed.

By virtue of the presumption of innocence, the burden of proof in criminal proceedings rests on the prosecutor and demands serious evidence, beyond reasonable doubt, that a criminal activity has been committed. Such presumption presupposes that a person is innocent until proven guilty. By contrast, data-driven pushes law enforcement in the opposite direction. The presumption of innocence comes along with the notion of equality of arms in criminal proceedings, as well as the safeguard of privacy against unwarranted investigative techniques, and with the right to non-discrimination as a way to protect individuals against prejudice and unfair bias.

Are algorithms in their current state amount to 'risk forecasting' rather than actual crime prediction?[64] The identification of the future location of criminal activities could be possible by studying where and why past times patterns have developed over time. However, forecasting the precise identity of future criminals is not evident.

If suspicion based on correlation, instead of evidence, could successfully lead to the identification of areas where crime is likely to be committed (on the basis of property and place-based predictive policing), it might be insufficient to point at the individual who is likely to commit such crime (on the basis of person-focused technology).[65]

A Hunt, 'Risk, Pre-emption, and the Limits of the Criminal Law' in K Doolin et al. (eds), *Whose Criminal Justice? State or Community?* (Waterside Press 2011), 51.

62 Proactive/anticipative criminal investigations have a primary preventive function, combined with evidence gathering for the purpose of an eventual prosecution. See MFH Hirsch Ballin (n 25).

63 Ferguson (n 56).

64 Walter P. Perry and others, *Predictive Policing. The Role of Crime Forecasting in Law Enforcement Operations* (Rand 2013).

65 Ferguson (n 56).

7.3.3 *Preventive Justice*

Predictive policing could be seen as a feature of preventive justice. Policy-making and crime-fighting strategies are increasingly concerned with the prediction and prevention of future risks (in order, at least, to minimise their consequences) rather than the prosecution of past offences.[66] Zedner describes a shift towards a society 'in which the possibility of forestalling risks competes with and even takes precedence over responding to wrongs done',[67] and where 'the post-crime orientation of criminal justice is increasingly overshadowed by the pre-crime logic of security'.[68] Pre-crime is characterised by 'calculation, risk and uncertainty, surveillance, precaution, prudentialism, moral hazard, prevention and, arching over all of these, there is the pursuit of security'.[69] An analogy has been drawn with the precautionary principle developed in environmental law in relation to the duties of public authorities in a context of scientific uncertainty, which cannot be accepted as an excuse for inaction where there is a threat of serious harm.[70]

Although trends certainly existed prior to September 11, the counter-terrorism legislation enacted since then has certainly expanded all previous trends towards anticipating risks. The aim of current counter-terrorism measures is mostly that of a preventive identification, isolation, and control of individuals and groups who are regarded as dangerous and purportedly represent a threat to society.[71] The risk in terms of mass casualties resulting from a terrorist attack is thought to be so high that the traditional due process safeguards are deemed unreasonable or unaffordable and prevention becomes a political imperative.[72]

Current developments, combined with preventive justice, lead to the so-called predictive reasonable suspicion. In a model of preventive justice, and specifically in the context of speculative security,[73] individuals are targets of public authorities' measures; information is gathered irrespective of whether and how it could be used

[66] L Zedner, 'Fixing the Future?' in S Bronnit et al. (eds), *Regulating Deviance* (Hart Publishing 2008).

[67] L Zedner, 'Pre-crime and Post-criminology?' (2007) 11 *Theoretical Criminology* 261.

[68] Ibid., 262.

[69] Ibid.

[70] See E Fisher, 'Precaution, Precaution Everywhere' (2002) 9 *Maastricht Journal of European and Comparative Law* 7. The analogy is made by L Zedner, 'Preventive Justice or Pre-punishment?' (2007) 60 *CLP* 174, 201.

[71] L Amoore and M de Goede (eds), *Risk and the War on Terror* (Routledge 2008); L Amoore, 'Risk before Justice: When the Law Contests Its Own Suspension' (2008) 21(4) *Leiden Journal of International Law* 847; C Aradau and R van Munster, 'Governing Terrorism through Risk: Taking Precautions, (Un)knowing the Future' (2007) 13(1) *European Journal of International Relations* 89; U Beck, 'The Terrorist Threat: World Risk Society Revisited' (2002) 19(4) *Theory, Culture and Society* 39.

[72] A Ashworth and L Zedner, 'Prevention and Criminalization: Justifications and Limits' (2012) 15 *New Crim LR* 542. By contrast, with reference to automated decision-making, see also DK Citron and F Pasquale, 'The Scored Society: Due Process for Automated Prediction Easy' (2014) 89 *Washington Law Review* 1.

[73] See M De Goede, *Speculative Security* (University of Minnesota Press 2012).

to charge the suspect of a criminal offence or use it in criminal proceedings and eventually at trial.

Law enforcement authorities can thus act not only in the absence of harm but even in the absence of suspicion. Thus there is a grey area for the safeguard of rights of individuals who do not yet fall into an existing criminal law category but are already subject to a measure which could lead to criminal law-alike consequences. At the same time, individual rights (e.g., within the realm of private or administrative law) are not fully actionable/enforceable unless a breach has been committed. However, in order for information to become evidence in court, gathering, sharing, and processing should respect criminal procedure standards. This is often at odds with the use of technologies in predictive policing.

7.4 CONCLUDING REMARKS

Law enforcement authorities and intelligence services have already embraced the assumed benefits of big data analyses. It is yet difficult to assess how and to what extent big data are applied to the field of security, irrespective of exploring whether or not their use fosters efficiency or effectiveness. This is also because of secrecy often surrounding law enforcement operations, the experimental nature of new means, and authorities' understandable reluctance to disclose their functioning to public opinion. 'Algorithms are increasingly used in criminal proceedings for evidentiary purposes and for supporting decision-making. In a worrying trend, these tools are still concealed in secrecy and opacity preventing the possibility to understand how their specific output has been generated',[74] argues Palmiotto, addressing the Exodus case,[75] while questioning whether opacity represents a threat to fair trial rights.

However, there is still a great need for an in-depth debate about the appropriateness of using algorithms in machine-learning techniques in law enforcement, and more broadly in criminal justice. In particular, there is a need to assess how the substance of legal protection may be weakened by the use of tools such as algorithms and artificial intelligence.[76]

Moreover, given that big data, automation, and artificial intelligence remain largely under-regulated, the extent to which data-driven surveillance societies could erode core criminal law principles such as reasonable suspicion and the presumption of innocence ultimately depends on the design of the surveillance

[74] F Palmiotto, 'Algorithmic Opacity as a Challenge to the Rights of the Defense', Robotic & AI Law Society, blog post, 6 September 2019 https://ai-laws.org/en/2019/09/algorithmic-opacity-challenge-to-rights-of-the-defense/.

[75] C Anesi et al., 'Exodus, gli affari dietro il malware di stato che spiava gli italiani', Wired, 18 November 2019, www.wired.it/attualita/tech/2019/11/18/exodus-malware-affari-italia/, accessed 27 July 2020.

[76] A Sachoulidou, 'The Transformation of Criminal Law in the Big Data Era: Rethinking Suspects' and Defendants' Rights using the Example of the Right to Be Presumed Innocent', EUI Working Paper, MWP, RSN 2019/35.

infrastructures. There is thus a need to develop a regulatory framework adding new layers of protection to fundamental rights and safeguards against their erroneous use.

There are some improvements which could be made to increase the procedural fairness of these tools. First, more transparent algorithms could increase their trustworthiness. Second, if designed to remove pre-existing biases in the original data sets, algorithms could also improve their neutrality. Third, when algorithms are in use profiling and (semi-)automated decision-making should be regulated more tightly.[77]

Most importantly, the ultimate decision should always be human. The careful implementations by humans involved in the process could certainly mitigate the vulnerabilities of automated systems. It must remain for a human decision maker or law enforcement authority to decide how to act on any computationally suggested result.

For instance, correlation must not be erroneously interpreted as a causality link, so that 'suspicion' is not confused with 'evidence'. Predictions made by big data analysis must never be sufficient for the purpose of initiating a criminal investigation.

Trust in algorithms both in fully and partially automated decision processes is grounded on their supposed infallibility. There is a tendency (as has been the case in the use of experts in criminal cases[78]) among law enforcement authorities to blindly follow them. Rubberstamping algorithms' advice could also become a trick to minimise the responsibility of decision maker.

Algorithm-based decisions require time, context, and skills to be adequate in each individual case. Yet, given the complexity of algorithms, judges and law enforcement authorities can at times hardly understand the underlying calculus, and it is thus difficult to question their accuracy, effectiveness, or fairness. This is linked with the transparency paradox surrounding the use of big data:[79] citizens become increasingly transparent to government, while the profiles, algorithms, and methods used by government organisations are hardly transparent or comprehensible to citizens.[80] This results in a shift in the balance of power between state and citizen, in favour of the state.[81]

77 D Spiegelhalter, 'Should We Trust Algorithms?', *Harvard Data Science Review*, https://hdsr.mitpress.mit.edu/pub/56lnenzj/release/1, accessed 27 July 2020.

78 PW Grimm, 'Challenges Facing Judges Regarding Expert Evidence in Criminal Cases' (2018) 86(4) *Fordham Law Review* 1601.

79 N Richards and H King, 'Three Paradoxes of Big Data' (2013) 66 *Stanford Law Review Online* 41, http://ssrn.com/abstract=2325537.

80 According to Palmiotto, there is a risk to transform the criminal justice system in a 'system of machinery' where individuals only what machines are yet uncapable of pursuing. See F Palmiotto, 'The Blackbox on Trial. The Impact of Algorithmic Opacity on Fair Trial Right in Criminal Proceedings' in M Ebers and M Cantero-Gamito (eds), *Algorithmic Governance and Governance of Algorithms* (Springer 2020).

81 See F Pasquale, *The Black Box Society* (Harvard University Press 2015); S Zuboff, *The Age of Surveillance Capitalism* (Public Affairs 2019).

PART II

Regulation and Policy

8

Algorithms and Regulation

Amnon Reichman and Giovanni Sartor

8.1 SETTING UP THE FIELD

Algorithms – generally understood as sequences of precise instruction unambiguously specifying how to execute a task or solve a problem – are such a natural ingredient of regulation that some may wonder whether regulation could even be understood without recognising its algorithmic features, and without realising algorithms as a prime subject for regulation. In terms of the algorithmic features of regulation, somewhat simplistically and without suggesting in any way that the algorithmic language captures regulation in its entirety – far from it – algorithms are relevant to the three dimensions of regulation: the regulatory process, the modalities of regulation, and the regulatory approaches (or attitudes). By the regulatory process, we refer to the process that, stylistically, commences with political and economic pressures to find a solution to a certain problem and continues with the formation of policy goals, data gathering, and the mapping of possible regulatory responses to achieve these goals (which ought to include the sub-processes of regulatory impact assessment upon choosing the preferred measure). The chosen measures are translated into regulatory norms and implemented (or enforced), resulting, if all went well, with some improvement of the conditions related to the initial social problem (as can be analysed by a back-end regulatory impact assessment). By regulatory modalities, we mean the set of regulatory measures available to the state (or, more accurately, to state agencies acting as regulators): regulation through (and of) information, permits and licensing, civil, administrative and criminal liability, taxes and subsidies, or insurance schemes. By regulatory approaches, or attitudes, we mean the top-down command and control attitude, performance-based regulation, and the managerial approach, with the latter two also including co-regulation or private regulation.

Algorithms are relevant to all three dimensions of regulation, as they may assist most, if not all, stages of the regulatory process, may inform or even be a component of the regulatory modalities, and may similarly inform and be integrated into the regulatory attitudes. Conversely, algorithms may be the subject matter of regulation.

Their development and deployment may be considered (as part of) the social problem triggering the regulatory process; they may then enlist one or more of the regulatory modalities to address the structure of incentives that generate harmful use of algorithms, and stand at the focal point of the policy question regarding which regulatory attitude fits best to address the host of risks associated with algorithms, and in particular with machine learning and AI.

In the following section, we will first introduce a general concept of an algorithm, which then can be applied both to human action and to computer systems. On this basis, we shall consider the jurisprudential debate on prospects and limits of 'algorithmicisation' or 'mechanisation' of law and government.

We shall then address computer algorithms and consider the manner in which they have progressively entered government. We shall focus on artificial intelligence (AI) and machine learning, and address the advantages of such technologies, but also the concerns their adoption raises. The motivation of this analysis is to shed an important light on the relationship between the state and AI, and on the need to consider regulating the state's recourse to algorithms (including via attention to the technology itself, usually referred to as 'regulation by design').

8.2 ALGORITHMIC LAW BEFORE COMPUTERS

An algorithm, in the most general sense, is a sequence of instructions (a plan of action, or a recipe) that univocally specifies the steps to be accomplished to achieve a goal, as well as the order over such steps.[1] It must be directed to executors that are able to exactly perform each of the steps indicated in the algorithm, in their prescribed order. The order may include structures such as sequence (first do A, then B), conditional forks (if A is true then do to B, otherwise do C), or repetitions (continue doing B until A is true).

The execution of an algorithm should not require a fresh cognitive effort by the executor, when the latter is provided with a suitable input: every action prescribed by the algorithm should either be a basic action in the repertoire of the executor (such as pushing a button or adding two digits) or consist of the implementation of an algorithm already available to the executor. Algorithms, in this very broad sense, may be directed to humans as well as to automated systems.

Precise and univocal instructions to use hardware or software devices, install appliances, get to locations, or make mathematical calculations, can be viewed as algorithms. There is, however, a special connection between algorithms and computations. The term 'algorithm' in fact derives from the name of a Persian scholar, Muhammad ibn Mūsā al-Khwārizmī, who published in the 9th century a foundational text of algebra, providing rules for solving equations, with practical applications, in particular in the division of inheritance. The idea of a mathematical

[1] See David Harel and Yishai Feldman, *Algorithmics: The Spirit of Computing* (Addison-Wesley, 2004).

algorithm however is much earlier. For instance, the Greek mathematician Euclid is credited with having invented, in the 4th century BC, an algorithm for finding the greatest common divisor between two integer numbers.

In any case, algorithms, as plans meant to have a 'mechanical' implementation (i.e., whose execution does not require a fresh cognitive effort nor the exercise of discretion), should always lead to the same outcome for the same input, whenever they are entrusted to a competent executor. This idea is often expressed by saying that algorithms are deterministic or repeatable (though, as we shall see, some algorithms go beyond this idea; i.e., they also include elements of randomness).

The idea that at least some state activities could be governed by algorithms in a broad sense – unambiguous and repeatable impersonal procedures, leading to predictable decisions according to precise rules – was viewed as a characteristic feature of modern bureaucracies by the social theorist Max Weber according to whom: 'The modem capitalist enterprise rests primarily on calculation and presupposes a legal and administrative system, whose functioning can be rationally predicted, at least in principle, by virtue of its fixed general norms, just like the expected performance of a machine.'[2]

The same Weber, however, also observed an opposite tendency in contemporary administration and adjudication, namely, the pressure toward 'material justice', which evades air-tight codification because it is concerned with the effective pursuit of interests and values. Approaching the exercise of administrative and judicial power as a goal-directed activity, meant to satisfy certain interests or values rather than satisfying exact application of rules, involves, to some extent, an original cognitive effort by decision makers. Some discretion in the identification of the interests or values to be pursued, as well as choices regarding the means to achieve them, cannot be avoided. This cognitive presence, in turn, is a site of agency, representing substantive, or material, moral reasoning (and, it seems, not only rationality but also empathy, and perhaps other virtuous sensibilities and emotions). We will return to this matter when we further discuss machine-generated (i.e., learnt) algorithms (sometimes referred to as AI).

Focusing on adjudication – a key function of the state in exercising its official power – the ideal of a mechanical (or algorithmic, as we say today) approach has most often been the target of critique. Adjudication in many cases cannot, and indeed should not, be reduced to the application of precisely defined rules. The very term 'mechanical jurisprudence' was introduced, more than a century ago, by US legal theorist Roscoe Pound,[3] in a critical essay where he argued that judicial decision-making should not consist of the 'automatic' application of precedents' rulings, legislative rules, and legal conceptions. Pound stated that such an approach,

[2] Max Weber, *Economy and Society: An Outline of Interpretive Sociology* (University of California Press, 1978), 1194.

[3] Roscoe Pound, 'Mechanical Jurisprudence' (1908) 8 *Columbia Law Review* 605–623.

to the extent that it is viable, would have the law depart from shared ideas of correctness and fair play, as understood by citizens, and would lead to the law being 'petrified', and more generally unable to meet new challenges emerging in society, to 'respond to the needs of present-day life'.

A similar criticism against a 'mechanical' application of the law can be found via a famous US justice at the time, Oliver Wendell Holmes, who made two related somewhat polemical claims: the claim that 'general propositions do not decide concrete cases'[4] and the claim that 'the life of the law has not been logic: it has been experience'.[5] These two claims clarify that Holmes is attacking the view that the application of the law is a mere matter of deductive inference, namely, a reasoning process that only derives, relative to the facts of a case, what is entailed by pre-existing general premises and concepts. Holmes argued that, on the contrary, the application of law should be geared toward the social good, which requires officers, and in particular judges 'to consider and weigh the ends of legislation, the means of attaining them, and the cost'.[6] However, if considered more carefully, Holmes's perspective while rejecting the algorithmic application of the law (premised on mechanical jurisprudence), as it requires decision makers to obtain knowledge that is not included in legal sources, still adopts a restrictive approach to legal decision-making (premised on optimising a given object, based on past practice). Following this idea, the interpretation and application of the law only require fresh knowledge of social facts – that is, a better understanding (data and analysis) of experience, a clear formulation of the ends of legislation, and a good formula for assessing costs of applying the means towards these ends. It does not involve a creative and critical normative assessment of the goals being pursued and the side-effects of their pursuit, in the given social contexts.

A number of different currents in legal thinking have developed providing descriptive and prescriptive arguments that judges do not and indeed should not apply the law mechanically; they do, and should, rather aim to achieve values, pertaining to the parties of a case and to society at large. We cannot here do justice to such approaches; we can just mention, as relevant examples, the following: legal realism, sociological jurisprudence, interest-jurisprudence, value jurisprudence, free law, critical legal studies, and so forth. According to some of these approaches, the objections against rigid or static approaches to the law have gone beyond the advocacy of teleological reasoning as opposed to the application of given rules and concepts. Rather, it has been argued that legal problem solving, properly understood, goes beyond optimising the achievement of given goals, especially when such goals are limited to a single purpose such as economic efficiency or even welfare.[7] On the contrary, legal reasoning also includes the reflective assessment

[4] *Lochner* v. *New York*, 198 U.S. 45, 76 (1905) (Holmes, J., dissenting).
[5] Oliver Wendell Holmes, *The Common Law* (1881), 1.
[6] Oliver Wendell Holmes, 'The Path of the Law' (1896–1897) 10 *Harvard Law Review* 474.
[7] See Louis Kaplow and Steven Shavell, *Fairness versus Welfare* (Harvard University Press, 2002).

and balancing, of multiple social and individual values, which often presuppose moral or political evaluations and processes of communication and justification, inspired by deliberative ideas of integrity and meaningful belonging in a community.[8]

The view that the application of the law is not algorithmic or deductive has also been endorsed by authors that argued that the (private) law should not serve political aims, but rather focus on its 'forms', namely, on the internal coherence of its concepts, and its ability to reflect the nature of legal relations and the underlying theory of justice.[9]

A criticism of mechanical approaches to adjudication (and administrative decision-making) can also be found in analytical legal theorists. Hans Kelsen made the radical claim that legal norms never determine a single outcome for individual cases: they only provide a frame for particular decisions; their application requires discretion since 'every law-applying act is only partly determined by law and partly undetermined'.[10] For Kelsen, the relationship between a rule and the application in a particular case is always a site for judgment. More cautiously, H. L. A. Hart affirmed that it is impossible to make 'rules the application of which to particular cases never calls for a further choice'. Enacted laws are meant to address the prototypical cases that the legislator had envisaged; un-envisaged cases may require a different solution that has to be found outside of the legislative 'algorithm', by exercising choice or discretion, that is, by 'choosing between the competing interests in the way which best satisfies us'.[11] For Hart, then, cases that fall in greyer areas (relative to the core paradigmatic cases envisioned by the norm-giver) are sites of greater discretion. The question then becomes how to differentiate between the core and the penumbra – whether based solely on a conventional understanding of the words used by the rule, or whether also based on the purpose of the rule. A teleological approach may be needed since legal rules are performative (i.e., require action by those governed by the rules), so that the purpose of a rule may inform its meaning. In the latter case, applying the rule requires discretion regarding which application would further the purpose, and whether exceptions exist (either because the conventional meaning may disrupt the purpose or because a non-conventional meaning would further the purpose better).

This brief survey of leading approaches to jurisprudence demonstrates that the application of law is not merely algorithmic, but rather relies upon the discretion of the decision maker, whenever the norms (embedded in legislation or case-law) do not dictate a single outcome to a decisional problem. It is true that some authors have strongly reiterated the view that in order to effectively direct and coordinate the

8 Different, and even opposed, approaches to legal reasoning share this fundamental idea; see Ronald M. Dworkin, *Law's Empire* (Kermode, Fontana Press, 1986); Duncan Kennedy, *A Critique of Adjudication* (Harvard University Press, 1997).

9 Ernest Weinrib, *The Idea of Private Law* (Harvard University Press, 1995). For expansion of this theme, see Amnon Reichman, *Formal Legal Pluralism* (manuscript with authors).

10 Hans Kelsen, *The Pure Theory of Law* (University of California Press, 1967), 349.

11 Herbert L. A. Hart, *The Concept of Law*, 2nd ed. (Oxford University Press, [1961] 1994).

action and the expectations of citizens and officers, the law should provide clear if-then rules specifying the link between operative facts and corresponding rights and obligations (and other legal effects).[12] However, there is an apparent consensus that legal decision-making cannot be fully driven by rules (or algorithms) alone; it calls for teleological and value-based reasoning and for the assessment of uncertain factual situations, with regard to the specific cases at stake.[13] Other authors have observed that even when the application of a general norm to given facts is needed, matching the general terms in the norm to the features of specific factual situations involves a 'concretisation' of the norm itself, namely, it requires enriching the indeterminate content of such terms, as needed to determine whether they apply or not to the given facts.[14] Applying the law, therefore, requires that the decision-maker engages in a genuine cognitive effort. This effort may involve interlinked epistemic and practical inquiries: determining the relevant facts and correlation between them, assessing accordingly the impacts that alternative choices may have on relevant interests and values, and determining accordingly which choice is preferable, all things considered. Discretion may also include honing the contours of the values or interests to be pursued, as well as their relative importance. This broad idea of discretion also includes proportionality assessments under constitutional law, which aim to determine whether an infringement of constitutional rights is justified by pursuing non-inferior advantages with regard to other constitutional rights and values, and by ensuring that no less- infringing choice provides a better trade-off.[15]

So far, we have focused on algorithmic approaches to judicial decision-making, which usually involves disputes about the facts of a case or about the interpretation of the applicable legal norms, so that reasoned choices are needed to come to a definite outcome. But legal decisions, on a daily basis, are entered not only – in fact, not predominantly – by judges. Rather, public agencies (sometimes referred to as 'administrative' or 'bureaucratic' agencies) apply the law routinely, on a large scale. In some domains, such as tax and social security, a complex set of rules, often involving calculations, is designed to minimise discretion and therefore appears to be amenable to 'algorithmic' application (even before the computerisation of public administration). Even though controversies are not to be excluded in the application of such regulations, often the facts (i.e., data) are available to the agency per each case (usually as a result of rather precise rules governing the submission of such

[12] See, for instance, Niklas Luhmann, 'Der Politische Code' (1974) 21(3) *Zeitschrift Für Politik* 353; Frederick Schauer, *Playing by the Rules: A Philosophical Examination of Rule-Based Decision-Making in Law and Life* (Clarendon Press, 1991). For the comparative assessment of rules and standards in law, see Louis Kaplow, 'Rules versus Standards: An Economic Analysis' (1992) 42 *Duke Law Journal* 557.

[13] On legal argumentation in interpretation, see recently Douglas Walton, Fabrizio Macagno, and Giovanni Sartor, *Statutory Interpretation. Pragmatics and Argumentation* (Cambridge University Press, 2021).

[14] Karl Larenz and Claus-Wilhelm Canaris, *Methodenlehre der Rechtswissenschaft* (Springer-Lehrbuch, 1995), 1.3.c

[15] On proportionality, see Aharon Barak, *Proportionality* (Cambridge University Press, 2012).

data), to which precise rules can then be applied, to provide definite outcomes that in standard cases will withstand challenge (if the rules are applied correctly).

In these domains too, however, fully eliminating discretion may undermine the purpose of the scheme and thus not only be counter-productive but also potentially raise legal validity concerns, to the extent the legal system includes more general legal principles according to which particular rules incompatible with the purpose of the statutes (or the values of the constitution) are subject to challenge. More specifically, a tension may emerge on occasion between the strict application of rules and a call, based on the purposes of the empowering statute (or on more general legal principles and values), to take into account unenumerated particular circumstances of individual cases. For instance, in social security, there may be a tension between taking into account the conditions of need of benefit claimants and applying a law that appears prima-facie not to include such claimants.

More generally, we may observe that algorithms – whether computerised or not – are less applicable when the legal terrain is not paved fully by rules but is interspersed with standards, which by definition are more abstract and thus less amenable to codification based on the clear meaning of the language (more on that in Section 8.10). Moreover, analytically, algorithms are less applicable when more than one norm applies (without a clear binary rule on which norm trumps in case of potential clashes). This is often the case, as various rules on different levels of abstraction (including, as mentioned, standards) may apply to a given situation. Lastly, it should be noted that the debate on mechanical application of the law has thus far assumed a rather clear distinction between the application of a legal norm and the generation (or enactment) of the norm. At least in common law jurisdictions, this distinction collapses, as application of norms (precedents or statutes) is premised on interpretation, which may lead to refining the existing doctrine or establishing a novel doctrine. Norm-generation is even less amenable to algorithmicising, as it is difficult (for humans) to design rules that optimise this process, given the value-laden nature of generating legal norms.

The general conclusion we can derive from this debate is that the application of the law by humans is governed by algorithmic instructions only to a limited extent. Instructions given to humans concern the substance of the activities to be performed (e.g., the legal and other rules to be complied with and implemented, the quantities to be calculated, the goals to be aimed at, in a certain judicial or administrative context). They do not address the general cognitive functions that have to be deployed in executing such activities, such as understanding and generating language, visualising objects and situations, determining natural and social correlations and causes, and understanding social meaning. In particular, the formation and application of the law requires engaging with facts, norms, and values in multiple ways that evade capture by human-directed algorithmic instructions. Consider the following: determining what facts have happened on the basis of evidence and narratives; ascribing psychological attitudes, interests, and motivations to individuals and groups on the basis of behavioural clues; matching facts and states of mind against abstract rules; assessing the impacts of alternative interpretations/applications of such rules; making analogies; choosing means to achieve goals and values in new settings; determining the contours of such goals and values; quantifying the extent to which they may be promoted or demoted by alternative choices; assessing possible trade-offs. Even when officers are provided with plans to achieve a task, such plans include high-level instructions, the implementation of which by the competent officers requires human cognitive activities, such as those listed previously, which are not performed by implementing handed-down algorithmic commands. Such activities pertain to the natural endowment of the human mind, enhanced through education and experience, and complemented with the intelligent use of various techniques for analysis and calculations (e.g., methods for general and legal argumentation, statistics, cost-benefit analysis, multicriteria decision-making, optimisation, etc.). They result from the unconscious working of the neural circuitry of our brain, rather than from the implementation of a pre-existing set of algorithmic instructions, though qualitative and quantitative models can also be used in combination with intuition, to analyse data, direct performance, detect mistakes, and so forth.

But the question remains: does the problem lie with algorithms, in the sense that algorithms are inherently unsuited for tasks involving learning or creativity, or with humans, in the sense that the human condition (the way we acquire and process information, based on our natural endowment) is incompatible with engaging in such tasks by following algorithmic instructions? Put differently: is it the case that no set of algorithmic instructions, for any kind of executor, can specify how to execute such tasks, or rather that humans are unable to engage with such tasks by diligently executing algorithmic specifications given to them, rather than by relying on their cognitive competence?

A useful indication in this regard comes from the psychologist David Kahneman, who distinguishes two aspects of the human mind:

- System 1 operates automatically (i.e., without the need of a conscious choice and control) and quickly, with little or no effort and no sense of voluntary control.
- System 2 allocates attention to the effortful mental activities that demand it, including complex computations.[16]

If following algorithmic instructions for humans requires exploiting the limited capacities of system 2 (or in any case the limited human capacity to learn, store and execute algorithms), then the human capacity for following algorithmic instructions is easily overloaded, and performance tends to degrade, also with regard to tasks that can be effortlessly performed when delegated to system 1. Therefore, some of the

[16] Daniel Kahneman, *Thinking: Fast and Slow* (Allen Lane, 2011).

tasks that system 1 does automatically – those tasks that involve perception, creativity, and choice – cannot be performed, at the human level, by implementing algorithmic instructions handed in to a human executor. However, this does not mean, in principle, that such instructions cannot be provided for execution to a machine, or to a set of high-speed interconnected machines.[17]

As we shall see in the following sections, machines can indeed be provided with algorithmic specifications (computer programs), the execution of which enables such machines to learn, in particular by extracting knowledge from vast data sets. This learned knowledge is then embedded in algorithmic models that are then used for predictions (and even decisions). As machines can learn by implementing algorithmic instructions, contrary to humans, the algorithmic performance of state functions though machines could expand beyond what is algorithmically possible to humans. Algorithms for learning can provide machines with the ability to adapt their algorithmic models to complex and dynamic circumstances, predict the outcome of alternative courses of action, adjust such predictions based on new evidence, and act accordingly.

Nevertheless, this does not mean that all tasks requiring a fresh cognitive effort by their executors can be successfully performed in this way today or in the near (or even mid-range) future; some can, and others cannot. We will address such issues in the following sections, as we turn our attention to state activities and the possible integration of algorithms into the apparatus of state agencies.

8.3 COMPUTER ALGORITHMS BEFORE AI

In the previous section, we considered the possibility of adopting an 'algorithmic approach' toward human activities concerned with the formation and application of the law, and more generally to state functions concerned with the administration of official functions. We have observed that such an algorithmic approach to decision-making within government existed much before the introduction of computers, but that it had a limited application. In this section, we consider the changes that have taken place following the automation of the execution of algorithms within government with the assistance of computer systems. Before moving into that, we need to discuss the nature of computer algorithms. Computer algorithms correspond to the general notion of an algorithm introduced previously, with the proviso that since such algorithms are directed to a computer system, the basic actions they include must consist of instructions that can be executed by such a system.

To make an algorithm executable by a computer, it must be expressed in a programming language, namely, in language that provides for a repertoire of exactly defined basic actions – each of which has a clear and univocal operational

[17] This idea was developed by Marvin Minsky, who sees mind as a 'society' resulting from the interaction of simpler non-intelligent modules doing different kinds of computations; see Marvin Minsky, *The Society of Mind* (Simon and Schuster, 1988).

meaning – and for a precise syntax to combine such actions. Different programming languages exist, which have been used at different times and are still used for different purposes. In every case, however, the instructions of all such languages are translated into operations to be performed by the computer hardware, namely, in arithmetical operations over binary numbers. This translation is performed by software programs that are called compilers or interpreters. The automated execution of algorithms has much in common with the human execution of algorithms, when seen at a micro-level (i.e., at the level of single steps and combinations of them). This analogy, however, becomes more and more tenuous when we move to the macro level of complex algorithms, executed at super-high speed and interacting with one another.

The variety of algorithms (computer programs) which are and have been used within public administrations for different functions is amazingly vast. However, it may be possible to distinguish three key phases: a computer revolution, an Internet revolution, and finally an AI revolution, each of which has brought about a qualitative change in state activities.

The computer revolution consisted in the use of computers to perform what could be taken as routine tasks within existing state procedures, typically for making mathematical calculations, storing, retrieving data, and processing data. The history of computing is indeed, from its very beginning, part of the history of the modern states. Many of the first computers or proto-computers were built in connection with public activities, in particular in relation to warfare, such as decoding encrypted messages (e.g., the Colossus, developed in the UK in 1942) and computing ballistic trajectories (e.g., Harvard Mark I and Eniac in the US). Other state tasks to be conferred to computers were concerned with censuses (IBM was born out of the company that automated the processing of population data before computers were available) and the related statistics, as well as with scientific and military research (e.g., for space missions).

However, it was the use of computers for keeping vast sets of data (databases), and the retrieval and processing of the data, that really made a difference in more common governmental operations. Databases were created in all domains of public action (population, taxation, industries, health, criminal data, etc.), and these data sets and the calculations based on them were used to support the corresponding administrative activities. This led to a deep change in the governmental information systems, namely, in those socio-technical structures – comprised of human agents, technologies, and organisational norms – that are tasked with providing information to governments. The ongoing collecting, storing, and processing of data were thus integrated into the operational logic of the modern state (characterised by providing basic services and regulating the industry as well as the provision of these services). In a few decades, states have moved from relying on human information systems, based on paper records created and processed by humans, to hybrid information systems in which humans interact with computer systems. Multiple computer systems have been deployed in the public sphere to support an increasing range of administrative tasks, from taxation, to social security, to accounting, to the management of contracts, to the administration of courts and the management of proceedings[18]. As of the 1980s, personal computers entered all public administrations, providing very popular and widespread functions as text processing and spreadsheets, which increased productivity and facilitated digitisation. However, this technological advance did not, in and of itself, change the fundamental division of tasks between humans and automated devices, computers being limited to routine tasks supporting human action (and providing data to humans).[19]

The emergence of networks, culminating with the Internet (but comprising of other networks as well), brought a fundamental change in the existing framework, as it integrated computational power with high-speed communications, enabling an unprecedented flow of electronic data. Such flow takes place between different government sections and agencies, but also between government and citizens and private organisations (and of course within the private sphere itself). Even though the private sector was the driving force in the development of the Internet, it would be a mistake to ignore the significant role of the government and the deep impact of digitised networks for the manner in which public institutions go about their business. Recall that the initial thrust for the Internet was generated by the Defence Advanced Research Projects (DARPA) of the US government. The security establishment has not withdrawn from this realm ever since (although its activities remain mostly behind the scenes, until revealed by whistle-blowers, such as Snowden). Focusing on the civil and administrative facets of modern governments, and in particular on the tools of government in the digital era, Hood and Margetts observed that all different modalities through which the government may exercise influence on society were deeply modified by the use of computers and telecommunication. They distinguish the four basic resources which the government can use to obtain information from and make an impact on the world: nodality (being at the centre of societal communication channels), authority (having legal powers), treasure (having money and other exchangeable properties), and organisation (having administrative structures at their service). They note that in the Internet era, the flow of information from government to society has increased due to the ease of communications and the availability of platforms for posting mass amounts of information online.

Moreover, and perhaps more importantly, the provision of public services through computer systems has enabled the automated collection of digital information as well as the generation of automated messages (e.g., pre-compiled tax forms, notices

18 Amnon Reichman, Yair Sagy, and Shlomi Balaban, 'From a Panacea to a Panopticon: The Use and Misuse of Technology in the Regulation of Judges' (2020) 71 *Hastings Law Review* 589.

19 For an account of the early evaluation of the use of ICT in public administration, see United Nations, 'Government Information Systems: A Guide to Effective Use of Information Technology in the Public Sector of Developing Countries', Tech. Report ST/TCD/SER.E/28, 1995. For subsequent developments, see Christopher C. Hood and Helen Z. Margetts, *The Tools of Government in the Digital Age* (Palgrave, 2007).

about sanctions, deadlines, or the availability of benefits) in response to queries. The exercise of authority has also changed in the Internet age, as the increased possession of digital information about citizens enables states to automatically detect certain unlawful or potentially unlawful behaviour (e.g., about tax or traffic violations) and trigger corresponding responses. Tools to collect and filter information offline and online enable new forms of surveillance and control. Regarding the treasury, payment by and by the government has increasingly moved to electronic transfers. Moreover, the availability of electronic data and the automation of related computation has facilitated the determination of entitlements (e.g., to tax credits or benefits) or has allowed for automated distinctions in ticketing (e.g., automatically sanctioning traffic violations, or charging for transportation fees according to time of the day or age of the passenger).

Finally, the way in which governmental organisations work has also evolved. Not only the internal functioning of such organisations relies on networked and computerised infrastructures, but digital technologies are widely used by governmental agencies and services to collect and process information posted online (e.g., intercept telecommunications, analyse Internet content), as well as deploying other networked sensors (e.g., street cameras, satellites and other tools to monitor borders, the environment, and transfers of goods and funds).

To sum up this point, we may say that in the Internet era the internal operation of the state machinery (in particular, the bureaucracy), and the relation between government and civil society is often mediated by algorithms. However, this major development, in which considerable segments of the daily activities of the government are exercised through computer networks (i.e., algorithms), is primarily confined to routine activities, often involving calculations (e.g., the determination of taxes and benefits, given all the relevant data). This idea is challenged by the third wave of algorithmic government, still underway: the emergence of AI, to which we now turn.

8.4 ALGORITHMS AND AI

The concept of AI covers a diverse set of technologies that are able to perform tasks that require intelligence (without committing to the idea that machine intelligence is 'real' intelligence), or at least tasks that 'require intelligence if performed by people'.[20] AI systems include and possibly integrate different aspects of cognition, such as perception, communication (language), reasoning, learning, and the ability to move and act in physical and virtual environments.

While AI has been around for a few decades – in 1950 Alan Turing pioneered the idea of machine intelligence,[21] and in 1956 a foundational conference took place in

[20] Raymond Kurzweil, *The Age of Spiritual Machines* (Orion, 1990), 14. On the notion of artificial intelligence, see Stuart J. Russell and Peter Norvig, *Artificial Intelligence: A Modern Approach*, 3rd ed. (Pearson, 2016), section 1.1.

[21] Alan M. Turing, 'Computer Machinery and Intelligence' (1950) 59 *Mind* 433–460.

Dartmouth, with the participation of leading scientists[22] – only recently is AI rising to play a dominant role in governments, following and complementing AI successes in the private sector. In fact, an array of successful AI applications have been built which have already entered the economy, and are thus used by corporations and governments alike: voice, image, and face recognition; automated translation; document analysis; question-answering; high-speed trading; industrial robotics; management of logistics and utilities; and so forth. AI-based simulators are often deployed as part of training exercises. The security establishment, it has been reported, has also developed AI systems for analysing threats, following the 9/11 attacks. We are now witnessing the emergence of autonomous vehicles, and soon autonomous unmanned flying vehicles may join. In fact, in very few sectors AI is not playing a role, as a component of the provision of services or the regulation of society, in the application and enforcement segments or the norm-generation stages.

The huge success of AI in recent years is linked to a change in the leading paradigm in AI research and development. Until a few decades ago, it was generally assumed that in order to develop an intelligent system, humans had to provide a formal representation of the relevant knowledge (usually expressed through a combination of rules and concepts), coupled with algorithms making inferences out of such knowledge. Different logical formalisms (rule languages, classical logic, modal and descriptive logics, formal argumentation, etc.) and computable models for inferential processes (deductive, defeasible, inductive, probabilistic, case-based, etc.) have been developed and applied automatically.[23] Expert systems – like computer systems including vast domain-specific knowledge bases, for example, in medicine, law, or engineering, coupled with inferential engines – gave rise to high expectations about their ability to reason and answer users' queries. The structure for expert systems is represented in Figure 8.1. Note that humans appear both as users of the system and as creators of the system's knowledge base (experts, possibly helped by knowledge engineers).

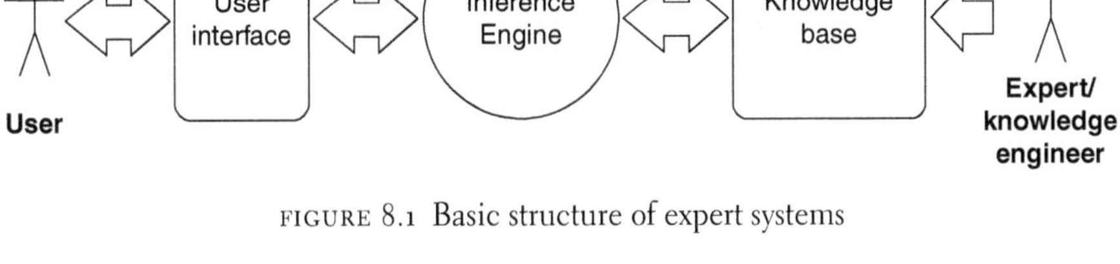

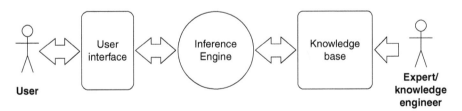

FIGURE 8.1 Basic structure of expert systems

[22] For the history of AI, see Nils J. Nilsson, *The Quest for Artificial Intelligence* (Cambridge University Press, 2010).

[23] Frank Van Harmelen et al., *Handbook of Knowledge Representation* (Elsevier, 2008).

Unfortunately, such systems were often unsuccessful or only limitedly successful: they could only provide incomplete answers, were unable to address the peculiarities of individual cases, and required persistent and costly efforts to broaden and update their knowledge bases. In particular, expert-system developers had to face the so-called *knowledge representation bottleneck:* in order to build a successful application, the required information – including tacit and common-sense knowledge – had to be represented in advance using formalised languages. This proved to be very difficult and, in many cases, impractical or impossible.

In general, only in some restricted domains have logical models led to successful application. In the legal domain, logical models of great theoretical interest have been developed – dealing, for example, with arguments,[24] norms, and precedents[25] – and some expert systems have been successful in legal and administrative practice, in particular in dealing with tax and social security regulations. However, these studies and applications have not fundamentally transformed the legal system and the application of the law. The use of expert systems has remained, in the application of legal norms, and more generally within governmental activity, confined to those routing tasks where other computer tools were already in use.

It may be useful to consider the connection between algorithms and expert systems. The 'algorithm' in a broad sense, of such systems, includes two components: the inferential engine and the knowledge base. Both have to be created, in all their details, by humans, and may be changed only by human intervention, usually to correct/expand the knowledge base. Thus the capacity of such systems to adequately address any new cases or issues depends on how well their human creators have been able to capture all relevant information, and anticipate how it might be used in possible cases. It is true that such systems can store many more rules than a human can remember and process them at high speed, but still humans must not only provide all such rules but also be able to understand their interactions, to maintain coherence in the system.

AI has made an impressive leap forward since it began to focus on the application of machine learning to mass amounts of data. This has led to a number of successful applications in many sectors – ranging from automated translation to industrial optimisation, marketing, robotic visions, movement control, and so forth – and some of these applications already have substantial economic and social impacts. In machine learning approaches, machines are provided with learning methods, rather than (or in addition to) formalised knowledge. Using such methods, computers can automatically learn how to effectively accomplish their tasks by extracting/inferring relevant information from their input data, in order to reach an optimised end.

24 Henry Prakken and Giovanni Sartor, 'Law and Logic: A Review from an Argumentation Perspective' (2015) 227 *Artificial Intelligence* 214.

25 Kevin D. Ashley, *Artificial Intelligence and Legal Analytics: New Tools for Law Practice in the Digital Age* (Cambridge University Press, 2017).

More precisely, in approaches based on machine learning, the input data provided to the system is used to build a *predictive model*. This model embeds knowledge extracted from the input data – that is, it consists of a structure that embeds generalisations over the data, so that it can be used to provide responses to new cases. As we shall see such responses are usually called 'predictions'. Different approaches exist, to construct such a model. For instance, the model may consist of one or more decision trees (i.e., combinations of choices), based on the features that a case may possess, leading to corresponding responses. Alternatively, it can consist of a set of rules, obtained through induction, which expresses connections between combinations of features and related responses. Or it can consist of a neural network, which captures the relation between case features and responses through a set of nodes (called neurons) and weighted connections between them. Under some approaches, the system's responses can be evaluated, and based on this evaluation the system can self-update. By going through this process again (and again), optimisation is approximated.

8.5 APPROACHES TO MACHINE LEARNING

Three main approaches to machine learning are usually distinguished: supervised learning, reinforcement learning, and unsupervised learning.

Supervised learning is currently the most popular approach. In this case, the machine learns through 'supervision' or 'teaching': it is given in advance a training set (i.e., a large set of answers that are assumed to be correct in achieving the task at hand). More precisely, the system is provided with a set of pairs, each linking the description of a case, in terms of a combination of features, to the correct response (prediction) for that case. Here are some examples: in systems designed to recognise objects (e.g., animals) in pictures, each picture in the training set is tagged with the

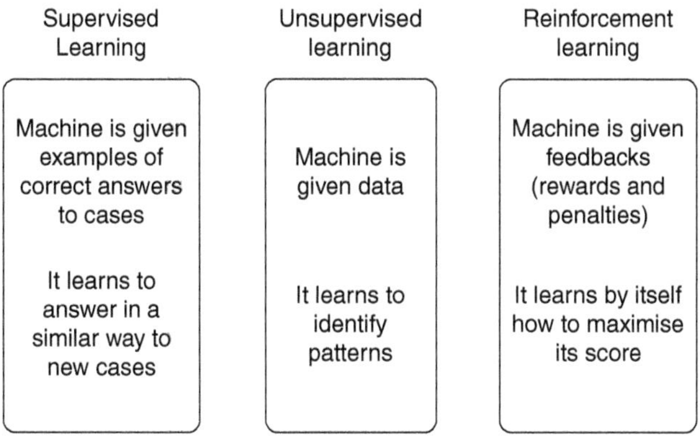
Supervised
Learning
Machine is given examples of correct answers to cases
It learns to answer in a similar way to new cases
Unsupervised
learning
Machine is given data
It learns to identify patterns
Reinforcement
learning
Machine is given feedbacks (rewards and penalties)
It learns by itself how to maximise its score

FIGURE 8.2 Kinds of learning

name of the kind of object it contains (e.g., cat, dog, rabbit); in systems for automated translation, each (fragment of) a document in the source language is linked to its translation in the target language; in systems for personnel selection, the description of each past applicants (age, experience, studies, etc.) is linked to whether the application was successful (or to an indicator of the work performance for appointed candidates); in clinical decision support systems, each patient's symptoms and diagnostic tests is linked to the patient's pathologies; in recommendation systems, each consumer's features and behaviour is linked to the purchased objects; in systems for assessing loan applications, each record of a previous application is linked to whether the application was accepted (or, for successful applications, to the compliant or non-compliant behaviour of the borrower). And in our context, a system may be given a set of past cases by a certain state agency, each of which links the features of a case with the decision made by the agency. As these examples show, the training of a system does not always require a human teacher tasked with providing correct answers to the system. In many cases, the training set can be the side product of human activities (purchasing, hiring, lending, tagging, deciding, etc.), as is obtained by recording the human choices pertaining to such activities. In some cases, the training set can even be gathered 'from the wild' consisting of the data which are available on the open web. For instance, manually tagged images or faces, available on social networks, can be scraped and used for training automated classifiers.

The learning algorithm of the system (its trainer) uses the training set to build a model meant to capture the relevant knowledge originally embedded in the training set, namely the correlations between cases and responses. This model is then used, by the system – by its predicting algorithm – to provide hopefully correct responses to new cases, by mimicking the correlations in the training set. If the

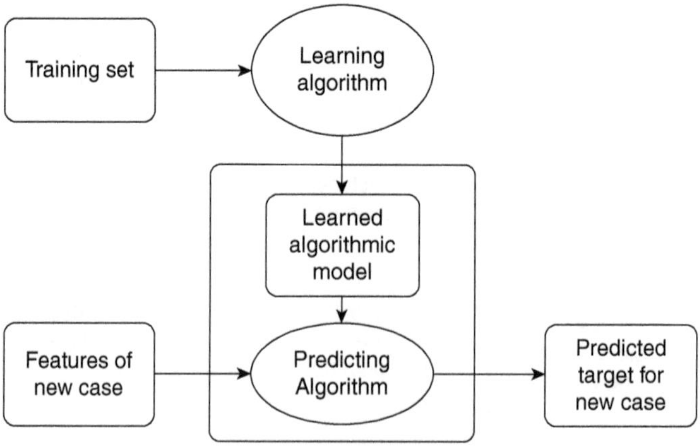

FIGURE 8.3 Supervised learning

examples in the training set that come closest to a new case (with regard to relevant features) are linked to a certain answer, the same answer will be proposed for the new case. For instance, if the pictures that are most similar to a new input were tagged as cats, the new input will also be tagged in the same way; if past applicants whose characteristics best match those of a new applicant were linked to rejection, the system will propose to reject also the new applicant; if the past workers who come closest to a new applicant performed well (or poorly), the system will predict that also the new applicant will perform likewise; if past people most similar to a convicted person turned out to be recidivists, the system will predict that the new convict will also re-offend.

Reinforcement learning is similar to supervised learning, as both involve training by way of examples. However, in the case of reinforcement learning the system also learns from the outcomes of its own actions, namely, through the rewards or penalties (e.g., points gained or lost) that are linked to such outcomes. For instance, in the case of a system learning how to play a game, rewards may be linked to victories and penalties to defeats; in a system learning to make investments, to financial gains and penalties to losses; in a system learning to target ads effectively, to users' clicks; and so forth. In all these cases, the system observes the outcomes of its actions, and it self-administers the corresponding rewards or penalties in order to optimise the relationship between the response and the goal. Being geared towards maximising its score (its utility), the system will learn to achieve outcomes leading to rewards (victories, gains, clicks), and to prevent outcomes leading to penalties. Note that learning from one's successes and failures may require some exploration (experimentation): under appropriate circumstances, the system may experiment with randomly chosen actions, rather than performing the action that it predicts to be best according to its past experience, to see if something even better can come up. Also note that reinforcement learning must include, at least to an extent, a predefined notion of what counts as a 'success'.

Finally, in unsupervised learning, AI systems learn without receiving external instructions, either in advance or as feedback, about what is right or wrong. The techniques for unsupervised learning are used, in particular, for clustering – that is, for grouping the set of items that present relevant similarities or connections (e.g., documents that pertain to the same topic, people sharing relevant characteristics, or terms playing the same conceptual roles in texts). For instance, in a set of cases concerning bail or parole, we may observe that injuries are usually connected with drugs (not with weapons as expected), or that people having prior record are those who are related to weapons. These clusters might turn out to be informative to ground bail or parole policies.

8.6 AI SYSTEMS AS PREDICTION MACHINES

Machine-learning systems are still based on the execution of algorithmic instructions, conveyed through software programs, as any computer is. In the end, such programs govern the functioning of a digital computer, and their execution is reduced to the simple operations of binary arithmetic performed by one or more processors. However, such algorithms are different, in an important way, from the non-learning algorithms we have described previously, including algorithms meant to govern the behaviour of humans (see Section 8.2) and algorithms directed to machines (see Sections 8.3 and 8.4).

As noted previously, the difference is that to create a non-learning algorithm, humans have to provide in advance all knowledge that is needed to address the task that the algorithm is meant to solve. Thus the use of such algorithms is restricted to the cases in which it is possible, for humans, to give in advance all such information. A further restriction comes from the extent to which a human is able to process this information (in the case of algorithms directed to humans) or to which a human is able to grasp connections and impose coherence over the information (in the case of algorithms directed to computers).

With regard to learning algorithms, we enter a different domain. Once given a training set (in supervised learning), relevant feedback (in reinforcement learning), or just a set of data (in unsupervised learning), the learning algorithm produces a predictive model (i.e., a set of rules or decision trees or a neural network) which embeds information extracted from the training set. This information basically consists of correlations between certain data on objects or events (i.e., the predictors to be used) and other data concerning the same objects or events (i.e., the targets that the system is meant to determine), based on the predictors. Thus, for instance, in a system dealing with recidivism, the model might embed the correlations between features of offenders (age, criminal record, socio-economic conditions, or any other factors) and the crimes they are expected to commit after being released.[26] In a system dealing with case law, the model may embed correlations between the textual content of the judge's opinions (plus possibly, further codified information on the case or may other information, regarding social, political, or economic events) and the corresponding decisions. We can consider the predictive model itself (in combination with the software that activates it) as a complex algorithm, an algorithm that is not constructed by humans (who may only specify some parameters and features of it), but by the learning algorithm. The predictive model can be applied to a new object or event, given the values of the predictors for that object or event, and asked to assign corresponding values for the target. It can evolve by being further modified by the learning algorithm, so as to improve its performance. Moreover, to the extent the learning process is given access to a very large (and ever-increasing) data set, it can find within this data set statistical patterns that predict given outcomes in ways that are difficult to foresee when the algorithm was first launched.

[26] As in the COMPAS system, which will be discussed in Section 8.14.

Thus, machine learning systems can be viewed as 'prediction machines'.[27] To understand their impact on public activities, we need to clarify this notion of prediction. Within machine learning, predicting a target datum based on a set of input data (predictors) just means to suggest what the target datum is likely to be, on account of its correlation with such input data; it consists in 'filling the missing information' based on the information we have.[28] Prediction in this sense does not always, though it does often, refer to future events. As examples of prediction focused on the present, consider an image recognition system that labels pictures (as dogs, cats, humans, etc.), face recognition systems that label faces (with people's names), or a diagnostic system that labels radiographies with possible pathologies. For predictions focused on the future, consider a system that predicts the likelihood that a person will have a certain health issue, or that a certain student admitted to a university will do well, that an applicant for parole will escape or engage in criminal activities, that a traffic jam will happen, or that crimes are likely to take place in a certain area of a city under certain circumstances.

Having systems that can make predictions, in a cheap and effective way, has three distinct implications:

- Predictions currently made by humans will, partially or completely, be delegated to machines, or in any case machine predictions will be integrated with human ones.
- A much larger number of predictions will be executed, in a broader set of domains.
- A much larger set of data will be collected to enable automated predictions.

Moreover, the learning process may reveal factors that we have not yet realised to be relevant to the 'correct' outcome or may even suggest a different outcome as a correct outcome, if such an outcome correlates better with other outcomes identified as preferable.

8.7 FROM PREDICTION TO ACTION

Automated predictions may empower decision makers by enabling them to better assess the situation at stake and take consequential actions. Alternatively, such actions too may be entrusted to an automated system. In certain cases, a system's prediction may be subject to human control ('human in the loop', or 'human over the loop'), in other cases, they may not be challenged by humans. For instance, the prediction that a patient suffers a pathology based on the automated analysis of his or her radiology is, to date, subject to endorsement by the doctor, for it to become the basis of subsequent treatment. Similarly, a prediction of recidivism has to be endorsed by a judge before it becomes the basis for a judgment. On the other

27 Ajay Agrawal, Joshua Gans, and Avi Goldfarb, *Prediction Machines: The Simple Economics of Artificial Intelligence* (Harvard Business Review Press, 2018).

28 Ibid., at page 32.

hand, the prediction that there is a pedestrian in the middle of the road, for obvious reasons of time, will lead directly to the action of an autonomous car (without necessarily removing human intervention from the autonomous car altogether).

The link between prediction and decision may take place in different ways. A human may have the task of deciding what to do based on the prediction – that is, of determining whether to grant bail, or whether to approve a loan (and at which rate), after the system has predicted the likelihood that the convict will escape or recommit a crime or the likelihood of default on the loan. The choice to entrust a certain decision to a human, even when prediction is delegated to a machine, is ultimately a normative choice. When decisions – including legal decisions by judicial or administrative bodies – involve selecting one course of action among alternatives, based on the way in which the selected alternative promotes or demotes the values (individual rights, public interests) at stake, the process often entails evaluating the comparative importance of these values. To date, no machine has the ability to make such an assessment, but this does not mean that such choices can never be delegated to a machine.

First, a hard-coded automated rule may specify that given a prediction, a certain decision is to be taken by the system (e.g., that a loan application has to be rejected if the applicant is predicted to default with a likelihood that is above a given threshold); similarly, an online filtering system may reject a message given the likelihood that it is unlawful or inappropriate.[29] This ex-ante choice (i.e., the decision rule specifying what the systems should do, given its prediction), of course, is where the normative work is being done, and hence we would expect it to be rendered by humans.

In case no hard-coded rules are available for linking predictions to choices, but the goals to be achieved , as well as their relative importance, are clear (again, in the sense that humans have made a prior decision regarding these goals), the system may also be entrusted with learning the best way to achieve such goals under the predicted circumstances, and implement it. For instance, in the case of online advertising, a system may learn what kind of messages are most likely to trigger a higher response by certain kinds of users (the maximisation of users' clicks or purchases being the only goal being pursued) and act accordingly. As this example shows, a problem arises from the fact that, in order to delegate a choice to a machine, the multiple values that are at stake (profit of the supplier, interests of the consumers, overall fairness etc.) are substituted by a single proxy (e.g., number of clicks or purchases) that is blindly pursued.

When even the goals are not clear, the system may still be delegated the task of suggesting or even taking actions, after it has acquired the ability to predict how a human would have acted under the given circumstances: the action to be taken is

[29] On online-filtering, see Giovanni Sartor and Andrea Loreggia, 'A Study: The Impact of Algorithms for Online Content Filtering or Moderation – Upload Filters' (European Parliament, 2020), www.europarl.europa.eu/RegData/etudes/STUD/2020/657101/IPOL_STU(2020)657101_EN.pdf.

simply the action that the system predicts that a human would have taken, after training itself on a relevant data set that captures the inputs humans receive and their subsequent decisions. For instance, a system may learn – on the basis of human-made translations, documents, or paintings – how to translate a text, write a document, or draw a painting, by predicting (after adequate training) how humans would translate the text, write the document, or draw the painting. Similarly, a system may forecast or suggest administrative or judicial decisions, after having been trained on data sets of such decisions, by predicting how a human administrator or judge would decide under the given circumstances. This is what is aimed at in the domain of predictive justice: the system should forecast or suggest decisions by predicting what a judge would do under the given circumstances.

A learning process needs to be calibrated on the manner in which a human would make a decision, whenever hard facts, ground truths, or clear consequences which distinguish a correct decision from a faulty decision are hard to come by. Contrast for instance medical and legal decision-making. In medical decision-making, the evolution of the physical conditions of a patient may tell whether a diagnosis was right or wrong, or whether a therapy was effective or not; in the law, matters are more complicated. Whereas we may have facts regarding recidivism or 'jumping bail' (which, however, may reflect societal inequities or biases in and of themselves), it is much more difficult to generate a factual method with which to evaluate whether a correct decision has been entered regarding the validity of a contract or a will, or on whether a certain interpretation of a statute is more correct than another. The methodological precondition that requires learning by mimicking human decision makers is obviously a double-edged sword: the AI system will learn to replicate the virtues and successes of humans but also their biases and failures.

On this basis, we may wonder to what extent AI (predicting machines) do and may contribute to state activity. As prediction is key to most if not all decision-making, it appears that a vast domain of possibilities exists. A learning system can provide indications that pertain to different domains that are relevant to the government. For instance, such a system may predict the chances that a person is going to re-commit an offence (i.e., has certain recidivist tendencies) or violate certain obligations, and on this basis, it can suggest measures to be adopted. It can predict where and at what time crimes are most likely to take place, so that appropriate measures can be taken. Or it may predict the occurrence of traffic jams, and possibly suggest how to direct the traffic in such a way that jams are avoided. Or it may predict the possibility of environmental issues, and possible responses to them. It may predict the spread of a disease and the effectiveness of measures to counter it. More generally, it may predict where social issues are going to emerge, and how to mitigate them. The context of the system's use often determines whether its proposals are interpreted as forecasts, or rather as suggestions. For instance, a system's 'prediction' that a person's application for bail or parole will be accepted can be viewed by the defendant (and his lawyer) as a prediction of what the judge will do, and by the judge as a suggestion for her decision (assuming that she prefers not to depart from previous practice). The same applies to a system's prediction that a loan or a social entitlement will be granted. Depending on the context and on the technology used, such predictions can be associated (or not) with a probability score. In any case, such predictions are uncertain, being grounded on the data in the input set provided to the system, and on the statistical correlations between such data.

However, we must not forget that the fact that a machine is able to make predictions at a human and even at a superhuman level does not mean that the machine knows what it is doing. For instance, a system for automated translation does not know the meaning of the text in the input language, nor the meaning of the output in the target language; it has no idea of what the terms in the two languages refer to in the physical or social world. It just blindly applies the correlations – learned from previous translations – between textual expressions in the source and target language. It has indeed been argued that the success of automated translation does not show that machines today understand human language, since it rather consists of 'bypassing or circumventing the act of understanding language'.[30] Similarly, a machine predicting appeal decisions – based on the text of the appealed sentence and the arguments by the parties – does not know what the case is about. It is just blindly applying correlations linking textual patterns (and other data) to possible outcomes; it is suggesting legal outcomes by bypassing or circumventing the act of understanding laws and facts.[31]

It is true that the impacts of a choice on the real world may be fed back to, and taken into account by, a learning machine, but only to the extent that such impacts are linked to quantities that the machine can maximise. This may the case for investment decisions, where a quantification of the financial return of the investment may be fed back, or even directly captured by the machine (e.g., in the stock market); the situation is more difficult in most instances of administrative and judicial decision-making, where the multiple goals, values, and interests at stake have to be taken into account. Completely relaying decisions to the 'blind' machine assessment may involve a violation of the rule of law (as will be further discussed in Section 8.9, where we will address other concerns the recourse to AI raises).

8.8 ALGORITHMIC MACHINE LEARNING AS A REGULATORY AND POLICY-FORMATION INSTRUMENT

In this section, we will consider how algorithms can assist governmental agencies in exercising executive functions, focusing first on algorithms as part of the

[30] See recently Douglas Hofstadter, 'The Shallowness of Google Translate' (*The Atlantic*, 30 January 2018) On the automated generation of language, see also Luciano Floridi and Massimo Chiriatti, 'Gpt-3: Its Nature, Scope, Limits, and Consequences' (2020) 30 *Minds and Machines* 681.

[31] The idea of 'blind thought' goes back to Leibniz, who speaks of blind (or symbolic) thinking to characterise the kind of thinking through which we 'reason in words, with the object itself virtually absent from our mind'. See Leibniz, *Meditations on Knowledge, Truth, and Ideas* (Acta Eruditorum, 1684).

administrative and regulatory apparatus, rather than as a subject for regulation. The state, it should be recalled, acts in three capacities: it is an operator, or an actor (when, for example, it goes to war or uses other forms of direct action); it is an administrative entity (when administering, or implementing, a regulatory scheme, for example, when providing services to citizens and residents); and it also has legislative powers (primary and secondary) to devise a policy and then enact a regulatory regime (which may apply to the state or to the industry). Algorithms can play a part in all three prongs.

First, as a direct actor, or operator, the state may harness AI for its war powers (autonomous or semi-autonomous weapons)[32] or police powers (when it resorts to AI in the law enforcement context for deploying its forces)[33] or other operational decisions, including logistics and human resources. In the policing domain, with surveillance sensors expanding to include online cameras, neural network technologies can be used for facial recognition,[34] and access to law enforcement agencies' databases may provide real-time predictive policing, for assisting officers in making operational decisions in response or in anticipation of risks. More specifically, predictive policing systems are used to determine the locations and times in which different kinds of criminal activities are more likely to take place, so that a timely preventive action can be undertaken by police forces.

The police power of the state encompasses also the second prong of state power – the administration of a regulatory regime designed to achieve certain regulatory purposes. In that respect, predictive policing is not different from other types of predictive tools, designed to give implementing agencies more efficient capacities. To the extent that algorithmic instructions reach the desired outcome or rigorously reflect the legal criteria underlying a given regulatory scheme,[35] and so long as the factual input upon which the instructions are then implemented is sound, such algorithms can facilitate the day-to-day bureaucratic machinery, which is faced with the challenge of addressing a large number of decisions pursuant to a regulatory scheme. Among other duties, regulatory agencies perform monitoring routines; publish state-certified information; grant or withdraw permits and licenses; levy fines; assess, collect, and refund fees, taxes, and subsidies; and execute decisions of judicial bodies. Recall that many of these 'application algorithms' discussed previously need not necessarily include a machine-learning component, at least to the extent that the language of the legal codes may be translated into computer code and applied in a manner that does not require machine 'discretion'. Depending on the specificity of the legal criteria undergirding the regulatory regime governing such

32 See Paul Scharre, *Army of None: Autonomous Weapons and the Future of War* (Norton, 2018).

33 Andrew G. Ferguson, 'Policing Predictive Policing' (2017) 94 *Washington University Law Review* 1109.

34 Susan Fourtané, 'AI Facial Recognition and IP Surveillance for Smart Retail, Banking and the Enterprise', *Interesting Engineering*, 27 January 2020, https://interestingengineering.com/ai-facial-recognition-and-ip-surveillance-for-smart-retail-banking-and-the-enterprise.

35 For information about using algorithms as bureaucratic agencies, see Chapter 5 in this book.

duties, many such routine decisions are candidates for being coded and translated into algorithms, thereby relieving some of the administrative burden associated with these decisions, as well as assisting in achieving greater consistency in the application of the law to concrete cases. Moving beyond 'simple' algorithms, an AI component allows for optimisation of the decision-making process when only some facts are known but not all the facts are easily discernible. In such cases, one (or more) of the basic approaches to machine learning (described in Section 8.5) may be relevant for sifting through a large number of cases and detecting the cases in which the exercise of the regulatory function is most likely appropriate.

For example, when the state agencies are called upon to perform the basic function of ensuring compliance by the industry with rules, procedures, or outcomes, the question of how to allocate compliance resources may be one in which AI may assist and suggest possible resources that may be enlisted to assist. Consider the allocation of financial or other resources to citizens and organisations pursuant to some self-reporting: predicting which cases probably meet the criteria and therefore require fewer checks may promote the overall social good.[36] The technology may also be used to anticipate who may drop out of school. More generally, it may identify people who, in the near future, may require other forms of governmental assistance, or, for that matter, certain medical treatments. Similarly, AI may be used to assist the grading of public tenders, or other forms of public contracts. In the enforcement context, examples include detecting money laundering by relying on technological approaches such as those used by PayPal, banks, and credit card companies that seek to spot irregular activities based on established spending patterns.[37] Similarly, governments may use AI to detect welfare frauds[38] (and tax frauds more generally). Enforcement may also capture relevant online communications (e.g., organised crimes, or terrorism, but also, in authoritarian states, proscribed opinions).

More fundamentally, algorithms can be harnessed to play a role not only in the implementation of regulatory schemes, technical or discretionary, but also in their evaluation and eventually in formation process of alternative schemes. The development of the predictive algorithms may be useful in assessing not only a particular case, but the more general relationship between regulatory means and ends. It may shed light on what measure is likely to work, and under what conditions. It may also inform the policy makers with respect to the probable cost-benefit analysis of achieving certain policy

[36] Kate Crawford and Jason Schultz, 'AI Systems as State Actors' (2019) 119 *Columbia Law Review* 1941, 1948–1957, shows few case studies of tasks performed by algorithms, including 'Medicaid' and disability benefit assessment, public teacher employment evaluation, criminal risk assessment, and unemployment benefit fraud detection; Maria Dymitruk, 'The Right to a Fair Trial in Automated Civil Proceedings' (2019) 13(1) *Masaryk University Journal of Law & Technology* 27, on the possibility of an algorithm carrying judicial procedures.

[37] Penny Crosman, 'How PayPal Is Taking a Chance on AI to Fight Fraud', *American Banker*, 1 September 2016, www.americanbanker.com/news/how-paypal-is-taking-a-chance-on-ai-to-fight-fraud.

[38] Bernard Marr, 'How the UK Government Uses Artificial Intelligence to Identify Welfare and State Benefits Fraud' https://bernardmarr.com/default.asp?contentID=1585.

goals. Such algorithms may be conceptualised as 'policy algorithms', since the problem they are designed to solve is the overall risk allocation in a given socio-economic field, or the adequacy (likelihood) of a certain regulatory scheme as applied to achieve its goals, compared to (tested) alternatives. Obviously, such algorithms can also be designed so that they 'learn' and adapt, as they analyse policy decisions at the aggregate level, to detect those with greater probabilities of achieving a desired goal (and lower probability for achieving unintended negative consequences).

More specifically, then, to the extent a state agency was able to distil the objectives it seeks to optimise, or to identify key factors underlying a social problem (or which may affect such a problem), the agency may resort to the technology for designing policy, by focusing on what the technology may tell the policymaker regarding the relationship between means and ends.[39] For example, it may harness machine learning in public health for predicting risks and susceptibility to diseases and illnesses and for predicting which regulatory responses may optimise desired outcomes.[40] Similarly, machine learning may be used in education, where AI systems can predict educational performance,[41] including the correlation between such performance and different regulatory approaches. In transportation and urban planning, machine learning may be used to predict traffic, capacity, or urbanisation patterns, and their correlation with different planning policies.[42] In predicting external events or situations that are relevant to the activities of state agencies, environmental patterns should also be mentioned.[43] Note that in these cases as well, AI is not concerned with the overall set of values the policy is set to promote, but rather is placed at the level of optimising the means for achieving these goals. Furthermore, we can appreciate that predicting recidivism, crimes, financial frauds, and tax evasion are not only of interest to the law enforcement agency – they are also relevant for the policy formation segments of the state. Similarly, anticipating environmental, sanitary, or financial difficulties; reviewing purchases or other contractual arrangements; predicting the flow of traffic or the consumption of energy are relevant not only for real-time response, but are also valuable in the policy formation process, including for optimising the logistics in civil and military domains.

In conclusion of this section, machine learning holds the potential of going beyond what we currently identify as legally relevant criteria. To the extent the design of the algorithmic 'production line' includes access to big data, not classified

39 See Crawford and Shultz (n 38).

40 Sanjay Das, 'How Artificial Intelligence Could Transform Public Health', *Sd Global*, 26 March 2020, www.sdglobaltech.com/blog/how-artificial-intelligence-could-transform-public-health; Brian Wahl et al., 'Artificial Intelligence (AI) and Global Health: How Can AI Contribute to Health in Resource-Poor Settings?' (2018) 3(4) *BMJ Global Health*.

41 See the discussion in Carlo Perrotta and Neil Selwyn, 'Deep Learning Goes to School: Toward a Relational Understanding of AI in Education' (2020) 45(3) *Learning, Media and Technology* 251.

42 See the discussion in Elisabete Silva and Ning Wu, 'Artificial Intelligence Solutions for Urban Land Dynamics: A Review' (2010) 24(3) *Journal of Planning Literature* 246.

43 Jackie Snow. 'How Artificial Intelligence Can Tackle Climate Change', *National Geographic*, 18 July 2018, www.nationalgeographic.com/environment/2019/07/artificial-intelligence-climate-change/.

according to any legally relevant criteria, the algorithm may come up with alternative criteria, which are based on statistical probabilities of certain correlated facts in a given instance. In this sense, the learning algorithm is not merely an 'application algorithm', which contends itself with the technical application of a predetermined set of instructions. Rather, a learning algorithm can be understood as a 'discretionary algorithm', since it may devise the criteria upon which a state decision may be based. These criteria are those embedded in the predictive model constructed by the learning algorithm of the system, regardless of whether such criteria have a linguistic form (as in system based on inferred rules or decision trees), or whether they are coded at the sub-symbolic level (as in the weighted connections within a neural network). This holds the potential to expand the ability of the state agency (or agencies, to the extent a regulatory regime involves multiple organs). It comes, however, with its own set of legal difficulties.

It is worthwhile to note AI is not a single technology, but rather a vast bundle of diverse methods, approaches, and technologies. Within that bundle, there are learning algorithms that may be designed to generate cognitive responses (rational and emotional) that nudge people – whether they are conscious of the manipulation or not – to behave or react in a certain way. This feature may be combined with algorithms that seek, upon mining big data, to ascertain what achieves a preferred outcome without necessarily following pre-ordained legal criteria.[44] Nudging algorithms, are relevant as a regulatory measure, precisely because of their ability to nudge people to react, form opinions/emotions, and invest their attention one way (or not invest it in another), and therefore they offer regulators the ability to channel the behaviour of an unspecified public by micro-targeting segments thereof. Their deployment also clearly raises considerable ethical and right-based questions. And we should also realise that automated nudging may be deployed by the regulated industry so as to prompt a certain reaction from the agency (and the decision makers therein).

8.9 THE ALGORITHMIC STATE – SOME CONCERNS

With all their promise, algorithms – application algorithms, discretionary algorithms, and policy-analysis (or policy-formation) algorithms – challenge our understanding of regulation in two dimensions, both rather obvious. The first is that the integration of algorithms into the regulatory process comes with some serious drawbacks. The second is that algorithms are not only (or primarily) integrated into the regulatory process; they emerge as the backbone of the modern, data-driven industries, and as such call for regulation by the (algorithmic) state. As noted previously, they are the subject of regulation, and hence a tension may arise.

44 See Karen Yeung, 'Algorithmic Regulation: A Critical Interrogation' (2017) *Regulation & Governance* 6–11, for a discussion regarding the capabilities and possible classifications for algorithmic regulations.

On a fundamental level, and in reference to the analysis of the different functions of government, we may observe that AI systems could be deployed to enhance the influence of government over information flows (nodality). AI systems have indeed been used to filter the information that is available to citizens (as happens most often in repressive regimes), to analyse the information generated by citizens (and not necessarily reveal such analysis to the general public), and to provide personalised answers to citizen's queries, or otherwise target individuals, in a manner that may be manipulative. Furthermore, as has been identified by many, AI may be used by for-profit or not-for-profit entities to further enhance existing socio-political cleavages. By nudging activities within echo-chambers in a manner that alters priorities, perceptions, and attitudes, a degree of social control may be obtained in a manner that is inconsistent with underlying presumptions regarding deliberative discourse and the ongoing formation of values. To the extent the state fails to regulate such deployment of AI by for-profit or not-for-profit organisations, AI can be used to undermine democratic values.

8.10 ALGORITHMS AND LEGAL (PERFORMATIVE) LANGUAGE

The drawbacks of algorithmic regulation have been noted by many. But before we outline some such key concerns, any serious discussion between jurists and computer scientists on algorithms (or machine learning or AI) reaches the issue of language and rules. Recall that algorithms are a form of prescriptive language, and as such share this feature with law. Yet as philosophers of law teach us, 'the law' – itself a rather complex term – is greater than the sum of its rules. The legal universe is also comprised of standards, principles, and values – which by definition are not 'finite' and as such evade codification into an algorithm. Moreover, the relationship between the rule (as a general norm) and the application of the rule (to one particular case) is not trivial. It would appear that by definition a rule must include a set of cases greater than one for it to be a rule of general application. Yet as soon as we shift our focus from the rule to the particular case, at least two things happen. The first is that we have to inquire whether other legal norms may be applicable, and since as noted the legal system includes standards and values, with relatively far-reaching application, the answer is almost always yes. This creates a built-in tension, as there are no easily available rules to solve the potential clash between a rule of general application and the more general standard or value. The second, more nuanced issue that arises relates to the very notion of 'application', which requires a certain form of judgement which cannot be reduced, in law, to a cut and dry, mechanical syllogism. This is because conceptually, language does not apply itself, and normatively built into the rule is its purpose, which may call, in the particular case, for generating an exception to the rule or otherwise refresh the understading of the rule to address its particular 'application' in a manner consistent with the purpose of the rule.

In other words, in law the relationship between the rule and its application is dialectic: the very essence of the rule is that it will be 'binding' and apply to the particular cases captured by the language of the rules, yet at the same time part of the DNA of the language of the rules is that the application in the particular case, while fitting a certain analytic structure is also consonant with the underlying purpose and function the rule is there to fulfil. Because in law rules do not self-apply, some form of judgment is inherent. Viewed slightly differently, there is always, again, because of the nature of human language, an ingredient of interpretation regarding the meaning of the words that construct the rule. Such interpretation may be informed by the core (conventional) meaning of a certain phrase, but it may also be informed by the penumbra, where the meaning is more vague. The line between the core and the penumbra is itself open to interpretation. Some even question the clear distinction between the core and the penumbra, suggesting that drawing such a line reflects normative considerations of purpose and aesthetic considerations of fit.

Be it as it may, normatively, we do not want to erase the tension between the rule and the exception because discretion, even when highly restricted, is nonetheless an integral part of what makes law worthy of our moral respect; it connects the operative words to their (otherwise morally appropriate) purpose. At least some leading jurists suggest that law provides a distinct reason for abiding by its prescriptions, and that reason at least at some level ties back to the notion of the moral legitimacy of the rule as part of a legitimate set of rules, and ultimately of a legal system and its processes.

Moreover, central to the notion of law in a liberal democracy is its human nature: it is a product of human agency, its values and goals should reflect care for human agency, and its application should ultimately be at the hands of humans exercising agency. The aforementioned legitimacy therefore is enhanced with the exercise of judgment as a matter of moral agency (and seeing right from wrong) by the person who applies the law. Some jurists suggest that the question of legal validity, scope, and operative meaning of a particular rule as considered for application in a given set of facts cannot be fully separated from the underlying values embedded in the rule (as part of a set of rules and principles, governing a given field of human interaction). If this is indeed the case, discretion is a feature, not a bug. It is not clear that we can fully separate the question of 'what is the operative meaning of the rule with respect to a particular set of facts' from the question 'should we enforce that meaning in the given set of facts'.

In that respect, would we rather have bureaucrats fully automated, without seeing the unique circumstances before them – the human being (not only the case number), applying for the exercise of state power (or its withdrawal) in a particular case? Certainly, there is a risk that relaxing the technical commitment to the conventional meaning of rules will result in biases or favouritisms, as may be the case when human judgment is exercised. But the alternative, namely removing all ambiguity from the system, may result in detaching law from its human nature, by removing agency and by supposing that codes can adequately cover all circumstances, and that human language is capable of capturing 'the reality' in a transparent, technical manner. The latter assumption is difficult to support.

On some abstract level, the law is 'quantic'. Contrary to our everyday understanding, in the marginal cases it evades being reduced to yes-no answers, and we may never know what the rule is until past its application (and then we know what the application has been, not necessarily how the rule will be applied in the next marginal case). The presence of the marginal cases radiates back to the core cases, such that even in some core cases irregular application may ensue, and thus an internal tension always exists between the rule and its application.

Algorithms it would seem, have a different logic: as a general matter, a clear binary answer is what makes an algorithm sound. In cases where such a binary answer is unavailable, it is replaced with an approximation, and then this approximation is reduced to a yes-no complex flow chart.

Even though AI system may be able to learn from past examples and from feedback to randomly select and test new solutions, and to model competing arguments and criteria for choosing between these solutions, it is still difficult to conceive – at least accordingly to the present state of the art – of a dialectic algorithm which adequately captures the internal tension between rule and exception, or the general rule and the particular case, built into law. As noted previously, even the most advanced predictive systems do not have an understanding of language; they can only harness 'blind thought' (i.e., in unreflected data manipulation), lacking the capacity to link language to reality, and in particular link legal provisions to the social and human issues that such provisions are meant to regulate. Consequently, delegating the application of the law to an automated system in a manner that eliminates human discretion (and fully removes the human from the loop, including from above the loop) entails, fundamentally, the displacement of a certain question from the legal realm to the technical/bureaucratic realm. This does not mean that certain matters cannot be so displaced, but it does mean that such displacement, to the extent it involves the exercise of state power, generates a call for a process of legal contestation, for reasons related to the rule of law. Hence, the law is reintroduced and the potential for human intervention is brought back.

An interesting, albeit highly speculative development in this domain suggests that we should reconfigure our understanding of general rules by introducing the concept of personalised law.[45] The idea is there to use AI to predict the relevant features of individual citizens, and to select accordingly the law that applies to them. For instance, if it is possible to distinguish automatically between skilful or incapable drivers, or between vulnerable or knowledgeable, consumers, each individual should be applied the law that fits his or her features, with regard to the achievement of the required level of care (e.g., speed limits), advertising messages, or privacy notices. Similarly, with regard to default rules (e.g., in matters of inheritance,), each one may be subject, by default, to the legal rule that fits his or her predicted

45 Christoph Busch and Alberto De Franceschi, *Algorithmic Regulation and Personalized Law: A Handbook* (Hart Publishing, 2020).

preferences.[46] It remains to be seen not only whether this would indeed be technically feasible, but also whether it may challenge our understanding of the relationship between general norms and their application, including the relationship between rules and standards on the one hand, and rules and particular exceptions on the other.

8.11 RULE OF LAW

Moving to a less abstract level, resorting to algorithms as a regulatory tool may generate conflicts with the demands of the rule of law, to the extent the recourse to algorithms amounts to delegation of legal authority either to the state-run algorithm, or to private companies that own the data or the algorithm (or both). Clearly, to the extent that private entities play a key role in algorithmic regulation (of others), the issue of delegation of state power is a serious concern.[47] Considerable attention has been devoted to the public-private interface, sometimes referred as a 'partnership', although such partnership already assumes a model of co-regulation, which then raises concerns of self-dealing or the potential capture of either the policy formation or the enforcement processes, or both. But even if the private entities only play a supportive role (or play no role at all), the rule-of-law problem remains.

As noted previously, under the analysis of legal language, the rule of law, as a concept, is not the rule of machines. This is not a mere matter of legal technicality: the idea of the rule of law is premised on the conscious and intentional articulation and deployment of legal categories and concepts, reflecting certain values, to address specific and more general distributive and corrective decisions. Such premise holds at the level of norm-setting (thereby is relevant to policy-analysis algorithms) but also at the level of implementation (and is thereby relevant to implementation and discretionary algorithms). Contrary to a simplified meaning, according to which the rule of law is posited as the opposite of the rule of men, the rule of law is not a rule detached from humans. Rather, it is a rule formed through human interaction, governing human interaction, for the benefit of humans. The rule of law therefore is a mechanism to counter the rule of whim, desire, arbitrariness, or corrupted self-interest, which may follow from constructing the state as if it can do no wrong, and the rulers as if they are entitled to pursue whatever they deem through whatever means they chose.[48] It is not a mechanism designed to replace moral agency with automated decision-making, even if such automated decision-making may reduce negative outcomes.

46 Anthony J. Casey and Anthony Niblett, 'A. Framework for the New Personalization of Law' (2019) 86 *University of Chicago Law Review* 333.

47 For an example of a discussion regarding the delegation of state power in risk assessment algorithms, see Andrea Nishi, 'Privatizing Sentencing: A Delegation Framework for Recidivism Risk Assessment' (2017) 119 *Columbia Law Review* 1617.

48 John Locke, *Two Treatises of Government* (1689), 163–166; Lon Fuller, *The Morality of Law* (1964), 33–39.

Since the rule of law is an expression of autonomy and agency, and since agency is a rather complex term which includes the exercise of empathy, it appears that the rule of law demands a rule laid down and then implemented by moral agents, at least so long as an algorithmic rule (and application) will result in some errors (defined as rules or applications which fail to optimise the fit between legitimate regulatory purposes and the means used, or fail to be consistent with underlying values and the analytic logic of technical legal concepts). Granted that algorithms may reduce such errors, compared to human-made rules and applications, the errors caused by machines are more difficult to justify for those who suffer from their consequence than errors caused as a product of processes through which deliberative moral agency is exercised. A human error can be accepted, or tolerated, because collective decision-making – and legal rules and their implementations are examples of decisions made by some and then applied to others – is premised on a certain degree of solidarity, which stems from a shared notion of what it feels like to suffer from the harm errors cause. Such solidarity, and the premise of empathy, are not present when decisions are made by machines, even if machines may reach fewer decisions that cause such errors. In other words, the concept of the rule of law requires a human in or over the loop, even if we reach a position that AI is fully developed to pass a legal Turing Test (i.e., be indistinguishable from a competent human decision maker) for its ability to integrate purposes and the means achieve consistency between underlying values, on the one hand, and technical legal concepts, on the other. To date, we should be reminded, we are still some ways away from that demanding benchmark. In the law as in other domains, at least in the foreseeable future, it is most likely (and normatively appropriate) that complex tasks, including those requiring creativity and insight, are approached through a hybrid or symbiotic approach that combines the capacities of humans and machines.[49]

Moreover, the issues of legal competence (who gets to call the shots?), of process (how is the decision reached?), and of discretion (what are the relevant considerations, and their respective weight?) are central because they reflect social experience regarding the use of power (and law is a form of power). A rather intricate system of checks and controls is usually in place to ensure the four heads of legal competence (over the matter, the person exercising power, the territory, and the time frame) are checked and often distributed to different entities. What would it mean for algorithms to reflect the need to distribute power when rules are promulgated and applied? Algorithms are designed to integrate and optimise. Should we rather design algorithms so as to check on other algorithms? Similarly, the process that produces legal norms and particular legal decisions is

[49] The idea of a man-machine symbiosis in creative tasks was anticipated by J. Licklider, 'Man-Computer Symbiosis' (March 1960) 4 *IRE Transactions on Human Factors in Electronics, HFE-1*. For a view that in the legal domain too software systems can succeed best as human–machine hybrid, see Tim Wu, 'Will Artificial Intelligence Eat the Law? The Rise of Hybrid Social-Ordering Systems' (2019) 119 *Columbia Law Review*.

itself regulated, with principles of due process in mind. How would a due-process algorithm be designed?

And, lastly, the modern public law has developed rather extensive structures for managing executive discretion (at the policy-formation, norm-giving and then implementing stages), based upon a paradigm which stipulates that (a) certain considerations are 'irrelevant' to the statutory purpose or even 'illegitimate' to any purpose, and (b) the relevant or legitimate considerations are to be given a certain weight. The latter is premised on the language of balancing and proportionality, central to which is the structured duty for justifying the relationship between means to achieve the chosen goal, the lack of a less restrictive mean, and the overall assessment that the benefit (to the protection of rights and public interests) expected to be gained by the application of measure is not clearly outweighed by the harm the measure will cause (to protected rights and public interests). This language of proportionality, notwithstanding its rational structure, is rather difficult to code, given the absence of reliable data, unclear causal lines, and the lack of agreed-upon numbers with which to determine when something is clearly outweighed by something else.

This is not to say that algorithms cannot assist in determining where data is missing (or otherwise diluted or corrupt), whether less restrictive means may be available, and what may be the overall cost-benefit analysis. Banning access to proportionality-related algorithms is not warranted, it seems, by the principles of the rule of law, nor would it be a sound policy decision. But fully relying on such algorithms as if their scientific aura places them as a superior tool of governance is neither warranted nor reconcilable with the underlying premise of proportionality, namely that the judgement call will be made by a moral agent capable of empathy.

To sum up this point, a robust delegation of authority is, to date, compatible with the principles of the rule of law only in the most technical applications of clearly defined norms, where the matter under consideration is of relatively minor importance, the data in the particular case is relatively straightforward and verifiable, and an appeal processes (to other machines and ultimately to humans) is available. In such cases, machine learning (and AI more generally) may be relevant in the periphery, as a tool for identifying regimes where decisions are processed by the administration as technical decisions, and therefore as candidates for 'simple' algorithmic processing. Learning, in the sense that the algorithm will devise the predictive model to be applied, will be relevant to the technical, binary decisions discussed in this paragraph, mostly with regard to the assessment of relevant facts (e.g., recognising images and people in the context of traffic fines, identifying potential frauds or risks of violation in the tax of financial domain).

8.12 RESPONSIVE LAW

As machines cannot be expected to understand the values and interests at stake in administrative and judicial decisions, we can conclude that, left alone, they would not be able to make improvements over the law, but just reproduce the existing practice, leading to the 'petrification' about which Roscoe Pound complained, as we observed previously, and about which modern scholars have expressed concerns.[50] Some aspects of this critique attracted possible rebuttals, suggesting that the force of the concern may depend on the manner in which the AI system is designed, and the manner in which it is used.[51] Researchers in AI and law have suggested that there may be computational models of legal reasoning going beyond deduction that involve the generation of multiple defeasible arguments,[52] possibly concerning alternative interpretations, on the basis of cases and analogies.[53] The advent of machine learning may advance these, or similar approaches by overcoming the technical difficulty of formalising such models, but at the same time, the opacity of machine learning systems proves counterproductive for generating meaningful debate regarding alternative norms.

A possible example on point may be what has been called predictive justice (but the same idea can also be applied both to the judiciary and to administration). The key idea is that systems can be trained on previous judicial or administrative decisions (on the relation between the features of such cases and the corresponding decisions), in such a way that such systems predict what a new decision may be, on the basis of the features of the case to be decided. The results so far obtained have limited significance, as accuracy is low. Some systems base their predictions on extra-legal features (e.g., identity of the parties, lawyers, and judges),[54] others on the text of case documents. Some of the experiments made no real prediction of the outcome of future cases, but rather the decision of an already decided case is

50 John Morison and Adam Harkens, 'Re-engineering Justice? Robot Judges, Computerized Courts and (Semi) Automated Legal Decision-Making' (2019) 39(4) *Legal Studies* 618. The authors develop the idea that such automated systems would make more rigid the application of the law: legal norms would be interpreted once and for all, and this task would be delegated to the knowledge engineers creating the knowledge base of the system, who would produce once for the logical formalisation to be automatically applied (by the inferential engine of the system) to any new case. No space would the left for arguments supporting alternative interpretation, nor for the consideration of features of individual cases that were not captured by the given formalisation. The law would be 'petrified' and applied regardless of the social context and dynamics.

51 A possible reply to Morison and Harkens's critique would observe that by giving to the adopted interpretation a logical form, contestation would rather be facilitated, being given a clear target (i.e., the interpretation of norms that has been formalised in the system). Moreover, the use of intelligent systems in the legal domain could promote a legal and organisational context which would ensure the accurate consideration of individual cases and the revisability of rules. Finally, improvement in the rules, once embedded in the system's knowledge base, would be spread to all users of the system, ensuring learning and equality of application. See Surend Dayal and Peter Johnson, 'A Web-Based Revolution in Australian Public Administration?' (2000) 1 *The Journal of Information, Law and Technology*.

52 Henry Prakken and Giovanni Sartor, 'Law and Logic: A Review from an Argumentation Perspective' (2015) 227 *Artificial Intelligence* 214.

53 Kevin D. Ashley (n 27).

54 Daniel Martin Katz, Michael J. Bommarito, and Josh Blackman, 'A General Approach for Predicting the Behavior of the Supreme Court of the United States' (2017) 12(4) *PLoS ONE*.

predicted based on sections of the opinion on that case.[55] Moreover, it can be argued that the task of judicial or administrative decision makers does not consist of predicting what they would do, nor what their colleagues would do (though this may be relevant for the sake of coherence), but in providing an appropriate decision based on facts and laws, supported by an appropriate justification.[56] However, looking into the future, we may consider the possibility that outcomes of decisions may be reliably forecasted and we may wonder how this would affect the behaviour of the parties, officers, and judges. We may wonder whether this would reduce litigation and induce more conformism in the behaviour of officers and judges, so contributing to legal certainty, but also favouring the 'petrification 'of law.

8.13 HUMAN RIGHTS

Beyond rule of law and responsive law concerns, recourse to algorithmic regulation may infringe protected rights, primarily human dignity, due process, privacy, and equality. Human dignity can be infringed upon to the extent a person is reduced to being a data object rather than a fully embodied moral agent, deserving meaningful choice, reasoning, and a decision by another moral agent. We will expand on a variant of this argument below. Due process can be infringed upon to the extent the decision cannot be meaningfully contested as either the data or the explanation behind the decision are opaque.[57] Privacy can be infringed upon to the extent the algorithm relied on data mined without full and free consent (including consent for the application of the particular data for the purpose it was used) or to the extent the algorithm was used in a manner that inhibited decisional autonomy by nudging a person without full disclosure.[58] Finally, equality can be infringed upon to the extent the algorithm relies on what turns out to be discriminatory factors, reflects existing discriminatory practices in society, or generates discriminatory impact. As noted, the proportionality analysis, which is designed to check whether the

55 Nikolaos Aletras et al., 'Predicting Judicial Decisions of the European Court of Human Rights' (2016) *PeerJ Computer Science*; Masha Medvedeva, Michel Vols, and Martijn Wieling, 'Using Machine Learning to Predict Decisions of the European Court of Human Rights' (2019) *Artificial Intelligence and Law*; For a critical discussion, see Frank Pasquale and Glyn Cashwell, 'Prediction, Persuasion, and the Jurisprudence of Behaviourism' (2018) 68(1) *University of Toronto Law Journal* 63.

56 Floris Bex and Henry Prakken, 'The Legal Prediction Industry: Meaningless Hype or Useful Development?' (2020), https://webspace.science.uu.nl/~prakk101/pubs/BexPrakkenAA2020English.pdf.

57 For a detailed discussion about using AI in the Law enforcement field and its impact , see Chapters 3 and 6 in this book.

58 For a discussion of autonomy and human dignity with regard to emotion-recognition algorithms, see Chapter 4 in this book. Amazon for example used a matching tool based on resumes submitted to the company over a ten-year period. This matching tool eventually favoured male candidates over females, giving every woman a lower rank. Jeffery Dastin, 'INSIGHT – Amazon Scraps Secret AI Recruiting Tool That Showed Bias against Women (*Reuters*, 10 October 2018), www.reuters.com/article/amazoncom-jobs-automation/insight-amazon-scraps-secret-ai-recruiting-tool-that-showed-bias-against-women-idUSL2N1VB1FQ?feedType=RSS&feedName=companyNews.

infringement on individual rights may nonetheless be justified, with regard to other rights or social values, is difficult to run, in part because the key aspects of a proportionality assessment – the availability of alternative means, the overall benefit generated by recourse to algorithmic machine learning, and the extent to which the benefit outweighs the harm – are neither easy to concretise nor reasonably assess.

More specifically, the very increase in predictive capacity provided by machines can contribute to fixing and solidifying or even increasing inequalities and hardship embedded in social relations, rather than enabling solutions designed to overcome such inequalities. This is likely to happen when an unfavourable prediction concerning an individual – the prediction that the person is likely to have a health problem, to commit crime, to have inferior performance in education, and so forth – leads to a further disadvantage for the concerned individuals (increased insurance costs, heavier sentences, exclusion from education), rather than to a remedial action to mitigate the social causes of the predicted unfavourable outcome. For this to be avoided, prediction has to be complemented with the individuation of socially influenceable causes and with the creative identification of ways to address them or spread risks.

It should be noted that supporters of the use of predictive systems argue that the baseline for assessing the performance of automated predictors should be human performance rather than perfection: biased computer systems still contribute to fairness when their biases are inferior to those of human decision makers. They argue that automated decision-making can be controlled and adjusted much more accurately than human decision-making: automated prediction opens the way not only for more accuracy but also for more fairness,[59] since such systems can be 'calibrated' so that their functioning optimises, or at least recognises, the idea of fairness that is desired by the community.[60]

A more general issue pertains to the fact that the possibility to use AI to make accurate predictions on social dynamics pertaining to groups and or individuals, based on vast sets of data sets, provides a powerful incentive toward the massive collection of personal data. This contributes to lead toward what has been called the 'surveillance state', or the 'information state', namely a societal arrangement in which 'the government uses surveillance, data collection, collation, and analysis to identify problems, to head off potential threats, to govern populations, and to deliver valuable social services'.[61] The availability of vast data set presents risks in itself, as it

59 Jon Kleinberg, Jens Ludwig, Sendhil Mullainathan, and Cass Sunstein, 'Discrimination in the Age of Algorithm' (2019) 10 *Journal of Legal Analysis* 113–174; Cass Sunstein, 'Algorithms, Correcting Biases' (2019) 86 *Social Research: An International Quarterly* 499–511.

60 Jon Kleinberg, Sendhil Mullainathan, and Manish Raghavan, 'Inherent Trade-Offs in the Fair Determination of Risk Scores' in Christos C. Papadimitriou (ed.), *8th Innovations in Theoretical Computer Science Conference* (ITCS, 2017).

61 Jack M. Balkin, 'The Constitution in the National Surveillance State' (2008) 93 *Minnesota Law Review* 1–25.

opens the possibility that such data are abused for purposes pertaining to political control and discrimination.

In the context of the availability of massive amounts of data, AI enables new kinds of algorithmic mediated differentiations between individuals, which need to be strictly scrutinised. While in the pre-AI era differential treatments could be only based on the information extracted through individual interactions (interviews, interrogation, observation) and human assessments, or on few data points whose meaning was predetermined, in the AI era differential treatments can be based on vast amounts of data enabling probabilistic predictions, which may trigger algorithmically predetermined responses. In many cases, such differential treatment can be beneficial for the concerned individuals (consider for instance how patients may benefit from personalised health care, or how individuals in situations of social hardship can profit from the early detection of their issues and the provision of adequate help). However, such a differential treatment may on the contrary exacerbate the difficulties and inequalities that it detects. The impacts of such practices can go beyond the individuals concerned, and affect important social institutions, in the economical as well as in the political sphere. An example on point is the recourse to AI for generating grades based on past performance for students in the UK, given the inability to examine students on the relevant materials they should have learned during the COVID-19 crisis. Students reacted negatively to the decision, in part because the very idea of an exam is based on individual performance at the exam itself and substituting this data point by going to past practices, reproduces past group-based inequalities.[62]

8.14 OPAQUENESS AND EXPLAINABILITY (DUE PROCESS AND FAIRNESS)

A key issue concerning the use of machine learning in the public sector also concerns the fact that some of the most effective technologies for learning (in a particular neural network) tend to be opaque – that is, it is very difficult to explain, according to human-understandable reasons, their predictions in individual cases (e.g., why the machine says that an application should be rejected or that a person is likely to escape from parole). So not only can such machines fail to provide adequate justifications to the individuals involved, but their opacity may also be an obstacle to the identification of their failures and the implementation of improvements.[63]

An example for this conflict is the discussion concerning 'COMPAS' (Correctional Offender Management Profiling for Alternative Sanctions) – a software used by several US courts, in which an algorithm is used to assess how and whether a defendant is

62 Alex Hern, 'Do the Maths: Why England's A-Level Grading System Is Unfair', *The Guardian*, 14 August 2020.

63 See Riccardo Guidotti, Anna Monreale, Franco Turini, Dino Pedreschi, and Fosca Giannotti, 'A Survey of Methods for Explaining Black Box Models' (2018) 51(5) *ACM Computing Surveys* 93, 1–42.

likely to become a recidivist. Critics have pointed both to the inaccuracy of the system (claiming that in a large proportion of cases, the predictions that released individuals would or would not engage in criminal activities were proved to be mistaken) and on its unfairness.[64] On the latter point, it was observed that the proportion of black people mistakenly predicted to reoffend (relative to all black people) was much higher than the corresponding proportion of white people. Thus it was shown that black people have a higher chance of being mistakenly predicted to reoffend and be subject to the harsh consequences of this prediction. Consequently, detractors of the system accused it of being racially biased. Supporters of the system replied by pointing out that the accuracy of the system had to be matched against the accuracy of human judgments, which was apparently inferior. On the point of fairness, they responded that the system was fair, from their perspective: it treated equally blacks and whites in the sense that its indication that a particular individual would reoffend was equally related, for both blacks and whites, to the probability that the person would in reality reoffend: the proportion of black people which were correctly predicted to reoffend (relative to all black people who were predicted, correctly or incorrectly to reoffend) were similar to the same proportions for white people. The same was the case with regard to those who were predicted not to reoffend.[65]

The use of COMPAS was the object of a judicial decision, in the *Loomis v. Wisconsin* case, where it was claimed that the opacity of the system involved a violation of due process, and that the system might have been racially biased. The Court, however, concluded that the use of the algorithm did not violate due process, since it was up to the judge, as part of his or her judicial discretion, to determine what use to make of the recidivism assessment, and what weight to accord to other data. The Court also stated that the judges should be informed of the doubts being raised about the racial fairness of the system.

As noted, COMPAS presented the problem of the opacity of the algorithm, since defendants faced considerable hurdles in understanding the basis upon which the assessment in their case has been reached. This issue is compounded by an additional problem – the IP rights of the private companies that developed the system. Invoking IP rights proved to be an obstacle in obtaining the code, which may be necessary for providing a meaningful opportunity for challenging the outcomes of the system.[66]

Further issues concerning automated decisions in the justice domain pertain not so much to the accuracy and fairness of automated predictions, but rather to the use

64 Julia Angwin et al., 'Machine Bias: There's Software Used across the Country to Predict Future Criminals. And It's Biased against Blacks', *ProPublica*, 23 May 2016, www.propublica.org/article/machine-bias-risk-assessments-in-criminal-sentencing.

65 William Dieterich, Christina Mendoz, and Tim Brennan, 'Compas Risk Scales: Demonstrating Accuracy Equity and Predictive Parity: Performance of the Compas Risk Scales in Broward County', *Technical report, Northpointe Inc. Research Department*, 8 July 2016, https://go.volarisgroup.com/rs/430-MBX-989/images/ProPublica_Commentary_Final_070616.pdf.

66 Cynthia Rudin et al., 'The Age of Secrecy and Unfairness in Recidivism Prediction' (2020) 2(1) *Harvard Data Science Review*, https://doi.org/10.1162/99608f92.6ed64b30.

of such predictions. It has been argued that predictions of recidivism should be integrated by causal analyses of modifiable causes of recidivism. This would open the space for interventions meant to mitigate the risk of recidivism, rather than using the predictions only for aggravating the condition of the concerned individuals.[67]

The debate on automated decision-making within the justice system is part of a broader discussion of the multiple criteria for measuring the fairness of a predictive system relative to the equal treatment of individuals and groups,[68] a debate which adds a level of analytical clarity to the discussion on fairness and affirmative action, not only in connection with algorithms.[69]

Some initiatives to mitigate the issues related to automated decision models, by both public and private actors, were introduced in recent years. The European General Data Protection Regulations (GDPR)[70] – the goal of which is to 'supervise' the movement of data in the European Union, and mostly to protect the 'fundamental rights and freedoms of natural persons and in particular their right to the protection of personal data – addresses automated decision-making at Article 22. It establishes the right 'not to be subject to a decision based solely on automated processing, including profiling, which produces legal effects concerning him or her or similarly significantly affects him or her'. However, automated decision-making is permissible when explicitly consented by the data subject, when needed for entering into or performing a contract, or when 'authorised by Union or Member State law to which the controller is subject'. The laws that authorise automated decision-making must lay down 'suitable measures to safeguard the data subject's rights and freedoms and legitimate interests'. Thus a legality requirement for the use of automated decision-making by state authorities is established.

Another idea is Explainable Artificial Intelligence (xAI): this concept seeks to alleviate the 'black box' problem,[71] at least to an extent, by providing some human-understandable meaning to the process of decision-making and data analysis. Thus it

67 Chelsea Barabas et al., 'Interventions over Predictions: Reframing the Ethical Debate for Actuarial Risk Assessment' (2018) arXiv:1712.08238.

68 Richard Berk et al., 'Fairness in Criminal Justice Risk Assessments: The State of the Art' (2017) 50(1) *Mathematics, Psychology, Sociological Methods & Research* 3.

69 Solon Barocas and Andrew D. Selbst, 'Big Data's Disparate Impact' (2016) 104 *California Law Review* 671–732.

70 Regulation (EU) 2016/679 of the European Parliament and of the Council of 27 April 2016 on the protection of natural persons with regard to the processing of personal data and on the free movement of such data, and repealing Directive 95/46/EC (General Data Protection Regulation), OJ L119/1, art. 1. For the question of the compatibility of the GDPR with AI, see Giovanni Sartor and Francesca Legioia, 'Study: The Impact of the General Data Protection Regulation on Artificial Intelligence' (European Parliament: Panel for the Future of Science and Technology, 2020), 86–89; and for a rather different opinion on the matter, see Tal Zarsky, 'Incompatible: The GDPR in the Age of Big Data' (2017) 47(4) *Seton Hall Law Review* 995.

71 'Black Box' refers to the part of the algorithm that is hidden. This is generally occurring in machine-learning algorithms, when the major part of the algorithm, being the processing of the data, becomes so complex and so independent that it becomes almost impossible to understand what logical process was bringing the algorithm to a specific output and to what rationale it may correspond.

may contribute to reducing the due-process problem. This approach may also address problems of machine-learning bias[72], as in the COMPAS example noted previously, and answer questions of fairness in an algorithm's decision-making process. This approach is not free from difficulties, in particular relating to the question of the scope of the desired explanations. Do we wish, for example, for the explanation to be an 'everyday' explanation, that would lack in scientific, professional details, but provide an accessible explanation any individual would be able to understand? Or would we rather have a 'scientific' explanation, only meaningful to certain proficient and sufficiently educated individuals, though by far more reflective of the process? Related, is the question of process: do we need to know the exact process that led to the decision, or are we satisfied that an ex-post-facto explanation is available, namely that a backward-looking analysis can find a match between the decision reached and demonstrable salient factors, that can be understood by the data subject as relevant? There is also a question whether an explanation should be provided regarding the entire model or only to the specific decision or prediction. Furthermore, some explanations have the potential of being misleading, manipulative, or incoherent.[73]

Others also argue that human decision-making itself suffers from a lack of explainability, in the sense that one never fully knows what a human truly thought about while making a decision. Yet explanation and reason-giving are required especially because humans tend to suffer from bias and errors; the prior knowledge that they are required to provide an explanation for their decision offers a path for accountability, as it generates awareness and focuses the attention of the decision-maker, at the very least, on the need to reach a decision that fits criteria that can be explained, given the facts of the case.[74] Another argument stipulates that the main importance of the duty to provide reasoning is not having a 'casual' or a 'scientific' explanation – but having a *legal* explanation – claiming that an algorithm should be able to explain the rationale behind its decision and fulfil the legal requirements for an explanation, due process and other obligations set by administrative law or any other law.[75] Therefore, a fully detailed explanation does not necessarily provide

[72] For instance, the Australian government has been advised to introduce laws that ensure the explainability of AI. For a critical perspective, emphasising that where an AI algorithm cannot give a reasonable explanation it cannot be used where decisions can infringe human rights , see Angela Daly et al., *Artificial Intelligence Governance and Ethics: Global Perspectives* (2019), 4–5, https://arxiv.org/abs/1907.03848; GDPR emphasising 'right to explanation' in order to justify a decision made by ML model Commission Regulation 2016/679, art. 13(2)(f), 2016 O.J. (L 119) 1.

[73] See Brent Mittelstadt et al., 'Explaining Explanations in AI', Conference on Fairness, Accountability, and Transparency (2019). The article provides an extensive discussion on the question of the explanation in xAI. It also gives a rather important perspective regarding the nature of 'everyday' explanations and some of their downsides – being comparative, for example, and thus vulnerable to manipulation. See also Arun Rai, 'Explainable AI: From Black Box to Glass Box' (2020) *Journal of the Academy of Marketing Science* 48, 137–141, for a discussion concerning a two-dimensional approach to explanation techniques.

[74] For a wide discussion about reasons for explaining, see Katherine J. Strandburg, 'Rulemaking and Inscrutable Automated Decision Tools' (2020) 119(185) *Columbia Law Review* 1851, 1864.

[75] See Chapter 11 in this book.

a legal explanation. Attention should be paid also to the specific justification requirements for administrative and judicial decision-making (i.e., in particular, that a decision is grounded in legally acceptable rationales, based on legal sources).

Lastly, some argue that too much transparency may be bad. From an explainability perspective, more transparency does not mean better explainability. Informing an individual about every minor calculation does the exact opposite of what the idea of explainable AI is seeking to achieve: it saturates and ends up obfuscating. Moreover, too much transparency could reveal private data collected by the machine-learning software, hence infringing the right to privacy for many individuals and in this sense doing more harm than good. Some also claim that increased transparency will reduce private incentives and delay progress by forcing the exposure of certain key elements of a developer's intellectual property.[76] These problems are important to keep in mind when thinking about xAI.

8.15 THE SPECIFIC PROBLEMS OF 'ZERO PRICE' AND 'THE SCORE' (OR 'THE PROFILE')

Of particular concern is the lack of valuation of data for citizens/users/consumers, given that the collection of data is not attached to any tangible price. In most services online, whether offered by the industry or the state, there is no option to obtain the service while paying for the data not to be collected and analysed or rather to obtain the service without those aspects of it (e.g., personalised recommendations) that require our personal data.[77] The sense that we are getting an optimised service by giving up our private data and by subjecting ourselves to personalised information that would be fed back to us seems like a good deal in part because we have no way of fully understanding the value, in monetary terms, of the data we provide the system, and the value, in monetary terms, of the nudging that may be associated with the manner in which the personalised information is presented to us. We may be aware, of course, that the data lumps us with "people like us", thereby creating a filter buble, but it is almost impossible to figure out how much are would we be willing to pay in order to ascertain better control over this batching process. In other words, our consent is given in a highly suboptimal context: we lack important anchors for making an informed decision. Moreover, some may even argue that since we are already immersed in a saturated environment premised on surveillance capitalism, it is not easy to ensure that we have not been nudged to accept the loss of privacy (in both senses, the collection of data and the feedback of analysed data) as inevitable.

Furthermore, as noted, the logic of the algorithmic eco-system is that providing the data enhances the service. Each data point provided by users/citizens assists both

[76] Adrian Weller, 'Transparency: Motivations and Challenges', in Wojciech Samek et al., *Explainable AI: Interpreting, Explaining and Visualizing Deep Learning* (Springer, 2019), 23, 30.

[77] Frederik J. Zuiderveen Bourgesius et al., 'Tracking Walls, Take-It-or-Leave-It Choices, the GDPR, and the ePrivacy Regulation' (2017) 3(3) *European Data Protection Law Review* 353–368.

the data subject and other data subjects. In our daily lives, we seem to acquiesce by participating in the AI ecosystem, which is premised on constant surveillance, data collection, and data analysis, which is then fed back to us in correlation with the filter bubble to which we belong, thereby further shaping, nudging, and sculpting our outlook, attitude, mood, and preferences.

But with it comes a hidden price related to the accumulation of data and, more importantly, to the construction of a profile (often including a 'score'). The matter of the 'score' is pernicious. Attaching a certain number to a person, indicating the extent to which that person is predicted to have a certain desired or undesired feature, attitude, or capacity, brings to the fore a clash between the underlying feature of a liberal democracy – premised on the unrestricted authorship of any individual to write her or his own life story, express, experience, and expand their agency by interacting with others in a meaningful manner – with the bureaucratic logic of the regulatory state, even when this logic aims at achieving certain liberal goals (particularly the promotion of collective goods and the protection of human rights, including, ironically, the optimisation of human dignity). As soon as such goal-driven attitude is translated into a 'score', broadly understood (a classification as a good or bad customer or contractor, a quantification of a probability or propensity, such as the likelihood of recidivism, or a grade, as is the assessment of the merit of citizens or officers), and as soon such a score is attached to any move within the social matrix or to any individual interacting with another or with a state agency, then a dignitary component is lost. Yet without that score (or classification, or grade), we may be worse off, in the sense that the value brought about by the AI revolution may be sub-optimal, or lost altogether. Given this tension, greater attention needs to be given not only to the processes through which these 'scores' (or classifications, or grades, or profiles) are generated, including the power to understand and contest, and not only to the spheres and contexts in which such scores may be used, but also to the social meaning of the score, so that it is clear that we are not governed by a profile, but are seeking ways to constantly write, change, and challenge it.

An extreme example of the usage of 'score' would be the Chinese Social Credit System (SCS).[78] This system, used by the Chinese government, creates an extremely extensive database of personal data for every citizen, regarding most aspects of one's life. This data is then used to create a social credit score, which rates an individual's 'trustworthiness' and is then used by both authorities and business entities for their benefit.[79] A lower social credit score may lead to legal, economic, and reputational sanctions, while a higher social credit score would allegedly provide an individual

[78] For a thorough description of the Chinese credit system, its development, and implications on privacy and human rights, see Yongxi Chen and Anne Sy Cheung, 'The Transparent Self under Big Data Profiling: Privacy and Chinese Legislation on the Social Credit System' (2017) 12 *The Journal of Comparative Law* 356.

[79] Ibid., at 356–360.

with more opportunities and a better life.[80] This almost dystopian reality may seem to be a distant problem, relevant only to non-democratic societies such as China, but many believe that these ideas and especially technologies are not very unlikely to 'leak' into democratic Western societies as well.[81] The credit score systems used in most Western democracies for assessing the reliability of prospective borrowers, although less invasive and thorough, may not be as different from the SCS as one might think: In both systems, credit score is an index for an individual's reputation or trustworthiness. Also, both credit systems have many similar implications on an individual's life for good or for bad.[82]

8.16 THE DATA (AND AI DERIVATIVES)

On a more basic level, to date, it is not clear that the data sets used for training and calibrating the algorithms are sufficiently sound, in the sense that the data is not corrupt by either being inaccurate or reflecting past or pre-existing wrongs which, normatively, should be discounted and not reinforced.[83] For example, as noted previously, criticisms were raised against the extent to which predictive systems might reproduce and expand social bias. Various critics observed that systems trained on human decisions affected by prejudice (e.g., officers treating with harshness the member of certain groups), or on data sets that reflected different attitudes relative to different groups (e.g., data sets of past convictions, given different level of control over subpopulations), or on variables that disregarded the achievements of certain groups (e.g., results obtained in less selective educational environments) could lead to replicate iniquities and prejudice.

80 Ibid., at 362.

81 See Daithí Mac Síthigh and Mathias Siems, 'The Chinese Social Credit System: A Model for Other Countries?' (2019) 82 *Modern Law Review* 1034, for a discussion regarding the SCS, its relevance to Western societies, and its likelihood to influence them. The article also discusses different 'score' systems applied by Western democracies, with an emphasis on 'creditworthiness' ratings.

82 Ibid., at 5–11. Although a major difference is that unlike the SCS, Western credit scores encompass only the financial aspects of an individual's life, or perfomance at work (e.g., when work activities are managed through platforms, as for Uber drivers). Nevertheless, some are considering that twenty-first-century technology, along with ever-changing and growing economies, drive Western credit scores to encompass more and more aspects of our lives. See also John Harris, 'The Tyranny of Algorithms Is Part of Our Lives: Soon They Could Rate Everything We Do', *The Guardian*, 5 March 2018, www.theguardian.com/commentisfree/2018/mar/05/algorithms-rate-credit-scores-finances-data. See also Karen Yeung, 'Algorithmic Regulation: A Critical Interrogation' (2017) *Regulation & Governance*, 20–22, for another perspective of the so-called 'western, democratic type of surveillance society', along with some concerns and consequences.

83 See Angwin and others (n 66); Joy Buolamwini and Timnit Gebru, 'Gender Shades: Intersectional Accuracy Disparities in Commercial Gender Classification' (2018) *Proceedings of Machine Learning Research* 81. For research showing that by relying on non-reflective databases, a facial recognition algorithm showed far greater accomplishments among lighter-skinned males, with an overwhelming 99.2 per cent success rate, compared to as low as 63.3 per cent of success among darker-skinned females, see Strandburg (n 76).

The state of the data, therefore, casts serious doubts regarding the reasonableness of relying on the assumption that the algorithm is capable of achieving the preferred result, taking into consideration broader concerns of overall dignity and equal, meaningful membership in a society of moral agents. It then becomes a policy question of comparing the propensity of the algorithm to get it wrong because of corrupt data, to the propensity of humans to get it wrong on account of other errors, including bias, as well as our ability to generate social change so as to recognise past wrongs and work towards their remedy, rather than reification.

Data-related issues do not end here. The data may be problematic if it is not sufficiently reflective (or representative). This may be a product of a data market in which the data-collecting pipelines (and sensors) are owned or otherwise controlled by entities that erect barriers for economic reasons. The logic of surveillance capitalism tends to lead to the amalgamation of collection lines up to a point, precisely because the value of the data is related to it being reflective and therefore useful. But when a data-giant emerges – an entity the data it owns is sufficiently 'big' to allow for refined mining and analysis – the incentive to further collaborate and share data decreases. To the extent that data giants (or 'super-users') already have sufficient control over a certain data market, they may have an incentive to freeze competition out. Such access barriers may hamper optimised regulation.[84]

The dependence on data raises further concerns: data has to be continuously updated (for the algorithms to keep 'learning'). While with respect to some algorithms, the marginal utility of more data may be negligible (and in that sense, the algorithm has already 'learned' enough), the dynamic changes in technology, and more importantly, the changes in society as it interacts with technological developments and with new applications – many of which are designed to 'nudge' or otherwise affect people and thus generate further change – suggest that the demand for data (and updated AI based on that data) is un likely to diminish, at least in some contexts. This leads to accelerating pressures towards surveillance capitalism and the surveillance state. It also raises data-security concerns: data stored (for the purposes of 'learning') attracts hackers, and the risk for data breaches is ever-present. The state then has to decide on a data collection and retention policy: would it be agency specific? Or may agencies share data? The answer is far from easy. On the one hand, generating one database from which all state agencies draw data (and use these data for algorithmic purposes) is more efficient. It is easier to protect and to ensure all access to the data is logged and monitored. It also saves contradictions among

84 The lack of cooperation is not the only barrier raised in the big-data market. While most barriers are economic by their nature, some are more complicated to bypass, even given a sufficient economic cushion to work with. See, for example, Michal Gal and Daniel Rubinfeld, 'Access Barriers to Big Data' (2017) 59 *Arizona Law Review* 339. Also, some barriers were raised intentionally by governments in the past, with the intention to pursue a common good. For example, see also Michael Birnhack and Niva Elkin-Koren, 'The Invisible Handshake: The Reemergence of the State in the Digital Environment' (2003) 8(6) *SSRN Electronic Journal*, on public-private cooperation in fighting terrorism, resulting in a more concentrated information market.

different state agencies and, one may assume, reduces the rate of erroneous data, as it increases the chances of wrong data being corrected by citizens or by a state agency. To the extent that the data are indeed 'cleaner', the data analysis will be less prone to error. On the other hand, consolidating all data in one place (or allowing access to many or all agencies to data collected and stored by co-agencies) increases the allure for hackers, as the prize for breach is greater. Moreover, the consolidation of data raises separation-of-powers concerns. Access to data is power, which may be abused. The algorithmic state can be captured by special interests and/or illiberal forces, which may use algorithms for retaining control. Algorithms may assist such forces in governance as they may be used to manage public perception and nudge groups in an illiberal fashion. In other words, algorithms make social control easier. They may also be used to provide preferential treatment to some or discriminate against others. And they may infringe fundamental rights. Consequently, concentrating data in one central pot increases the risk of capture. Reasons underlying separation of powers – between the three branches, between state and federal powers, and within the various executive agencies – call for 'data federalism' whereby checking mechanisms are applied prior to data-sharing within various state agencies. Such sharing requires justification and should allow for real-time monitoring and ex-post review. The price is clear: access to data will be more cumbersome, and monitoring costs will increase. More importantly, the technical protocols will have to support effective review, so as to increase the likelihood of detecting, at least ex post, illegitimate use. To the best of our knowledge, the regulatory incentives are such that to date this field is under-developed.

8.17 PREDICTING PREDICTIONS

Rule of law concerns, fundamental rights infringements, and data-regulation questions are not the only issues facing the state. At this point in time, as the 'predictive' agencies are beginning to flex their algorithmic muscles, another use for predictive machine learning emerges: one that predicts how agencies make decisions. This approach can be deployed by the industry – as will be discussed later – but also by the state agencies themselves. In order to better manage their regulatory resources, and ease regulatory burden, agencies are seeking ways to separate the wheat from the chaff by knowing which regulatory problems deserve regulatory attention, versus other tasks that can be managed as a matter of routine. '97% of cases like that are decided in this or that way' is a message that is attached now to certain agency procedures, a product of an algorithm that follows state practice and designed to assist bureaucrats in deciding on which issues or decisions to focus, and which can be summarily decided one way or another. This approach is premised on the importance of having a human in the loop, or over the loop, so that decisions are not fully made by machines, but algorithms may nonetheless reflect useful information to the decision makers.

Such predictive algorithms, often designed and run by private entities, raise not only the familiar 'private-public-interface' conundrum, as the agencies partner with the industry, but also pose an interesting problem of path dependency: to the extent that the algorithm captures the bureaucratic practice as it is currently administered, and to the extent the predictive information it provides is indeed followed by state officials, the normative power of the actual is solidified, not necessarily as a product of thorough consideration, and in any event, in a manner that affects the path of future developments. As noted previously with regard to predictive justice (the use of algorithms to predict judicial decisions based on past cases), it remains to be seen how such algorithms will influence the expectations of those interacting with officers, as well as the behaviour of officers themselves. Algorithms developed by private entities and used by governments can create an accountability gap regarding the government's lack of ability to understand or explain the decision that has been made.[85]

As noted previously, the second main concern with the rise of the algorithmic society is that algorithms are (also, if not mainly) used by the regulated industry. Therefore, their use must also be regulated by checking the degree to which it conflicts with the regulatory regime (including statutory or constitutional rights). In that respect, the algorithmic state is facing the challenge to regulate the algorithmic industry, and determine the appropriate way to go about this task, given regulatory challenges related to informational asymmetries, intellectual property rights of the regulated industry, and privacy rights of its customers.

8.18 REGULATING THE INDUSTRY, REGULATING THE EXECUTIVE – REGULATING ALGORITHMS WITH ALGORITHMS?

The challenge of regulating the algorithmic market by the algorithmic state is technological, administrative, and legal. Technological, in the sense that the development of auditing tools for algorithms, or of statistical equivalents thereof, becomes an integral part of the evidence-gather process upon which any auditing regulatory scheme is premised. Recall that the state currently develops algorithms to audit the non-algorithmic activities of industries – for example, it develops auditing tools to monitor health-related records, or pollution-related records, or, for that matter, any record that is relevant for its auditing capacity. It now faces a challenge to develop auditing tools (algorithmic or non-algorithmic) in order to audit algorithmically developed records. The challenge is to have the technological tools to uncover illegal algorithms, namely algorithms that deploy processes or criteria that violate the law or algorithms that are used to pursue outcomes that violate the law. Technologically, this is a complex task, but it may be feasible. Put differently, if algorithms are the problem, they may also be the solution, provided the relevant ecosystem is developed and nurtured. It is also administratively challenging, because it requires qualified personnel, person-hours, and other resources, as well as the

85 Crawford and Shultz (n 38) suggest filling this gap by applying the state action doctrine to vendors who supply AI systems for government decision-making.

awareness and institutional incentives to follow through. Legally, it is challenging both institutionally and normatively. Institutionally, it may be the case that some procedures may need to be tweaked or modified in order to provide judicial or quasi-judicial bodies with the necessary procedural infra-structure with which inquiries into the misuses of algorithms can be conducted. This is not to suggest that a wholesale revolution is necessary, but neither is it to say that the current procedural tools are necessarily optimal. Normatively, it may be the case that some new rules may need to be introduced, in order to align the modalities of regulation with the challenges of regulating the algorithmic industry.[86]

More specifically, the risks – some of which identified in this chapter – need to be defined in a manner precise enough to enable the regulators to design appropriate regulatory means. This may be taxing, given the polycentric nature of the problem, as various goals – sometimes conflicting – may be at play. For example, as has been stated, data-driven AI markets tend to concentrate, and hence generate competition-related harms, but also democracy-related risks. Such concentration, and the potential to 'nudge' people within certain echo-chambers by deploying AI-driven manipulations, are certainly a challenge, to the extent we care about the integrity of the democratic process. Addressing each concern – the anti-trust challenge and the social-control worry – may point to different regulatory approaches.

Turning our attention to the available modalities, regulating information sharing seems to be important, in order to cut down disruptive information barriers by defining the relevant informational communities that should have access to certain information regarding regulated algorithms (defined as including the data pipelines that feed them and the output they produce). Some information should be shared with the state agency, while others with the customers/users. Similarly, licensing regimes may be relevant, to the extent that some algorithms require meeting some defined standards (such as privacy or accountability by design). This modality may apply also to the state regulating its own licensing agencies. Furthermore, the structure of civil and criminal liability may have to be refined, in order to match the responsibility of the relevant agents, as well as their incentives to comply. Criminal liability specifically might pose a serious problem with the further development of artificial intelligence and might require both the lawmakers and the court to find new solutions that will fit the technological changes.[87] Tax and subsidy modalities also come to mind, as the state may resort to taxing elements of the algorithmic eco-system (e.g., taxing opacity or providing subsidies for greater explainability[88]). In that respect, it would appear that an algorithm that tracks other algorithms in order to detect the saliency of certain criteria may be useful.

86 See Andrew Tutt, 'An FDA for Algorithms' (2017) 69 *Administrative Law Review* 83, for a possibly controversial solution of establishing a state agency in charge of assessing and approving algorithms for market use.

87 Nora Osmani, 'The Complexity of Criminal Liability in AI Systems' (2020) 14 *Masaryk U. J.L. & Tech.* 53.

88 See the discussion in Section 8.14 of this chapter.

And, finally, insurance may be a relevant regulatory factor, both as a tool to align incentives of the industry, and because insurance itself is algorithmic (in the sense that the insurance industry itself relies on machine learning to predict individualised risks and determine corresponding insurance premiums, which may affect risk-sharing).

In short, as the regulator and an actor itself, the state may be pulled by the algorithmic logic state in different directions. As an executive, it may seek to flex its algorithmic muscles so as to optimise its executive function. As a regulator, it may seek to harness algorithms in order to tame their far-reaching and perhaps unintended consequences. This requires policy formation processes that are attuned to the different pulls, as well as to the different modalities that can be put to bear in order to align the incentives.

8.19 REGULATION AND THE MARKET – THE BACKGROUND OF CIVIL LIABILITY

Before concluding, it is important to revisit regulation and policy making by situating these concepts in a larger context. According to some voices, technology at large and algorithms in particular are better off being 'deregulated'. We want to resist these calls not only for normative reasons (namely, that regulation is a good thing) but mainly because the term 'de-regulation' is misleading. There is always at least one regulatory modality which covers any field of human activity. At the very least, any human interaction raises questions of civil liability. The contours of such liability are a form of regulation, from the perspective of the state. If state agencies are still debating how to proceed with a specialised regulatory regime (including modalities other than civil liability), the residual nature of property, tort, contract, and unjust enrichment is always present.

Take two examples. To the extent the state does not regulate the production, distribution, and deployment of malicious software (which detects and exploits vulnerabilities algorithmically), at the end of the day a civil lawsuit may generate the boundaries of liability. This is exemplified by the civil suit brought by Facebook against NSO, for using the Facebook platform in order to plant malicious software (worms) which allow the attackers the ability to access information on the attacked device. This, of course, is a subject matter upon which a certain regulatory agency should have a say. But to the extent it does not, regulation is still present – in the form of civil liability. Likewise, a civil lawsuit opposed the pharmaceutical company Teva against Abbot Israel (the importer and distributor of Similac, a baby-food formula) and Agam Leaders Tech, a marketing firm. The suit alleges that the defendants engaged in a 'mendacious and covert slur campaign' by using fake profiles to distribute false information about Teva's product (Nutrilon) which caused Teva considerable damage. Such marketing campaigns rely on algorithms to detect relevant 'conversations' where either fake profiles or real people are rallied to put forward a certain position, almost always without the audience (or other participants in the conversation) being aware of the algorithmic rally being deployed (let alone being deployed for money). In such cases, a civil lawsuit will have to determine the boundaries of such algorithmic campaigns (and the potential duties to disclose their source) and the relevant regime of civil liability (including consumer protection).

8.20 CONCLUSION

While in legal literature usually a very sceptical approach is adopted toward a mechanical application of rules, different indications come from other disciplines, which focus on the limits of intuitive judgments. For instance, the economist and psychologist Daniel Kahneman observes that in many cases, simple algorithms provide better results than human intuition, even when human capacities and attitudes have to be assessed.[89] What should be the procedures and norms according to which the state ought to regulate the adoption of AI to its own decision and assessment infrastructure? Should there be a difference between mere application AI, relevant for implementation decisions in highly codified contexts, to discretionary AI, which is designed to address regulatory decisions in a more open legal landscape, to policy-making algorithms, which are designed to assist in the policy formation level?

In the previous section, we considered in detail many issues emerging from the intermingling of AI and government, concluding that the law and its principles such as human rights and the rule of law are not averse to AI-based innovation, but that nonetheless serious concerns emerge. AI, where appropriately deployed, can contribute to more informed, efficient, and fair state action, provided some safeguards are maintained. For this purpose, human judgment must not be substituted by the 'blind thought' of AI systems, which process whatever kind of information is provided to them without understanding its meaning and the human goals and values at stake. Humans must be in the loop or at least over the loop in every deployment of AI in the public domain, and should be trained so as to be mindful of the potential risks associated with being influenced by scores and profiles in a manner inconsistent with what must ultimately be human judgment. The level of human involvement should therefore be correlated to the extent to which essentially human capacities are required, such as empathy, value judgments, and capacity to deal with unpredictable circumstances and exceptions.

A broader speculation concerns whether, or to what extent, the impact of AI will generate a change in the manner by which we are governed. More specifically, it concerns whether the law, as we understand it now, particularly in connection with the value of the rule of law, may be supplemented or even substituted by different ways to guiding human action, driven by the extensive deployment of AI.[90]

89 Kahneman (n 16).

90 See Mireille Hildebrandt, *Smart Technologies and the End(s) of Law: Novel Entanglements of Law and Technology* (Elgar, 2016).

The law, in its current form, is based on authoritative verbal messages, which are enacted in written form by legislative and administrative bodies. Such messages usually convey general instructions which order, prohibit or permit certain courses of action, and in so doing also convey a normative or moral position with respect to these actions. Interwoven within the legal apparatus are further norms that perform ancillary functions, by ascribing legal outcomes (or sanctions), qualifications to people and objects, as well as by creating institutional facts, institutions, and procedures. Legislation and administration are complemented by other written verbal messages, namely judicial or quasi-judicial decisions – which apply the law to specific cases, developing and specifying it – as well as by doctrinal writings which interpret and develop the norms, close gaps between the code and social life, and again generate expressive content pertaining to morality and identity. To become active, such verbal messages have to be understood by humans (the addressees of legal provisions), and this may require an act of interpretation. An act of human understanding is also required to comprehend and apply non-written sources of the law, such as customs and other normative practices. Once that the citizens or officers concerned have understood what the law requires from them in their circumstances, they will usually comply with the law, acting as it requires, but they may also choose to evade or violate the law (though this may entail the possibility of suffering the consequences of violation) or otherwise sidestep the legal rule by relying on a standard which may conflict with the rule or potentially mute its application. They may also approve or disapprove of the norms in question and voice their opposition. Thus, the law assumes, at least in a democratic state, that citizens are both free agents and critical reasoners.

It is unclear whether the law will preserve this form in the future, as AI systems are increasingly deployed by the state. This is problematic. In a world in which the governance of human action is primarily delegated to AI, citizens could either no longer experience genuine legal guidance (or experience it to a lesser extent), being rather nudged or manipulated to act as desired (and thus the law as such would be rendered irrelevant or much less relevant), or they would only or mainly experience the law through the mediation of AI systems.

The first option – the substitution of normativity with technology – would take place if human action were influenced in ways that prescind from the communication of norms.[91] The state might rather rely on 'technoregulation'.[92] Such an architecture may open or preclude possibilities to act (enable or disable actions, as when access to virtual or digital facilities require automated identification), open or preclude possibilities to observe human action (enable or disable surveillance), facilitate or make more difficult, or more or less accessible certain opportunities

[91] As noted by Lawrence Lessig, *Code Version 2.0* (Basic Books, 2006).

[92] Roger Brownsword, 'What the World Needs Now: Techno-regulation, Human Rights and Human Dignity' in Roger Brownsword (ed.), *Global Governance and the Quest for Justice. Volume 4: Human Rights* (Hart Publishing, 2004), 203–234.

(as it is the case for default choices which nudge users into determined options), directly perform action that impacts on the interests of concerning individuals (e.g., apply a tax or a fine, disabling the functioning of a device, such as a car, etc.), or may direct individuals through micro-targeted rewards and punishments towards purposes that may not be shared by or that are not even communicated to the concerned individuals. This is troubling, even dystopian, to the extent we care about human agency (and human dignity) as currently understood.

The second option, AI-mediated normativity, would take place if the state were to delegate to AI systems the formulation of concrete indications to citizens – on the predicted outcome of cases, or the actions to be done or avoided in a given context – without citizens having access to understandable rules and principles that support and justify such concrete indications. The citizens would just know that these concrete indications have been devised by the AI system itself, in order to optimise the achievement of the policy goals assigned to it. Citizens would be in a situation similar to that of a driver being guided step by step by a GPS system, without having access to the map showing the territory and the available routes toward the destination. Again, the implications regarding agency, meaningful participation in a community of moral agents, and human dignity are obvious (and troubling).

In summary, if these scenarios materialise, and especially if they materialise in a concentrated market (characterised by states and monopolies), we fear that humans may lose a significant component of control over the normative framework of their social action, as well as the ability to critically address such a normative framework. In this context, the state may no longer address its citizens (and lower officers as well) as fully autonomous agents, capable of grasping the law's commands (and acting accordingly, based on such understanding, and on the reasons they have for complying).[93] This concern holds also for office-holders, who are often the direct subject of such instructions.[94] Moreover, it is unclear whether the state would still consider its citizen as agents capable of critical reflection, able to grasp the rationales of the commands (or instructions) and subject them to scrutiny, debate, and deliberation. Such a transformation entails a fundamental shift in the structure of communication[95] underlying the legal system and thus raises significant moral legitimacy concerns.

We believe therefore that it is essential that the state continues to express its regulatory norms in human language, and that the human interpretation of such instructions, in the context of legal principles and political values, represents the

[93] Gerald Postema, 'Law as Command: The Model of Command in Modern Jurisprudence' (2001) 11 *Philosophical Issues* 18.

[94] Meir Dan Cohen, 'Decision Rules and Conduct Rules: Acoustic Separation in Criminal Law' 97 *Harv. L. Rev* 625 (1983–1984); Edward L. Rubin, 'Law and Legislation in the Administrative State' 89 *Colum. L. Rev*. 369 (1989).

[95] Mark Van Hoecke, 'Law as Communication' (Hart Publishing, 2001), engaging with the theory of Niklas Luhmann (System Theory), as further expounded by Gunter Tuebner (Law as an Autopoietic System).

reference for assessing the way in which the law is applied through AI systems, and more generally, the way in which the operation of such systems affects individual interests and social values.

In conclusion, AI puts forward significant opportunities but also a deep challenge to the state, as the latter debates the uses and misuses of AI.

9

AI, Governance and Ethics

Global Perspectives

*Angela Daly, Thilo Hagendorff, Li Hui, Monique Mann, Vidushi Marda, Ben Wagner, and Wayne Wei Wang**

9.1 INTRODUCTION

Artificial intelligence (AI) is a technology which is increasingly being utilised in society and the economy worldwide, but there is much disquiet over problematic and dangerous implementations of AI, or indeed even AI itself deciding to do dangerous and problematic actions. These developments have led to concerns about whether and how AI systems currently adhere to and will adhere to ethical standards, stimulating a global and multistakeholder conversation on AI ethics and the production of AI governance initiatives. Such developments form the basis for this chapter, where we give an insight into what is happening in Australia, China, the European Union, India and the United States.

We commence with some background to the AI ethics and regulation debates, before proceedings to give an overview of what is happening in different countries and regions, namely Australia, China, the European Union (including national level activities in Germany), India and the United States. We provide an analysis of these country profiles, with particular emphasis on the relationship between ethics and law in each location.

Overall we find that AI governance and ethics initiatives are most developed in China and the European Union, but the United States has been catching up in the last eighteen months. India remains an outlier among these 'large jurisdictions' by

* This chapter is a revised and updated version of a report the authors wrote in 2019: Angela Daly, Thilo Hagendorff, Li Hui, Monique Mann, Vidushi Marda, Ben Wagner, Wayne Wei Wang and Saskia Witteborn, 'Artificial Intelligence, Governance and Ethics: Global Perspectives' (The Chinese University of Hong Kong Faculty of Law Research Paper No. 2019-15, 2019).

We acknowledge the support for this report from Angela Daly's Chinese University of Hong Kong 2018–2019 Direct Grant for Research 2018–2019 'Governing the Future: How Are Major Jurisdictions Tackling the Issue of Artificial Intelligence, Law and Ethics?'.

We also acknowledge the research assistance for the report from Jing Bei and Sunny Ka Long Chan, and the comments and observations from participants in the CUHK Law Global Governance of AI and Ethics workshop, 20–21 June 2019.

not articulating a set of AI ethics principles, and Australia hints at the challenges a smaller player may face in forging its own path. The focus of these initiatives is beginning to turn to producing legally enforceable outcomes, rather than just purely high-level, usually voluntary, principles. However, legal enforceability also requires practical operationalising of norms for AI research and development, and may not always produce desirable outcomes.

9.2 AI, REGULATION AND ETHICS

AI has been deployed in a range of contexts and social domains, with mixed outcomes, including in finance, education, employment, marketing and policing.[1] At this relatively early stage in AI's development and implementation, the issue has arisen of AI adhering to certain ethical principles.[2] The ability of existing laws to govern AI has emerged as another key question as to how future AI will be developed, deployed and implemented.[3] While originally confined to theoretical, technical and academic debates, the issue of governing AI has recently entered the mainstream with both governments and private companies from major geopolitical powers including the United States, China and the European Union formulating statements and policies regarding AI and ethics.[4]

A host of questions are raised by these developments. For one, what are the ethical standards to which AI should adhere? The transnational nature of digitised technologies, the key role of private corporations in AI development and implementation and the globalised economy give rise to questions about which jurisdictions and actors will decide on these standards. Will we end up with a 'might is right' approach where it is these large geopolitical players which set the agenda for AI regulation and ethics for the whole world? Further questions arise regarding the enforceability of ethics statements regarding AI, both in terms of whether they reflect existing fundamental legal principles and are legally enforceable in specific jurisdictions,

[1] See, e.g., Cathy O'Neil, *Weapons of Math Destruction: How Big Data Increases Inequality and Threatens Democracy*. (Penguin Random House 2016); Andrew Guthrie Ferguson, *The Rise of Big Data Policing Surveillance, Race and the Future of Law Enforcement* (NYU Press 2017).

[2] See, e.g., Ronald Arkin, 'Ethical Robots in Warfare' (2009) 28(1) *IEEE Technology & Society Magazine* 30; Richard Mason, 'Four Ethical Issues of the Information Age' in John Wekert (ed), *Computer Ethics* (Routledge 2017).

[3] See, e.g., Ronald Leenes and Federica Lucivero, 'Laws on Robots, Laws by Robots, Laws in Robots: Regulating Robot Behaviour by Design' (2014) 6(2) *Law, Innovation & Technology* 193; Ryan Calo, 'Robotics and the Lessons of Cyberlaw' (2015) 103(3) *California Law Review* 513; Sandra Wachter, Brett Mittelstadt and Luciano Floridi, 'Transparent, Explainable, and Accountable AI for Robotics' (2017) 2(6) *Science Robotics* 6080.

[4] See, e.g., European Commission, 'European Group on Ethics in Science and New Technologies Statement on Artificial Intelligence, Robotics and "Autonomous" Systems' (2018) https://ec.europa.eu/research/ege/pdf/ege_ai_statement_2018.pdf accessed 21 June 2020; Sundar Pichai, 'AI at Google: Our Principles' (7 June 2018) www.blog.google/technology/ai/ai-principles/ accessed 21 June 2020.

and the extent to which the principles can be operationalised and integrated into AI systems and applications in practice.

Ethics itself is seen as a reflection theory of morality or as the theory of the good life. A distinction can be made between fundamental ethics, which is concerned with abstract moral principles, and applied ethics.[5] The latter also includes ethics of technology, which contains in turn AI ethics as a subcategory. Roughly speaking, AI ethics serves for the self-reflection of computer and engineering sciences, which are engaged in the research and development of AI or machine learning. In this context, dynamics such as individual technology development projects, or the development of new technologies as a whole, can be analysed. Likewise, causal mechanisms and functions of certain technologies can be investigated using a more static analysis.[6] Typical topics are self-driving cars, political manipulation by AI applications, autonomous weapon systems, facial recognition, algorithmic discrimination, conversational bots, social sorting by ranking algorithms and many more.[7] Key demands of AI ethics relate to aspects such as research goals and purposes, research funding, the linkage between science and politics, the security of AI systems, the responsibility for the development and use of AI technologies, the inscription of values in technical artefacts, the orientation of the technology sector towards the common good and much more.[8]

In this chapter, we give an overview of major countries and regions' approaches to AI, governance and ethics. We do not claim to present an exhaustive account of approaches to this issue internationally, but we do aim to give a snapshot of how some countries and regions, especially large ones like China, the European Union, India and the United States, are (or are not) addressing the topic. We also include some initiatives at the national level, of EU Member State Germany and Australia, all of which can be considered as smaller (geo)political and legal entities. In examining these initiatives, we look at one particular aspect, namely the extent to which these ethics/governance initiatives from governments are legally enforceable. This is an important question given concerns about 'ethics washing': that ethics and governance initiatives without the binding force of law are mere 'window dressing' while unethical uses of AI by governments and corporations continue.[9]

These activities, especially of the 'large jurisdictions', are important given the lack of international law explicitly dealing with AI. There has been some activity from

5 Otfried Höffe, *Ethik: Eine einführung* (C. H. Beck 2013).

6 Iyad Rahwan et al., 'Machine Behaviour' (2019) 568(7753) *Nature* 477.

7 Thilo Hagendorff, "The Ethics of AI Ethics. An Evaluation of Guidelines' (2020) 30 *Minds & Machines* 99.

8 Future of Life Institute, 'Asilomar AI Principles' (2017) https://futureoflife.org/ai-principles accessed 21 June 2020.

9 Ben Wagner, 'Ethics as an Escape from Regulation: From Ethics-Washing to Ethics-Shopping?' in Mireille Hildebrandt (ed), *Being Profiled. Cogitas ergo sum* (Amsterdam University Press 2018).

international organisations such as the OECD's Principles on AI, which form the basis for the G20's non-binding guiding principles for using AI.[10] There are various activities that the United Nations (UN) and its constituent bodies are undertaking which relate to AI.[11] The most significant activities are occurring at UNESCO, which has commenced a two-year process 'to elaborate the first global standard-setting instrument on ethics of artificial intelligence', which it aims to produce by late 2021.[12] However, prospects of success for such initiatives, especially if they are legally enforceable, may be dampened by the fact that an attempt in 2018 to open formal negotiations to reform the UN Convention on Certain Conventional Weapons to govern or prohibit fully autonomous lethal weapons was blocked by the United States and Russia, among others.[13] In June 2020, various states – including Australia, the European Union, India, the United Kingdom and the United States, but excluding China and Russia – formed the Global Partnership on Artificial Intelligence (GPAI), an 'international and multistakeholder initiative to guide the responsible development and use of AI, grounded in human rights, inclusion, diversity, innovation, and economic growth'.[14] GPAI's activities, and their convergence or divergence with those in multilateral fora such as UN agencies, remain to be seen.

In the following sections, we give overviews of the situation in each country/region and the extent to which legally binding measures have been adopted. We have specifically considered government initiatives which frame and situate themselves in the realm of 'AI governance' or 'AI ethics'. We acknowledge that other initiatives, from corporations, NGOs and other organisations on AI ethics and governance, and other initiatives from different stakeholders on topics relevant to 'big data' and the 'Internet of Things', may also be relevant to AI governance and ethics. Further work should be conducted on these and on 'connecting the dots' between some predecessor digital technology governance initiatives and the current drive for AI ethics and governance.

[10] OECD, 'OECD Principles on AI' (2019) www.oecd.org/going-digital/ai/principles/ accessed 21 June 2020; G20, 'Ministerial Statement on Trade and Digital Economy' (2019) https://trade.ec.europa.eu/doclib/docs/2019/june/tradoc_157920.pdf accessed 21 June 2020.

[11] ITU, 'United Nations Activities on Artificial Intelligence' (2018) www.itu.int/dms_pub/itu-s/opb/gen/S-GEN-UNACT-2018-1-PDF-E.pdf accessed 21 June 2020.

[12] UNESCO, 'Elaboration of a Recommendation on Ethics of Artificial Intelligence' https://en.unesco.org/artificial-intelligence/ethics accessed 21 June 2020.

[13] Janosch Delcker, 'US, Russia Block Formal Talks on Whether to Ban "Killer Robots"' (*Politico*, 1 September 2018) www.politico.eu/article/killer-robots-us-russia-block-formal-talks-on-whether-to-ban/ accessed 21 June 2020.

[14] Government of Canada, 'Joint Statement from Founding Members of the Global Partnership on Artificial Intelligence' (15 June 2020) www.canada.ca/en/innovation-science-economic-development/news/2020/06/joint-statement-from-founding-members-of-the-global-partnership-on-artificial-intelligence.html?fbclid=IwAR0QF7jyy0ZwHBm8zkjkRQqjbIgiLd8wt939PbZ7EbLICPdupQwR685dlvw accessed 21 June 2020.

9.3 COUNTRY/REGION PROFILES

Australia

While Australia occupies a unique position as the only western liberal democracy without comprehensive enforceable human rights protections,[15] there has been increasing attention on the human rights impacts of technology and the development of an AI ethics framework.

The Australian AI Ethical Framework was initially proposed by Data 61 and CSIRO in the Australian Commonwealth (i.e., federal) Department of Industry, Innovation and Science in 2019.[16] A discussion paper from this initiative commenced with an examination of existing ethical frameworks, principles and guidelines and included a selection of largely international or US-based case studies, which overshadowed the unique Australian socio-political-historical context. It set out eight core principles to form an ethical framework for AI. The proposed framework was accompanied by a 'toolkit' of strategies, as attempts to operationalise the high-level ethical principles in practice, including impact and risk assessments, best practice guidelines and industry standards. Following a public consultation process, which involved refinement of the eight proposed principles (for example, merging two and adding a new one), the Australian AI Ethics Principles are finalised as: human, social and environmental wellbeing; human-centred values; fairness; privacy protection and security; reliability and safety; transparency and explainability; contestability; and accountability.[17] The Principles are entirely voluntary and have no legally binding effect. The Australian government released some guidance for the Principles' application, but this is scant compared to other efforts in, for example, Germany (as discussed later).[18]

One further significant development is the Human Rights and Technology project that is being led by the Australian Human Rights Commissioner Edward Santow, explicitly aimed at advancing a human rights–based approach to regulating

[15] See Monique Mann, Angela Daly, Michael Wilson and Nicolas Suzor, 'The Limits of (Digital) Constitutionalism: Exploring the Privacy-Security (Im)balance in Australia' (2018) 80(4) *International Communication Gazette* 369; Monique Mann and Angela Daly, '(Big) Data and the North-*in*-South: Australia's Informational Imperialism and Digital Colonialism' (2019) 20(4) *Television & New Media* 379.

[16] Australian Government Department of Industry, Innovation and Science (2019), *Artificial Intelligence: Australia's Ethics Framework* (7 November 2019) https://consult.industry.gov.au/strategic-policy/artificial-intelligence-ethics-framework/ accessed 22 June 2020.

[17] Australian Government Department of Industry, Science, Energy and Resources, 'AI Ethics Principles' www.industry.gov.au/data-and-publications/building-australias-artificial-intelligence-capability/ai-ethics-framework/ai-ethics-principles accessed 22 June 2020.

[18] Australian Government Department of Industry, Science, Energy and Resources, 'Applying the AI Ethics Principles' www.industry.gov.au/data-and-publications/building-australias-artificial-intelligence-capability/ai-ethics-framework/applying-the-ai-ethics-principles accessed 22 June 2020.

AI.[19] The Australian Human Rights Commission (AHRC) has made a series of proposals, including: the development of an Australian National Strategy on new and emerging technologies; that the Australian government introduce laws that require an individual to be informed where AI is used and to ensure the explainability of AI-informed decision-making; and that where an AI-informed decision-making system does not produce reasonable explanations, it should not be deployed where decisions can infringe human rights. The AHRC has also called for a legal moratorium on the use of facial recognition technology until an appropriate legal framework has been implemented. There is the potential for these proposals to become legally binding, subject to normal parliamentary processes and the passage of new or amended legislation.

China

China has been very active in generating state-supported or state-led AI governance and ethics initiatives along with its world-leading AI industry. Until the 2019 Trump Executive Order stimulating AI governance and ethics strategy development in the United States, China combined both this very strong AI industry with governance strategising, contrasting with its main competitor.

In 2017, China's State Council issued the New-Generation AI Development Plan (AIDP), which advanced China's objective of high investment in the AI sector in the coming years, with the aim of becoming the world leader in AI innovation.[20] An interim goal, by 2025, is to formulate new laws and regulations, and ethical norms and policies related to AI development in China. This includes participation in international standard setting, or even 'taking the lead' in such activities as well as 'deepen[ing] international cooperation in AI laws and regulations'.[21] The plan introduced China's attitude towards AI ethical, legal and social issues (ELSI), and prescribed that AI regulations should facilitate the 'healthy development of AI'.[22] The plan also mentioned AI legal issues including civil and criminal liability, privacy and cybersecurity. Its various ethical proposals include a joint investigation into AI behavioural science and ethics, an ethical multi-level adjudicative structure and an ethical framework for human-computer collaboration.

To support the implementation of 'Three-Year Action Plan to Promote the Development of a New Generation of Artificial Intelligence Industry (2018–2020)', the 2018 AI Standardization Forum released its first White Paper on AI

19 Australian Human Rights Commission, 'Human Rights and Technology' (17 December 2019) www.humanrights.gov.au/our-work/rights-and-freedoms/projects/human-rights-and-technology accessed 22 June 2020.

20 FLIA. (2017). *China's New Generation of Artificial Intelligence Development Plan* (30 July 2017) https://flia.org/notice-state-council-issuing-new-generation-artificial-intelligence-development-plan/ accessed 22 June 2020.

21 Ibid.

22 Ibid.

Standardization.[23] It signalled that China would set up the National AI Standardization Group and the Expert Advisory Panel. Public agencies, enterprises and academics appear to be closely linked to the group, and tech giants like Tencent, JD, Meituan, iQiyi, Huawei and Siemens China are included in the Advisory Panel on AI ethics. The 2019 report on AI risks then took the implications of algorithms into serious consideration by building upon some declarations and principles proposed by international, national and technical communities and organisations concerning algorithmic regulation.[24] The report also proposes two ethical guidelines for AI. The first is the principle of human interest, which means that AI should have the ultimate goal of securing human welfare; the second is the principle of liability, which implies that there should be an explicit regime for accountability in both the development and deployment of AI-related technologies.[25] In a broader sense, liability ought to be considered as an overarching principle that can guarantee transparency as well as consistency of rights and responsibilities.[26]

There have been further initiatives on AI ethics and governance. In May 2019, the Beijing AI Principles were released by the Beijing Academy of Artificial Intelligence, which depicted the core of its AI development as 'the realization of beneficial AI for humankind and nature'.[27] The Principles have been supported by various elite Chinese universities and companies including Baidu, Alibaba and Tencent. Another group comprising top Chinese universities and companies and led by the Ministry of Industry and Information Technology's (MIIT's) China Academy of Information and Communications Technology, the Artificial Intelligence Industry Alliance (AIIA) released its Joint Pledge on Self Discipline in the Artificial Intelligence Industry, also in May 2019. While the wording is fairly generic when compared to other ethics and governance statements, Webster points to the language of 'secure/safe and controllable' and 'self-discipline' as 'mesh[ing] with broader trends in Chinese digital governance'.[28]

23 中国电子技术标准化研究院 (China Electronics Standardization Institute), '人工智能标准化白皮书 (White Paper on AI Standardization)' (January 2018) www.cesi.cn/images/editor/20180124/20180124135528742.pdf accessed 22 June 2020.

24 国家人工智能标准化总体组 (National AI Standardization Group), '人工智能伦理风险分析报告 (Report on the Analysis of AI-Related Ethical Risks)' (April 2019) www.cesi.cn/images/editor/20190425/20190425142632634001.pdf accessed 22 June 2020. The references include (1) ASILOMAR AI Principles; (2) the Japanese Society for Artificial Intelligence Ethical Guidelines; (3) Montréal Declaration for Responsible AI (draft) Principles; (4) Partnership on AI to Benefit People and Society; (5) the IEEE Global Initiative on Ethics of Autonomous and Intelligent Systems.

25 Huw Roberts et al., 'The Chinese Approach to Artificial Intelligence: An Analysis of Policy and Regulation' (2020) *AI & Society* (forthcoming).

26 国家人工智能标准化总体组 (National AI Standardization Group) (n 24) 31–32.

27 Beijing Academy of Artificial Intelligence, 'Beijing AI principles' (28 February 2019) www.baai.ac.cn/blog/beijing-ai-principles accessed 22 June 2020.

28 Graham Webster, 'Translation: Chinese AI alliance drafts self-discipline "Joint Pledge" (*New America Foundation*, 17 June 2019) www.newamerica.org/cybersecurity-initiative/digichina/blog/translation-chinese-ai-alliance-drafts-self-discipline-joint-pledge/ accessed 22 June 2020.

An expert group established by the Chinese Government Ministry of Science and Technology released its eight Governance Principles for the New Generation Artificial Intelligence: Developing Responsible Artificial Intelligence in June 2019.[29] Again, international cooperation is emphasised in the principles, along with 'full respect' for AI development in other countries. A possibly novel inclusion is the idea of 'agile governance', that problems arising from AI can be addressed and resolved 'in a timely manner'. This principle reflects the rapidity of AI development and the difficulty in governing it through conventional procedures, for example through legislation which can take a long time to pass in China, by which time the technology may have already changed. While 'agile policy-making' is a term also used by the European Union High-Level Expert Panel, it is used in relation to the regulatory sandbox approach, as opposed to resolving problems, and is also not included in the Panel's Guidelines as a principle.

While, as mentioned previously, Chinese tech corporations have been involved in AI ethics and governance initiatives both domestically in China and internationally in the form of the Partnership on AI,[30] they also appear to be internally considering ethics in their AI activities. Examples include Toutiao's Technology Strategy Committee, which partially acts as an internal ethics board.[31] Tencent also has its AI for Social Good programme and ARCC (Available, Reliance, Comprehensible, Controllable) Principles but does not appear to have an internal ethics board to review AI developments.[32]

Although the principles set by these initiatives initially lacked legal enforcement/enforceability and policy implications, China highlighted in the 2017 AIDP three AI-related applied focuses, namely international competition, economic growth and social governance,[33] which have gradually resulted in ethical and then legal debates.

First, China's agile governance model is transforming AI ethics interpreted in industrial standards into the agenda of national and provincial legislatures. After the birth of a gene-edited-baby caused the establishment of the National Science and Technology Ethics Committee in late 2019, the Ethics Working Group of the Chinese Association of Artificial Intelligence is planning to establish and formulate

29 China Daily, 'Governance Principles for the New Generation Artificial Intelligence–Developing Responsible Artificial Intelligence' (17 June 2020) www.chinadaily.com.cn/a/201906/17/WS5d07486ba3103dbf14328ab7.html accessed 22 June 2020.

30 However, the Chinese representative, Baidu, which is the largest search giant in China, has recently left the Partnership on AI amid the current US-China tension. See Will Knight, 'Baidu Breaks Off an AI Alliance Amid Strained US-China Ties' (*Wired*, 18 June 2020) www.wired.com/story/baidu-breaks-ai-alliance-strained-us-china-ties/ accessed 13 August 2020.

31 新京报网 (BJNews), '人工智能企业要组建道德委员会，该怎么做 (Shall AI Enterprises Establish an Internal Ethics Board? And How?)' (2019) www.bjnews.com.cn/feature/2019/07/26/608130.html accessed 15 May 2020.

32 J. Si *Towards an Ethical Framework for Artificial Intelligence* (2018) https://mp.weixin.qq.com/s/_CbBsrjrTbRkKjUNdmhuqQ.

33 Roberts et al. (n 25).

various ethical regulations for AI in different industries, such as self-driving, data ethics, smart medicine, intelligent manufacturing and elders-aiding robot specifications.[34] National and local legislation and regulation have been introduced or are being experimented upon to ensure AI security in relation to drones, self-driving cars and fintech (e.g., robot advisors).[35]

Second, AI ethics has had a real presence in social issues and judicial cases involving human-machine interaction and liability. One instance has involved whether AI can be recognised as the creator of works for copyright purposes, where two courts in 2019 came to opposing decisions on that point.[36] Another has involved regulatory activity on the part of the Cyberspace Administration of China to address deepfakes. It has issued a draft policy on Data Security Management Measures which proposes requiring as part of their platform liability service providers that use AI to automatically synthesise 'news, blog posts, forum posts, comments etc', to clearly signal such information as 'synthesized' without any commercial purposes or harms to others' pre-existing interests.[37]

European Union

Perceived to be lacking the same level of industrial AI strength as China and the United States, the European Union has been positioning itself as a frontrunner in the global debate on AI governance and ethics from legal and policy perspectives. The General Data Protection Regulation (GDPR), a major piece of relevant legislation, came into effect in 2018, and has a scope (Art 3) which extends to some organisations outside of the European Union in certain circumstances,[38] and provisions on the Right to Object (Article 21) and Automated Individual Decision-Making Including Profiling (Article 22). There is significant discussion as to precisely what these provisions entail in practice regarding algorithmic

[34] 中新网 (ChinaNews), '新兴科技带来风险 加快建立科技伦理审查制度 (As Emerging Technologies Bring Risks, the State Should Accelerate the Establishment of a Scientific and Technological Ethics Review System)' (9 August 2019) https://m.chinanews.com/wap/detail/zw/gn/2019/08-09/8921353.shtml accessed 22 June 2020.

[35] 全国信息安全标准化技术委员会 (National Information Security Standardization Technical Committee), '人工智能安全标准化白皮书 (2019版) (2019 Artificial Intelligence Security Standardization White Paper)' (October 2019) www.cesi.cn/images/editor/20191101/20191101115151443.pdf accessed 22 June 2020.

[36] Kan He, '*Feilin* v. *Baidu*: Beijing Internet Court Tackles Protection of AI/Software-Generated Work and Holds that Copyright Only Vests in Works by Human Authors' (*The IPKat*, 9 November 2019) http://ipkitten.blogspot.com/2019/11/feilin-v-baidu-beijing-internet-court.html accessed 22 June 2020. 'AI Robot Has IP Rights, Says Shenzhen Court' (*Greater Bay Insight*, 6 January 2020) https://greaterbayinsight.com/ai-robot-has-ip-rights-says-shenzhen-court/ accessed 22 June 2020.

[37] Ibid.

[38] Benjamin Greze, 'The Extra-territorial Enforcement of the GDPR: A Genuine Issue and the Quest for Alternatives' (2019) 9(2) *International Data Privacy Law* 109.

decision-making, automation and profiling and whether they are adequate to address the concerns that arise from such processes.[39]

Among other prominent developments in the European Union is the European Parliament Resolution on Civil Law Rules on Robotics from February 2017.[40] While the Resolution is not binding, it expresses the Parliament's opinion and requests the European Commission to carry out further work on the topic. In particular, the Resolution 'consider[ed] that the existing Union legal framework should be updated and complemented, where appropriate, by guiding ethical principles in line with the complexity of robotics and its many social, medical and bioethical implications'.[41]

In March 2018, the European Commission issued a Communication on Artificial Intelligence for Europe, in which the Commission set out 'a European initiative on AI' with three main aims: of boosting the European Union's technological and industrial capacity, and AI uptake; of preparing for socio-economic changes brought about by AI (with a focus on labour, social security and education); and of ensuring 'an appropriate ethical and legal framework, based on the Union's values and in line with the Charter of Fundamental Rights of the European Union'.[42]

The European Union High-Level Expert Group on Artificial Intelligence, a multistakeholder group of fifty-two experts from academia, civil society and industry produced the Ethics Guidelines for Trustworthy AI in April 2019, including seven key, but non-exhaustive, requirements that AI system ought to meet in order to be 'trustworthy'.[43] The Expert Group then produced Policy and Investment Recommendations for Trustworthy AI in June 2019.[44] Among the recommendations (along with those pertaining to education, research, government use of AI and investment priorities) is strong criticism of both state and corporate surveillance using AI, including that governments should commit not to engage in mass surveillance and the commercial surveillance of individuals

39 See , e.g., Lilian Edwards and Michael Veale, 'Slave to the Algorithm? Why a 'Right to an Explanation' Is Probably Not the Remedy You Are Looking For' (2017) 16(1) *Duke Law & Technology Review* 18; Sandra Wachter, Brett Mittelstadt and Luciano Floridi, 'Why a Right to Explanation of Automated Decision-Making Does Not Exist in the General Data Protection Regulation' (2017) 7(2) *International Data Privacy Law* 76.

40 European Parliament, 'Resolution of 16 February 2017 with Recommendations to the Commission on Civil Law Rules on Robotics' (2015/2103(INL)) https://eur-lex.europa.eu/legal-content/EN/TXT/?uri=CELEX%3A52017IP0051 accessed 22 June 2020.

41 Ibid.

42 European Commission, 'Communication on Artificial Intelligence for Europe' (COM/2018/237 final, 2018) https://eur-lex.europa.eu/legal-content/EN/TXT/?uri=COM%3A2018%3A237%3AFIN accessed 22 June 2020.

43 European Commission Independent High-Level Expert Group on Artificial Intelligence, *Ethics Guidelines for Trustworthy AI* (Final Report, 2019) https://ec.europa.eu/digital-single-market/en/news/ethics-guidelines-trustworthy-ai accessed 22 June 2020.

44 European Commission Independent High-Level Expert Group on Artificial Intelligence 'Policy and Investment Recommendations for Trustworthy AI' (26 June 2019) https://ec.europa.eu/digital-single-market/en/news/policy-and-investment-recommendations-trustworthy-artificial-intelligence accessed 22 June 2020.

including via 'free' services should be countered.[45] This is furthered by a specific recommendation that AI-enabled 'mass scoring' of individuals be banned.[46] The Panel called for more work to assess existing legal and regulatory frameworks to discern whether they are adequate to address the Panel's recommendations or whether reform is necessary.[47]

The European Commission released its White Paper on AI in February 2020, setting out an approach based on 'European values, to promote the development and deployment of AI'.[48] Among a host of proposals for education, research and innovation, industry collaboration, public sector AI adoption, the Commission asserts that 'international cooperation on AI matters must be based on an approach which promotes the respect of fundamental rights' and more bullishly asserts that it will 'strive to export its values across the world'.[49]

A section of the White Paper is devoted to regulatory frameworks, with the Commission setting out its proposals for a new risk-based regulatory framework for AI targeting 'high risk' applications. These applications would be subject to additional requirements including vis-à-vis: training data for AI; the keeping of records and data beyond what is currently required to verify legal compliance and enforcement; the provision of additional information than is currently required, including whether citizens are interacting with a machine rather than a human; ex ante requirements for the robustness and accuracy of AI applications; human oversight; and specific requirements for remote biometric identification systems.[50] The White Paper has been released for public consultation and follow-up work from the Commission is scheduled for late 2020.

Alongside this activity, the European Parliament debated various reports prepared by MEPs on civil liability, intellectual property and ethics aspects of AI in early 2020.[51] Issues such as a lack of harmonised approach among EU Member States and lack of harmonised definitions of AI giving rise to legal uncertainty were featured in the reports and debates, as well as calls for more research on specific frameworks

45 Ibid.

46 Ibid.

47 Ibid.

48 European Commission, 'White Paper on Artificial Intelligence – A European Approach to Excellence and Trust' (COM(2020) 65 final, 2020) https://ec.europa.eu/info/sites/info/files/commission-white-paper-artificial-intelligence-feb2020_en.pdf accessed 22 June 2020.

49 Ibid.

50 Ibid.

51 European Parliament Committee on Legal Affairs, 'Draft Report with Recommendations to the Commission on a Civil Liability Regime for Artificial Intelligence' (2020/2014(INL), 2020); European Parliament Committee on Legal Affairs, 'Draft Report with Recommendations to the Commission on a Framework of Ethical Aspects of Artificial Intelligence, Robotics and Related Technologies' (2020/2012(INL), 2020); European Parliament Committee on Legal Affairs, 'Draft Report on Intellectual Property Rights for the Development of Artificial Intelligence Technologies' (2020/2015(INI), 2020).

such as IP.[52] MEPs are due to debate and vote on amendments to the reports later in 2020. It is unclear whether COVID-19 disruptions will alter these timelines.

In addition to this activity at the supranational level, EU Member States continue with their own AI governance and ethics activities. This may contribute to the aforementioned divergence in the bloc, a factor which may justify EU-level regulation and standardisation. Prominent among them is Germany, which has its own national AI Strategy from 2018.[53] In light of competition with other countries such as the United States and China, Germany – in accordance with the principles of the European Union Strategy for Artificial Intelligence – intends to position itself in such a way that it sets itself apart from other, non-European nations through data protection-friendly, trustworthy, and 'human centred' AI systems, which are supposed to be used for the common good.[54] At the centre of those claims is the idea of establishing the 'AI Made in Germany' 'brand', which is supposed to become a globally acknowledged label of quality. Behind this 'brand' is the idea that AI applications made in Germany or, to be more precise, the data sets these AI applications use, come under the umbrella of data sovereignty, informational self-determination and data safety. Moreover, to ensure that AI research and innovation is in line with ethical and legal standards, a Data Ethics Commission was established which can make recommendations to the federal government and give advice on how to use AI in an ethically sound manner.

The Data Ethics Commission issued its first report written by 16 Commission experts, intended as a group of ethical guidelines to ensure safety, prosperity and social cohesion amongst those affected by algorithmic decision-making or AI.[55] Among other aims promoting human-centred and value-oriented AI design, the report introduces ideas for risk-oriented AI regulation, aimed at strengthening Germany and Europe's 'digital sovereignty'. Seventy-five rules are detailed in the report to implement the main ethical principles the report draws upon, namely human dignity, self-determination, privacy, security, democracy, justice, solidarity and sustainability. Operationalising these rules is the subject of a current report 'From Principles to Practice – An Interdisciplinary Framework to Operationalize AI ethics', resulting from the work of the interdisciplinary expert Artificial Intelligence Ethics Impact Group (AIEIG), which describes in detail how organisations conducting research and development of AI applications can implement ethical

[52] Samuel Stolton, 'MEPs Chart Path for a European Approach to Artificial Intelligence' (*EurActiv*, 12 May 2020) www.euractiv.com/section/digital/news/meps-chart-path-for-a-european-approach-to-artificial-intelligence/ accessed 22 June 2020.

[53] Bundesministerium für Bildung und Forschung; Bundesministerium für Wirtschaft und Energie; Bundesministerium für Arbeit und Soziales, 'Strategie Künstliche Intelligenz der Bundesregierung' (15 November 2018) www.bmwi.de/Redaktion/DE/Publikationen/Technologie/strategie-kuenstliche-intelligenz-der-bundesregierung.html accessed 22 June 2020.

[54] European Commission (n 45).

[55] Datenethikkommission der Bundesregierung, 'Gutachten der Datenethikkommission der Bundesregierung' (2019) www.bmjv.de/SharedDocs/Downloads/DE/Themen/Fokusthemen/Gutachten_DEK_DE.pdf?__blob=publicationFile&v=3 accessed 22 June 2020.

precepts into executable practice.[56] Another example of this practical approach can be seen in the recent Lernende Systeme (German National Platform for AI) report launching certification proposals for AI applications, which are aimed at inter alia creating legal certainty and increasing public trust in AI through, for example, a labelling system for consumers.[57] These certification proposals may serve as predecessors for future legal requirements, such as those which may be proposed at the EU level.

India

India's approach to AI is substantially informed by three initiatives at the national level. The first is Digital India, which aims to make India a digitally empowered knowledge economy;[58] the second is Make in India, under which the government of India is prioritising AI technology designed and developed in India;[59] and the third is the Smart Cities Mission.[60]

An AI Task Force constituted by the Ministry of Commerce and Industry in 2017 looked at AI as a socio-economic problem solver at scale. In its report, it identified ten key sectors in which AI should be deployed, including national security, financial technology, manufacturing and agriculture.[61] Similarly, a National Strategy for Artificial Intelligence was published in 2018 that went further to look at AI as a lever for economic growth and social development, and considers India as a potential 'garage' for AI applications.[62] While both documents mention ethics, they fail to meaningfully engage with issues of fundamental rights, fairness, inclusion and the limits of data-driven decision-making. These are also heavily influenced by the private sector, with civil society and academia, rarely, if ever, being invited into these discussions.

56 Sebastian Hallensleben et al., *From Principles to Practice. An Interdisciplinary Framework to Operationalise AI Ethics* (Bertelsmann Stiftung 2020).

57 Jessica Heesen, Jörn Müller-Quade and Stefan Wrobel, *Zertifizierung von KI-Systemen* (München 2020).

58 Government of India Ministry of Electronics & Information Technology, 'Digital India Programme' https://digitalindia.gov.in/ accessed 22 June 2020.

59 Government of India Ministry of Finance, 'Make in India' www.makeinindia.com/home/ accessed 22 June 2020.

60 Government of India Ministry of Housing and Urban Affairs, 'Smart Cities Mission' www.smartcities.gov.in/content/ accessed 22 June 2020; Vidushi Marda, 'Artificial Intelligence Policy in India: A Framework for Engaging the Limits of Data-Driven Decision-Making' (2018) 376(2133) *Philosophical Transactions of the Royal Society A: Mathematical, Physical and Engineering Sciences*.

61 Government of India Ministry of Commerce and Industry, 'Report of the Artificial Intelligence Task Force' (20 March 2018) https://dipp.gov.in/sites/default/files/Report_of_Task_Force_on_ArtificialIntelligence_20March2018_2.pdf accessed 22 June 2020.

62 NITI Aayog, 'National Strategy for Artificial Intelligence' (discussion paper, June 2018) https://niti.gov.in/writereaddata/files/document_publication/NationalStrategy-for-AI-Discussion-Paper.pdf accessed 22 June 2020.

The absence of an explicit legal and ethical framework for AI systems, however, has not stalled deployment. In July 2019, the Union Home Ministry announced plans for the nationwide Automated Facial Recognition System (AFRS) that would use images from CCTV cameras, police raids and newspapers to identify criminals, and enhance information sharing between policing units in the country. This was announced and subsequently developed in the absence of any legal basis. The form and extent of the AFRS directly violates the four-part proportionality test laid down by the Supreme Court of India in August 2017, which laid down that any violation of the fundamental right to privacy must be in pursuit of a legitimate aim, bear a rational connection to the aim and be shown as necessary and proportionate.[63] In December 2019, facial recognition was reported to have been used by Delhi Police to identify 'habitual protestors' and 'rowdy elements' against the backdrop of nationwide protests against changes in India's citizenship law.[64] In February 2020, the Home Minister stated that over a thousand 'rioters' had been identified using facial recognition. [65]

These developments are made even more acute given the absence of data protection legislation in India. The Personal Data Protection Bill carves out significant exceptions for state use of data, with the drafters of the bills themselves publicly expressing concerns about the lack of safeguards in the latest version. The current Personal Data Protection Bill also fails to adequately engage with the question of inferred data, which is particularly important in the context of machine learning. These issues arise in addition to crucial questions for how sensitive personal data is currently processed and shared. India's biometric identity project, *Aadhaar*, could also potentially become a central point of AI applications in the future, with a few proposals for use of facial recognition in the last year, although that is not the case currently.

India recently became one of the founding members of the aforementioned Global Partnership on AI.[66] Apart from this, there is no ethical framework or principles published by the government at the time of writing. It is likely that ethical

[63] Vidushi Marda, 'Every Move You Make' (*India Today*, 29 November 2019) www.indiatoday.in/magazine/up-front/story/20191209-every-move-you-make-1623400-2019-11-29 accessed 22 June 2020.

[64] Jay Mazoomdaar, 'Delhi Police Film Protests, Run Its Images through Face Recognition Software to Screen Crowd' (*The Indian Express*, 28 December 2019) https://indianexpress.com/article/india/police-film-protests-run-its-images-through-face-recognition-software-to-screen-crowd-6188246/ accessed 22 June 2020.

[65] Vijaita Singh, '1,100 Rioters Identified Using Facial Recognition Technology: Amit Shah' (*The Hindu*, 12 March 2020) https://economictimes.indiatimes.com/news/economy/policy/personal-data-protection-bill-can-turn-india-into-orwellian-state-justice-bn-srikrishna/articleshow/72483355.cms accessed 22 June 2020.

[66] *The New India Express*, 'India Joins GPAI as Founding Member to Support Responsible, Human-Centric Development, Use of AI' (15 June 2020) www.newindianexpress.com/business/2020/jun/15/india-joins-gpai-as-founding-member-to-support-responsible-human-centric-development-use-of-ai-2156937.html accessed 22 June 2020.

principles will emerge shortly, following global developments in the context of AI, and public attention on data protection law in the country.

United States of America

Widely believed to rival only China in its domestic research and development of AI,[67] the US government had been less institutionally active regarding questions of ethics, governance and regulation compared to developments in China and the European Union, until the Trump Administration Executive Order on Maintaining American Leadership in Artificial Intelligence in February 2019.[68] Prior to this activity, the United States had a stronger record of AI ethics and governance activity from the private and not-for-profit sectors. Various US-headquartered/-originating multinational tech corporations have issued ethics statements on their AI activities, such as Microsoft and Google Alphabet group company DeepMind. Some US-based not-for-profit organisations and foundations have also been active, such as the Future of Life Institute with its twenty-three Asilomar AI Principles.[69]

The 2019 Executive Order has legal force, and created an American AI Initiative guided by five high-level principles to be implemented by the National Science and Technology Council (NSTC) Select Committee on Artificial Intelligence.[70] These principles include the United States driving development of 'appropriate technical standards' and protecting 'civil liberties, privacy and American values' in AI applications 'to fully realize the potential for AI technologies for the American people'.[71] Internationalisation is included with the view of opening foreign markets for US AI technology and protecting the United States's critical AI technology 'from acquisition by strategic competitors and adversarial nations'. Furthermore, executive departments and agencies that engage in AI-related activities including 'regulat[ing] and provid[ing] guidance for applications of AI technologies' must adhere to six strategic objectives including protection of 'American technology, economic and national security, civil liberties, privacy, and values'.

The US Department of Defense also launched its own AI Strategy in February 2019.[72] The Strategy explicitly mentions US military rivals China and Russia investing in military AI 'including in applications that raise questions regarding international norms and human rights', as well as the perceived 'threat' of these

67 Stephen Cave and Sean ÓhÉigeartaigh, 'An AI Race for Strategic Advantage: Rhetoric and Risks' (AI Ethics And Society Conference, New Orleans, 2018).

68 US White House, 'Executive Order on Maintaining American Leadership in Artificial Intelligence' (11 February 2019) www.whitehouse.gov/presidential-actions/executive-order-maintaining-american-leadership-artificial-intelligence/ accessed 22 June 2020.

69 Future of Life Institute (n 8).

70 US White House (n 69).

71 Ibid.

72 US Department of Defense, 'Summary of the 2018 Department of Defense Artificial Intelligence strategy: Harnessing AI to Advance Our Security and Prosperity' (2019) https://media.defense.gov/2019/Feb/12/2002088963/-1/-1/1/SUMMARY-OF-DOD-AI-STRATEGY.PDF accessed 22 June 2020.

developments to the United States and 'the free and open international order'. As part of the Strategy, the Department asserts that it 'will articulate its vision and guiding principles for using AI in a lawful and ethical manner to promote our values', and will 'continue to share our aims, ethical guidelines, and safety procedures to encourage responsible AI development and use by other nations'. The Department also asserted that it would develop principles for AI ethics and safety in defence matters after multistakeholder consultations, with the promotion of the Department's views to a more global audience, with the seemingly intended consequence that its vision will inform a global set of military AI ethics.

In February 2020, the White House Office of Science and Technology Policy published a report documenting activities in the previous twelve months since the Executive Order was issued.[73] The report frames activity relating to governance under the heading of 'Remove Barriers to AI Innovation', which foregrounds deregulatory language but may be contradicted in part by the need for the United States to 'providing guidance for the governance of AI consistent with our Nation's values and by driving the development of appropriate AI technical standards'.[74] However, there may be no conflict if soft law non-binding 'guidance' displaces hard law binding regulatory requirements. In January 2020, the White House published the US AI Regulatory Principles for public comment, which would establish guidance for federal agencies 'to inform the development of regulatory and non-regulatory approaches regarding technologies and industrial sectors that are empowered or enabled by artificial intelligence (AI) and consider ways to reduce barriers to the development and adoption of AI technologies'.[75] Specifically, federal agencies are told to 'avoid regulatory or non-regulatory actions which needlessly hamper AI innovation and growth', they must assess regulatory actions against the effect on AI innovation and growth and 'must avoid a precautionary approach'.[76] Ten principles are set out to guide federal agencies' activities (reflecting those in the Executive Order), along with suggested non-regulatory approaches such as 'voluntary consensus standards' and other activities outside of rulemaking which would fulfil the direction to reduce regulatory barriers (such as increasing public access to government-held data sets).[77]

During 2019 and 2020, the US Food and Drug Administration (FDA) proposed regulatory frameworks for AI-based software as a medical device and draft guidance for clinical decision support software.[78] The US Patent and Trademark Office

[73] US White House Office for Science and Technology Policy, 'American Artificial Intelligence: Year One Annual Report' (February 2020) www.whitehouse.gov/wp-content/uploads/2020/02/American-AI-Initiative-One-Year-Annual-Report.pdf accessed 22 June 2020.

[74] Ibid.

[75] 'Guidance for Regulation of Artificial Intelligence Applications' www.whitehouse.gov/wp-content/uploads/2020/01/Draft-OMB-Memo-on-Regulation-of-AI-1-7-19.pdf accessed 22 June 2020.

[76] Ibid.

[77] Ibid.

[78] US Food and Drug Administration, 'Artificial Intelligence and Machine Learning in Software as a Medical Device' (28 January 2020) www.fda.gov/medical-devices/software-medical-device-samd

(USPTO) issued a public consultation on whether inventions developed by AI should be patentable. These activities could be framed as attempts to clarify how existing frameworks apply to AI applications but do not appear to involve the 'removal' of regulatory 'barriers'.

9.4 ANALYSIS

From the country and region profiles, we can see that AI governance and ethics activities have proliferated at the government level, even among previously reticent administrations such as the United States. India remains an outlier as the only country among our sample with no set of articulated AI governance or ethics principles. This may change, however, with India's participation in the GPAI initiative.

Themes of competition loom large over AI policies, as regards competition with other 'large' countries or jurisdictions. The AI competition between China and the United States as global forerunner in research and development may be reflected in the United States Executive Order being framed around preserving the United States's competitive position, and also China's ambition to become the global AI leader in 2030. We now see the European Union entering the fray more explicitly with its wish to export its own values internationally. However, there are also calls for global collaboration on AI ethics and governance, including from all of these actors. In practice, these are not all taking place through traditional multilateral fora such as the UN, as can be seen with the launch of GPAI. Smaller countries such as the Australian example show how they may be 'followers' rather than 'leaders' as they receive ethical principles and approaches formulated by other similar but larger countries.

In many of the AI ethics/governance statements, we see similar if not the same concepts reappear, such as transparency, explainability, accountability and so forth. Hagendorff has pointed out that these frequently encountered principles are often 'the most easily operationalized mathematically', which may account partly for their presence in many initiatives.[79] Some form of 'privacy' or 'data protection' also features frequently, even in the absence of robust privacy/data protection laws as in the United States example. In India, AI ethical principles might follow the development of binding data protection legislation which is still pending. Nevertheless, behind some of these shared principles may lie different cultural, legal and philosophical understandings.

/artificial-intelligence-and-machine-learning-software-medical-device accessed 22 June 2020; US Food and Drug Administration, 'Clinical Decision Support Software' (September 2019) www.fda.gov/regulatory-information/search-fda-guidance-documents/clinical-decision-support-software accessed 22 June 2020.

79 Hagendorff (n 7).

There are already different areas of existing law, policy and governance which will apply to AI and its implementations including technology and industrial policy, data protection, fundamental rights, private law, administrative law and so forth. Increasingly the existence of these pre-existing frameworks is being acknowledged in the AI ethics/governance initiatives, although more detailed research may be needed, as the European Parliament draft report on intellectual property and AI indicates. It is important for those to whom AI ethics and governance guidelines are addressed to be aware that they may need to consider, and comply with, further principles and norms in their AI research, development and application, beyond those articulated in AI-specific guidelines. Research on other novel digital technologies suggests that new entrants may not be aware of such pre-existing frameworks and may instead believe that their activities are 'unregulated'.[80]

On the question of 'ethics washing' – or the legal enforceability of AI ethics statements – it is true that almost all of the AI ethics and governance documents we have considered do not have the force of binding law. The US Executive Order is an exception in that regard, although it constitutes more of a series of directions to government agencies rather than a detailed set of legally binding ethical principles. In China and the European Union, there are activities and initiatives to implement aspects of the ethical principles in specific legal frameworks, whether pre-existing or novel. This can be contrasted with Australia, whose ethical principles are purely voluntary, and where discussions of legal amendment for AI are less developed.

However, the limits of legal enforceability can also be seen in the United States example, whereby there is the paradox of a legally enforced deregulatory approach mandated by the Executive Order and the processes it has triggered for other public agencies to forbear from regulating AI in their specific domains unless necessary. In practice, though, the FDA may be circumventing this obstacle by 'clarifications' of its existing regulatory practices vis-à-vis AI and medical devices.

In any event, the United States example illustrates that the legal enforceability of AI governance and ethics strategies does not necessarily equate to substantively better outcomes as regards actual AI governance and regulation. Perhaps in addition to ethics washing, we must be attentive towards 'law washing', whereby the binding force of law does not necessarily stop unethical uses of AI by government and corporations; or to put it another way, the mere fact that an instrument has a legally binding character does not ensure that it will prevent unethical uses of AI. Both the form and substance of the norms must be evaluated to determine their 'goodness'.[81]

80 Antonia Horst and Fiona McDonald, 'Personalisation and Decentralisation: Potential Disrupters in Regulating 3D Printed Medical Products' (2020) working paper.

81 See Angela Daly, S. Kate Devitt and Monique Mann (eds), *Good Data* (Institute of Network Cultures 2019).

Furthermore, legal enforceability of norms may be stymied by a lack of practical operationalisation by AI industry players – or that it is not practical to operationalise them. We can see that some governments have taken this aspect seriously and implemented activities, initiatives and guidance on these aspects, usually developed with researchers and industry representatives. It is hoped that this will ensure the practical implementation of legal and ethical principles in AI's development and avoid situations where the law or norms are developed divorced from the technological reality.

9.5 CONCLUSION

In this chapter, we have given an overview of the development of AI governance and ethics initiatives in a number of countries and regions, including the world AI research and development leaders China and the United States, and what may be emerging as a regulatory leader in form of the European Union. Since the 2019 Executive Order, the United States has started to catch up China and the European Union regarding domestic legal and policy initiatives. India remains an outlier, with limited activity in this space and no articulated set of AI ethical principles. Australia, with its voluntary ethical principles, may show the challenges a smaller jurisdiction and market faces when larger entities have already taken the lead on a technology law and policy topic.

Legal enforceability of norms is increasingly the focus of activity, usually through an evaluation of pre-existing legal frameworks or the creation of new frameworks and obligations. While the ethics-washing critique still stands to some degree vis-à-vis AI ethics, the focus of activity is moving towards the law – and also practical operationalisation of norms. Nevertheless, this shift in focus may not always produce desirable outcomes. Both the form and substance of AI norms – whether soft law principles or hard law obligations – must be evaluated to determine their 'goodness'.

A greater historical perspective is also warranted regarding the likelihood of success for AI ethics/governance initiatives, whether as principles or laws, by, for instance, examining the success or otherwise of previous attempts to govern new technologies, such as biotech and the Internet, or to insert ethics in other domains such as medicine.[82] While there are specificities for each new technology, different predecessor technologies from which it has sprung, as well as different social, economic and political conditions, looking to the historical trajectory of new technologies and their governance may teach us some lessons for AI governance and ethics.

A further issue for research may arise around regulatory or policy arbitrage, whereby organisations or researchers from a particular country or region which

82 Brett Mittelstadt, 'Principles Alone Cannot Guarantee Ethical AI' (2019) 1(11) *Nature Machine Intelligence* 501.

does have AI ethics/governance principles engage in 'jurisdiction shopping' to a location which does not or has laxer standards to research and develop AI with less 'constraints'. This offshoring of AI development to 'less ethical' countries may already be happening and is something that is largely or completely unaddressed in current AI governance and ethics initiatives.

10

EU By-Design Regulation in the Algorithmic Society

A Promising Way Forward or Constitutional Nightmare in the Making?

Pieter Van Cleynenbreugel

10.1 INTRODUCTION

Algorithmic decision-making fundamentally challenges legislators and regulators to find new ways to ensure algorithmic operators and controllers comply with the law. The European Union (EU) legal order is no stranger to those challenges, as self-learning algorithms continue to develop at an unprecedented pace.[1] One of the ways to cope with the rise of automated and self-learning algorithmic decision-making has been the introduction of by-design obligations.

By-design regulation refers to the array of regulatory strategies aimed at incorporating legal requirements into algorithmic design specifications. Those specifications would have to be programmed/coded into existing or newly developed algorithms.[2] That may be a necessity, as the European Commission in its February 2020 White Paper on Artificial Intelligence recognised the insufficiency of existing EU legislation on product safety and the protection of fundamental rights in that context.[3] Against that background, different open questions remain as to the modalities of this kind of regulation, ranging from who is competent to how to ensure compliance with those specifications. Those obligations demand economic operators to program their algorithms in such a way as to comply with legal norms. Related to existing co-regulation initiatives, by-design obligations present a new and potentially powerful

[1] See, on the rise of automated decision-making and on the challenges this raises, Frank Pasquale, *The Black Box Society: The Secret Algorithms That Control Money and Information* (Harvard University Press, 2015). See also Karen Yeung, 'Hypernudge: Big Data as a Mode of Regulation by Design', (2017) 20 *Information, Communication & Society* 118–136. On artificial intelligence in particular, Nicolas Petit, 'Artificial Intelligence and Automated Law Enforcement: A Review Paper', *SSRN Working Paper* 2018 https://papers.ssrn.com/sol3/papers.cfm?abstract_id=3145133 accessed 29 February 2020.

[2] According to the European Commission, Independent High Level Expert Group on Artificial Intelligence, Ethics Guidelines for Trustworthy AI, 8 April 2019, p. 8 https://ec.europa.eu/futurium/en/ai-alliance-consultation accessed 29 February 2020, compliance with EU law is a prerequisite for ethical behaviour.

[3] See European Commission, White Paper on Artificial Intelligence – A European Approach to Excellence and Trust, COM (2020) 65 final, https://ec.europa.eu/info/sites/info/files/commission-white-paper-artificial-intelligence-feb2020_en.pdf accessed 29 February 2020, pp. 11 and 14.

way to push economic operators more directly into ensuring respect for legal norms and principles.

This chapter will explore the potential for a more developed by-design regulatory framework as a matter of EU constitutional law. To that extent, it first conceptualises by-design regulation as a species of co-regulation, which is a well-known EU regulatory technique. The first part of this chapter revisits the three most common EU co-regulation varieties and argues that each of them could offer a basis for more enhanced by-design obligations. The second part of the chapter identifies the opportunities and challenges EU constitutional law would present in that context. In revisiting some basic features and doctrines of the EU constitutional order, this chapter aims to demonstrate that by-design regulation could be implemented if and to the extent that certain constitutional particularities of the EU legal order are taken into account.

10.2 BY-DESIGN OBLIGATIONS AS A SPECIES OF CO-REGULATION

Although by-design regulation sounds novel, it actually constitutes a species of a well-known regulatory approach of co-regulation (Section 10.2.1). That approach appears in at least three varieties in the EU legal order (Section 10.2.2), each lending itself to algorithmic by-design regulatory approaches (Section 10.2.3).

10.2.1 *By-Design Regulation as Co-regulation*

The notion of by-design regulation may appear vague and perhaps confusing at first glance.[4] In its very essence, however, by-design regulation refers to nothing more than an obligation imposed on businesses, as a matter of law, to program or code their technologies in such ways that they comply automatically or almost automatically with certain legal obligations.[5] A pro-active form of compliance through regulation, the law basically requires businesses to design or redesign their technologies so that certain values or objectives are respected by the technology itself. In algorithmic design, this regulatory approach would require translating legal obligations into algorithmic specifications. By-design regulation would thus require, as a matter of hard law, developers/designers to translate legal obligations into workable engineering or design specifications and principles.[6]

4 As also mentioned in Pagona Tsormpatzoudi, Bettina Berendt, and Fanny Coudert, 'Privacy by Design: From Research and Policy to Practice – The Challenge of Multi-disciplinarity' in Bettina Berendt, Thomas Engel, Demosthenes Ikonomou, Daniel Le Métayer, and Stefan Schiffner (eds.), *Privacy Technologies and Policy* (Springer, 2017) 199.

5 To some extent, this idea is closely related to the theory that the infrastructure of cyberspace limits possibilities in itself. In that regard, code is law as well; see Lawrence Lessig, *Code and Other Laws of Cyberspace* (Basic Books, 1999) 6. The idea of by-design regulation demands designers/developers to code in certain values so as to limit that technology would keep defying certain legal values or obligations. See also Karen Yeung, n. 1, 121.

6 Compare with Ira Rubinstein, 'Privacy and Regulatory Innovation: Moving beyond Voluntary Codes', (2011) *I/S: a Journal of Law and Policy for the Information Society* 371.

The origins of by-design obligations as a regulatory technique originate in the privacy by design approach. According to that approach, respect for privacy must ideally become any (business) organisation's default mode of operation.[7] When setting up technical and physical infrastructure and networks, privacy has to be designed into the operations of those networks.[8] More particularly, it was proposed to businesses to have in place privacy-enhancing technologies (PETs).[9] Within the context of its General Data Protection Regulation (GDPR), the EU additionally imposed data protection via design obligation on data processors.[10]

The successful implementation of privacy by design faces two difficulties. First, given the varying conceptions of privacy maintained in different legal orders, questions arose quickly as to the exact requirements that needed to be implemented.[11] Second, beyond the difficulties to envisage the implementation of privacy by design, questions equally arose as to the liability of those designers and operators not having made or implemented a privacy-enhancing technological framework. The idea of privacy by design is appealing, yet without a legal obligation on particular businesses or public authorities to implement it and to oversee its application, the whole idea rests on shaky ground.

Despite the practical by-design problems highlighted here, the classification of by-design obligations is less complicated from a regulatory theory perspective. It is submitted indeed that by-design obligations in their very essence always imply some form of co-regulation. Co-regulation essentially refers to a regulatory framework that involves both private parties and governmental actors in the setting, implementation, or enforcement of regulatory standards.[12] The EU is familiar with this type of regulation and has been promoting it consistently over the course of past decades. It cannot therefore be excluded that the EU could be willing further to develop and refine that approach in the context of algorithmic design obligations as well.

7 European Network and Information Security Agency (ENISA), *Privacy and Data Protection by Design – From Policy to Engineering*, available at www.enisa.europa.eu/publications/privacy-and-data-protection-by-design accessed 29 February 2020, 2014 Report, 2.

8 Ann Cavoukian and Marc Dixon, 'Privacy and Security by Design: An Enterprise Architecture Approach', available at www.ipc.on.ca/wp-content/uploads/Resources/pbd-privacy-and-security-by-design-oracle.pdf accessed 29 February 2020.

9 For a review of such technologies, see Yun Shen and Siani Pearson, *Privacy Enhancing Technologies: A Review*, available at www.hpl.hp.com/techreports/2011/HPL-2011-113.pdf accessed 29 February 2020.

10 See Article 25 Regulation 2016/679 of the European Parliament and of the Council of 27 April 2016 on the protection of natural persons with regard to the processing of personal data and on the free movement of such data, and repealing Directive 95/46/EC (General Data Protection Regulation), [2016] O.J. L119/1 (hereafter GDPR).

11 Seda Gürses, Carmela Troncoso, and Claudia Diaz, 'Engineering Privacy-by-Design', available at www.esat.kuleuven.be/cosic/publications/article-1542.pdf accessed 29 February 2020, p. 2.

12 See, for a most basic definition, http://ec.europa.eu/smart-regulation/better_regulation/documents/brochure/brochure_en.pdf. See also Christopher Marsden, *Internet Co-Regulation* (Cambridge University Press, 2011) 46; Michèle Finck, 'Digital Co-regulation: Designing a Supranational Legal Framework for the Platform Economy', (2018) 43 *European Law Review* 47, 65.

10.2.2 *Co-regulation within the European Union*

The EU's former 2003 Interinstitutional Agreement on Better Lawmaking refers to co-regulation as 'the mechanism whereby a [Union] legislative act entrusts the attainment of the objectives defined by the legislative authority to parties which are recognised in the field (such as economic operators, the social partners, non-governmental organisations, or associations)'.[13] In contrast with self-regulation, where private actors have been entrusted overall responsibility to determine the content, applicability, and enforcement of different rules, co-regulation still accords a certain role to governmental actors.

Within the EU legal order, one can distinguish three implicitly present formats of co-regulation currently present. Those formats differ on the basis of three distinguishing criteria: the actual norm-setter, the implementation of co-regulatory obligations, and the enforcement of respect for the regulatory requirements.[14]

The first format concerns the framework applicable in the context of technical standardisation. It is well-known that, at the EU level, standards to a large extent are being developed by so-called standardisation bodies. Those bodies, essentially of a private nature, have been mandated by the EU institutions to adopt norms that have some force of law. The EU's new approach to technical harmonisation[15] best illustrates that tendency. In this standardised co-regulation scheme, standardisation organisations play a pivotal role as norm-setters. They assemble different experts and ask those experts to set up and design a standard. Their regulatory mandate justified by them assembling experts to design technical and technocratic standards, the EU legislator can suffice in delegating to those organisations the task to come up with those highly technical standards. Following and implementing a standard thus creates a presumption that the product is safe. This system has remained in place

[13] European Parliament, Council, Commission, Interinstitutional Agreement on better law-making, OJ2003, C 321/01, point 18. This agreement has been replaced by a new 2016 interinstitutional agreement ([2016] O.J. L123/1), in which the notion of co-regulation no longer explicitly features that notion. That does not mean, however, that the EU no longer relies on co-regulation. Quite on the contrary, best practices and guiding principles for better co-regulation have still been developed in 2015; see https://ec.europa.eu/digital-single-market/sites/digital-agenda/files/CoP%20-%20Principles%20for%20better%20self-%20and%20co-regulation.pdf.

[14] I have found those implicit three criteria to underlie the conceptualisations made by Linda Senden, 'Soft Law, Self-Regulation and Co-Regulation in European Law: Where Do They Meet?, 9 *Electronic Journal of Comparative Law* (2005), and Ira Rubinstein, 'The Future of Self-Regulation Is Co-regulation' in Evan Salinger, Jules Polonetsky and Omer Tene (eds.), *The Cambridge Handbook of Consumer Privacy* (Cambridge University Press, 2018) 503–523. I do, however, take responsibility for limiting my typology to a distinction on the basis of those three criteria. I would like to state, as a caveat, that this typology could be refined; yet is taken as a starting point for further reflections on the possibilities for by-design co-regulation in the EU legal order.

[15] See, on the EU's new approach from a constitutional perspective, Harm Schepel, *The Constitution of Private Governance – Product Standards in the Regulation of Integrating Markets* (Hart, 2005). See also Noreen Burrows, 'Harmonisation of Technical Standards: Reculer Pour Mieux Sauter?', (1990) 53 *Modern Law Review* 598.

ever since, even though a 2012 update has sought to increase the transparency over the standard-setting process.[16] Within that framework, the Court of Justice has stated that harmonised European standards, though adopted by private standardisation bodies, are to be assimilated to acts of the EU institutions.[17]

The second format of EU co-regulation introduces a certification-centred approach. That approach is related closely to how the EU legislator has envisaged data protection by design in its GDPR. In that format of co-regulation, there is no pre-defined norm setter. The legislator sets out particular values or principles to be designed into certain technologies, but further leaves it up to designers or importers of technologies to ensure compliance with those values. As co-regulation allows for a more intensified administrative or judicial review over co-set standards or rules, this format presumes an ex post control of public authorities over the rules adopted. Although businesses may create or rely on standardisation organisations to translate the predetermined values into workable principles, respect for such standards does not automatically trigger a presumption of conformity. In this format, the intervention of standardisation organisations is not sufficient to trigger a presumption of conformity with the predetermined values. On the contrary, a lack of respect for the principles and values laid out by the legislator may result in a command-and-control type of sanctioning. In that case, a public authority can impose sanctions by means of a decision, which could be contested before the courts. As such, the actual content of the decision remains to be determined by the businesses responsible, yet the enforcement fully enters the traditional command and control realm.

A third possible format goes beyond the voluntary standardisation or certification approaches by allowing the legislator to impose certain designs on technology developers. More particularly, this format would see the EU institutions outline themselves in more detail than the previous varieties the values that need to be protected by and coded into the technology at hand. It would then fall upon the designers/developers concerned to implement those values. In doing so, they would respect the legal norms posited by the EU legislator. Those by-design obligations would most likely be inserted in instruments of delegated or implementing legislation. A similar approach is taken in the context of financial services regulation.[18] It would be perfectly imaginable to envisage expert groups or expert bodies assisting the European Commission in developing and fine-tuning by-design obligations in

16 Regulation 1025/2012 of the European Parliament and of the Council of 25 October 2012 on European standardisation, amending Council Directives 89/686/EEC and 93/15/EEC and Directives 94/9/EC, 94/25/EC, 95/16/EC, 97/23/EC, 98/34/EC, 2004/22/EC, 2007/23/EC, 2009/23/EC, and 2009/105/EC of the European Parliament and of the Council and repealing Council Decision 87/95/EEC and Decision No. 1673/2006/EC of the European Parliament and of the Council, [2012] O.J. L316/12. See also Harm Schepel, 'The New Approach to the New Approach: The Juridification of Harmonized Standards in EU Law', (2013) *Maastricht Journal of European and Comparative Law* 523.

17 CJEU, Case C-613/14, *James Elliott Construction*, EU:C:2016:821, para. 34.

18 See, for that framework, Niamh Moloney, 'The Lamfalussy Legislative Model: A New Era for the EC Securities and Investment Services Regime', (2003) 52 *International and Comparative Law Quarterly* 510.

the realm of algorithmic decision-making as well. This could be coupled with a mix of traditional command and control enforcement techniques (administrative and judicial enforcement) currently also in place within that context.[19] It would indeed not seem impossible that those governance structures could also accompany the setup of by-design obligations.

The three varieties distinguished here should be understood as ideal-typical features resembling somehow similar regulatory initiatives in the EU. Those varieties actually reflect a sliding scale of regulatory possibilities, as the following table shows.

Co-regulation varieties	*Norm-setting*	*Implementation*	*Enforcement*
Standardisation	Standardisation bodies	Non-binding harmonised general interest standards	Presumption of conformity + supplementary judicial enforcement
Certification	Businesses themselves (aided by certification bodies)	Non-binding individualised or certified general interest standards	Subsidiary administrative and judicial enforcement?
Control-centred co-regulation	EU institutions (delegated or implementing acts, involving stakeholders)	Binding technical rules + ex ante approval of technologies?	Administrative and judicial enforcement

10.2.3 *Room for Enhanced By-Design Co-regulation Strategies at the EU Level?*

All three co-regulation varieties start from the premise that designers/developers have to construct or structure their algorithms in order to ensure compliance with applicable legal norms. If that starting point is accepted, the three varieties depict a variety of intensities with which compliance with those obligations into the design of algorithms can be guaranteed. Overall, they represent different degrees of public intervention in determining the scope and in enforcing the way in which algorithms have been designed. Given the prevalence of those different regulatory strategies in different fields of EU policy, it would seem that those varieties of by-design co-regulation could also be introduced or developed within the context of algorithmic decision-making.

19 On this framework in EU financial services regulation, see Pieter Van Cleynenbreugel, *Market Supervision in the European Union. Integrated Administration in Constitutional Context* (Brill, 2014) 52–55.

That framework of standard-setting by standardisation bodies clearly lends itself to the context of algorithmic regulation and the imposition of by-design obligations on their developers/designers. It can indeed be imagined that EU legislation would require any coder, programmer, or developer to respect all privacy, individual liberty, or other protective values the EU as an organisation holds dear. Those 'general interest' requirements, as they would be referred to under the New approach,[20] would have to be respected by every producer seeking to make available or use a certain algorithm to customers falling within the scope of EU law. The actual implementation and coding-in of those values into the algorithms concerned would have to take place in accordance with general interest standards adopted by standardisation organisations. It is not entirely impossible to envisage that similar bodies to CEN, CENELEC, or ETSI could be designated to develop general interest standards in the realm of algorithmic governance.

In the same way, a certification mechanism could be set up. By way of example, the GDPR refers to the possibility of having in place a certification mechanism that would include data protection concerns in the standardisation process of technologies. In order for that system to work, data protection certification bodies have to be set up. Those private bodies would be responsible for reviewing and attesting to the conformity of certain data protection technologies with the values and principles of the GDPR.[21] So far, those mechanisms are still in the process of being set up and much work needs to be done in order to extract from the GDPR a set of workable principles that would have to be integrated in the technologies ensuring data processing and in the algorithms underlying or accompanying those technologies.[22]

The more enhanced control-centred co-regulation framework could also be made to fit algorithmic by-design regulation. In that case, the EU legislator or the European Commission, or any other type of EU executive body that would be responsible for the drafting and development of by-design obligations, would need to be involved in the regulation of algorithms. It could be expected that some type of involvement of businesses concerned would be useful in the drafting of the by-design obligations. Ex ante approval mechanisms or ex post enforcement structures could be envisaged to guarantee that businesses comply with those requirements.

20 Annex II of the 1985 New Approach Resolution refers to essential safety requirements or other requirements in the general interest which can be translated into harmonised technical standards.

21 Article 43 GDPR.

22 European Network and Security Information Agency, 'Privacy by Design in Big Data. An Overview of Privacy Enhancing Technologies in the Era of Big Data Analytics', December 2015 Report, www.enisa.europa.eu/publications/big-data-protection accessed 29 February 2020, and European Data Protection Supervisor, 'Preliminary Opinion on Privacy by Design', 31 May 2018, https://edps.europa.eu/sites/edp/files/publication/18-05-31_preliminary_opinion_on_privacy_by_design_en_0.pdf accessed 29 February 2020 (hereafter EDPS Opinion 2018), p. 16.

10.3 BY-DESIGN-ORIENTED CO-REGULATION: A PROMISING WAY FORWARD OR EU CONSTITUTIONAL LAW NIGHTMARE IN THE MAKING?

It follows from the previous section that, in light of its co-regulation experiences, the EU legal order would not be as such hostile to the introduction of by-design obligations. In order for a regulatory approach to be made operational, regulatory strategists have to ensure a sufficient amount of constitutional fit,[23] if only to legitimise the regulatory approach offered in this context.

It is submitted that at least three challenges in an increasing order of relevance can be highlighted in that regard. First, the principle of competence conferral may impose constraints on the introduction and development of by-design obligations, which deserve to be qualified (Section 10.3.1). Second, in the same way, the by-design system setup would amount to a delegation of certain powers to private or public actors. From that point of view, concerns regarding compliance with the so-called *Meroni* doctrine arise (Section 10.3.2). Third, and most fundamentally, however, the major challenge of by-design regulation lies in its enforcement. In a constitutional order characterised itself by the lack of a common administrative enforcement framework, questions can be raised regarding the effectiveness of control over the respect of by-design regulations (Section 10.3.3). Although the EU constitutional framework raises challenges in this regard, it is submitted that those challenges are not in themselves insurmountable. As a result, by-design regulation could become a complementary and useful regulatory strategy aimed at responding to challenges raised by the algorithmic society (Section 10.3.4).

10.3.1 *Competence Conferral Challenges*

A first constitutional challenge that the setting-up of a more developed by-design regulation framework would encounter concerns the EU's system of competence conferral.[24] The Treaty contains different legal bases which could grant the Union the competence to set up a co-regulatory framework focused on by-design obligations.

The principal challenge with those different legal bases is that one has to verify what kind of values one wants to programme into algorithms as a matter of EU law. Absent any discussion so far beyond data protection, that remains a very important preliminary issue to be determined. It could be submitted that values of non-discrimination, consumer protection, free movement principles, or others would have to be coded in. In this respect, it will appear that the EU can go farther in some domains than in others.

[23] For that argument in the context of technical standards, Linda Senden, 'The Constitutional Fit of European Standardization Put to the Test', (2017) 44 *Legal Issues of Economic Integration* 337.

[24] Art. 4(1) and 5 of the Treaty on European Union (TEU).

The most appropriate Treaty bases are the transversal provisions containing a list of values that need to be protected across the board by EU policies and offering the EU the power to take action to protect those values. It would seem that those values could also be developed into technical specifications to be coded into algorithmic practice.

First, Article 10 of the Treaty on the Functioning of the European Union (TFEU) holds that in defining and implementing its policies and activities, the Union shall aim to combat discrimination based on sex, racial or ethnic origin, religion or belief, disability, age, or sexual orientation. Article 18 TFEU complements that provision by stating that within the scope of application of the Treaties, and without prejudice to any special provisions contained therein, any discrimination on grounds of nationality shall be prohibited. To that extent, the European Parliament and the Council, acting in accordance with the ordinary legislative procedure, may adopt rules designed to prohibit such discrimination. Article 19 adds that the Council, acting unanimously in accordance with a special legislative procedure and after obtaining the consent of the European Parliament, may take appropriate action to combat discrimination based on sex, racial or ethnic origin, religion or belief, disability, age, or sexual orientation. In that context, the European Parliament and the Council, acting in accordance with the ordinary legislative procedure, may adopt the basic principles of Union incentive measures, excluding any harmonisation of the laws and regulations of the Member States, to support actions taken by the Member States in order to contribute to the achievement of the objectives of non-discrimination. To the extent that non-discrimination is one of the key values of the European Union, it can take action either to harmonise non-discrimination on the basis of nationality, or to incentivise Member States to eradicate all forms of discrimination. The notion of incentivising is important here; it would indeed appear that, under the banner of non-discrimination, the EU could take measures to stimulate non-discriminatory by-design approaches. At the same time, however, the EU may not harmonise laws regarding non-discrimination on grounds other than nationality. It follows from this that EU rules could only incite Member States to take a more pro-active and by-design oriented compliance approach. A full-fledged ex ante or ex post algorithmic design control approach in the realm of non-discrimination would potentially go against Article 19 TFEU. It would thus appear that the EU is competent to put in place particular incentive mechanisms, yet not necessarily to set up a complete law enforcement framework in this field. Regarding discrimination on the basis of nationality, setting up such a by-design framework would still be constitutionally possible, as Article 18 TFEU grants broader legislative powers to the EU institutions.

Second, Article 11 TFEU holds that environmental protection requirements must be integrated into the definition and implementation of the Union policies and activities, in particular, with a view to promoting sustainable development. Article 12 refers to consumer protection. Both provisions are accompanied by specific legal bases that would allow for co-regulatory by-design mechanisms to be set up.[25]

Third, Article 16 refers to the right to personal data protection. According to that provision, the European Parliament and the Council, acting in accordance with the ordinary legislative procedure, shall lay down the rules relating to the protection of individuals with regard to the processing of personal data by Union institutions, bodies, offices and agencies, and by the Member States when carrying out activities which fall within the scope of Union law, and the rules relating to the free movement of such data. Compliance with these rules shall be subject to the control of independent authorities. This provision constituted the legal basis for the GDPR and the data protection by design framework outlined in that Regulation.[26] Neither during negotiations, nor after its entry into force, has the choice of a legal basis for this type of by-design obligations been contested. It could be concluded, therefore, that this provision could serve as a legal basis for data protection by design measures. Beyond data protection, however, this provision would be of no practical use.

Fourth, Articles 114 and 352 TFEU seem to be of limited relevance. Article 114 TFEU allows the EU to adopt the measures for the approximation of the provisions laid down by law, regulation, or administrative action in Member States which have as their object the establishment and functioning of the internal market. That provision essentially aims at harmonising Member States' regulatory provisions rather than imposing specific design obligations on algorithmic designers. However, it cannot be excluded that the imposition of specific obligations can be a means to avoid obstacles to trade from materialising. In that understanding, this provision may serve as an additional basis to adopt measures setting up a co-regulatory by-design framework.[27] Article 352 states that if action by the Union should prove necessary, within the framework of the policies defined in the Treaties, to attain one of the objectives set out in the Treaties. According to the Court,

> recourse to Article [352 TFEU] as a legal basis is ... excluded where the Community act in question does not provide for the introduction of a new protective right at Community level, but merely harmonises the rules laid down in the laws of the Member States for granting and protecting that right.[28]

In other words, Article 352 TFEU can be relied on to create a new Union right, or body, that leaves the national laws of the member states unaffected and imposes additional rights.[29] That provision seems less relevant for the introduction of

[25] See indeed also Art. 169 and 191–193 TFEU.
[26] See EDPS 2018 Opinion, pp. 18–19.
[27] As confirmed by CJEU, Case C-270/12, *United Kingdom* v. *Parliament and Council*, EU:C:2014:18.
[28] CJEU, Case C-436/03, *European Parliament* v. *Council*, EU:C:2006:277, para. 37.
[29] Ibid., paras. 44–45.

by-design obligations. Those obligations essentially aim to implement certain policies and to ensure better compliance with certain rights, rather than to create new ones.

It follows from the foregoing analysis that the Treaty does contain several values and legal bases allowing those values to be protected in a by-design way. From the previous cursory overview, it now seems more than ever necessary to catalogue the values the EU holds dear and to question what actions the EU could take in terms of by-design regulation for them. In addition, the Charter of Fundamental Rights, a binding catalogue of EU fundamental rights, could play a complementary role in that regard.[30]

10.3.2 *Implementation and Delegation Challenges*

The setup of by-design regulatory mechanisms requires the involvement of either government actors or private bodies (standardisation or certification bodies). Even when the European Union has the competence to set up a particular regulatory framework which includes the imposition of by-design obligations, EU constitutional law also limits or circumscribes the delegation of powers conferred on the EU to public (Section 10.3.2.1) or private bodies (Section 10.3.2.2). In both instances, delegation is not entirely impossible, yet additional conditions need to be met.

10.3.2.1 Delegation of Technical Rules to the Commission and Expert Committees

According to Article 290 TFEU, a legislative act may delegate to the Commission the power to adopt non-legislative acts of general application to supplement or amend certain non-essential elements of the legislative act.[31] A delegation of power under that provision confers power on the Commission to exercise the functions of the EU legislature, in that it enables it to supplement or amend non-essential elements of the legislative act. Such a supplementary or amending power needs to emanate from an express decision of the legislature and its use by the Commission needs to respect the bounds the legislature has itself fixed in the basic act. For that purpose, the basic act must, in accordance with that provision, lay down the limits of its conferral of power on the Commission, namely the objectives, content, scope, and duration of the conferral.[32] In addition, Article 291 TFEU states

[30] Charter of Fundamental Rights in the European Union, [2012] O.J. C236/391. The Charter does not give the EU additional competences, yet at the same time affirms the key values the EU wants to promote throughout its policies. It could therefore be imagined indeed that those values constitute the background against which value-inspired specifications will be developed that would be part of the by-design co-regulatory enterprise.

[31] Paul Craig, 'Delegated Acts, Implementing Acts and the New Comitology Regulation', (2011) 36 *European Law Review* 675.

[32] CJEU, Case C-696/15 P, *Czech Republic* v. *Commission*, EU:C:2017:595, para. 55.

that where uniform conditions for implementing legally binding Union acts are needed, those acts shall confer implementing powers on the Commission. A 2011 Regulation outlines the basic framework for doing so.[33] Any delegation to the Commission or to an expert committee has to respect that framework.[34]

10.3.2.2 Delegation to Private Standardisation Bodies?

The questions noted previously all remain regarding the delegation of by-design standardisation or certification powers to private organisations, such as standardisation bodies. Those questions go back to case law dating from 1958. In its *Meroni* judgment, the Court invalidated a *delegation* of *discretionary* regulatory competences by the European Commission to a private body.[35] *Meroni* limited the delegation of regulatory powers to private bodies in two ways. First, it limited the *delegation* of powers. Delegation of rule-making powers was to be expressly provided for in a legal instrument, only powers retained by a delegating body could be delegated, the exercise of these powers was subject to the same limits and procedures as they would have been within the delegating body and such delegation needed to be necessary for the effective functioning of the delegating institution.[36] Second, the judgment limited the *scope of powers* delegated. It maintained that the powers delegated could only include *clearly defined executive powers* that were capable of being objectively reviewed by the delegating body.[37] A delegation of powers by the High Authority to a private body outside the realm of supranational law would not fit that image. The 1981 *Romano* judgment was said to have confirmed that position in relation to the Council, although that judgment focused on public authorities to which powers delegated would escape judicial review as to their compliance with EU law.[38]

The *Meroni* doctrine may be problematic from the point of view of setting up a by-design regulation framework.[39] The delegation of standardisation or certification powers to private bodies without any possibility of judicial oversight by the EU Courts has been considered particularly problematic in this regard. Although the

33 Regulation 182/2011 of the European Parliament and of the Council of 16 February 2011 laying down the rules and general principles concerning mechanisms for control by Member States of the Commission's exercise of implementing powers, [2011] O.J. L55/13.

34 Joana Mendes, 'The EU Administration' in Pieter-Jan Kuijper et al. (ed.), *The Law of the European Union*, 5th edition (Kluwer, 2018) 267–311.

35 CJEU, Case 9/56, *Meroni* v. *High Authority*, EU:C:1958:7 at p. 152.

36 CJEU, Case 9/56, *Meroni*, at 150–151. See, for a schematic overview, Takis Tridimas, 'Financial Supervision and Agency Power' in Niamh Nic Shuibhne and Lawrence Gormley (eds.), *From Single Market to Economic Union. Essays in Memory of John A. Usher* (Oxford University Press, 2012) 61–62.

37 CJEU, Case 9/56, *Meroni*, at 152.

38 CJEU, Case 98/80, *Giuseppe Romano* v. *Rijksinstituut voor Ziekte- en Invaliditeitsverzekering*, EU:C:1981:104, 1241, para. 20 on the prohibition to take binding decisions by an administrative commission.

39 See Opinion of Advocate General Jääskinen of 12 September 2013 in Case C-270/12, *United Kingdom* v. *Council and European Parliament*, EU:C:2013:562, para. 68.

EU framework of delegating standardisation powers to private organisations in the realm of product safety has been in operation for more than thirty years, its compatibility with EU law has recently come under scrutiny.[40] It is to be remembered that the Court of Justice in that context held that standards adopted by private organisations following an EU mandate to do so, are to be considered norms which can be reviewed by the Court of Justice, despite them formally not being EU legal acts.[41] Although the practical consequences of those rulings remain far from clear, the Court has succeeded in opening a debate on the constitutionality of delegation to private organisations. In the wake of this case law, it now seems that standards set up by private organisations should by some means be subject to judicial control.

That background is of direct relevance to discussions on the possibility to introduce by-design obligations. To the extent that delegation of standard-setting powers to private standardisation bodies is problematic under EU law, the setup of a standardised co-regulatory by-design regime would be a less likely choice to make. Prior to setting up this kind of legal regime, additional guarantees will have to be put in place in order to ascertain some kind of judicial oversight over those standards. Given that it is unclear at present how far such oversight should go, setting up a standardisation-based regime seems more difficult to attain. The alternative of certification-based co-regulation, which asks every designer/developer individually to integrate the EU law-compatible values into their algorithms, avoids such delegation and would seem a more viable alternative in the current state of EU law, should the control-centred model and the accompanying delegation to public authorities be considered a less preferred option.

10.3.3 *Enforcement Challenges*

A third EU constitutional law challenge concerns the enforcement of the by-design regimes set up. Even when the EU is competent and when certain by-design regulatory tasks can be delegated to public or private authorities, the actual application and enforcement of those by-design obligations are likely to raise additional constitutional law problems. It is to be remembered in this regard that the EU has not set up an administrative enforcement system to guarantee the application and implementation of its norms. Quite on the contrary, Article 291 TFEU explicitly obliges the Member States to guarantee this.[42] As a result, it falls in principle upon Member States to set up and organise surveillance and sanctioning mechanisms. This has resulted in a wide diversity of institutional and organisational practices, giving rise to EU law enforcement being differently structured and understood in different Member States.[43]

40 Linda Senden, n. 23, 350.

41 CJEU, Case C-613/14, *James Elliott Construction*, EU:C:2016:821.

42 According to Robert Schütze, 'From Rome to Lisbon: "Executive federalism" in the (New) European Union', (2010) 47 *Common Market Law Review* 1418.

43 See also Pieter Van Cleynenbreugel, n. 19, 209 for an example as to how the EU tried to overcome such diversity.

In order to overcome somehow the Member States' diversity in this realm, the European Union has in some domains tried to streamline the enforcement of EU rules. To that extent, EU agencies or networks of Member States' supervisory authorities have been set up.[44] Within those agencies or networks, representatives of Member States' authorities assemble and determine policy priorities or decide upon non-binding best practices.[45] In the realm of financial services regulation, EU agencies representing all Member States' authorities even have the power to impose sanctions in cases where Member States' authorities are unable or unwilling to do so.[46] As such, a complex regime of coordinated or integrated administration is set up.[47] Alternatively, the European Commission itself has taken on responsibility for the direct enforcement of EU law, whenever it has been conferred such role by the Treaties. In the field of EU competition law, the Commission thus plays a primary role in that regard.[48] Decisions taken by the Commission and/or EU agencies are subject to judicial oversight by the EU Courts, oftentimes following an internal administrative review procedure.[49] To a much more marginal extent, the EU envisages the private enforcement of its norms. Under that scheme, private individuals would invoke EU norms in their private interest, thus resulting in those norms being enforced against perpetrators of them. It generally falls upon national judges to apply the law in those contexts. The fields of competition law and consumer protection law are particularly open to this kind of enforcement,[50] which nevertheless remains of a subsidiary nature compared to public enforcement. The presence

44 See also Joana Mendes, n. 34, 283 and 295.

45 For an example, see Article 16 of Regulation 1093/2010 of the European Parliament and of the Council of 24 November 2010 establishing a European Supervisory Authority (European Banking Authority) amending Decision 716/2009/EC and repealing Commission Decision 2009/78/EC, *O.J.* L 331/12; Regulation 1094/2010 of the European Parliament and of the Council of 24 November 2010 establishing a European Supervisory Authority (European Insurance and Occupational Pensions Authority) amending Decision 716/2009/EC and repealing Commission Decision 2009/79/EC, *O.J.* L 331/ 48; Regulation 1095/2010 of the European Parliament and of the Council of 24 November 2010 establishing a European Supervisory Authority (European Securities and Markets Authority) amending Decision 716/2009/EC and repealing Commission Decision 2009/77/EC, *O.J.* L 331/84. All three regulations established the so-called European Supervisory Authorities in EU financial services supervision, establishing bodies that assemble representatives of different Member States' authorities. Collectively, they are referred to as the ESA Regulations.

46 By way of example, Regulation (EU) 236/2012 of the European Parliament and of the Council of 14 March 2012 on short selling and certain aspects of credit default swaps, [2012] OJ L86/1.

47 Pieter Van Cleynenbreugel, 'EU Post-Crisis Economic and Financial Market Regulation: Embedding Member States' Interests within "More Europe"' in Marton Varju (ed.), *Between Compliance and Particularism. Member State Interests and European Union Law* (Springer, 2019) 79–102.

48 See Article 103 TFEU and Article 11 of Council Regulation 1/2003 of 16 December 2002 on the implementation of the rules on competition laid down in Articles 81 and 82 of the Treaty, [2003] OJ L 1/1.

49 For an example, see Article 58 ESA Regulations.

50 In the realm of EU competition law, see most notably Directive 2014/104/EU of the European Parliament and of the Council of 26 November 2014 on certain rules governing actions for damages under national law for infringements of the competition law provisions of the Member States and of

of those different frameworks allows one to conclude that a patchwork of different EU enforcement frameworks has been set up, depending on the policy domain and the felt need for coordinated application of EU legal norms.

The existence of this patchwork of enforcement frameworks has an impact on debates on whether and how to set up a by-design enforcement structure. Three observations can be made in that respect.

First, a standardisation-focused co-regulation framework would rely on essentially private standards and a presumption of conformity. That presumption could be invoked before Member States' courts and authorities to the extent that it has been established by an EU legislative instrument. This form of essentially private enforcement has worked for technical standards, yet has recently come under scrutiny from the Court, calling for some kind of judicial oversight over the process through which norms are set. Questions can therefore be raised to what extent this system would also fit by-design obligations as envisaged here. It would be imaginable that the EU legislator would decide to set up a two-step enforcement procedure in this regard. On the one hand, it would delegate the setting of by-design specifications translating EU legal obligations to a standardisation body. The procedures of that body would have to be transparent, and norms adopted by it could be subject to judicial – or even administrative – review. Once the deadline for such review would have passed, the norms are deemed valid and compliance with them in the design of algorithms would trigger a presumption of legality, which could be rebutted on the basis of concrete data analysis. As this system would mix public and private enforcement to some extent, it would seem likely that it can be made to fit the EU's enforcement system. It is essential, however, that the legal instrument establishing the features of by-design regulation clearly establishes how the different enforcement features would relate to each other.

Second, a more control-centred EU enforcement framework could also be envisaged. In order to set up that kind of framework, it is important to take stock of the limits of the EU enforcement structure. In essence, the imposition of fines will generally have to be entrusted to Member States' authorities, as the GDPR showcases.[51] Those authorities' powers and procedures can be harmonised to some extent,[52] and their operations could be complemented by a formal network of national authorities or an EU agency overseeing those activities.[53] As other sectors have demonstrated, it does take time, however, before such a regime is operational and functions smoothly.[54]

the European Union, [2014] O.J. L349/1. In the realm of consumer protection law, see the Proposal for a Directive on representative actions for the protection of the collective interests of consumers, and repealing Directive 2009/22/EC, COM 2018/184 final, available at https://eur-lex.europa.eu/legal-content/EN/TXT/?uri=COM:2018:184:FIN.

51 Article 83 GDPR.

52 Article 58 GDPR.

53 Article 65 GDPR – the European Data Protection Board has a role in the resolution of disputes between supervisory authorities.

54 See, in that context, Eillis Ferran, 'The Existential Search of the European Banking Authority', (2016) *European Business Organisation Law Review* 285–317.

From that point of view, it could also be questioned whether it would not be a good idea to entrust the European Commission with sanctioning powers in this field. Article 291 TFEU could be interpreted as allowing for this to happen by means of secondary legislation, if a sufficient majority is found among the Member States.[55] Entrusting the European Commission with those powers would require a significant increase in terms of human and financial resources. It remains to be questioned whether the Member States would indeed be willing to allocate those resources to the Commission, given that this has not happened in other policy fields. More generally, however, whatever institution would apply and enforce those rules, in-depth knowledge of both law and of coding/programming would be required, in order meaningfully to assess how the by-design obligations would have been integrated into an algorithm's functioning. That again would require a significant investment in training both programmers and lawyers to work at the EU level in the general interest.

Third, what is often lacking in discussions on EU law enforcement is the attention that needs to be paid to compliance with legal rules. Compliance refers to the act of obeying an order, rule, or request,[56] and is a preliminary step in ensuring effective enforcement. If one can ensure an addressee of a legal norm respects that norm, no ex post enforcement by means of fines or other sanctions would be possible. It is remarkable, therefore, that EU administrative governance pays little transversal attention to compliance. In some domains, such as the free movement of goods produced lawfully in one Member State[57] or in the realm of competition law,[58] the EU has taken some modest steps to ensure compliance. It is submitted, however, that compliance needs to be the keystone of any enforcement framework, should the EU indeed wish to pursue a by-design regulatory approach on a more general scale. By-design obligations by their very nature are indeed meant to ensure compliance with EU legal norms. By coding into existing or new algorithms certain specifications that would lead to lawfully functioning algorithms, by-design regulation essentially seeks to avoid that people are harmed by algorithms and would have to claim compensation or other types of sanctions ex post. From that point of view, by-design regulatory obligations are in themselves a form of compliance. It thus would appear strange to emphasise too much the possibility of sanctions or other public enforcement tools, without giving a central place to the need for businesses to implement the specifications in their algorithms. In that context, it could be imagined that the EU would like to put in place some kind of ex ante authorisation mechanism. Technical specifications or designs authorised by the European Commission would then be presumed to be legal, triggering the presumption of

[55] Provided that Article 114 TFEU would be relied upon, a qualified majority would be required in this regard.

[56] See indeed https://dictionary.cambridge.org/dictionary/learner-english/compliance.

[57] See https://eur-lex.europa.eu/legal-content/EN/HIS/?uri=COM:2017:795:FIN for a proposal in this regard currently in development at the level of the Parliament and Council.

[58] See http://ec.europa.eu/competition/antitrust/compliance/index_en.html.

conformity as well. Such authorisation mechanisms exist in other fields of European Union law. It would seem that, at least in theory, the introduction of a similar mechanism would also be possible in this context as well.

It follows from those observations that the introduction of a by-design regulatory framework would necessitate a debate on how those obligations will be enforced, what the relationship will be between compliance programmes and ex post sanctions, and how the different enforcement approaches would relate to each other. No matter what by-design framework would be opted for, discussions on compliance and the tools to ensure and enforce such compliance would have to be laid out in a more developed way. An ex ante authorisation mechanism appears to offer the possibility to ensure compliance of certain technical specifications with EU values from the very outset. Integrating those authorised tools in newly designed algorithms could thus be conceived of as a valuable strategy for enhancing the enforcement of by-design obligations.

10.4 CONCLUSION

This chapter analysed to what extent the EU would have the competence to set up a by-design regulatory approach and, if so, whether the EU constitutional framework would pose certain limits to it. Although the EU has not been conferred explicit competences in the realm of algorithmic by-design regulation, different legal bases may be relied on in order to establish a more general by-design co-regulatory framework. That does not mean, however, that the EU constitutional framework would not tolerate any new by-design regulatory frameworks. If certain key principles are taken into account, the EU may very well proceed with the development of those frameworks. It thus would only require a certain political will to proceed in this regard. Should that will exist, one can conclude there is a strong chance to integrate by-design obligations better in the EU regulatory framework.

11

What's in the Box?

The Legal Requirement of Explainability in Computationally Aided Decision-Making in Public Administration

Henrik Palmer Olsen,[*] *Jacob Livingston Slosser,*[**] *and Thomas Troels Hildebrandt*[†]

11.1 INTRODUCTION

As the quality of AI[1] improves, it is increasingly applied to support decision-making processes, including in public administration.[2] This has many potential advantages: faster response time, better cost-effectiveness, more consistency across decisions, and so forth. At the same time, implementing AI in public administration also raises a number of concerns: bias in the decision-making process, lack of

[*] Associate Dean for Research, Professor of Jurisprudence, iCourts (Danish National Research Foundation's Centre of Excellence for International Courts) at the University of Copenhagen, Faculty of Law; henrik.palmer.olsen@jur.ku.dk. This work was produced in part with the support of Independent Research Fund Denmark project PACTA: Public Administration and Computational Transparency in Algorithms, grant number: 8091–00025

[**] Carlsberg Postdoctoral Fellow, iCourts (Danish National Research Foundation's Centre of Excellence for International Courts) at the University of Copenhagen, Faculty of Law; jacob.slosser@jur.ku.dk. This work was produced in part with the support of the Carlsberg Foundation Postdoctoral Fellowship in Denmark project COLLAGE: Code, Law and Language, grant number: CF18-0481.

[†] Professor of Computer Science, Software, Data, People & Society Research Section, Department of Computer Science (DIKU), University of Copenhagen; hilde@di.ku.dk. This work was produced in part with the support of Independent Research Fund Denmark project PACTA: Public Administration and Computational Transparency in Algorithms, grant number: 8091–00025 and the Innovation Fund Denmark project EcoKnow.org.

[1] AI is here used in the broad sense, which includes both expert systems and machine learning as well as hybrid models. Various webpages contain information about how AI and Machine Learning may be understood. For an example, see www.geeksforgeeks.org/difference-between-machine-learning-and-artificial-intelligence/.

[2] See also Jennifer Cobbe, 'Administrative Law and the Machines of Government: Judicial Review of Automated Public-Sector Decision-Making' (2019) 39 *Legal Studies* 636; Monika Zalnieriute, Lyria Bennett Moses, and George Williams, 'The Rule of Law and Automation of Government Decision-Making' (2019) 82 *The Modern Law Review* 425. Zalnieriute et al. conduct four case studies from four different countries (Australia, China, Sweden, and United States), to illustrate different approaches and how such approaches differ in terms of impact on the rule of law.

transparency, and elimination of human discretion, among others.[3] Sometimes, these concerns are raised to a level of abstraction that obscures the legal remedies that exist to curb those fears.[4] Such abstract concerns, when not coupled with concrete remedies, may lead to paralysis and thereby unduly delay the development of efficient systems because of an overly conservative approach to the implementation of ADM. This conservative approach may hinder the development of even safer systems that would come with wider and diverse adoption. The fears surrounding the adoption of ADM systems, while varied, can be broadly grouped into three categories: the argument of control, the argument of dignity, and the argument of contamination.[5]

The first fear is the loss of control over systems and processes and thus of a clear link to responsibility when decisions are taken.[6] In a discretionary system, someone must be held responsible for those decisions and be able to give reasons for them. There is a legitimate fear that a black box system used to produce a decision, even when used in coordination with a human counterpart or oversight, creates a system that lacks responsibility. This is the fear of the rubber stamp: that, even if a human is in the loop, the deference given to the machine is so much that it creates a vacancy of accountability for the decision.[7]

The second fear of ADM systems is that they may lead to a loss of human dignity.[8] If legal processes are replaced with algorithms, there is a fear that humans will be

3 See, among various others, Virginia Eubanks, *Automating Inequality: How High-Tech Tools Profile, Police, and Punish the Poor* (St Martin's Press 2018); Cathy O'Neil, *Weapons of Math Destruction: How Big Data Increases Inequality and Threatens Democracy* (Broadway Books 2017).

4 We find that some of the ethical guidelines for AI use, such as the European Commission's Ethics Guidelines for Trustworthy AI (https://ec.europa.eu/digital-single-market/en/news/ethics-guidelines-trustworthy-ai) raise general concerns, but do not provide much guidance on how to address the concerns raised.

5 These categories are generally sketched from Bygrave's analysis of the *travaux préparatoires* of Art 22 of the General Data Protection Regulation, which concerns explanation in automated processing and the Commission's reticence towards implementing fully automated systems exemplified in Art 15 of the Data Protection Directive. See the draft version at p 6–7 of the chapter on Art. 22: Lee A Bygrave, 'Article 22', 2019 *Draft Commentaries on 6 Articles of the GDPR (From Commentary on the EU General Data Protection Regulation)* (Oxford University Press 2020) https://works.bepress.com/christopher-kuner/2/download.

6 A related but more legal technical problem in regards to the introduction of AI public administration is the question of *when* exactly a decision is made. Associated to this is also the problem of *delegation*. If a private IT developer designs a decision-system for a specific group of public decisions, does this mean that those decisions have been delegated from the public administration to the IT developer? Are future decisions *made* in the process of writing the code for the system? We shall not pursue these questions in this chapter, but instead proceed on the assumption that decisions are made when they are issued to the recipient.

7 Elin Wihlborg, Hannu Larsson, and Karin Hedstrom, '"The Computer Says No!" – A Case Study on Automated Decision-Making in Public Authorities', *2016 49th Hawaii International Conference on System Sciences (HICSS)* (IEEE 2016) http://ieeexplore.ieee.org/document/7427547/.

8 See e.g., Corinne Cath et al., 'Artificial Intelligence and the "Good Society": The US, EU, and UK Approach' [2017] *Science and Engineering Ethics* http://link.springer.com/10.1007/s11948-017-9901-7.

reduced to mere 'cogs in the machine'.[9] Rather than being in a relationship with other humans to which you can explain your situation, you will be reduced to a digital representation of a sum of data. Since machines cannot reproduce the whole context of the human and social world, but only represent specific limited data about a human (say age, marital status, residence, income, etc.), the machine cannot *understand* you. Removing this ability to understand and to communicate freely with another human and the autonomy which this represents can lead to alienation and a loss of human dignity.[10]

Third, there is the well-documented fear of 'bad' data being used to make decisions that are false and discriminatory.[11] This fear is related to the ideal that decision-making in public administration (among others) should be neutral, fair, and based on accurate and correct factual information.[12] If ADM is implemented in a flawed data environment, it could lead to systematic deficiencies such as false profiling or self-reinforcing feedback loops that accentuate irrelevant features that can lead to a significant breach of law (particularly equality law) if not just societal norms.[13]

While we accept that these fears are not unsubstantiated, they need not prevent existing legal remedies from being acknowledged and used. Legal remedies should be used rather than the more cursory reach towards general guidelines or grand and ambiguous ethical press releases, that are not binding, not likely to be followed, and do not provide much concrete guidance to help solve the real problems they hope to address. In order to gain the advantages of AI-supported decision-making,[14] these concerns must be met by indicating how AI can be implemented in public administration without undermining the qualities associated with contemporary administrative procedures. We contend that this can be done by focusing on how ADM can be introduced in such a way that it meets the requirement of explanation as set out in administrative law at the standard calibrated by what we expect legally out of human explanation.[15] In contradistinction to much recent literature, which focuses on the

9 Meg Leta Jones, 'The Right to a Human in the Loop: Political Constructions of Computer Automation and Personhood' (2017) 47 *Social Studies of Science* 216.

10 Karl M. Manheim and Lyric Kaplan, 'Artificial Intelligence: Risks to Privacy and Democracy' (Social Science Research Network 2018) *SSRN Scholarly Paper ID 3273016* https://papers.ssrn.com/abstract=3273016.

11 For discussion of this issue in regards to AI supported law enforcement, see Rashida Richardson, Jason Schultz, and Kate Crawford, 'Dirty Data, Bad Predictions: How Civil Rights Violations Impact Police Data, Predictive Policing Systems, and Justice' [2019] *New York University Law Review Online* 192.

12 Finale Doshi-Velez et al., 'Accountability of AI Under the Law: The Role of Explanation' [2017] *arXiv:1711.01134 [cs, stat]* http://arxiv.org/abs/1711.01134.

13 See, among others, Pauline T. Kim, 'Data-Driven Discrimination at Work' (2016) 58 *William & Mary Law Review* 857.

14 See Zalnieriute, Moses, and Williams (n 2) 454.

15 By *explanation*, we mean here that the administrative agency gives reasons that support its decision. In this chapter, we use the term *explanation* in this sense. This is different from *explainability*, as used in relation to the so-called 'black box problem'; see Cynthia Rudin, 'Stop Explaining Black Box Machine Learning Models for High Stakes Decisions and Use Interpretable Models Instead' (2019) 1 *Nature*

right to an explanation solely under the GDPR,[16] we add and consider the more well-established traditions in administrative law. With a starting point in Danish law, we draw comparisons to other jurisdictions in Europe to show the common understanding in administrative law across these jurisdictions with regard to assuring administrative decisions are explained in terms of the legal reasoning on which the decision is based.

The chapter examines the explanation requirement by first outlining how the explanation should be understood as a *legal* explanation rather than a *causal* explanation (Section 11.2). We dismiss the idea that the legal requirement to explain an ADM-supported decision can be met by or necessarily implies mathematical transparency.[17] To illustrate our point about legal versus causal explanations, we use a scenario based on real-world casework.[18] We consider that our critique concerns mainly a small set of decisions that focus on legal decision-making: decisions that are based on written preparation and past case retrieval. These are areas where a large number of similar cases are dealt with and where previous decision-making practice plays an important role in the decision-making process (e.g., land use cases, consumer complaint cases, competition law cases, procurement complaint cases, applications for certain benefits, etc.). This scenario concerns an administrative decision regarding the Danish law on the requirement on municipalities to provide compensation for loss of earnings to a parent (we will refer to them as Parent A) who provides care to a child with a permanent reduced physical or mental functioning (in particular whether an illness would be considered 'serious, chronic or long-term'). The relevant legislative text reads:

> Persons maintaining a child under 18 in the home whose physical or mental function is substantially and permanently impaired, or who is suffering from serious, chronic or long-term illness [shall receive compensation]. Compensation shall be subject to the condition that the child is cared for at home as a necessary consequence of the impaired function, and that it is most expedient for the mother or father to care for the child.[19]

Machine Intelligence 206. As we explain later, we think the quest for black-box explainability (which we call *mathematical transparency*) should give way to an explanation in the public law sense (giving grounds for decisions). We take this to be in line with Rudin's call for interpretability in high-stakes decisions.

[16] See e.g., Sandra Wachter, Brent Mittelstadt, and Luciano Floridi, 'Why a Right to Explanation of Automated Decision-Making Does Not Exist in the General Data Protection Regulation' (2017) 7 *International Data Privacy Law* 76; Margot E. Kaminski, 'The Right to Explanation, Explained' (2019) 34 *Berkeley Tech. LJ* 189.

[17] See the debate regarding transparency outlined in Brent Daniel Mittelstadt et al., 'The Ethics of Algorithms: Mapping the Debate' (2016) 3(2) *Big Data & Society* 6–7.

[18] See the Ecoknow project: https://ecoknow.org/about/.

[19] § 42 (1) of the Danish Consolidation Act on Social Services, available at http://english.sm.dk/media/14900/consolidation-act-on-social-services.pdf. For a review of the legal practice based on this provision (in municipalities), see Ankestyrelsen, 'Ankestyrelsens Praksisundersøgelse Om Tabt Arbejdsfortjeneste Efter Servicelovens § 42 (National Board of Appeal's Study on Lost Earnings According to Section 42 of the Service Act)' (2017) https://ast.dk/publikationer/ankestyrelsens-praksisundersogelse-om-tabt-arbejdsfortjeneste-efter-servicelovens-ss-42.

We will refer to the example of Parent A to explore explanation in its causal and legal senses throughout.

In Section 11.3, we look at what the explanation requirement means legally. We compare various national (Denmark, Germany, France, and the UK) and regional legal systems (EU law and the European Convention of Human Rights) to show the well-established, human standard of explanation. Given the wide range of legal approaches and the firm foundation of the duty to give reasons, we argue that the requirements attached to the existing standards of explanation are well-tested, adequate, and sufficient to protect the underlying values behind them. Moreover, the requirement enjoys democratic support in those jurisdictions where it is derived from enacted legislation. In our view, ADM can and should be held accountable under those existing legal standards and we consider it unnecessary to public administration if this standard were to be changed or supplemented by other standards or requirements for ADM and not across all decision makers, whether human or machine. ADM, in our view, should meet the same minimum explanation threshold that applies to human decision-making. Rather than introducing new requirements designed for ADM, a more dynamic communicative process aimed at citizen engagement with the algorithmic processes employed by the administrative agency in question will be, in our view, more suitable to protecting against the ills of using ADM technology in public administration. ADM in public administration is a phenomenon that comes in a wide range of formats: from the use of automatic information processing for use as one part of basic administrative over semi-automated decision-making, to fully automated decision-making that uses AI to link information about facts to legal rules via machine learning.[20] While in theory a full spectrum of approaches is possible, and fully automated models have attracted a lot of attention,[21] in practice most forms of ADM are a type of hybrid system. As a prototype of what a hybrid process that would protect against many of the fears associated with ADM might look like, we introduce a novel solution, that we, for lack of a better term, call the 'administrative Turing test' (Section 11.4). This test could be used to *continually validate and strengthen* AI-supported decision-making. As the name indicates, it relies on comparing solely human and algorithmic decisions, and only allows the latter when a human cannot immediately tell the difference between the two. The administrative Turing test is an instrument to ensure that the existing (human) explanation requirement is met in practice. Using this test in ADM systems aims at ensuring the continuous quality of explanations in ADM and advancing what some research suggests is the

20 There is indeed also a wide range of ways that an automated decision can take place. For an explanation of this, see the working version of this paper at section 3, http://ssrn.com/abstract=3402974.

21 Perhaps most famous is O'Neil (n 3), but the debate on Technological Singularity has attracted a lot of attention; see, for an overview, Murray Shanahan, *The Technological Singularity* (MIT Press 2015).

best way to use AI for legal purposes – namely, in collaboration with human intelligence.[22]

11.2 EXPLANATION: CAUSAL VERSUS LEGAL

As mentioned previously, we focus on legal explanation – that is, a duty to give reasons/justifications for a legal decision. This differs from causal explainability, which speaks to an ability to explain the inner workings of that system beyond legal justification. Much of the literature on black-box AI has focused on the perceived need to open up the black box.[23] We can understand that this may be because it is taken for granted that a human is by default explainable, where algorithms in their many forms are not, at least in the same way. We propose that, perhaps counter-intuitively, that even if we take the blackest of boxes, it is the legal requirement of explanation in the form of sufficient reasons that matter for the protection of citizens. It is, in our view, the ability to challenge, appeal, and assess decisions against their legal basis, which ensures citizens of protection. It is not a feature of being able to look into the minutiae of the inner workings of a human mind (its neuronal mechanisms) or a machine (its mathematical formulas). The general call for explainability in AI – often conflated with complete transparency – is not required for the contestation of the decision by a citizen. This does not mean that we think that the quest for transparent ADM should be abandoned. On the contrary, we consider transparency to be desirable, but we see this as a broader and more general issue that links more to overall trust in AI technology as a whole[24] rather than something that is necessary to meet the explanation requirement in administrative law. The requirement of explanation for administrative decisions can be found, in one guise or another, in most legal systems. In Europe, it is often referred to as the 'duty to give reasons' – that is, a positive obligation on administrative agencies to provide an explanation ('begrundelse' in Danish, 'Begründung' in German, and 'motivation' in French) for their decisions. The explanation is closely linked to the right to legal remedies. Some research indicates that its emergence throughout history has been driven by the need to enable the citizen affected by an administrative decision to effectively challenge it before a court of

[22] See Saul Levmore and Frank Fagan, 'The Impact of Artificial Intelligence on Rules, Standards, and Judicial Discretion' (2019) 93 *Southern California Law Review*.

[23] See, for example, Riccardo Guidotti et al., 'A Survey of Methods for Explaining Black Box Models' (2018) 51 *ACM Computing Surveys (CSUR)* 1. Similarly, Cobbe (n 2), who makes a distinction between 'how' and 'why' a decision was made, says 'just as it is often not straightforward to explain *how* an ADM system reached a particular conclusion, so it is also not straightforward to determine *why* that system reached that conclusion'. Our point is that these are the wrong questions to ask, because even in a human non-ADM system, we will never know 'why that system reached that conclusion'. We cannot know. What we can *do*, however, is to judge whether or not the explanation given was sufficiently accurate and sufficient under the given legal duty to give reasons.

[24] Amina Adadi and Mohammed Berrada, 'Peeking Inside the Black-Box: A Survey on Explainable Artificial Intelligence (XAI)' (2018) 6 *IEEE Access* 52138.

law.[25] This, in turn, required the provision of sufficient reasons for the decision in question: both towards the citizen, who as the immediate recipient should be given a chance to understand the main reasoning behind the decision, and the judges, who will be charged with examining the legality of the decision in the event of a legal challenge. The duty to give reasons has today become a self-standing legal requirement, serving a multitude of other functions beyond ensuring effective legal remedies, such as ensuring better clarification, consistency, and documentation of the decisions, self-control of the decision-makers, internal and external control of the administration as a whole, as well as general democratic acceptance and transparency.[26]

The requirement to provide an explanation should be understood in terms of the law that regulates the administrative body's decision in the case before it. It is not a requirement that *any* kind of explanation must or should be given but rather a *specific kind* of explanation. This observation has a bearing on the kind of explanation that may be required for administrative decision-making relying on algorithmic information analysis as part of the process towards reaching a decision. Take, for instance, our example of Parent A. An administrative body issues a decision to Parent A in the form of a rejection explaining that the illness the child suffers from does not qualify as *serious* within the meaning of the statute. The constituents of this explanation would generally cover a reference to the child's disease and the qualifying components of the category of *serious illness* being applied. This could be, for example, a checklist system of symptoms or a reference to an authoritative list of formal diagnoses that qualify combined with an explanation of the differences between the applicant disease and those categorised as applicable under the statute. In general, the decision to reject the application for compensation of lost income would explain the legislative grounds on which the decision rests, the salient facts of the case, and the most important connection points between them (i.e., the discretionary or interpretive elements that are attributed weight in the decision-making

25 Uwe Kischel, *Die Begründung: Zur Erläuterung Staatlicher Entscheidungen Gegenüber Dem Bürger*, vol 94 (Mohr Siebeck 2003) 32–34.

26 Franz-Joseph Peine and Thorsten Siegel, *Allgemeines Verwaltungsrecht* (12th ed., C.F. Müller2018) 160, mn. 513; Schweickhardt, Vondung, and Zimmermann-Kreher (eds), *Allgemeines Verwaltungsrecht* (10th ed., Kohlhammer 2018) 586–588; Kischel (n 25) 40–65; H. C. H. Hofmann, G. C. Rowe, and A. H. Türk, *Administrative Law and Policy of the European Union* (Oxford University Press 2011), 200–202; CJEU, *Council of the European Union* v. *Nadiany Bamba*, 15 November 2012, Case C-417 / 11, para. 49; N. Songolo, 'La motivation des actes administratifs', 2011, www.village-justice.com/articles/motivation-actes-administratifs,10849.html; J.-L. Autin, La motivation des actes administratifs unilatéraux, entre tradition nationale et évolution des droits européens 'RFDA' 2011, no. 137–138, 85–99. We do not engage in a deeper analysis of the underlying rationale for the existence of the requirement to provide an explanation, as this is not the aim of our chapter. For this discussion in administrative law, see Joana Mendes, 'The Foundations of the Duty to Give Reasons and a Normative Reconstruction' in Elizabeth Fisher, Jeff King, and Alison Young (eds), *The Foundations and Future of Public Law* (Oxford University Press 2020).

process).[27] It is against this background that the threshold for what an explanation requires should be understood.

In a human system, at no point would the administrative body be required to describe the neurological activity of the caseworkers that have been involved in making the decision in the case. Nor would they be required to provide a psychological profile and biography of the administrator involved in making the decision, giving a history of the vetting and training of the individuals involved, their educational backgrounds, or other such information, to account for all the inputs that may have been explicitly or implicitly used to consider the application. When the same process involves an ADM system, must the explanation open up the opaqueness of its mathematical weighting? Must it provide a technical profile of all the inputs into the system? We think not. In the case of a hybrid system with a human in the loop, must the administrators set out – in detail – the electronic circuits that connect the computer keyboard to the computer hard drive and the computer code behind the text-processing program used? Must it describe the interaction between the neurological activity of the caseworker's brain and the manipulation of keyboard tabs leading to the text being printed out, first on a screen, then on paper, and finally sent to the citizen as an explanation of how the decision was made? Again, we think not.

The provided examples illustrate the point that causal explanation can be both insufficient and superfluous. Even though it may be empirically fully accurate, it does not necessarily meet the requirement of *legal* explanation. It gives an explanation – but it does likely not give the citizen the explanation he or she is looking for. The problem, more precisely, is that the explanation provided by causality does not, in itself, normatively connect the decision to its legal basis. It is, in other words, not possible to see the *legal reasoning* leading from the facts of the case and the law to the legal decision, unless, of course, such legal reasoning is explicitly coded in the algorithm. The reasons that make information about the neurological processes inside the brains of decision-makers irrelevant to the legal explanation requirement are the same that can make information about the algorithmic processes in an administrative support system similarly irrelevant. This is not as controversial of a position as it might seem on first glance.

Retaining the existing human standard for explanation, rather than introducing a new standard devised specifically for AI-supported decision-making, has the extra advantage that the issuing administrative agency remains fully responsible for the decision no matter how it has been produced. From this also follows that the administrative agency issuing the decision can be queried about the decision in ordinary language. This then assures a focus on the *rationale* behind the explanation being respected, even if the decision has been arrived at through some algorithmic

[27] Making sure that the connection relies on 'clean' data is obviously very important, but it is a separate issue that we do not touch on in this chapter. For a discussion of this issue in regards to AI-supported law enforcement, see Richardson, Schultz, and Crawford (n 11).

calculation that is not transparent. If the analogy is apt in comparing algorithmic processes to human neurology or psychological history, then requiring algorithmic transparency in legal decisions that rely on AI-supported decision-making would fail to address the explanation requirement at the right level. Much in line with Rahwan et al., who argue for a new field of research – the study of machine behaviour akin to human behavioural research[28] – we argue that the inner workings of an algorithm are not what is in need of explanation but, rather, the human interaction with the *output* of the algorithm and the biases that lie in the *inputs*. What is needed is not that algorithms should be made more transparent, but that the standard for intelligibility should remain undiminished.

11.3 EXPLANATION: THE LEGAL STANDARD

A legal standard for the explanation of administrative decision-making exists across all main jurisdictions in Europe. We found, when looking at different national jurisdictions (Germany, France, Denmark, and the UK) and regional frameworks (EU law and European Human Rights law), that explanation requirements differ slightly among them but still hold as a general principle that never requires the kind of full transparency advocated for. While limited in scope, the law we investigated includes a variety of different legal cultures across Europe at different stages of developing digitalised administrations (i.e., both front-runners and late-comers in that process). They also diverge on how they address explanation: in the form of a general duty in administrative law (Denmark and Germany) or a patchwork of specific legislation and procedural safeguards, partly developed in legal practice (France and the UK). Common for all jurisdictions is that the legal requirement put on administrative agencies to provide reasons for their decisions has a threshold level (minimum requirement) that is robust enough to ensure that if black box technology is used as part of the decision-making process, recipients will not be any worse off than if decisions were made by humans only. In the following discussion, we will give a brief overview of how the explanation requirement is set out in various jurisdictions.[29]

In Denmark, The Danish Act on Public Administration contains a section on explanation (§§22-24).[30] In general, the explanation can be said to entail that the citizen to whom the decision is directed must be given sufficient information about the grounds of the decision. This means that the explanation must fully cover the decision and not just explain parts of the decision. The explanation must also be truthful and in that sense correctly set forth the grounds that support the decision. Explanations may be limited to stating that some factual requirement in the case is

28 See Iyad Rahwan et al., 'Machine Behaviour' (2019) 568 *Nature* 477.

29 For a longer detailed analysis, see the working paper version of this chapter: http://ssrn.com/abstract=3402974.

30 The full text at www.retsinformation.dk/forms/r0710.aspx?id=161411#Kap6.

not fulfilled. For example, in our parent A example, perhaps a certain age has not been reached, a doctor's certificate is not provided, or a spouse's acceptance has not been delivered in the correct form. Explanations may also take the form of standard formulations that are used frequently in the same kind of cases, but the law always requires a certain level of concreteness in the explanation that is linked to the specific circumstances of the case and the decision being made. It does not seem to be possible to formulate any specific standards in regards to how deep or broad an explanation should be in order to fulfil the minimum requirement under the law. The requirement is generally interpreted as meaning explanations should reflect the most important elements of the case relevant to the decision. Similarly, in Germany, the general requirement to explain administrative decisions can be found in the Administrative Procedural Code of 1976.[31] Generally speaking, every written (or electronic) decision requires an explanation or a 'statement of grounds'; it should outline the essential factual and legal reasons that gave rise to the decision.

Where there was not a specific requirement for explanation,[32] we found – while perhaps missing the overarching general administrative duty – a duty to give reasons as a procedural safeguard. For example, French constitutional law does not by itself impose a general duty on administrative bodies to explain their decisions. Beyond sanctions of a punitive character, administrative decisions need to be reasoned, as provided by a 1979 statute[33] and the 2016 Code des Relations entre le Public et l'Administration (CRPA). The CRPA requires a written explanation that includes an account of the legal and factual considerations underlying the decision.[34] The rationale behind the explainability requirement is to strengthen transparency and trust in the administration, and to allow for its review and challenge before a court of law.[35] Similarly, in the UK, a recent study found, unlike many statements to the contrary and even without a *general* duty, in most cases, 'the administrative decision-maker being challenged [regarding a decision] was under a *specific statutory duty* to compile and disclose a specific statement of reasons for its decision'.[36] This research

[31] §39 VwVfG. Specialised regimes, e.g., for taxes and social welfare, contain similar provisions.

[32] We found that in neither France nor the UK is there a general duty for administrative authorities to give reasons for their decisions. For French law, see the decision by Conseil Constitutionnel 1 juillet 2004, no. 2004–497 DC ('les règles et principes de valeur constitutionnelle n'imposent pas par eux-mêmes aux autorités administratives de motiver leurs décisions dès lors qu'elles ne prononcent pas une sanction ayant le caractère d'une punition'). For UK law, see the decision by House of Lords in *R* v. *Secretary of State for the Home Department, ex parte Doody*, 1993 WLR 154 ('the law does not at present recognise a general duty to give reasons for an administrative decision').

[33] Loi du 11 juillet 1979 relative à la motivation des actes administratifs et à l'amélioration des relations entre l'administration et le public.

[34] Art. L211-5 ('La motivation exigée par le présent chapitre doit être écrite et comporter l'énoncé des considérations de droit et de fait qui constituent le fondement de la decision').

[35] N. Songolo, 'La motivation des actes administratifs, 2011', www.village-justice.com/articles/motivation-actes-administratifs,10849.html.

[36] Joanna Bell, 'Reason-Giving in Administrative Law: Where Are We and Why Have the Courts Not Embraced the "General Common Law Duty to Give Reasons"?' *The Modern Law Review* 9 http://

is echoed by Jennifer Cobbe, who found that 'the more serious the decision and its effects, the greater the need to give reasons for it'.[37]

In both the UK as well as the above countries, there are ample legislative safeguards that provide specific calls for reason giving. What is normally at stake is the *adequacy* of reasons that are given. As Marion Oswald has pointed out, the case law in the UK has a significant history in spelling out what is required when giving reasons for a decision.[38] As she recounts from *Dover District Council*, 'the content of [the duty to give reasons] should not in principle turn on differences in the procedures by which it is arrived at'.[39] What is paramount in the UK conception is not a differentiation between man and machine but one that stands by enshrined and tested principles of being able to mount a meaningful appeal, 'administrative law principles governing the way that state actors take decisions via human decision-makers, combined with judicial review actions, evidential processes and the adversarial legal system, are designed to counter' any ambiguity in the true reasons behind a decision.[40]

The explanation requirement in national law is echoed and further hardened in the regional approaches, where for instance Art. 41 of the Charter of Fundamental Rights of the European Union (CFR) from 2000 provides for a *right to good administration*, where all unilateral acts that generate legal consequences – and qualify for judicial review under Art. 263 TFEU – require an explanation.[41] It must 'contain the considerations of fact and law which determined the decision'.[42] Perhaps the most glaring difference that would arise between automated and non-automated scenarios is the direct application of Art. 22 of the General Data Protection Regulation (GDPR), which applies specifically to 'Automated individual decision making, including profiling.' Art. 22 stipulates that a data subject 'shall have the right not to be subject to a decision based solely on automated processing, including profiling, which produces legal effects concerning him or her or similarly significantly affects him or her',[43] unless it is proscribed by law with 'sufficient

onlinelibrary.wiley.com/doi/abs/10.1111/1468-2230.12457 accessed 19 September 2019 original emphasis.

37 Cobbe (n 2) 648.

38 Marion Oswald, 'Algorithm-Assisted Decision-Making in the Public Sector: Framing the Issues Using Administrative Law Rules Governing Discretionary Power' (2018) 376 *Phil. Trans. R. Soc. A* https://ssrn.com/abstract=3216435.

39 *Dover District Council (Appellant)* v. *CPRE Kent (Respondent) CPRE Kent (Respondent)* v. *China Gateway International Limited (Appellant)* [2017] UKSC 79, para. 41. See, in particular, *Stefan* v. *General Medical Council* [1999] 1 WLR 1293 at page 1300G.

40 Oswald (n 38) 6.

41 Case C-370/07 *Commission of the European Communities* v. *Council of the European Union*, 2009, ECR I-08917, recital 42 ('which is justified in particular by the need for the Court to be able to exercise judicial review, must apply to all acts which may be the subject of an action for annulment').

42 Jürgen Schwarze, *European Administrative Law* (Sweet & Maxwell 2006) 1406.

43 Reg (EU) 2016/679 of the European Parliament and of the Council of 27 April 2016 on the protection of natural persons with regard to the processing of personal data and on the free movement of such data, and repealing Dir 95/46/EC (General Data Protection Regulation) 2016, Art. 22(1).

safeguards' in place,[44] or by 'direct consent.'[45] These sufficient safeguards range from transparency in the input phase (informing and getting consent) to the output-explanation phase (review of the decision itself).[46] The GDPR envisages this output phase in the form of external auditing through Data Protection Authorities (DPAs), which have significant downsides in terms of effectiveness and efficiency.[47] Compared to this, we find the explanation standard in administrative law to be much more robust, for it holds administrative agencies to a standard for intelligibility irrespective of whether they use ADM or not. Furthermore, under administrative law, the principle of 'the greater interference on the recipients life a decision has, the greater the need to give reasons in justification of the decision' applies. Furthermore, the greater the discretionary power of the decision maker, the more thorough the explanation has to be.[48] Focusing on the process by which a decision is made rather than the gravity of its consequences seems misplaced. By holding on to these principles, the incentive should be to develop ADM technology that can be used under this standard, rather than inventing new standards that fit existing technologies.[49]

ADM in public administration does not and should not alter existing explanation requirements. The explanation is not different now that it is algorithmic. The duty of explanation, although constructed differently in different jurisdictions, provides a robust foundation across Europe for ensuring that decision-making in public administration remains comprehensible and challengeable, even when ADM is applied. What remains is asking how ADM could be integrated into the decision-making procedure in the organisation of a public authority to ensure this standard.

11.4 ENSURING EXPLANATION THROUGH HYBRID SYSTEMS

Introducing a machine-learning algorithm in public administration and using it to produce *drafts* of decisions rather than final decisions to be issued immediately to citizens, we suggest, would be a useful first step. In this final section of the chapter, we propose an idea that could be developed into a proof of concept for how ADM could be implemented in public authorities to support decision-making.

In contemporary public administration, much drafting takes place using templates. ADM could be coupled to such templates in various ways. Different

44 Ibid., Art. 22(2)b.

45 Ibid., Art. 22(2)c.

46 For a longer detailed analysis, see the working paper version of this chapter: http://ssrn.com/abstract=3402974.

47 See Antoni Roig, 'Safeguards for the Right Not to Be Subject to a Decision Based Solely on Automated Processing (Article 22 GDPR)' (2017) 8(3) *European Journal of Law and Technology*.

48 Schwarze (n 42) 1410.

49 See also Zalnieriute, Moses, and Williams (n 2), who conclude (at p. 454) after conducting four case studies that only one system (the Swedish student welfare management system) succeeds in reaping benefits from automation while remaining sensitive to rule of law values. They characterize this as 'a carefully designed system integrating automation with human responsibility'.

templates require different kinds of information. Such information could be collected and inserted into the template automatically, as choices are made by a human about what kind of information should be filled into the template. Another way is to rely on automatic legal information retrieval. Human administrators often look to previous decisions of the same kind as inspiration for deciding new cases. Such processes can be labour intensive, and the same public authority may not all have the same skills in finding a relevant, former decision. Natural Language Processing technology may be applied to automatically retrieve relevant former decisions, if the authority's decisions are available in electronic form in a database. This requires, of course, that the data the algorithm is learning from is sufficiently large and that the decisions in the database are generally considered to still be relevant 'precedent'[50] for new decisions. Algorithmically learning from historical cases and reproducing their language in new cases by connecting legal outcomes to given fact descriptions is not far from what human civil servants would do anyway: whenever a caseworker is attending to a new case, he or she will seek out former cases of the same kind to use as a compass to indicate how the new case should be decided.

One important difference between a human and an algorithm is that humans have the ability to respond more organically to past cases because they have a broader horizon of understanding: They are capable of contextualizing the understanding of their task to a much richer extent than algorithms, and humans can therefore adjust their decisions to a broader spectrum of factors – including ones that are hidden from the explicit legislation and case law that applies to the case at hand.[51] Resource allocation, policy signals, and social and economic change are examples of this. This human contextualisation of legal text precisely explains why new practices sometimes develop under the same law.[52]. Algorithms, on the other hand operate, without such context and can only relate to explicit texts. Hence they cannot evolve in the same way. Paradoxically, then, having humans in the legal loop serves the purpose of relativizing strict rule-following by allowing sensitivity to context.

This limited contextualization of algorithmic 'reasoning' will create a problem if *all* new decisions are drafted on the basis of a machine learning algorithm that reproduces the past, and if those drafts are only subjected to minor or no changes by

50 We are well aware that such decisions do not formally have the character of precedent, what we refer to here is the de facto tendency in the administrative process to make new decisions that closely emulate earlier decisions of the same kind.

51 Even deciding what former decisions are relevant to a new case can sometimes be a complex problem that requires a broader contextual understanding of law and society that is not attainable by algorithms.

52 See also Carol Harlow and Richard Rawlings, 'Proceduralism and Automation: Challenges to the Values of Administrative Law' in E. Fisher, J. King, and A. Young (eds), *The Foundations and Future of Public Law (in Honour of Paul Craig)* (Oxford University Press 2019) (at 6 in the SSRN version) https://papers.ssrn.com/abstract=3334783, who note that 'Administrative Law cannot be static, and the list of values is not immutable; it varies in different legal orders and over time'.

its human collaborator[53]. Once the initial learning stage is finalized and the algorithm is used in output mode to produce decision drafts, then new decisions will be produced in part by the algorithm. One of two different situations may now occur: One, the new decisions are fed back into the machine-learning stage. In this case, a feedback loop is created in which the algorithm is fed its own decisions.[54] Or, two, the machine-learning stage is blocked after the initial training phase. In this case, every new decision is based on what the algorithm picked up from the original training set, and the output from the algorithm will remain statically linked to this increasingly old data set. None of these options are in our opinion optimal for maintaining an up-to-date algorithmic support system.

There are good reasons to think that a machine learning algorithm will only keep performing well in changing contexts (which in this case is measured by the algorithm's ability to issue usable drafts of a good legal quality) – if it is constantly maintained by fresh input which reflects those changing contexts. This can be done in a number of different ways, depending on how the algorithmic support system is implemented in the overall organization of the administrative body and its procedures for issuing decisions. As mentioned previously, our focus is on models that engage AI and human collaboration. We propose two such models for organizing algorithmic support in an administrative system that aim at issuing decisions that we think are particularly helpful because they address the need for intelligible explanations of the outlined legal standard.

In our first proposed model, the caseload in an administrative field that is supported by ADM assistance is randomly split into two loads, such that one load is fed to an algorithm for drafting and another load is fed to a human team, also for drafting. Drafts from both algorithms and humans are subsequently sent to a senior civil servant (say a head of office), who finalizes and signs off on the decisions. All final decisions are pooled and used to regularly update the algorithm used.

By having an experienced civil servant interact with algorithmic drafting in this way, and feeding decisions, all checked by human intelligence, back into the machine-learning process, the algorithm will be kept fresh with new original decisions, a percentage of which will be written by humans from scratch. The effect of splitting the caseload and leaving one part to through a 'human only' track is that the previously mentioned sensitivity to broader contextualization is fed back into the algorithm and hence allows a development in the case law that could otherwise not

53 Research has identified a phenomenon known as *automation bias*. This is the propensity for humans to favour suggestions from automated decision-making systems and to ignore contradictory information made without automation, even if it is correct. See Mary Cummings, 'Automation Bias in Intelligent Time Critical Decision Support Systems', *AIAA 1st Intelligent Systems Technical Conference* (2004); Asia J Biega, Krishna P Gummadi, and Gerhard Weikum, 'Equity of Attention: Amortizing Individual Fairness in Rankings', *The 41st International ACM SIGIR Conference on Research & Development in Information Retrieval* (2018). In implementing ADM in public administration, we follow this research by recommending processes that seek to reduce such bias.

54 See O'Neil (n 3) for a discussion of the problem with feedback loops.

happen. To use our Parent A example as an illustration: Over time, it might be that new diseases and new forms of handicaps are identified or recognized as falling under the legislative provision because it is being diagnosed differently. If every new decision is produced by an ADM system that is not updated with new learning on cases that reflect this kind of change, then the system cannot evolve to take the renewed diagnostic practices into account. To avoid this 'freezing of time', a hybrid system in which the ADM is constantly being surveyed and challenged is necessary. Furthermore, if drafting is kept anonymous, and all final decisions are signed off by a human, recipients of decisions (like our Parent A) may not know how his/her decision was produced. Still, the explanation requirement assures that recipients can at any time challenge the decision, by inquiring further into the legal justification.[55] We think this way of introducing algorithmic support for administrative decisions could advance many of the efficiency and consistency (equality) gains sought by introducing algorithmic support systems, while preserving the legal standard for explanation.

An alternative method – our second proposed model – is to build into the administrative system itself a kind of continuous administrative Turing test. Alan Turing, in a paper written in 1950,[56] sought to identify a test for artificial intelligence. The test he devised consisted of a setup in which (roughly explained) two computers were installed in separate rooms. One computer was operated by a person; the other was operated by an algorithmic system (a machine). In a third room, a human 'judge' was sitting with a third computer. The judge would type questions on his computer, and the questions would then be sent to both the human and the machine in the two other rooms for them to read. They would then in turn write replies and send those back to the judge. If the judge could not identify which answers came from the person and which came from the machine, then the machine would be said to have shown the ability to think. A model of Turing's proposed experimental setup is seen in Figure 11.1:

Akin to this, an administrative body could implement algorithmic decision support in a way that would imitate the setup described by Turing. This could be done by giving it to both a human administrator and an ADM. Both the human and the ADM would produce a decision draft for the same case. Both drafts would be sent to a human judge (i.e., a senior civil servant who finalizes and signs off on the decision). In this setup, the human judge would not know which draft came from the ADM and which came from the human,[57] but would proceed to finalize the decision based on which draft was most convincing for deciding the case and

55 Whether recipients can or should be able to demand insight into the underlying neurological or algorithmic computations of caseworkers (human or robotic) is a separate question that we do not seek to answer here. Suffice it to say there may be many reasons why a human might ask for an explanation, including not caring what the justification is but simply wanting a change of outcome.

56 A. M. Turing, 'Computing Machinery and Intelligence' (1950) 49 *Mind* 433–460.

57 Formats for issuing drafts could also be formalized so as to reduce the possibility of guessing merely by recognizing the style of the drafter's language.

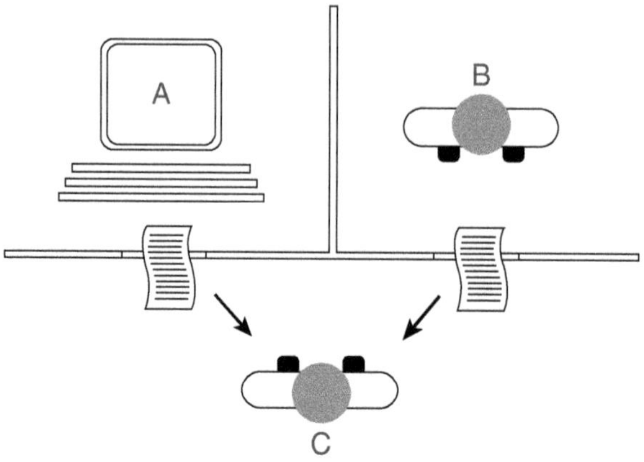

FIGURE 11.1 Turing's experimental setup (Source: https://en.wikipedia.org/wiki/Turing_test)

providing a satisfactory explanation to the citizen. This final decision would then be fed back to the data set from which the ADM system learns.

The two methods described previously are both hybrid models and can be used either alone or in combination to assure that ADM models are implemented in a way that is both productive, because drafting is usually a very time-consuming process and safe (even if not mathematically transparent) because there is a human overseeing the final product and a continuous human feedback to the data set from which the ADM system learns. Moreover, using this hybrid approach helps overcome the legal challenges that a fully automated system would face from both EU law (GDPR) and some domestic legislation.

11.5 CONCLUSION

Relying on the above models keeps the much-sought-after 'human in the loop' and does so in a way that is systematic and meaningful because our proposed models take a specific form: they are built around the idea of continuous human-AI collaboration in producing explainable decisions. Relying on this model makes it possible to develop ADM systems that can be introduced to enhance the effectiveness, consistency (equality) without diminishing the quality of explanation. The advantage of our model is that it allows ADM to be continuously developed and fitted to the legal environment in which it is supposed to serve. Furthermore, such an approach may have further advantages. Using ADM for legal information retrieval allows for analysis across large numbers of decisions that have been handed down across time. This could grow into a means for assuring better detection of hidden biases and other structural deficiencies that would otherwise not be discoverable. This approach may help allay the fears of the black box.

In terms of control and responsibility, our proposed administrative Turing test allows for a greater scope of review of rubber stamp occurrences by being able to compare differences in pure human and pure machine decisions by a human arbiter. Therefore the model may also help in addressing the concern raised about 'retrospective justifications'.[58] Because decisions in the setup we propose are produced in collaboration between ADM and humans, the decisions issued are likely to be more authentic than either pure ADM or pure human decision-making, since the use of ADM allows for a more efficient and comprehensive inclusion of existing decision-making practice as inputting the new decision-making through automated information retrieval and recommendation. With reference to human dignity, our proposed model retains human intelligibility as the standard for decision-making. The proposed administrative Turing model also continually adds new information into the system, and undergoes a level of supervision that can protect against failures that are frequently associated with ADM systems. Applying the test developed in this chapter to develop a proof of concept for the implementation of ADM in public administration today is the most efficient way of overcoming the weaknesses of purely human decision-making tomorrow.

ADM does not solve the inequalities built into our societal and political institutions, nor is it their original cause. There are real questions to be asked of our systems, and we would rather not bury those questions with false enemies. To rectify those inequalities, we must be critical of our human failings and not hold hostage the principles we have developed to counter injustice. If those laws are deficient, it is not the fault of a new technology. We are, however, aware that this technology can not only reproduce but even heighten injustice if it is used thoughtlessly. But we would also like to flag that the technology offers an opportunity to bring legal commitments like the duty of explanation up to a standard that is demanded by every occurrence of injustice: a human-based standard.

[58] Cobbe remarks that black box technology that 'their inexplicability is therefore a serious issue' and therefore decisions issued by such systems will likely not pass judicial review. She then adds that 'some public bodies may attempt to circumvent this barrier by providing retrospective justifications'. She flags that Courts and reviewers should be 'aware of this risk and should be prepared to exercise the appropriate level of scrutiny . . . against such justifications.' Cobbe (n 2) 648.

12

International Race for Regulating Crypto-Finance Risks

A Comprehensive Regulatory Framework Proposal

*Yaiza Cabedo**

12.1 REGULATORY RESPONSES TO FINANCIAL INNOVATION FROM A REGULATORY COMPETITION PERSPECTIVE

States are in continuous competition to attract business, wealth and innovation through the quality of their administration and courts and their capacity to provide specialised, innovative and efficient regulatory solutions to ensure a level playing field and an adequate level of protection for their citizens.[1] In this international regulatory race, the US legal system was a pioneer in regulating new rights, such as civil rights, women's rights, environmental regulations or traffic safety rights – all successful regulatory innovations that other countries imported. The US administrative model was inspired by the German and English administrative law principles, and at a later time, the US functioning between the fifty states and the federal government also inspired the functioning of the European Union and globalisation through what we call the *globalisation of law* phenomenon.[2]

The European Union (EU), with its regulatory initiatives and the development of its own process for regional and global integration, also became progressively an essential element for global checks and balances, able to correct and prevent distortions to the US legal and federal principles, such as antitrust law and the control of monopolies, deeply entrenched in the political and legal tradition of economic federalism.[3] The European Commissioner for Competition, Vestager,

* I am grateful to Manuel Ballbé Mallol for his great support and valuable contribution to an earlier draft. The views expressed in this article are privately held by the author and cannot be attributed to the European Securities and Markets Authority (ESMA).

1 See Ballbé, M. ; Padrós, C. Estado competitivo y armonización europea. Ariel. Barcelona, 1997. See also Ballbé, M.; Cabedo, Y. La necesidad de administraciones reguladoras en Latinoamérica para prevenir los ataques especulativos, los riesgos financieros y la defensa de los consumidores. Revista del CLAD Reforma y Democracia. No 57. Caracas, October 2013.

2 Ballbé, M.; Martinez, R. Law and globalization: between the United States and Europe in global administrative law. Towards a lex administrativa. Eds. Robalino-Orellana, J.; Rodriguez-Arana, J. Cameron May. 2010.

3 Ballbé, M.; Martinez, R. (2010).

and the antitrust case against Google illustrates the EU as a countervailing power to limit US companies' malpractice.[4]

One of the most potent administrative innovations in the United States since its Constitution is the independent regulatory agency (or authority as it is referred to in the EU). While the 'Constitution was designed to make lawmaking cumbersome, representative, and consensual[,] the regulatory agency was a workaround, designed to make lawmaking efficient, specialized, and purposeful' with fewer internal hierarchy conflicts and with pre-ordained missions.[5]

Wilson's presidency in the United States laid the foundations for an innovative decentralised system of independent regulatory agencies; the Massachusetts Board of Railroad Commissioners (1869) was the first of its kind. The Commission was formed to request information and issue recommendations without holding any enforcement power yet with capacity for publicity and admonition, which proved to be a more powerful antidote for corruption than force and compulsion.[6] This system was reproduced at state and federal levels and across sectors, creating a new regulatory model (e.g., the Federal Trade Commission, created in 1914, or the Federal Reserve, created in 1913).[7]

President Roosevelt, when reforming financial markets after the 1929 crash, created the Federal Deposit Insurance Corporation in 1933 and the Securities Exchange Commission (SEC) in 1934. Similarly, President Obama, after the 2008 crisis caused by the deregulation of over-the-counter (OTC) markets, expanded the powers of the SEC and the Commodity Futures Trading Commission (CFTC) and set up the Consumer Protection Financial Bureau (CPFB) for the protection of financial consumers as part of its Dodd-Frank Act reform package.[8]

In the EU, the 2008 financial crisis fostered the creation of supranational and very specialised administrations for the early detection and prevention of financial risks, less bureaucratised bodies than the three EU co-legislators[9] and able adapt quickly to new market challenges. The Single Resolution Board or the three European Supervisory Authorities – the European Securities and Markets Authority (ESMA) in charge of regulation and supervision of securities and financial markets, the European Banking Authority (EBA) for the supervising banking entities and the European Insurance and Occupational Pensions Authority (EIOPA) – are good examples. At the same time, the post-crisis reform also reinforced the EU decentralised regulatory model for financial markets, expanding the scope of action of each

4 See Commission fines Google €1.49 billion for abusive practices in online advertising https://ec.europa.eu/commission/presscorner/detail/en/IP_19_1770

5 DeMuth, C. ; The regulatory state. National Affairs. Summer 2012.

6 Eastman, J. B. The public service commission of Massachusetts. The Quarterly Journal of Economics. Vol. 27. No. 4 (August, 1913). Oxford University Press.

7 Ballbé, M.; Martinez, R. (2010).

8 Ballbé, M., Cabedo, Y.; (2013).

9 The European Commission, Parliament and Council.

EU Member State's independent regulatory agencies for the surveillance and regulation of financial products and markets.

From an international regulatory competition perspective, the system of independent regulatory agencies is a solid structure to enable countries to anticipate responses to risks and opportunities stemming from financial innovation and technological developments such as crypto-finance. Countries with the most advanced regulatory framework and most efficient and specialised regulatory bodies and courts will attract crypto-finance businesses and investors. ESMA's advice to the European Commission on ICOs and cryptocurrencies points out this competition between two financial blocs – the European Union and the United States – which may not be on the same page, with the European Union seeing mostly risks for regulators, investors and markets, and the United States being more open to the blockchain technology and crypto-assets.[10]

Indeed, states, far away from a passive-supervisory role, can and do play an essential role as precursors and innovation pioneers. Moreover, states can go well beyond the mere race for attracting business and rather contribute to generating new markets.[11] Crypto-finance is yet another example of states' driven innovation, and one of the technological key components of blockchain, the unique 'fingerprint' or hash[12] of each block of information in the chain, is generated using the standard cryptographic hashing functions invented by the US National Security Agency,[13] an administration whose research is financed with public funds.

Ultimately, economic development and financial stability depend on states' capacity to anticipate needs and prevent emerging risks by reaching innovative solutions. DLT systems such as blockchain, thanks to their immutability of records, traceability and transparency, offer potential enhancements of legal, financial and administrative processes for private companies and also for governments.[14] However, this transition to DLT-based systems requires new regulatory actors and legal changes. In this regulatory race, states can choose to join a race to the top and use

10 Brummer, C. EU reports on cryptoasset regulation could have global reverberations. Watchdogs urge EU-wide rules. 9 January 2019 www.rollcall.com/2019/01/09/eu-reports-on-cryptoasset-regulation-could-have-global-reverberations/

11 Mazzucato, M. The entrepreneurial state: debunking public vs. private sector myths. Anthem Press. London, 2013.

12 A hash provides a way to represent the bundle of transactions in a block as a string of characters and numbers that are uniquely associated with that block's transactions. De Filippi, P., Wright, A. Blockchain and the law: the rule of code. Harvard University Press. Massachusetts, 2018.

13 De Filippi, P., Wright, A. Blockchain and the law: the rule of code. Harvard University Press. Massachusetts, 2018.

14 For example, see Delaware law amendments to allow corporations to issue shares through blockchain in Reyes, C.L. Cryptolaw for distributed ledger technologies: a jurisprudential framework. Journal of Law Science and Technology. Spring 2018. Vol. 58 Issue 3. See also the Australian Stock Exchange transition to DLT for equity transactions https://cointelegraph.com/news/covid-19-forces-aussie-stock-exchange-to-delay-dlt-overhaul-to-2023

these technologies to compete in excellence or, on the contrary, go for a race to the bottom and compete in lenient and more permissive regulatory frameworks.

Innovative financial markets have always been a challenge and an opportunity for regulators from a competitive and regulatory perspective. The last paradigmatic example of a transformation of financial markets driven by the combination of financial innovation and lack of specific regulation or specialised surveillance bodies occurred with the rise of OTC derivatives markets, which consequently put at risk the global financial stability,[15] with a cost of trillions of dollars for taxpayers around the world.[16]

12.2 THE UNREGULATED OTC DERIVATIVE MARKETS AND THE TBTF[17]: LESSONS FROM A REGULATORY RACE TO THE BOTTOM

In 1933, after the 1929 crash, Roosevelt introduced a package of regulatory measures to reform financial markets and increase their transparency and resilience. In addition, the SEC was created as a specialised independent regulatory agency for the surveillance and regulation of securities markets, and the Securities Exchange Act was enacted to regulate securities transactions, laying the foundations for the prosecution of insider trading. The SEC's A-1 form, the first disclosure document introduced, required issuers of stocks to provide

> a narrative description of their businesses, details of corporate incorporation, management, properties, capital structure, terms of outstanding debt, the purpose of the new issue and associated expenses. It also demanded disclosure of topics not contained in listing applications, including management's compensation, transactions between the company and its directors, officers, underwriters and promoters, a list of principal shareholders and their holdings and a description of any contracts not made in the ordinary course of business.[18]

The SEC's success inspired the creation in 1974 of the CFTC, another specialised independent regulatory agency for the surveillance and regulation of futures markets.

Roosevelt's reform introduced principles for a regulated, more transparent and accountable capitalism, which provided financial stability and are still applicable

15 For further analysis on the causes of the crisis, see Lastra, R.M.; Wood, G. The crisis of 2007–09: nature, causes, and reactions. Journal of International Economic Law 13(3). See also Ballbé, M.; Cabedo, Y. (2013).

16 For figures on the bail-out costs of some EU financial institutions, see Ballbé, M.; Cabedo, Y. El ataque alemán deshaucia a España. 29 November 2012. In the United States, the Troubled Asset Relief Program initial budget amounted to $350 billion.

17 Too Big to Fail banks.

18 Mahoney, P.G.; Mei, J. Mandatory versus contractual disclosure in securities markets: evidence from the 1930s. Working Paper, 23 February 2006. Cited in Brummer, C.; et al. What should be disclosed in an initial coin offering? 29 November 2018. Cryptoassets: Legal and Monetary Perspectives, Oxford University Press, Forthcoming. Draft 24 February 2019.

today. However, starting from the late eighties in the UK[19] and in the mid- to late nineties in the United States, new private markets in the form of OTC derivative markets emerged without administrative or judicial surveillance, introducing innovative and highly risky financial instruments that allowed betting on the future value of any underlying asset (stocks, interest rates, currencies, etc). These OTC markets have grown exponentially since 2000, reaching $680 trillion of notional value in 2008[20] and becoming an epicentre of systemic risk,[21] with New York and London concentrating 90 per cent of the market. This market transformation and its dramatic growth were possible due to a deregulatory race-to-the-bottom strategy.

In 1999, in the United States, the Gramm Act removed restrictions that prevented deposit-taking entities from acting as investment banks.[22] In 2000, the Commodities and Futures Modernisation Act permitted corporations other than banks to trade as investment banks. In addition, it was established that the regulatory and surveillance capacity of the SEC and the CFTC would not apply to OTC derivatives markets. Indeed, all disclosure and identification requirements for regulated markets (stocks and futures) did not apply in OTC derivative markets, and instruments and behaviours that would have been considered a crime on Wall Street and any other regulated market, such as insider trading, were not prosecuted in OTC markets. Another restriction on banks' power, limiting the territorial scope of their banking services,[23] was also lifted and generated a massive wave of mergers among financial institutions. While in 1970 12,500 small banks held 46 per cent of total US banking assets, by 2010, more than 7,000 small banks had disappeared and the few small banks still running only represented 16 per cent of all US banking assets.[24] This is how banks became TBTF,[25] so big and powerful that they could easily capture the system – either through revolving doors or through information asymmetry (releasing technical information only favourable to their interests),[26] and they succeeded in keeping regulators away.

19 In 1986, an amendment to the Game Act was approved to carve-out OTC derivatives. However, the boom of OTC derivatives markets took place later on, in 2000, once the United States had unwound all regulatory and supervisory checks for OTC derivative markets.

20 Bank for International Settlements. BIS quarterly review: international banking and financial markets development. December 2018.

21 Cabedo, Y. OTC regulatory reform: risks of the clearing obligation from a competition perspective. Risk & Regulation. London School of Economics, Centre for Analysis of Risk and Regulation. Summer 2016.

22 This fragmentation system had been implemented in 1933 with the adoption of the Glass-Steagall Act as a risk contention measure; in case an investment bank would fail, entities holding deposits would not be impacted.

23 US banks could not provide banking services beyond the limits of their home state. This was part of the Dual Banking System and was grounded on the US constitutional spirit of checks and balances and control of monopolies. In 1994, the Reagle Neal Act removed this territorial restriction allowing banks to merge with other banks in the other states.

24 Federal Reserve Bank of Dallas. Annual Report. 2011.

25 Or, as some authors like to say, 'too big to jail'.

26 Stigler, G. J. The theory of economic regulation. The Bell Journal of Economics and Management Science. Vol. 2 No. 1. Spring 1971.

In the absence of administrative regulation and the lack of surveillance of OTC markets, the major OTC derivatives market players created the International Swaps and Derivatives Association (ISDA),[27] which became the standards setter in OTC derivative markets, providing standardised documentation for OTC transactions and able to seduce governments to maintain OTC markets self-regulated. As ISDAs Chair said by then, 'Markets can correct excess far better than any government. Market discipline is the best form of discipline there is.'[28]

After the 2008 financial crisis, the Special Report of the United States Congressional oversight panel concluded:

> After fifty years without a financial crisis – the longest such stretch in the nation's history – financial firms and policy makers began to see regulation as a barrier to efficient functioning of the capital markets rather than a necessary precondition for success. This change in attitude had unfortunate consequences. As financial markets grew and globalised, often with breath-taking speed, the US regulatory system could have benefited from smart changes. But deregulation and the growth of unregulated, parallel shadow markets were accompanied by the nearly unrestricted marketing of increasingly complex consumer financial products that multiplied risk at every stratum of the economy, from the family level to the global level. The result proved disastrous.[29]

The regulatory response to prevent this from happening again was to regulate for disclosure with independent agencies and specialised regulation for OTC derivatives. International leaders agreed at the 2009 Pittsburgh Summit on a decentralised international regulatory framework; in the United States, the Dodd-Frank Act (2010) and in the EU the European Markets Infrastructure Regulation (2012) mandated the use of a Legal Entity Identifier or LEI (similar to an ID) for the identification of the parties to an OTC derivative contract and the obligation to report and make visible to competent authorities all OTC derivative transactions taking place in the market. In addition, systemic risk controls were adopted internationally, such as the clearing obligation for standardised OTC products and the need to provide guarantees when transacting bilaterally OTC derivatives.[30]

Initiatives for standardised transactional documentation for crypto-finance, such as the Simple Agreement for Future Tokens (SAFT), are being developed by market participants. Regulators should not miss the opportunity to engage since the start to introduce checks and balances and to further develop specialised knowledge while providing legal and contractual certainty to investors.

An argument used to advocate for self-regulation in OTC derivative markets was complexity. New technological developments such as blockchain and crypto-finance

[27] ISDA gathers all major participants in OTC derivatives markets.

[28] 'Fools Gold' by Gillian Tett, Little Brown. 2009 p. 36. Cit. in Thomas, T. The 2008 global financial crisis: origins and response. 15th Malasyan Law Conference, 29–31 July. Kuala Lumpur. 2010.

[29] Congressional Oversight Panel. Special report on regulatory reform. January 2009.

[30] Cabedo, Y. (2016).

are also highly complex systems. As Supreme Court Justice Louis Brandeis warned a century ago:

> Business men have been active in devising other means of escape from the domain of the courts, as is evidenced by the widespread tendency to arbitrate controversies through committees of business organisations. An inadequate Remedy. The remedy so sought is not adequate, and may prove a mischievous one. What we need is not to displace the courts, but to make them efficient instruments of justice; not to displace the lawyer, but to fit him for his official or judicial task. And indeed, the task of fitting the lawyer and the judge to perform adequately the functions of harmonising law with life is a task far easier of accomplishment than that of endowing men, who lack legal graining, with the necessary qualifications.[31]

The emergence of new and innovative financial markets is an opportunity to apply lessons learned and prevent abuses arising from new and sophisticated crypto-assets. In addition, there is an increasing presence of tech giants in payment systems and crypto markets that will require new regulatory solutions. Big tech companies (e.g., Alibaba, Amazon, Facebook, Google and Tencent) have the potential to loom systemically relevant financial institutions very quickly; their business model builds on their large number users' data to offer a range of financial services that exploit natural network effects, generating further user activity.[32] *The Economist* warns they can be too BAADD (big, anti-competitive, addictive and destructive to democracy),[33] as they are a data-opoly[34] with the potential to bring together new ways of tyranny.

12.3 THE EMERGENCE OF CRYPTO-FINANCE: A RACE TO THE TOP OR A RACE TO THE BOTTOM?

Crypto-finance uses DLT systems such as blockchain to trade assets or 'crypto-assets'. At its core, blockchain is a decentralised database maintained by a distributed network of computers that use a variety of technologies, including peer-to-peer networks, cryptography and consensus mechanisms. The consensus mechanism is the set of strict rules for validating blocks that makes it difficult and costly for any one party to unilaterally modify the data stored, ensuring the orderly recordation of information and enhancing security.[35,36] Participants in the network are incentivised to proceed according to the protocol by a fee paid per block validated by the transaction originator. Miners select the unprocessed transactions and engage in

31 Brandeis, L.D. The living law. 1917, p. 468.
32 BIS. Big tech in finance. Opportunities and risks. Annual Report 2019.
33 How to tame the tech titans. The Economist. 18 January 2018.
34 Stucke, M.E. Should we be concerned about data-opolies? 2 Geo. L. Tech. Rev. 275. 2018.
35 De Filipi, P., Wright, A. (2018).
36 See Werbach, K.; Trust, but verify: Why the blockchain needs the law. Berkeley Technology Law Journal. Vol. 33.

computations until the first miner emerges with a valid proof-of-work which allows the miner to add a block of transactions to the blockchain, collecting the reward fees.[37] The new blockchain is shared among the network of miners and other users, who verify the proof-of-work, the signatures and the absence of double-spending. If this new blockchain emerges as the consensus version, the majority of miners keep on adding to it.[38]

DLT systems are built upon a cryptographic system that uses a public key, publicly known and essential for identification, and a private key (similar to a password that enables to transfer assets) kept secret and used for authentication and encryption.[39] Losing this password is equivalent to losing the right to access or move these assets. Blockchains are pseudonymous, and the private key does not reveal a 'real life' identity.[40]

How does owner X transfer a crypto-asset to Y? X generates a transaction including X and Y's address and X's private key (without disclosing the private key). The transaction is broadcast to the entire network, which can verify thanks to X's private key that X has the right to dispose of the crypto assets at a given address. What makes the system safe is the impossibility of inferring the public key from the address or inferring the private key from the public key. Meanwhile, the entire network can derive the public key from the private key and hence authenticate a given transaction.[41]

By combining blockchains with 'smart contracts', computer processes which can execute autonomously, people can construct their own systems of rules enforced by the underlying protocol of a blockchain-based network. These systems create order without law and implement what can be thought of as private regulatory frameworks or *lex cryptographica*.[42] As the CFTC Commissioner Quintez notes,

> Smart contracts are easily customized and are almost limitless in their applicability. For example, individuals could create their own smart contracts to bet on the outcome of future events, like sporting events or elections, using digital currency. If your prediction is right, the contract automatically pays you the winnings.... This could look like what the CFTC calls a 'prediction market', where individuals use so-called 'event contracts', binary options, or other derivative contracts to bet on the occurrence or outcome of future events [which the CFTC generally prohibits in non-crypto markets].[43]

37 The most commonly used are Proof of Work, Proof of Stake, Proof of Burn, Proof of Authority, Proof of Capacity and Proof of Storage (new ones are being introduced). Depending on which consensus mechanism is chosen, users will make different uses of computational logic on blockchain.

38 Auer, R. Beyond the doomsday economics of 'proof-of work' in cryptocurrencies. BIS Working Papers No 765. January 2019.

39 ESMA. Advice on Initial Coin Offerings and Crypto-Assets. 9 January 2019.

40 Schrepel, T. Collusion by blockchain and smart contracts. Harvard Journal of Law & Technology. Vol. 33. Fall 2019.

41 ESMA (2019).

42 De Filippi, P.; Wright, A. (2018).

43 CFTC. Commissioner Brian Quintez at the 38th Annual GITEX Technology Week Conference. Public Statements & Remarks, 16 October 2018.

There are a wide variety of crypto-assets: the 'investment type' which has profit rights attached, like equities; the 'utility type' which provides some utility or consumption rights; and the 'payment type', which has no tangible value but the expectation to serve as means of exchange outside their ecosystem – and there are also hybrid types.[44] Examples range from so-called crypto-currencies like Bitcoin to digital tokens that are issued through Initial Coin Offerings (ICOs). Crypto-finance is rapidly evolving since Bitcoin was launched in 2009,[45] and Central Banks are under pressure to improve the efficiency of traditional payment systems.[46] According to the ESMA, as of the end of December 2018, there were more than 2,050 crypto-assets outstanding, representing a total market capitalisation of around EUR 110bn – down from a peak of over EUR 700bn in January 2018. Bitcoin represents half of the total, with the top 5 representing around 75 per cent of the reported market capitalisation.[47]

Blockchain-based finance is taking a bite out of public markets, as it enables parties to sell billions of dollars of cryptographically secured 'tokens' – some of which resemble securities – and trade OTC derivatives and other financial products by using autonomous and unregulated code-based exchanges. Moreover, 'these blockchain-based systems often ignore legal barriers supporting existing financial markets and undercut carefully constructed regulations aimed at limiting fraud and protecting investors'.[48] Blockchain allows for anonymity in transactional relationships governed solely by the network protocols, where *code is law*.[49] Moreover, crypto markets (like OTC derivative markets) are global and can avoid jurisdictional rules by operating transnationally. If not adequately regulated, crypto-finance can be used to circumvent the existing financial regulation and investors' protection safeguards to commit fraud and engage in money laundering, terrorist financing or other illicit activities.

Besides the obvious differences referred to the underlying technology, the emergence of crypto-finance represents, from a regulatory perspective, the emergence of the 'new over-the-counter market' with yet no specific regulation and no administrative surveillance. Instruments and behaviours that are no longer accepted neither in stock markets nor in the OTC derivative markets since their post-crisis reform are found in the new anomic crypto space.

The lessons learnt from the unregulated OTC derivative markets and how they became an epicentre of systemic risk should be applied to crypto-finance by regulating for disclosure and identification, setting up independent regulatory bodies with

44 ESMA. Advice on Initial Coin Offerings and Crypto-Assets. 9 January 2019.

45 ESMA. (2019).

46 A switch from public fiat toward private electronic money still leaves central banks unconvinced due to security, scalability and interoperability concerns. See Ward, O., Rochemont, S.; Understanding central bank digital currencies. Institute and Faculty of Actuaries. March 2019.

47 ESMA. (2019).

48 De Filippi, P.; Wright, A. (2018).

49 Lessig, L.; Code and other laws of cyberspace. Perseus Books, 1999.

highly specialised officials and international coordination plans for establishing mechanisms for checks and balances that strike a careful balance between encouraging digital innovations and addressing underlying risks.[50]

12.4 ATTEMPTS TO REGULATE CRYPTO-ASSETS

The assignment of an object to one category (or none) initiates a whole cascade of further legal consequences, and as not all crypto-assets have the same features, not all of them need the same legal consideration. Crypto-currencies resemble currency in that they are exchanged 'peer-to-peer' in a decentralised manner, rather than through the accounting system of a central institution, but are distinguished from currency (i.e., cash) in that they are created, transferred and stored digitally rather than physically; they are issued by a private entity rather than a central bank or other public authority; and they are not 'legal tender'.[51]

Most regulators first steps towards crypto consisted in the analogue application of existing regulations. While the SEC attempts to treat some crypto-assets as securities, Bitcoin and Ether are considered commodities. Both the head of the SEC and the chairman of the CFTC have said Bitcoin and Ether are exempt from Securities Law[52] application and that they should be considered commodities under the Commodity Exchange Act.[53] A recent decision from the trade court of Nanterre in France (*Tribunal de Commerce Nanterre*)[54] qualifies for the first time the legal nature of Bitcoin, considering it as an intangible and fungible asset that is interchangeable – like a grain of rice or a dollar note – implying it has the features of money.[55] In 2018, in *Wisconsin Central Ltd.* v. *United States*, the United States Supreme Court introduced a passing reference to Bitcoin, implying Bitcoin is a kind of money; Justice Breyer wrote 'what we view as money has changed over time.... Our currency originally included gold coins and bullion.... Perhaps one day employees will be paid in Bitcoin or other types of cryptocurrency'.

In relation to the tokens of an ICO, the SEC has been proactive in bringing ICOs within the scope of the Securities Act of 1933, mandating to comply with the extensive regulatory requirements in place when offering securities to the

[50] Malady, L., Buckley, R. P., Didenko, A., Tsang, C. A regulatory diagnostic toolkit for digital financial services in emerging markets. Banking & Finance Law Review, 34(1). 2018.

[51] Lastra, R. M., Allen, J. G. Virtual currencies in the Eurosystem: challenges ahead. Study Requested by the ECON Committee, European Parliament. July 2018.

[52] Rooney, K. SEC chief says agency won't change securities laws to cater to cryptocurrencies, CNBC. com. 11 June 2018.

[53] CFTC Release Number 8051–19: Chairman Tarbert Comments on Cryptocurrency Regulation at Yahoo! Finance All Markets Summit. 10 October 2019.

[54] Decision of 26 February 2020.

[55] Andrew Singer, French court moves the BTC chess piece. How will regulators respond? 15 March 2020 https://cointelegraph.com/news/french-court-moves-the-btc-chess-piece-how-will-regulators-respond

public.[56] An ICO is a pre-sell of tokens that allows a person to finance the creation of the infrastructure needed to develop an entrepreneurial project. Let's imagine we want to build a central infrastructure for the storage of data. To finance it, we issue a token. Users seeking storage would be incentivised to buy tokens to exchange them for storage space; other users would be incentivised to provide storage by the prospect of getting tokens. The designer of infrastructure would not have the property or the control over the infrastructure, but rather, it would be collectively run by the users. Nevertheless, providers would have incentives to do a good job – providing storage and maintaining the network – because if they want their tokens to be valuable, they need their network to be useful and well maintained.[57]

An ICO is to crypto-finance what an IPO (Initial Public Offering) is to the traditional or mainstream investment world, and both share the purpose of raising capital. However, they are not fully equivalent: in an IPO, a company offers securities to raise capital through middlemen (investment banks, broker dealers, underwriters), while in an ICO, a company offers digital tokens directly to the public. During the ICO boom of 2017 and 2018, nearly 1,000 enterprises raised more than $22 billion[58] while being largely unregulated. Yet they have also been associated with fraud, failing firms and alarming lapses in information sharing with investors.[59]

The SEC's investigation and subsequent DAO Report[60] in 2017 was the first attempt to address the treatment of ICOs. The DAO (a digital decentralised autonomous organisation with open-source code, and a form of investor-directed venture capital fund) was instantiated on the Ethereum blockchain, had no conventional management structure and was not tied to any particular state, yet its token's sale in 2016 set the record for the largest crowdfunding campaign in history. The SEC's Report argued that the tokens offered by the DAO were securities and that federal securities laws apply to those who offer and sell securities in the United States, regardless of whether (i) the issuing entity is a traditional company or a decentralised autonomous organisation, (ii) those securities are purchased using US dollars or virtual currencies, or (iii) they are distributed in certificated form or through DLT.[61]

Under US law, securities are identified using the 'Howey Test' according to the Supreme Court ruling on *SEC* v. *Howey*[62], which established that a security is a contract involving 'an investment of money in an enterprise with a reasonable expectation of profits to be derived from the entrepreneurial or managerial efforts of others'. Presumably, an investor buys tokens expecting an increase of the value,

[56] Brummer, C.; Kiviat, T.; Massari, J. (2018).
[57] Levine, M.; The SEC gets a token fight. Bloomberg. 28 January 2019.
[58] Whirty, T., Protecting innovation: the kin case, litigating decentralization, and crypto disclosures. 4 February 2019 https://www.alt-m.org/2019/02/01/protecting-innovation-the-kin-case-litigating-decentralization-and-crypto-disclosures/
[59] Brummer, C.; Kiviat, T.; Massari, J. (2018).
[60] See SEC. Investigative report concluding dao tokens, a digital asset, were securities. Release. 2017.
[61] SEC. (2017).
[62] *SEC* v. *W. J. Howey Co.* et al. 27 May 1946.

however, the reasonable expectation of profits derived from the efforts of others is more complex to analyse, as it varies case by case.[63]

In the EU, the definition of *securities* is less straightforward, where the term is defined differently in EU languages, against the background of national legal systems. Even harmonised definitions of securities such as those found in MiFiD, the Market Abuse Directive 2003/6/EC and the Prospectus Directive 2003/71/EC appear susceptible to different interpretations among Member States.[64]

Parangon and Airfox ICO's[65] were the first cases where the SEC imposed civil penalties for violation of rules governing the registration of securities. Both issuers settled the charges and agreed to return funds to harmed investors, register the tokens as securities, file periodic reports with the SEC and pay penalties of $250,000 penalties each. The SEC also initiated an inquiry into the ICO launched by Kik Service (which owns the messaging app Kik with over 300 million users worldwide[66]) and raised $100 million[67] in 2017 selling a crypto-asset called Kin.[68] Instead of settling, Kik responded to the SEC by defending Kik as a currency or 'utility token', designed as a medium of exchange within Kin's ecosystem, and citing that currencies are exempted from securities regulation. However, SEC regulators seek an early summary judgment against the firm, arguing the company was aware of issuing securities and had also assured investors the tokens could be easily resold. This case is relevant because if Kik carries on with its argumentation, the final decision would further clarify the boundaries of securities and currencies.

Despite the need for specific regulation for crypto-assets, fraud still remains fraud regardless of the underlying technology. In the action against 'Shopin',[69] the SEC alleged that the issuer, Shopin, and its CEO conducted a fraudulent and unregistered offering of digital securities, where tokens would raise capital to personal online shopping profiles that would track customers' purchase histories across numerous online retailers and link those profiles to the blockchain. However, Shopin allegedly never had a functioning product, and the company's pivot to the blockchain only resulted from its struggles to stay in business as a non-blockchain business.[70]

63 See US Securities and Exchange Commission. Framework for 'investment contract' analysis of digital assets. 3 April 2019.

64 Lastra, R. M.; Allen, J. G. (2018).

65 SEC. Two ICO issuers settle SEC registration charges, agree to register tokens as securities. Press release. 16 November 2018.

66 Whirty, T. (2019).

67 Morris, D. Z.; How Kik's looming SEC fight could define Blockchain's future. Breakermag. 30 January 2019.

68 *SEC* v. *Kik Interactive*. US District Court Southern District of New York Case No. 19-cv-5244. 04/06/2019.

69 *SEC* v. *Eran Eyal and United Data, Inc. doing business as 'Shopin'*, Case 1:19-cv-11325, filed 11 December 2019.

70 Nathan, D.; Fraud is fraud – sales of unregistered digital securities resemble classic microcap fraud. JDSupra, 18 December 2019.

Qualifying crypto-tokens as securities instead of working on customised regulatory solutions for crypto-assets risks failing to provide an adequate level of protection. In a decentralised model, where the entrepreneur does not aim to keep control over the network, but rather build it to release it, if it is required to furnish financial statements and risk factors about the enterprise to potential investors (as for securities), then these financial statements will only show some expenses and no revenues for the first quarters and, once the infrastructure is built, nothing forever, which does not serve the purpose of protecting investors.[71]

12.5 PROPOSAL FOR A COMPREHENSIVE ADMINISTRATIVE FRAMEWORK FOR CRYPTO-FINANCE

12.5.1 *A Crypto-Finance Specialised Regulation*

As illustrated by the cases presented and the attempts of financial regulators to bring crypto-assets under some of the existing regulations, new financial products and new forms of fraud and abuse involving crypto-assets justify a renewed demand (as following the stock market crash of 1929 or the 2008 financial crisis) for specialised crypto regulation and preventive action that enables investors to make better-informed capital allocation decisions and reduce their vulnerability to wrongdoers.

Regulatory action requires a full understanding of the specific characteristics of financial products based on DLT systems. Moreover, the determinants of utility token prices are not the same as in traditional securities like stocks and bonds, and therefore financial requirements on traditional securities fail to provide the kind of useful information an investor needs when investing in crypto-assets. It is in the general interest to set up standards for the quality of the information to make investors less vulnerable to scams and allow investors to decide based on economic fundamentals, instead of driven by factors such as popularity and social media marketing, as is the case for ICO investment according to academic studies.[72]

Designing a specialised disclosure framework that considers the specific characteristics of crypto-finance requires more than just extending an existing regulatory regime to a new asset class, but it does not require starting from scratch. One of the key aspects when designing regulations for crypto is how to identify who is responsible for ensuring that activity on the blockchain complies with the law. As the CFTC Commissionaire Brian Quintez notes,[73] in the past, the CFTC has supervised derivatives markets through the registration of market intermediaries. Indeed, much of the CFTC's regulatory structure for promoting market integrity and protecting customers revolves around the regulation of exchanges, swap dealers, futures commission merchants, clearinghouses and fund managers, and we need to

[71] Brummer, C.; Kiviat, T.; Massari, J. (2018).
[72] Brummer, C.; Kiviat, T.; Massari, J. (2018).
[73] CFTC. Commissioner Brian Quintez. (16 October 2018).

find new ways to preserve accountability in the disintermediated world of blockchain.

In addition, new financial service providers using DLT have entered the crypto financial market and may well require different regulatory treatment than traditional banks or non-bank financial institutions. The rapid growth of Big-Tech services in finance can enhance financial inclusion and contribute to the overall efficiency of financial services. Conversely, given large network effects and economies of scale and scope, Big Tech represents a concentration risk and could give rise to new systemic risks. These particularities need to be specifically addressed in the regulation.[74]

The SEC has named Valerie Szczepanik Senior Advisor for Digital Assets and Innovation, the first 'Crypto-Tsar'.[75] Szczepanik is optimistic about boosting the cryptocurrency market through better regulation. She highlights the importance of taking an initial principles-based approach towards new technologies while following and studying them closely to avoid a new precipitous regime. Acknowledging the international regulatory competition aspect at stake, even if some companies might go outside the United States in search of more lenient regulatory regimes – in her words – the real opportunity is with companies that abide by the stronger rules: 'There are benefits to doing it the right way. And when they do that they will be the gold standard.'[76] Allegedly, SEC's strategy for crypto-finance is looking towards a race to the top.

As G20 leaders agreed on a regulatory reform to increase transparency in OTC derivative markets and prevent future crises at the 2009 Pittsburgh Summit,[77] a joined international effort to regulate crypto-finance defining key principles would serve as the basis for establishing a decentralised regulatory framework for disclosure and for a coordinated surveillance of crypto-finance markets. In the same line, the International Organization of Securities Commissions (IOSCO) is working on key considerations to regulate crypto-assets,[78] ensuring minimal coordination without being prescriptive and allowing competent authorities to implement their own strategies to reach common goals, and the FATF, the global money laundering and terrorist financing watchdog, issued guidance for monitoring crypto-assets and service providers.[79] More needs to be done in this area.

74 Frost, J., Gambacorta, L., Huang, Y., Shin, H., Zbinden, P.; BigTech and the changing structure of financial intermediation. BIS. April 2019.

75 SEC. SEC Names Valerie A. Szczepanik Senior Advisor for Digital Assets and Innovation. Press release. 2018–102.

76 Dale, B. SEC's Valerie Szczepanik at SXSW: Crypto 'Spring' Is Going to Come. Coindesk.com. 15 Mars 2019.

77 G20 Leaders Statement: The Pittsburgh Summit. 24–25 September 2009.

78 See OICV-IOSCO. Issues, risks and regulatory considerations relating to crypto-asset trading platforms. February 2020. See also a compilation of Regulators' Statements on Initial Coin Offerings.

79 FATF. Guidance on a risk-based approach to virtual assets and virtual asset service providers. June 2019.

12.5.2 *An Independent Regulatory Agency Specialised in Crypto-Finance to Foster Innovation within a Safe Environment*

Regulatory agencies represent an independent regulatory power, more effective in solving new situations and preventing emerging risks thanks to its less bureaucratised structure combined with a high degree of expertise and specialisation among its officers. These agencies can adopt regulation and recommendations, yet in some cases, they lack the most stringent enforcement and punitive tools.[80] Nevertheless, guidance and recommendations can have a strong effect in shaping market participants' behaviour and can trigger peer-pressure mechanisms that intensify the agency's impact.

Notably, in the case of financial institutions, which are in constant interaction with the regulator, compliance with guidelines and recommendations has a greater impact because, on the one hand, regulatory agencies have licensing capacity, which is a powerful inducement to comply with guidance pronouncements. On the other hand, this continuous interaction between financial entities and agencies 'facilitates regulators' ability to retaliate on numerous dimensions through supervision and examination, in addition to their ability to bring enforcement actions for noncompliance with a specific policy'.[81] An agency overviewing crypto-finance should seek a constant interaction relationship with its supervised entities.

In addition, agencies are also a guarantee for transparency and market participation in the policy-making process. The US Administrative Procedure Act establishes that agencies' rule-making requires three procedural steps: information, participation and accountability.[82] The EU agencies or authorities apply the equivalent public consultation procedure. In addition, there is an extra step envisaged for the EU agencies that mandates the inclusion of a costs and benefits analysis for each proposed regulatory measure. As Professor Roberta Romano highlights, this participative administrative procedure is linked to the political legitimacy of rule-making, given its management by unelected officials. Public participation 'can illuminate gaps in an agency's knowledge and provide an understanding of real-world conditions, as well as assist an agency in gauging a rule's acceptance by those affected'.[83]

James M. Landis, advisor to President Roosevelt and one of the designers of the post-crash regulations, understood that market stability should come from the creation of agencies in charge of monitoring business day-to-day life. Leaving all control to Courts through judicial review of cases did not allow for precautionary

80 In the EU, enforcement powers remain with national authorities and the ESAs are mainly tasked with ensuring supervisory convergence. In specific cases, the ESAs are direct supervisors (e.g., ESMA in relation to trade repositories or credit-rating agencies).

81 Romano, R. Does agency structure affect agency decisionmaking? Yale Journal on Regulation. Vol. 36, 2019.

82 Kerwin, C. M.; Furlong, S. R. Rule-making: how government agencies write law and make policy, 53 2011. Cit in Romano (2019).

83 Romano (2019).

and preventive measures. Moreover, Courts and judges cannot carry out the constant task of following and analysing market trends as a dedicated agency can do. Landis asserted in *The Administrative Process*, published in 1938, that

> the administrative process is, in essence, our generation's answer to the inadequacy of the judicial and legislative processes. It represents our effort to find an answer to those inadequacies by some other method than merely increasing executive power. If the doctrine of the separation of power implies division, it also implies balance, and balance calls for equality. The creation of administrative power may be the means for the preservation of that balance.

In addition,

> efficiency in the processes of governmental regulation is best served by the creation of more rather than less agencies'. Administrative agencies should by all means be independent and not be simply an extension of executive power or of legislative power. This view is based upon the desire of obtaining supervision and exploration with 'uninterrupted interest in a relatively narrow and carefully defined area of economic and social activity.[84]

When speaking about an independent and specialised agency for crypto-finance, we do not necessarily imply the creation of new agencies from scratch. On the contrary, it proves more beneficial to build on the reputation of an existing specialised authority that is already known by the market, which broadens its scope to create a special arm or body within its remit and recruits crypto experts to focus exclusively on finding regulatory solutions to be applied in the crypto field. The LabCFTC, for instance, is set up to bring closer the Washington regulator (historically focused on commodity markets rather than digital assets) and Silicon Valley. The new director of LabCFTC, Melissa Netram, comes from the software company Intuit and illustrates CFTC Chairman Tarbert's philosophy that you 'can't really be a good regulator unless you are hiring people who actually know and understand these markets'.[85]

Crypto-finance also introduces new mechanics that can translate into new risks of collusion, which need to be understood and specifically addressed. Collusion needs trust between market players and blockchain can play a key role in this respect by allowing more cooperation between the players. The question then becomes whether blockchain can be used to set up a system of binding agreements, and accordingly, to change the game into a cooperative collusive one. Combined with smart contracts, blockchain makes colluders trust each other because the terms of the agreement are immutable. Competition and antitrust agencies' task is to create a prisoner's dilemma in which each player shares the same dominant strategy: to

[84] Landis, J. M. The administrative process. Yale University Press, 1938.
[85] CFTC Release 8051–19 (2019).

denounce the agreement. Blockchain can help the players to build a reserve of trust, which in turn requires a greater effort from competition agencies.[86]

12.5.2.1 Regulatory Sandboxes

A regulatory sandbox is a scheme set up by a competent authority that provides regulated and unregulated entities with the opportunity to test, pursuant to a testing plan agreed and monitored by the authority, innovative products or services related to the carrying out of financial services.[87] Sandboxes are an important cooperation mechanism that allows entrepreneurs to develop their projects while avoiding uncertainty regarding the applicable regulatory framework, and they provide regulators the knowledge and insights they need to prepare well-balanced regulation. As noted by the Basel Committee on Banking Supervision (BCBS), sandboxes may also imply the use of legally provided discretions by the relevant supervisor.[88]

As Judge Louis Brandeis said in the context of the creation of one of the Federal Trade Commission, knowledge and understanding must come before publicity and regulation:

> You hear much said of correcting most abuses by publicity. We need publicity; but as a pre-requisite to publicity we need knowledge. We must know and know contemporaneously what business – what big businesses – is doing. When we know that through an authoritative source, we shall gone very far toward the prevention of the evils which attend the conduct of business.[89]

The sandbox concept, as a decentralised system of experimentation, plays a key role for administrative and regulatory innovation. Judge Brandeis theorised this concept in *New State Ice Co.* v. *Liebmann*: 'It is one of the happy incidents of the federal system that a single courageous State may, if its citizens choose, serve as a laboratory; and try novel social and economic experiments without risk to the rest of the country.'[90] This analysis advocates for administrative decentralisation as a foster of innovation. Decentralisation allows for experimenting with creative solutions in controlled spaces (or sandboxes) without endangering the global stability, and when other jurisdictions see merit in an innovation, they will then implement it without risk. This, in essence, is the same spirit inspiring crypto sandboxes.

Among other cases, the UK FCA set up a regulatory sandbox consisting of a controlled environment to test and issue securities using blockchain so the FCA

[86] Schrepel, T. (2019).

[87] See European Supervisory Authorities. Report on FinTech: Regulatory sandboxes and innovation hubs. JC 2018–74.

[88] European Supervisory Authorities. (2018).

[89] Brandeis, L. The regulation of competition versus the regulation of monopoly by Louis D. Brandeis. An address to the Economic Club of New York, 1 November 1912. Cited in Ballbé, M.; Martinez, R. (2010).

[90] *New State Ice Co.* v. *Liebmann*, 285 US 262, 311 (1932) (Brandeis, J., dissenting).

and the firms learn about the impact of current regulations on new financial products. However, at this stage, one could argue a 'sandbox is no longer an instrument for mutual learning only, but that it is becoming an original device for regulatory design where the FCA "swaps" with firms the accreditation of digital products in the UK financial market for influence in shaping the algorithms in a way which is more investor-friendly. Arguably, this strategy is producing a form of win-win regulation'.'[91]

From an international regulatory competition perspective, FCA's strategy is also instigated by concerns about firms flying to offer digital securities in a more permissive market, while for a firm, being admitted to the sandbox represents an opportunity to be formally accredited by the FCA, which opens the door to one of the largest markets around the world. According to FCA, bespoke safeguards were put in place where relevant, such as requiring all firms in the sandbox to develop an exit plan to ensure the test can be closed down at any point while minimising the potential detriment to participating consumers.[92] This collaborative strategy is already paying off, and the UK is currently ahead in authorising electronic platforms to offer crypto derivatives, such as CFDs,[93] putting certain activities under the regulator's radar. Nevertheless, the FCA had warned in 2017 that 'cryptocurrency CFDs are an extremely high-risk, speculative investment. You should be aware of the risks involved and fully consider whether investing in cryptocurrency CFDs',[94] and consistent with this warning, it is to be expected that FCA, before granting authorisation to platforms trading crypto-CFDs, has implemented adequate investor's protection safeguards and enforcement procedures.

12.5.3 *The Principle of Judicial Deference in Favour of Independent Agencies' Interpretation*

The United States has long discussed the doctrine of the 'deference principle', which states courts should show deference in favour of specialised agencies (by dint of their expertise) when interpreting the ambiguity of a statute or law. As Cass Sunstein[95] notes, the deference principle is a two-step approach,[96] as established in

[91] Mangano, R.; Recent developments: The sandbox of the UK FCA as win-win regulatory device? Banking and Finance Law Review, Vol. 34, No. 1. December 2018.

[92] UK, Financial Conduct Authority, Regulatory sandbox lessons learned report FCA, 2017. Cited in Mangano, R. (2018).

[93] It is the case, for example, of B2C2, an electronic OTC trading firm and crypto liquidity provider, authorized by the FCA to offer OTC derivatives on cryptos. See Khatri, Y. UK firm gets regulatory green light to offer crypto derivatives. Coindesk.com. 1 February 2019.

[94] FCA Public statement. November 2017.

[95] Legal scholar and former Administrator of the Office of Information and Regulatory Affairs for the Obama administration.

[96] Solum, L.B.; Sunstein, C. Solum, L. B.; Sunstein, C. R. Chevron as construction. Preliminary draft 12 December 2018.

Chevron v. *NRDC*;'[97] Courts must apply the deference principle to agency interpretations referred to legal texts when the provisions are ambiguous or unclear, so long as such interpretation is reasonable (in the sense that it is reasonable according to the agency's remit to interpret on that matter).

This case is fundamental in the recognition and delimitation of power of independent administrative agencies. It confirms that specialisation of officers in these agencies should prevail over Courts' judgments when it comes to interpreting statutory principles. For a subject as complex as crypto-finance, this deference principle in favour of the specialised agency would ensure better judgments and represents a precious asset in the international race between jurisdictions for becoming a financial crypto-hub.

12.5.4 *An Activist Agency: The Case of the Consumer Financial Protection Bureau (CFPB)*

Harvard Law Professor and Senator Elizabeth Warren has fiercely advocated for the creation of a specialised agency for the protection of financial consumers and for the introduction of disclosure requirements regarding credit and loans. Robert Shiller, who received the Nobel Prize in Economy, noted that

> in correcting the inadequacies of our information infrastructure, as outlined by Elizabeth Warren, would be for the government to set up what she calls a financial product safety commission, modeled after the Consumer Product Safety Commission ... to serve as an ombudsman and advocate. It would provide a resource for information on the safety of financial products and impose regulations to ensure such safety.. . . The National Highway Traffic Safety Administration maintains data on highway and motor vehicle safety and statistics on accidents. In the same way, we must fund a government organization empowered to accumulate information on the actual experience that individuals have with financial products – and the 'accidents', rare as well as commonplace, that happen with them – with an eye toward preventing such accidents in the future.[98]

The Dodd-Frank Act mandated the creation of the Consumers Financial Protection Bureau (CFPB) to protect consumers from unfair, deceptive or abusive practices, arming people with the information they need to make smart financial decisions, by empowering, educating and following a very dynamic (activist) strategy. The CFPB consolidated in one agency functions that had previously been allocated across seven federal agencies. To ensure independence, the CFPB was given a comparatively anomalous autonomous structure for a US administrative agency. It is organised analogously to a cabinet department in that it has a single director, but in contrast, the CFPB director has statutory removal protection. The

[97] *Chevron, USA., Inc.* v. *Nat. Res. Def. Council, Inc.*, 467 US 837 (1984).

[98] Shiller, R. The subprime solution. Princeton, 2008, p. 129.

agency is further independent of the executive by location, as it was placed within the Fed System. However, Fed Board governors may not intervene in the CFPB's affairs; review or delay implementation of its rules; or consolidate the bureau, its functions or its responsibilities with any other division. Also, a feature that is unique to the CFPB is its funding arrangement: it is independent of both Congress and the president, for it is not subject to the annual appropriations process. The director sets his/her own budget, which is funded by the Fed (capped at 12 per cent of the Fed's total operating expenses). Although the CFPB director must file semi-annual reports with Congress, there is minimal leverage that Congress holds to influence the agency, given its lack of budgetary control – which is a key disciplining technique.[99]

The reaction of major market participants to an agency with such a degree of independence was categorical, as Warren condemned in 2009:

> The big banks are storming Washington, determined to kill the CFPB. They understand that a regulator who actually cares about consumers would cause a seismic change in their business model: no more burying the terms of the agreement in the fine print, no more tricks and traps. If the big banks lose the protection of their friendly regulators, the business model that produces hundreds of billions of dollars in revenue – and monopolizes profits that exist only in non-competitive markets – will be at risk. That's a big change.[100]

Pressure was such that although President Obama had first thought of Warren as the director of the agency, he needed to step back and look for another possible candidate with a lower profile in this matter.

There have been continuous efforts by opponents of the CFPB to restructure the agency, and the Republican House under Trump's administration passed a bill to make the CFPB more accountable. (What are they scared of?) The CFPB is an example of a quasi-activist agency dynamic and very specialised in protecting financial consumers' rights – a model that shall be emulated in other jurisdictions and whose strategies should inspire the creation of an activist agency for crypto-finance that not only monitors but most importantly makes information accessible to financial consumers in intelligible ways. This model is enough dynamic and participative to have forums that are constantly warning about new risks associated with crypto-assets, scams or any relevant information almost in real time.

12.5.5 *Administrative Judges Specialising in Crypto-Finance*

The US Supreme Court *Lucia* v. *SEC*[101] decision is key, as it consolidates the role of administrative judges instituting proceedings within specialised independent

99 Romano, R. (2019).

100 Warren, E. Real change: turning up the heat on non-bank lenders. *The Huffington Post*, 3 September 2009.

101 *Lucia et al.* v. *Securities Exchange Commission*. US Supreme Court decision. June 2018.

agencies such as the SEC. The decision reflects on the power of administrative law judges and provides clarification on their status. The Court resolved that administrative Law Judges at the SEC are 'officers of the United States' rather than 'mere employees' and therefore need to be subject to the Appointment Clause (i.e., appointed by the president or a person with delegated power). The Supreme Court recognises that administrative judges have an important role that needs to be appointed according to a higher standard procedure in the US administration, rather than using simpler contractual means that could embed fewer guarantees in the process.

According to the Court, SEC's administrative judges carry great responsibility and exercise significant authority pursuant to the laws of the United States (e.g., take testimony, conduct trials, rule on the admissibility of evidence and have the power to enforce compliance with discovery orders, important functions that judges exercise with significant discretion). Contrary to other specialised agencies, the SEC can decide not to review the judge's decision, and when it does so, the judge's decision becomes final and is deemed the action of the SEC. The SEC judge has, undoubtedly, discretion in its role and has enforcement power.[102]

This precedent should inspire the inclusion of specialised administrative judges in European authorities for aspects in which they hold direct powers of supervision and enforcement. Administrative judges of the highest qualification, as per the precedent in *Lucia* v. *SEC*, improve the quality and reputation of those agencies. At the same time, such a specialised administrative and judicial body represents a competitive advantage in any given regulatory field and notably in the case of emerging markets such as crypto-finance, where general courts' judges around the globe may lack specialised knowledge and may not yet be familiar with DLT systems.

12.5.6 *Regulatory Decentralisation as a Guarantee for Independence*

The global regulatory framework design for regulating crypto-assets and for the protection of consumers and investors from crypto-finance risks should be a decentralised model that promotes competition in cooperation, the so-called co-opetition. Supranational regulatory bodies representing global leaders should define international regulatory standards on crypto-finance risks and opportunities, as for instance IOSCO starts to do, leaving the implementation in the hands of each jurisdiction's regulator. In this way, the different regulatory bodies would cooperate to achieve the internationally agreed-upon standards while competing in terms of implementation strategies and thus promoting regulatory innovation. This co-opetition has proven a very powerful tool for countervailing capture and/or

[102] See *Lucia* v. *SEC*. *Harvard Law Review*, 287. 1 May 2019.

deliberated inaction from regulators, as centralised structures are more vulnerable to these deviations.

The US Supreme Court *Watters* v. *Wachovia Bank*[103] decision (2007) is the crowning of a pre-emption trend[104] initiated under the George W. Bush administration to prevent states from any regulatory or supervisory intervention in the banking sphere. This case is a good illustration of the risks of a centralised supervisory and regulatory approach and how it could incentivise corruption and laisser-faire behaviour.

Wachovia Mortgages, a subsidiary entity of Wachovia Bank in North Carolina, offered mortgages in Michigan and in the rest of the United States. Subsidiary entities were under the control and supervision of the federal administration. However, Michigan statutory regulation imposes the obligation for mortgage brokers and subsidiary entities to register at the State Office of Insurance and Financial Services (OIFS) of Michigan. Linda Watters, a commissioner of the OIFS, was in charge of the supervision and of handling complaints from financial consumers referred to subsidiary entities registered in Michigan, with power limited to complaints that were not properly addressed by the federal authority. Watters requested information from Wachovia Mortgages on some of those cases, and the entity replied that the commissioner had no supervisory powers to initiate any investigation because such powers had been pre-empted by the federal administration. After this incident, commissioner Watters withdrew Wachovia Mortgages' authorisation to operate as a mortgage lender in Michigan.

The federal administrations with competences over lending activities were, on one side, the Fed with competences referred to direct supervision of federal banks, financial consumer protection and regulatory powers for transparency in credits.[105] In addition, in 1994, the Home Ownership and Equity Protection Act (HOEPA) granted absolute power to the Fed to regulate for the prevention of fraud in lending contracts. On the other side, the Office of the Comptroller of the Currency (OCC) was in charge of the surveillance of currency transactions.

Traditionally, consumer protection was a state's domain, as the state's administration is closer to consumers and states' respective laws allowed for the supervision of financial institutions within each state. However, this changed under Greenspan's presidency in the Fed. He believed that capitalist markets without restrictions create wealth levels that stimulate a more civilised existence.[106] In parallel, the OCC,

103 See Ballbe, M., Martinez, R., Cabedo, Y. La crisis financiera causada por la deregulation de derecho administrativo americano. In book Administración y justicia: un análisis jurisprudencial. Coords. Garcia de Enterría, E., Alonso, R. Madrid, Civitas, Vol. 2. 2012.

104 Refers to the federal government enacting legislation on a subject matter and precluding the state from enacting laws on the same subject.

105 See the Truth in Lending Act of 1968.

106 Greenspan, A. International Financial Risk Management. Federal Reserve Board. 19 November 2002. Cit. in Ballbe, M., Martinez, R., Cabedo, Y. (2012).

under the presidency of Dugan, also started a race to the bottom, aimed at attracting banks regulated by states' agencies to the federal scope of the OCC. To achieve this, the OCC, an administration financed directly by the fees of the banks it supervises and notoriously conflicted, took a lenient approach, deciding not to initiate investigations against banks. Moreover, the OCC appeared in proceedings initiated by states' regulatory agencies (amicus brief) to support financial entities against the allegations of such agencies.

Not surprisingly, during this period, financial entities directly regulated by the federal administration grew rapidly in number, and major banks such as JP Chase, HSBC or Bank of Montreal switched from state to federal banks. These transfers alone translated into an increase of 15 per cent of OCC's total budget income. As the Congressional Report on Regulatory Reforms highlighted in 2009,

> Fairness should have been addressed though better regulation of consumer financial products. If the excesses in mortgage lending had been curbed by even the most minimal consumer protection laws, the loans that were fed into the mortgage backed securities would have been choked off at the source, and there would have been no 'toxic assets' to threaten the global economy.[107]

Instead, the OCC joined Wachovia Bank against the OIFs.

The Supreme Court decision, published in 2007 (just before the start of the financial crisis), declared that the supervision of abusive conduct against consumers was a monopoly of the federal administration. It evidenced that the Supreme Court might not had known the magnitude of the frauds and abuses taking place in the mortgage market in the United States, nor to which extent federal supervisory bodies were captured. It was only after the crisis exploded when the Supreme Court changed the precedent and in *Cuomo* v. *Clearinghouse*[108] (2009) overruled the pre-emption of States' powers, in favour of the competences of states for financial consumers' protection. Definitely, centralisation by pre-emption of regulatory powers made the capture of regulators easier and left citizens unprotected.

Following the same line, another recent example of the countervailing power of a decentralised regulatory model is the case of manipulation of the LIBOR,[109] the benchmark that should reflect the price at which London-based financial entities borrow money and which indirectly sets the interest rates that apply to credits and loans. After the revelation of collusive practices on its fix by an article in the *Wall Street Journal*,[110] European and UK authorities remained indifferent

107 The special report on regulatory reform of the Congressional oversight panel, January 2009.

108 Supreme Court US. *Cuomo, Attorney General of New York* v. *Clearing House Association, L.L.C., et al.* No 08–453. April 2009.

109 On this case, see Ballbe, M.; Cabedo, Y. (2013) and (2012).

110 Mollenkamp, C., Whitehouse, M. Study casts doubt on key rate. WSJ analysis suggests banks may have reported flawed interest data for libor. The Wall Street Journal. 29 May 2008.

and took no action. It was only after competing authorities in Canada, Switzerland, Tokyo and the United States initiated a formal investigation when the European Commission reacted. Again, international competition among regulators and peer-to-peer pressure proved the best way to foster regulatory action.

PART III

Roles and Responsibilities of Private Actors

13

Responsibilities of Companies in the Algorithmic Society

Hans-W. Micklitz and Aurélie Anne Villanueva

13.1 CONTEXT – NEW WINE IN OLD BOTTLES?

The major focus of the book is on the constitutional challenges of the algorithmic society. In the public/private divide type of thinking, such an approach puts the constitution and thereby the state into the limelight. There is a dense debate on the changing role of the nation-state in the aftermath of what is called globalization and how the transformation of the state is affecting private law and thereby private parties.[1] This implies the question of whether the public/private divide can still serve as a useful tool to design responsibilities on both sides, public and private.[2] If we ask for a constitutional framing of business activities in a globalized world, there are two possible approaches: the first is the external or the outer reach of national constitutions; the second the potential impact of a global constitution. Our approach is broader and narrower at the same time. It is broader as we do not look at the constitutional dimension alone, but at the public/private law below the constitution and at the role and impact on private responsibilities, it is narrower as we will neither engage in the debate on the external/outer reach of nation-state constitutions nor on the existence of a 'Global Constitution' or an 'International Economic Constitution', based on the GATT/WTO and international human rights.[3] Such

[1] Hans-Wolfgang Micklitz and Dennis Patterson, 'From the Nation-State to the Market : The Evolution of EU Private Law as Regulation of the Economy beyond the Boundaries of the Union?' in Bart Van Vooren, Steven Blockmans and Jan Wouters (eds), *The EU's Role in Global Governance: The Legal Dimension* (Oxford University Press 2013).

[2] Matthias Ruffert, *The Public-Private Law Divide: Potential for Transformation?* (British Institute of International and Comparative Law 2009). Lukas van den Berge, 'Rethinking the Public-Private Law Divide in the Age of Governmentality and Network Governance' (2018) 5 *European Journal of Comparative Law and Governance* 119. Hans-W. Micklitz, 'Rethinking the Public/Private Divide' in Miguel Poiares Maduro, Kaarlo Tuori and Suvi Sankari (eds), *Transnational Law: Rethinking European Law and Legal Thinking* (Cambridge University Press 2014).

[3] Cahier à Thème, Les Grandes Théories du Droit Transnational, avec contributions du K. Tuori, B. Kingsbury, N. Krisch, R. B. Stewart, H. Muir Watt, Ch. Joerges, F. Roedel, F. Cafaggi, R. Zimmermann, G.-P. Calliess, M. Renner, A. Fischer-Lescano, G. Teubner, P. Schiff Berman, Numéro 1–2, Revue Internationale de Droit Economique, 2013.

an exercise would require a discussion about global constitutionalization and global constitutionalism in and through the digital society and digital economy.[4]

Therefore, this contribution does not look at private parties through the lenses of the constitutions or constitutionalization processes but through the lenses of private parties, here companies. The emphasis is on the responsibilities of private companies, which does not mean that there is no responsibility of nation-states. Stressing private responsibilities below the surface of the constitution directs the attention to the bulk of national, European and international rules that are and that have been developed in the last decades and that in one way or the other are dealing with responsibility or perhaps even better responsibilities of private and public actors. Responsibility is a much broader term than legal civil liability as it includes the moral dimension,[5] which might or might not give space to give private responsibility a constitutional outlook or even more demanding a constitutional anchoring, be it in a nation-state constitution, the European or even the Global Constitution.[6] The culmination point of the constitutional debate is the question of whether human rights are addressing states alone or also binding private parties directly.[7] Again, this is not our concern. The focus is on the level below the constitution, the 'outer space' where private parties and public – mainly administrative – authorities are co-operating in the search for solutions that strike a balance between the freedom of private companies to do business outside state borders and their responsibility as well as those of the nation-states.

The intention is to deliver a rough overview of where we are standing politically, economically and legally, when we are discussing possible legal solutions that design the responsibility of private companies in the globalized economy. This is done against the background of Baldwin's[8] structuring of the world trade order along the line of the decline of first transportation costs and second communication costs. The two stages can be associated with two very different forms of world trade. The decline of transportation enabled the establishment of the post–World War II order.

4 Gunther Teubner, *Constitutional Fragments: Societal Constitutionalism and Globalization* (Oxford University Press 2012).

5 Hans Jonas, *Das Prinzip Verantwortung: Versuch Einer Ethik Für Die Technologische Zivilisation* (Suhrkamp 1984).

6 Hans-W. Micklitz, Thomas Roethe and Stephen Weatherill, *Federalism and Responsibility: A Study on Product Safety Law and Practice in the European Community* (Graham & Trotman/M Nijhoff; Kluwer Academic Publishers Group 1994).

7 For a detailed account, see Chiara Macchi and Claire Bright, 'Hardening Soft Law: The Implementation of Human Rights Due Diligence Requirements in Domestic Legislation' in Martina Buscemi et al. (eds), *Legal Sources in Business and Human Rights Evolving Dynamics in International and European Law* (Brill 2020). Liesbeth Enneking et al., *Accountability, International Business Operations and the Law: Providing Justice for Corporate Human Rights Violations in Global Value Chains* (Routledge 2019). Stéphanie Bijlmakers, *Corporate Social Responsibility, Human Rights, and the Law* (Routledge 2019). Angelica Bonfanti, *Business and Human Rights in Europe: International Law Challenges* (Routledge 2018).

8 Richard E. Baldwin, *The Great Convergence: Information Technology and the New Globalization* (The Belknap Press of Harvard University Press 2016).

Products and services could circulate freely without customs and non-tariff barriers to trade. The conditions under which the products were manufactured, however, were left to the nation-states. This allowed private companies to benefit from the economies of scales, from differences between labour costs and later environmental costs. The decline of communication costs changed the international trade order dramatically. It enabled the rise of global value chains often used as a synonym for global value chains. Here product and process regulation are interlinked through contract.[9] It will have to be shown that the two waves show superficially regarded similarities, economically and technologically, though there are differences which affect the law, and which will have to be taken into account when it comes to the search for solutions.

13.2 THE FIRST WAVE – DOUBLE STANDARDS IN UNSAFE PRODUCTS AND UNSAFE INDUSTRIAL PLANTS

Timewise, we are in the 1960s, 1970s. International trade is blossoming. The major beneficiaries are Western democratic states and multinationals, as they were then called. Opening the gateway towards the responsibility of multinationals 'beyond the nation-state'[10] takes the glamour away from the sparkling language of the algorithmic economy and society and discloses a well-known though rather odd problem which industrialized states had to face hand in hand with the rise of the welfare state in whatever form and the increase of protective legislation to the benefit of consumers, of workers and of the environment against unsafe products.

13.2.1 *Double Standards on the Export of Hazardous Products*

The Western democratic states restricted the reach of the regulation of chemicals, pharmaceuticals, pesticides and dangerous technical goods to their territory, paving the way for their industries to export products to the rest of the world, although their use was prohibited or severely restricted in the home country. The phenomenon became known worldwide as the policy of 'double standards' and triggered political awareness around the globe, in the exporting and importing states, in international organizations and in what could be ambitiously called an emerging global society.[11]

9 European Review of Contract Law, Special Issue: Reimagining Contract in a World of Global Value Chains, 2020 Volume 16 Issue 1 with contribution of Klaas Hendrik Eller, Jaakko Salminen, Fabrizio Cafaggi and Paola Iamiceli, Mika Viljanen, Anna Beckers, Laura D. Knöpfel, Lyn K. L. Tjon Soel Len, Kevin B. Sobel-Read, Vibe Ulfbeck and Ole Hansen. Society of European Contract Law (SECOLA), Common Frame of Reference and the Future of European Contract Law, conference 1 and 2 June 2007, Amsterdam.

10 Ralf Michaels and Nils Jansen, 'Private Law beyond the State – Europeanization, Globalization, Privatization' (2006) 54 *American Journal of Comparative Law* 843.

11 Barry Castleman, 'The Export of Hazardous Industries in 2015' (2016) 15 *Environmental Health* 8. Hans-W. Micklitz, *Internationales Produktsicherheitsrecht: Zur Begründung Einer Rechtsverfassung Für Den Handel Mit Risikobehafteten Produkten* (Nomos Verlagsgesellschaft 1995). Hans-W. Micklitz

Communication costs, however, determined the search for political solutions. It has to be recalled that until the 1980s telephone costs were prohibitive, fax did not yet exist and the only way to engage in serious exchange was to meet physically. The decrease in transportation costs rendered the international gathering possible. The level of action to deal with 'double standards' was first and foremost political.

The subject related international organizations, WHO with regard to pharmaceuticals, UNEP and FAO with regard to chemicals, pesticides, waste and the later abolished UN-CTC with regard to dangerous technical goods invested into the elaboration of international standards on what is meant to be 'hazardous' and equally pushed for international solutions tying the export of double-standard products to the 'informed' consent of the recipient states. Within the international organizations, the United States dominated the discussions and negotiations. That is why each and every search for a solution was guided by the attempt to seek the support of the United States, whose president was no longer Jimmy Carter but Ronald Reagan. At the time, the European Union (EU) was near to non-existent in the international sphere, as it had not yet gained the competence to act on behalf of the Member States or jointly with the Member States. The Member States were speaking for themselves, built around two camps: the hard-core free-trade apologists and the softer group of states that were ready to join forces with voices from what is called today the Global South, seeking a balance between free trade and labour, consumer and environmental protection. Typically, the controversies ended in soft law solutions, recommendations adopted by the international organizations if not unanimously but at the minimum with the United States abstaining.

There is a long way from the recommendations adopted in the mid-1980s and the Rotterdam Convention on the export of hazardous chemicals and pesticides adopted in 1998, which entered into force in 2004.[12] On the bright side, there is definitely the simple fact that multilateralism was still regarded as the major and appropriate tool for what was recognized as a universal problem, calling for universal solutions. However, there is also a dark side to be taken into consideration. The UN organizations channelled the political debate on double standards, which was originally much more ambitious. NGOs, environmental and consumer organizations, and civil society activists were putting political pressure on the exporting countries to abolish the policy of double standards. The highly conflictual question then was and still is, 'Is there a responsibility of the exporting state for the health and safety of the citizens of the recipient countries?' Is there even a constitutional obligation of nation-states to exercise some sort of control over the activities of 'their' companies, who are operating from their Western Homebase in the rest of

and Rechtspolitik, *Internationales Produktsicherheitsrecht: Vorueberlegungen* (Universität Bremen 1989).

12 Rotterdam Convention on the Prior Informed Consent Procedure for Certain Hazardous Chemicals and Pesticides in International Trade https://treaties.un.org/pages/ViewDetails.aspx?src=TREATY&mtdsg_no=XXVII-14&chapter=27.

the world? How far does the responsibility/obligation reach? If double standards are legitimate, are nation-states at least constitutionally bound to elaborate and to ensure respect for internationally recognized standards on the safety of products, of health and safety at work, as well as environmental protection?

The adoption of the Rotterdam Convention suffocated the constitutional debate and shifted the focus towards its ratification. The juridification of a highly political conflict on double standards ends in a de-politicization. The attention shifted from the public political fora to the legal fora. The Member States of the EU and the EU ratified the Convention through EU Regulation 304/2003, later 698/2008, today 649/2012.[13] The United States signed the Convention but never ratified it. In order to be able to assess the potential impact of the Rotterdam Convention or more narrowly the role and function of the implementing EU Regulation on the European Member States, one has to dive deep into the activities of the European Chemical Agency, where all the information from the Member States is coming together.[14] When comparing the roaring public debate on double standards with the non-existent public interest in its bureaucratic handling, one may wonder to what extent 'informed consent' has improved the position of the citizens in the recipient state. The problem of double standards has not vanished at all.[15]

13.2.2 *Double Standards on Industrial Plants*

The public attention seems to focus ever stronger on catastrophes which shatter the global world order – from time to time, but with a certain regularity. The level of action is not necessarily political or administrative; it is judicial. The eyes of the victims but also of NGOs, civil society organizations, consumer and environmental organizations were and are directed towards the role and function of courts. Dworkin published his book on Law's empire, where he relied on the 'Hercules judge' in 1986, exactly at a time, where even in the transnational arena national courts and national judges turned into key actors and had to carry the hopes of all those who were fighting against double standards. This type of litigation can be easily associated with Baldwin's distinction. The decline of transportation costs allowed Western-based multinationals to build subsidiaries around the world. Due to the economies of scale, it was cheaper for the multinationals to get the products manufactured in the subsidiaries and ship them back to the Western world to get them assembled. Typically, the subsidiaries were owned by the mother company,

[13] Regulation (EC) No 304/2003 of the European Parliament and of the Council of 28 January 2003 concerning the export and import of dangerous chemicals OJ L 63, 6. 3. 2003, p. 1–26. Today Regulation (EU) No 649/2012 of the European Parliament and of the Council of 4 July 2012 concerning the export and import of hazardous chemicals OJ L 201, 27. 7. 2012, p. 60–106.

[14] For details, see the website of the European Chemical Agency, https://echa.europa.eu/-/new-eu-regulation-for-export-and-import-of-hazardous-chemicals-enters-into-operation.

[15] Webinar 'Hazardous Pesticides and EU's Double Standards', 29. 9. 2020, www.pan-europe.info/resources/articles/2020/08/webinar-hazardous-pesticides-and-eus-double-standards.

having its business seat in the United States or in Europe, either fully or at least up to a 51 per cent majority.

Again, the story to tell is not new, but it is paradigmatic for the 1980s. In 1984, a US-owned chemical plant in Bhopal India exploded. Thousands of people died. The victims argued that the plant did not even respect the rather low Indian standards of health and safety at work and Indian environmental standards. They were seeking compensation from Union Carbide Corporation, the mother company, and launched tort action claims in the United States.[16] The catastrophe mobilized NGOs and civil society organizations, along with class-action lawyers in the United States who combined the high expectations of the victims with their self-interest in bringing the case before US courts. The catastrophe laid bare the range of legal conflicts which arise in North-South civil litigation. Is there a responsibility of US companies which are operating outside the US territory to respect the high standards of the export state or international minimum standards, if they exist? Or does it suffice to comply with the lower standards of the recipient state? Is the American mother company legally liable for the harm produced through its subsidiary to the Indian workers, the Indian citizens affected in the community and the Indian environment? Which is the competent jurisdiction, the one of the US or the one of India, and what is the applicable law, US tort and class action law with its high compensation schemes or the tort law of the recipient state? The litigation fell into a period where socio-legal research played a key role in the United States and where legal scholars heavily engaged in the litigation providing legal support to the victims. There was a heated debate even between scholars sympathizing with the victims of whether it would be better for India to instrumentalise Bhopal so as to develop the Indian judiciary through the litigation in India in accepting the risk that Indian courts could provide carte blanche to the American mother companies or whether the rights of the victims should be preserved through the much more effective and generous US law before US courts. One of the key figures was Marc Galanter from Wisconsin, who left the material collected over decades on the litigation in the United States and in India, background information on the Indian judiciary, and the role and function of American authorities to the Wisconsin public library.[17] It remains to be added that in 1986 the US district court declined jurisdiction of American courts as *forum non conveniens* and that the victims who had to refile their case before Indian courts were never adequately compensated – until today. There are variations of the Bhopal type of litigation; the last one so far which equally gained public prominence is *Kiobel*.[18]

The political and legal debate on double standards which dominated the public and legal fora in the 1980s differs in two ways from the one we have today on the

16 Daniel Augenstein, *Global Business and the Law and Politics of Human Rights* (Cambridge University Press, forthcoming).

17 https://repository.law.wisc.edu/s/uwlaw/page/about-marc-galanter.

18 *Kiobel* v. *Royal Dutch Petroleum* CO., 569 US 108(2013).

responsibility of private parties in the digital economy and society: first and foremost, the primary addressees of the call for action were the Western democratic states as well as international organizations. They were sought to find appropriate solutions for what could not be solved otherwise. There are few examples of existing case law on double standards. Bhopal, though mirroring the problem of double standards, is different due to the dimension of the catastrophe and to the sheer number of victims which were identifiable. It is still noteworthy though that the international community left the search for solutions in the hands of the American respectively the Indian judiciary and that there was no serious political attempt neither of the two states nor of the international community to seek extra-judicial compensation schemes. The American court delegated the problem of double standards back to the Indian state and the Indian society alone. Second, in the 1980s, human rights were not yet or at least to a much lesser extent invoked in the search for political as well as for judicial solutions. There was less emphasis on the 'rights' rhetoric, on consumer rights as human rights or the right to safety as a human right.[19] Health, safety and the environment were treated as policy objectives that had to be implemented by the states, either nationally or internationally. The 1980s still breathe a different spirit, the belief in and the hope for an internationally agreeable legal framework that could provide a sound compromise between export and import states or, put differently, between the free-trade ideology and the need for some sort of internationally agreeable minimum standards of protection.

13.3 THE SECOND WAVE – GAFAS AND GLOBAL VALUE CHAINS (GVCS)

When it comes to private responsibilities in the digital economy and society, the attention is directed to the GAFAs, to what is called the platform economy and their role as gatekeepers to the market. Here competition law ties in. National competition authorities have taken action against the GAFAs under national and European competition law mainly with reference to the abuse of a dominant position.[20] The EU, on the other hand, has adopted Regulation 2019/1150[21] business to platforms in order to 'create a fair, transparent and predictable business environment for smaller businesses and traders', which entered into force on 20 July 2020. The von der Leyen

[19] Hans-W. Micklitz, 'Consumer Rights' in Andrew Clapham, Antonio Cassese and Joseph Weiler (eds), *European Union – The Human Rights Challenge, Human Rights and the European Community: The Substantive Law* (Nomos 1991).

[20] There is a vibrant debate in competition law on the reach of Art. 102 TFEU and the correspondent provisions in national cartel laws . See Nicolas Petit, *Big Tech and the Digital Economy: The Moligopoly Scenario* (1st ed., Oxford University Press 2020). With regard to the customer dimension, see the following judgment of the Federal Supreme Court of Germany (BGH) on Facebook, KVR 69/19, 23. 6. 2020 openJur 2020, 47441.

[21] Regulation (EU) 2019/1150 of the European Parliament and of the Council of 20 June 2019 on promoting fairness and transparency for business users of online intermediation services PE/56/2019/REV/1, OJ L 186, 11. 7. 2019, pp. 57–79.

Commission has announced two additional activities: a sector-specific proposal which is meant to fight down potential anti-competitive effects by December 2020 and a Digital Services Act which will bring amendments to the e-commerce Directive 2001/43/EEC probably also with regard to the rights of customers. While platforms hold a key position in the digital economy and society, they form in Baldwin's scenario no more than an integral part of the transformation of the economic order towards GVCs. Platforms help reduce the communication cost, and they are opening up markets for small- and medium-sized companies in the Global South which had no opportunity to gain access to the market before the emergence of platforms.

The current chapter is not the ideal place to do justice to the various roles and functions of platforms or GVCs. There is not even an agreed-upon definition of platforms or GVCs. What matters in our context, is, however, to understand the GVCs as networks which are interwoven through a dense set of contractual relations, which cannot be reduced to a lead company that is organized by the chain upstream and downstream and that holds all the power in their hands. Not only the public attention but also the political attention is very much concentrated on the GAFAs and on multinationals, sometimes even identified and personalized. Steve Jobs served as the incarnation of Apple, and Mark Zuckerberg is a symbolic figure and even a public figure. The reference to the responsibility of private actors is in their various denominations, *sociétés*, corporations and multinationals. Digitization enabled the development of the platform economy. Communication costs were reduced to close to zero. Without digitalization and without the platforms, the great transformation of the global economy, as *Baldwin* calls it, would not have been possible. The results are GVCs being understood as complex networks, where SMEs equally may be able to exercise, let alone that the focus on the chain sets aside external effects of the contractualization on third parties.[22] That is why personalization of the GAFAs is as problematic as the desperate search for a lead company which can be held responsible upstream and downstream.[23]

The overview of the more recent attempts internationally, nationally and the EU lay the ground for discussion. The idea of holding multinationals responsible for their actions in third countries, especially down the GVCs, has been vividly debated in recent years. Discussions have evolved to cover not only the protection of human rights but also environmental law, labour law and good governance in general. Developments in the field and the search for accountability have been led to political action at the international level, to legislative action at the national and

[22] Jaakko Salminen, 'Contract-Boundary-Spanning Governance Mechanisms: Conceptualizing Fragmented and Globalized Production as Collectively Governed Entities' (2016) 23 *Indiana Journal of Global Legal Studies* 709.

[23] This comes clear from the methodology used by Jaakko Salminen and Mikko Rajavuori, 'Transnational Sustainability Laws and the Regulation of Global Value Chains: Comparison and a Framework for Analysis' (2019) 26 *Maastricht Journal of European and Comparative Law* 602.

European level and to litigation before national courts. Most of the initiatives fall short of an urgently needed holistic perspective, which takes the various legal fields into account, takes the network effects seriously and provides for an integrated regulation of due diligence in corporate law, of commercial practices, of standard terms and of the contractual and tortious liability, let alone the implications with regard to labour law, consumer law and environmental law within GVCs.[24]

13.3.1 *International Approaches on GVCs*

In June 2011 the United Nations Human Rights Council unanimously adopted the Guiding Principles on Business and Human Rights (UNGPs). This was a major step towards the protection of Human Rights and the evolution of the concept of Social Corporate Responsibility. The adoption of the UNGPs was the result of thirteen years of negotiations. The year 2008 marked another step in the work of the Human Rights Council with the adoption of the framework 'Protect, Respect and Remedy: A Framework for Business and Human Rights'.[25] The framework laid down three fundamental pillars: the duty of the state to protect against human rights violations by third parties, including companies; the responsibility of companies to respect human rights; and better access by victims to effective remedies, both judicial and non-judicial. The Guiding Principles, which are seen as the implementation of the Protect, Respect and Remedy Framework, further detail how the three pillars are to be developed. The Guiding Principles are based on the recognition of

> [the] State's existing obligations to respect, protect and fulfil human rights and fundamental freedoms; The role of business enterprises as specialized organs of society performing specialized function, required to comply with all applicable laws and to respect human rights; the need for rights and obligations to be matched to appropriate and effective remedies when breaches.[26]

The Guiding Principles not only cover state behaviours but introduce a corporate responsibility to respect human rights as well as access to remedies for those affected by corporate behaviour or activities. Despite its non-binding nature, the UN initiative proves the intention to engage corporations in preventing negative impacts of their activities on human rights and in making good the damage they would nevertheless cause.

24 For first attempt to at least systematically address the legal fields and the questions that require a solution, Anna Beckers and Hans-W. Micklitz, 'Eine ganzheitliche Perspektive auf die Regulierung globaler Lieferketten' (2020) volume 6 *Europäische Zeitschrift für Wirtschafts- und Steuerrecht*, 324–329.

25 United Nations Humans Rights Council, Protect, Respect and Remedy: A Framework for Business and Human Rights, 2008 A/HRC/8/5.

26 United Nations Human Rights Council, United Nations Guidelines on Business and Human Rights, 2011 A/HRC/17/31; for details, see Claire Bright, 'Creating a Legislative Level Playing Field in Business and Human Rights at the European Level: Is French Duty of Vigilance Law the Way Forward?' EUI working paper MWP 2020/01, 2020, 2.

Here is not the place to give a detailed account of the initiative taken at the international level, but it is relevant to stop on the case of the OECD. The OECD worked closely with the UN Human Rights Council in elaborating the OECD Guidelines for Multinational Enterprises.[27] The guidelines especially introduced an international grievance mechanism. The governments that adhere to the guidelines are required to establish a National Contact Point (NPC) which has the task of promoting the OECD guidelines and handling complaints against companies that have allegedly failed to adhere to the Guidelines' standards. The NCP usually acts as a mediator or conciliator in case of disputes and helps the parties reach an agreement.[28]

13.3.2 *National Approaches to Regulate GVCs*

Not least through the international impact and the changing global environment, national legislators are becoming more willing to address the issue of the responsibility of corporations for their actions abroad from a GVC perspective. They focus explicitly or implicitly on a lead company which has to be held responsible. None have taken the network effects of GVS seriously. In 2010, California passed the Transparency in Supply Chains Act,[29] the same year the United Kingdom adopted the UK Bribery Act, which creates a duty for undertakings carrying an economic activity in Britain to verify there is no corruption in the supply chain.[30] The Bribery Act was then complemented by the UK Modern Slavery Act 2015, which focuses on human trafficking and exploitation in GVCs.[31] In the same line, the Netherlands adopted a law on the duty of care in relation to child labour, covering international production chains.[32] Complemented by EU instruments, such legislation is useful and constitutes a step forward, particularly at the political and legislative levels. Nevertheless, their focus on a sector, a product or certain rights does not enable the body of initiative to be mutually reinforcing. There is a crucial need for a holistic network-related approach to the regulation of GVCs.

Legislation on the responsibility of multinationals for human rights, environment or other harms is being designed in different countries. Germany and Finland have announced being in the process of drafting due diligence legislation.[33] Switzerland had been working on a proposal, led by NGOs and left parties. The initiative was put to the *votation* in the last days of November 2020. A total of 47 per cent of the

[27] OECD Guidelines for Multinational Enterprises, 2011.

[28] S. Eickenjäger, *Menschenrechtsberichtserstattung durch Unternehmen* (Mohr Siebeck 2017) 274.

[29] California Transparency in Supply Chains Act of 2010 (SB 657).

[30] Bribery Act 2010 c. 23.

[31] Modern Slavery Act 2018, No. 153, 2018.

[32] Wet zorgplicht kinderarbeid, 14 May 2019. For a comparison of the legislation discussed above, see Salminen and Rajavuori (n 23).

[33] For a detailed overview of the status quo, see Macchi and Bright (n 7).

population participated, of which 50.73 per cent voted 'Yes'.[34] The project was rejected at the level of the cantons. Therefore this initiative will not go forward. At the time of writing, it seems to be a lighter initiative that will be discussed – one where responsibility is not imposed along the supply chain but for Swiss companies in third countries. The *votation* is nevertheless a performance in terms of the willingness to carry out such a project, participation and in terms of result. The result of the vote of the cantons can be partly explained by the lobby strategies multinationals have conducted from the beginning of the initiative.

The French duty of vigilance law was adopted in 2017 and introduced in the Code of Commerce among the provisions on public limited companies in the sub-part on shareholders assemblies.[35] They require shareholders of large public limited companies with subsidiaries abroad to establish a vigilance plan. A vigilance plan introduces vigilance measures that identify the risks and measures to prevent serious harm to human rights, health, security or environmental harm resulting from the activities of the mother company but also of the company it controls, its subcontractors and its suppliers. The text provides for two enforcement mechanisms. First, a formal notice (*mise en demeure*) can be addressed to the company that does not establish a vigilance plan or establishes an incomplete one. The company has three months to comply with its obligations. Second, there could be an action in responsibility (*action en responsabilité*) against the company. Here the company must repair the prejudice the compliance with its obligations would have avoided. French multinationals have already received letters of formal notice. This is the case of EDF and its subsidiary EDF Energies Nouvelles for human rights violations in Mexico.[36] The first case was heard in January 2020. It was brought by French and Ugandan NGOs against Total. The NGOs argue that the vigilance plan designed and put in place by Total is not in compliance with the law on due diligence and that the measures adopted to mitigate the risks are insufficient or do not exist at all.

13.3.3 *The Existing Body of EU Approaches on GVCs and the Recent European Parliament Initiative*

Sector-specific or product-specific rules imposed on GVCs have been adopted at the EU level and introduced due diligence obligations. The Conflict Minerals

34 www.bk.admin.ch/ch/f/pore/va/20201129/index.html accessed on 1 December 2020.

35 LOI no. 2017–399 du 27 mars 2017 relative au devoir de vigilance des sociétés mères et des entreprises donneuses d'ordre JORF no. 0074 du 28 mars 2017, S. Brabant and E. Savourey, 'French Law on the Corporate Duty of Vigilance: A Practical and Multidimensional Perspective', *Revue international de la compliance et de l'éthique des affairs*, 14 December 2017, www.bhrinlaw.org/frenchcorporateduty law_articles.pdf.

36 For further details, see Claire Bright, 'Creating a Legislative Level Playing Field in Business and Human Rights at the European Level: Is French Duty of Vigilance Law the Way Forward?' EUI working paper MWP 2020/01, 2020, 6.

Regulation[37] and the Regulation of timber products[38] impose obligations along the supply chain; the importer at the start of the GVC bears the obligations. The Directive on the Disclosure of Non-Financial and Diversity Information obliges large capital market-oriented companies to include in their non-financial statement information on the effects of the supply chain and the supply chain concepts they pursue.[39] The Market Surveillance Regulation extends the circle of obligated economic operators in the EU to include participants in GVCs, thus already regulating extraterritorially.[40] The Directive on unfair trading practices in the global food chain regulates trading practices in supply chains through unfair competition and contract law.[41] Although these bits and pieces of legislation introduce a form of due diligence along the supply chain, they remain product- or sector-specific, which prevents an overall legal approach to due diligence across sectors for all products. This concern is addressed by the latest Recommendation of the European Parliament.

Most recently, in September 2020, the JURI Committee of the European Parliament published a draft report on corporate due diligence and corporate accountability which includes recommendations for drawing up a Directive.[42] Although the European Parliament's project has to undergo a number of procedures and discussions among the European institutions and is unlikely to be adopted in its current form, a few aspects are relevant for our discussion. Article 3 defines due diligence as follows:

> '[D]ue diligence' means the process put in place by an undertaking aimed at identifying, ceasing, preventing, mitigating, monitoring, disclosing, accounting for, addressing, and remediating the risks posed to human rights, including social and labour rights, the environment, including through climate change, and to governance, both by its own operations and by those of its business relationships.

Following the model of the UN Guiding Principles, the scope of the draft legislation goes beyond human rights to cover social and labour rights, the environment, climate change and governance. Article 4 details that undertakings are to

37 Regulation 2017/821/EU of 17 March 2017 laying down supply chain due diligence obligations for Union importers of tin, tantalum, tungsten, their ores and gold originating from conflict-affected and high-risk areas, OJ L 130, 19. 5. 2017, p. 1–20.

38 Regulation 995/2010/EU of 20 October 2010 on the obligations of operators who place timber and timer products on the market, OJ L 295, 12. 11. 2010, p. 23–34.

39 Directive 2014/95/EU of 22 October 2014 amending Directive 2013/34/EU as regards the disclosure of non-financial and diversity information by certain large companies and groups, OJ L 330, 15. 11. 2014, p. 1–9.

40 Regulation 2019/1020/EU of 20 June 2019 on market surveillance and compliance of products and amending Directive 2004/42/EC and Regulations 765/2008/EC and 305/2011/EU, OJ L 169, 25. 6. 2019, p. 1–44.

41 Directive 2019/633/EU of 17 April 2019 on unfair trading practices in business-to-business relationships in the agricultural and food chain, OJ L 111, 25. 4. 2019, p. 59–72.

42 Committee on Legal Affairs, Draft Report with recommendations to the Commission on corporate due diligence and corporate accountability, 2020/2129(INL), 11. 09. 2020.

identify and assess risks and publish a risk assessment. This risk-based approach is based on the second pillar of the UN Guiding Principles; it is also followed in the French due diligence law. In case risks are identified, a due diligence strategy is to be established whereby an undertaking designs measures to stop, mitigate or prevent such risks. The firm is to disclose reliable information about its GVC, namely, names, locations and other relevant information concerning subsidiaries, suppliers and business partners.[43] The due diligence strategy is to be integrated in the undertaking's business strategy, particularly in the choice of commercial partners. The undertaking is to contractually bind its commercial partners to comply with the company's due diligence strategy.

13.3.4 *Litigation before National Courts*

Civil society, NGOs and trade unions are key players in making accountable multinationals for their actions abroad and along the GVC. They have supported legal actions for human rights violations beyond national territories. Such an involvement of the civil society is considerably facilitated through digitalization, through the use of the platforms and through the greater transparency in GVCs.[44] Courts face cases where they have to assess violations of human rights in third countries by multinationals and their subsidiaries and construct extraterritorial responsibility. There is a considerable evolution from the 1980s in that the rights rhetoric goes beyond human rights so as to cover labour law, environmental law, misleading advertising or corporate law. Although the rights rhetoric recognizes the moral responsibility of private companies and accounts for their gravity, the challenges before and during trials to turn a moral responsibility into a legal liability are numerous.

In France, three textile NGOs brought a complaint arguing that Auchan's communication strategy regarding its commitment to social and environmental standards in the supply chain constituted misleading advertising, since Auchan's products were found in the Rana Plaza factory in Bangladesh, a factory well-known for its poor working and safety conditions. The case was dismissed at the stage of the investigation. In another case, Gabonese employees of COMILOG were victims of a train accident while at work, which led to financial difficulties for the company. They were dismissed and promised compensation, which they never received. With the support of NGOs, they brought the case to a French employment tribunal,

[43] European Parliament Committee on Legal Affairs, Draft Report with recommendations to the Commission on corporate due diligence and corporate accountability, 2020/2129(INL), 11. 09. 2020, article 4.

[44] For an early account of the new opportunities, see Eric Brousseau, Meryem Marzouki and Cécile Méadel, *Governance, Regulations and Powers on the Internet* (Cambridge University Press 2012). Andrea Calderaro and Anastasia Kavada, 'Challenges and Opportunities of Online Collective Action for Policy Change' (2013) in Diane Rowland, Uta Kohl and Andrew Charlesworth (eds), *Information Technology Law* (5th ed., Routledge 2017).

claiming that COMILOG was owned by a French company. Their claim was dismissed but successful on appeal, where the court held COMILOG France and COMILOG international responsible for their own conduct and for the conduct of their subsidiaries abroad. On the merits, the court found that COMILOG had to compensate the workers. On appeal, the *Court de Cassation* annulled this finding, arguing that there was no sufficient evidence for the legally required strong link with the mother company in France.[45] There is a considerable number of cases with similar constellations, where courts struggle in finding a coherent approach to these legal issues.

In Total, the NGOs pretended that the vigilance plan is incomplete and does not offer appropriate mitigating measures or failing to adopt them. The court did not rule on the merits, as the competence lies with the commercial court, since the law on due diligence is part of the Commercial Code. Nevertheless, the court made a distinction between the formal notice procedure which is targeted at the vigilance plan and its implementation and the action in responsibility.[46] It is unclear whether the court suggested a twofold jurisdiction, a commercial one for due diligence strategies and another one for actions in responsibility. The case triggers fundamental questions as to what a satisfactory vigilance plan is and what appropriate mitigating measures are. It also requires clarifications about the relevant field of law applicable, the relevant procedure and the competent jurisdiction.

Even if there is an evolution as to the substance, today's cases carry the heritage of those from the 1980s. Before ruling on the merits, courts engage in complex procedural issues, just like in the context of the Bhopal litigation or *Kiobel*. Such legal questions have not yet been settled at the national level, and they are still examined on a case-by-case basis. This lack of consistency renders the outcome of litigation uncertain. The first barrier is procedural; it concerns the jurisdiction of the national court on corporate action beyond the scope of its territorial jurisdiction. The second relates to the responsibility of the mother companies for their subsidiaries. In the two Shell cases brought up in the UK[47] and in the Netherlands,[48] Nigerian citizens had suffered from environmental damages which affected their territory, water, livelihood and health. Here the jurisdiction of the national courts was not an issue, but the differentiation between the mother company and its subsidiary remained controversial.[49]

45 Cass. Civ. 14 sept. 2017 no. 15–26737 et 15–26738.

46 Tribunal Judiciaire de Nanterre, 30 January 2020, no. 19/02833.

47 High Court, The Bodo Community et al. v Shell Petroleum Development Company of Nigeria Ltd, (2014) EWHC 1973, 20 June 2014.

48 *Court of Appeal of the Hague, Eric Barizaa Dooh of Goi et al.* v. *Royal Dutch Shell Plc et al.*, 200. 126. 843 (case c) and 200. 126. 848 (case d), of 18 Decembre 2015.

49 Claire Bright, 'The Civil Liability of the Parent Company for the Acts or Omissions of Its Subsidiary The Example of the Shell Cases in the UK and the Netherlands' in Angelica Bonfanti (ed), *Business and Human Rights in Europe: International Law Challenges* (Routledge 2018).

The tour d'horizon indicates how fragile the belief in judicial activism still is. The adoption of due diligence legislation has not changed the level playing field. Courts are to design the contours and requirements of due diligence. Two methodological questions are at the heart of the ongoing discussions of the private responsibilities of companies in the GVCs. Who is competent? Who is responsible? Such are the challenges of the multilevel internationalized and digitalized environment where law finds itself unequipped to address the relevant legal challenges.

13.3.5 *Business Approaches to GVCs within and beyond the Law*

Recent initiatives suggest a different approach, one where legal obligations are placed on companies, not only to comply with their own obligations but to make them responsible for the respect of due diligence strategies along the GVC. The role and function of Corporate Social Responsibility and Corporate Digital Responsibility are in the political limelight.[50] Thereby firms have the potential to exercise impact over the GVC. This is particularly true in case a lead company can easily be identified. If the upstream lead company decides to require its downstream partners to comply with its due diligence strategy, the lead company might be able to ensure compliance.[51] In GVCs, contracts are turned into a regulatory tool to the benefit of the lead company and perhaps to the benefit of public policy goals. There are two major problems: the first results from the exercise of economic power, which might be for good, but the opposite is also true. The second relates to the organization of the GVC, which more often than not is lacking a lead company but is composed out of a complex network of big, small and medium-sized companies. Designing responsibilities in networks is one of the yet still unsolved legal issues.

A consortium of French NGOs has drafted a report on the first year of application of the law on due diligence, where they have examined eighty vigilance plans published by French corporations falling under the scope of the due diligence law.[52] The report is entitled 'Companies Must Do Better' and sheds light on questions we have raised before. As regards the publication and content of the due

[50] Monika Namysłowska, 'Monitoring Compliance with Contracts and Regulations: Between Private and Public Law' in Roger Brownsword, R. A. J. van Gestel and Hans-W. Micklitz (eds), *Contract and Regulation: A Handbook on New Methods of Law Making in Private Law* (Edward Elgar Publishing 2017); Anna Beckers, *Enforcing Corporate Social Responsibility Codes: On Global Self-Regulation and National Private Law* (Hart Publishing 2015).

[51] Walter van Gerven, 'Bringing (Private) Laws Closer to Each Other at the European Level' in Fabrizio Cafaggi, *The Institutional Framework of European Private Law* (Oxford University Press 1993). Fabrizio Cafaggi and Horatia Muir Watt (eds), *Making European Private Law: Governance Design* (Edward Elgar 2008).

[52] Actionaid, Les Amis de la Terre France, Amnesty International, Terre Solidaire, Collectif Étique sur l'Étiquette, Sherpa, The law on duty of vigilance of parent and outsourcing companies Year 1: Companies must do better (2019), 49.

diligence plans, not all companies have published their vigilance plans, some have incomplete ones, some have a lack of transparency and others seem to ignore the idea behind the due diligence plan. The report writes, 'The majority of plans are still focusing on the risks for the company rather than those of third parties or the environment.'[53] Along the different criteria of the vigilance plan analysed by the consortium of NGOs, it becomes clear that few companies have developed methodologies and appropriate responses in designing their due diligence strategy, identifying and mitigating risks. It is also noted that companies have re-used some previous policies and collected them to constitute due diligence. The lack of seriousness does not only make the vigilance plans unreadable; it denies any due diligence strategy of the firm. If multinationals do not take legal obligations seriously at the level of the GVC leading company, are they likely to produce positive spillover effects along the chain? It is too early to condemn the regulatory approach and the French multinationals. Once similar obligations will be adopted in most countries, at least in the EU, we might see a generalization and good practices emerge. Over the long term, we might witness competition arise between firms on the ground of their due diligence strategy.

Externally from the GVC, compliance can also be carried out by actors such as Trade Unions and NGOs. They have long been active in litigation and were consulted in the process of designing legislation. The European Parliament's Recommendation suggests their involvement in the establishment of the undertaking's due diligence strategies, similar to French law.[54] Further, due diligence strategies are to be made public. In France, few companies have made public NGOs or stakeholders contributing to the design of the strategy. If there is no constructive cooperation between multinationals and NGOs yet, NGOs have access to grievance mechanisms under the European Parliament's Recommendation, which resembles the letter of formal notice under the French law.[55] Stakeholders which are not limited to NGOs could thereby voice concerns as to the existence of risks which the undertakings would have to answer to and be transparent about through publication.

NGOs have a unique capacity for gathering information abroad on the ground. The European Parliament's text explicitly refers to the National Contact Point under the OECD framework. National Contact Points are not only entrusted with the promotion of the OECD guidelines; they offer a non-judicial platform for

[53] Actionaid, Les Amis de la Terre France, Amnesty International, Terre Solidaire, Collectif Étique sur l'Étiquette, Sherpa, The law on duty of vigilance of parent and outsourcing companies Year 1: Companies must do better (2019), 10.

[54] European Parliament Committee on Legal Affairs, Draft Report with recommendations to the Commission on corporate due diligence and corporate accountability, 2020/2129(INL), 11. 09. 2020, articles 5 and 8.

[55] European Parliament Committee on Legal Affairs, Draft Report with recommendations to the Commission on corporate due diligence and corporate accountability, 2020/2129(INL), 11. 09. 2020, articles 9 and 10.

grievance mechanisms.[56] The OECD conducts an in-depth analysis of the facts and publishes a statement as to the conflict and what it can offer to mediate it. Although such proceedings are non-binding, they do offer the possibility for an exchange between the parties and the case files are often relied on in front of courts. It seems that NGOs and other stakeholders have a role to play in compliance with the due diligence principles. They are given the possibility to penetrate the network and work with it from the inside. There are equally mechanisms that allow for external review of the GVC's behaviour.

13.4 THE WAY AHEAD: THE SNAKE BITES ITS OWN TAIL

The European Parliaments have discussed the introduction of an independent authority with investigative powers to oversee the application of the proposed directive – namely, the establishment of due diligence plans and appropriate responses in case of risks.[57] In EU jargon, this implies the creation of a regulatory agency or a form alike. Such an agency could take different forms and could have different powers; what is crucial is the role such an agency might play in the monitoring and surveillance of fundamental rights, the environment, labour rights, consumer rights and so on. A general cross-cutting approach would have a broader effect than isolated pieces of sector- or product-specific legislation. If such rights were as important as for instance competition law, the EU would turn into a leader in transmitting its values only to the GVCs at the international level. Playing and being the gentle civiliser does not mean that the EU does not behave like a hegemon, though.[58]

Does the snake bite its own tail? Despite the idealistic compliance mechanisms, a return to courts seems inevitable, and fundamental questions remain. Are multinationals responsible for their actions abroad? Let us flip a coin. Heads, yes, there is legislation, or it is underway. There is political will and civic engagement. There is a strong rights rhetoric that people, politicians and multinationals relate to. Heads of multinationals and politicians have said this is important. Firms are adopting due diligence strategies; they are mitigating the risks of their activities. They are taking their responsibility seriously. Tails, all the above is true, there has been considerable progress and there is optimism. Does it work in practice? Some doubts arise. There are issues of compliance and courts struggle. Multinationals and nowadays GAFAs

56 OECD Guidelines for Multinational Enterprises, 2011, part II, Procedural Approaches, Part C, Application of the guidelines in special cases.

57 European Parliament Committee on Legal Affairs, Draft Report with recommendations to the Commission on corporate due diligence and corporate accountability, 2020/2129(INL), 11. 09. 2020, articles 14 and 15.

58 H.-W. Micklitz, 'The Role of the EU in the External Reach of Regulatory Private Law – Gentle Civilizer or Neoliberal Hegemon? An Epilogue', in M. Cantero and H.-W. Micklitz (eds), *The Role of the EU in Transnational Legal Ordering: Standards, Contracts and Codes* (Edward Elgar Publishing 2020) 298–320.

have communication strategies to send positive messages. They do not have mailboxes; it is sometimes difficult to find them. Mostly, they might even own GVCs, and what happens there stays there. It is upon their desire to commit to their duty of due diligence; it is not upon the state. How will these parties react in the algorithmic society?

14

Consumer Law as a Tool to Regulate Artificial Intelligence

Serge Gijrath

14.1 INTRODUCTION

Ongoing digital transformation combined with artificial intelligence (AI) brings serious advantages to society.[1] Transactional opportunities knock: optimal energy use, fully autonomous machines, electronic banking, medical analysis, constant access to digital platforms. Society at large is embracing the latest wave of AI applications as being one of the most transformative forces of our time. Two developments contribute to the rise of the algorithmic society: (1) the possibilities resulting from technological advances in machine learning, and (2) the availability of data analysis using algorithms. Where the aim is to promote competitive data markets, the question arises of what benefits or harm can be brought to private individuals. Some are concerned about human dignity.[2] They believe that human dignity may be threatened by digital traders who demonstrate an insatiable hunger for data.[3] Through algorithms the traders may predict, anticipate and regulate future private individual, specifically consumer, behaviour. Data assembly forms part of reciprocal transactions, where these data are currency. With the deployment of AI, traders can exclude uncertainty from the automated transaction processes.

The equality gap in the employment of technology to automated transactions begs the question of whether the private individual's fundamental rights are warranted adequately.[4] Prima facie, the consumer stands weak when she is subjected to automatic processes – no matter if it concerns day-to-day transactions, like boarding

[1] Press Release 19 February 2019, *Shaping Europe's Digital Future: Commission Presents Strategies for Data and Artificial Intelligence.*

[2] M. Tekmark, *Life 3.0: Being Human in the Age of Artificial Intelligence*, New York, 2017.

[3] For consistency purposes, this article refers to 'traders' when referring to suppliers and services providers. Art. 2(2) Directive 2011/83/EU *OJ L 304, 22 November 2011* (Consumer Rights Directive). See also Directive (EU) 2019/2161 amending Council Directive 93/13/EEC (Unfair Contract Terms Directive) and Directives 98/6/EC, 2005/29/EC and 2011/83/EU as regards the better enforcement and modernisation of Union consumer protection rules, *OJ L 328, 18 December 2019* (Modernization of Consumer Protection Directive).

[4] Council of Europe research shows that a large number of fundamental rights could be impacted from the use of AI, https://rm.coe.int/algorithms-and-human-rights-en-rev/16807956b5.

a train, or a complex decision tree used to validate a virtual mortgage. When 'computer says no' the consumer is left with limited options: click yes to transact (and, even then, she could fail), abort or restart the transaction process, or – much more difficult – obtain information or engage in renegotiations. But, where the negotiations process is almost fully automated and there is no human counterpart, the third option is circular rather than complementary to the first two. Empirical evidence suggests that automated decisions will be acceptable to humans only, if they are confident the used technology and the output is fair, trustworthy and corrigible.[5] How should Constitutional States respond to new technologies on multisided platforms that potentially shift the bargaining power to the traders?

A proposed definition of digital platforms is that these are companies (1) operating in two or multisided markets, where at least one side is open to the public; (2) whose services are accessed via the Internet (i.e., at a distance); and (3) that, as a consequence, enjoy particular types of powerful network effects.[6] With the use of AI, these platforms may create interdependence of demand between the different sides of the market. Interdependence may create indirect network externalities. This leads to establishing whether and, if so, how traders can deploy AI to attract one group of customers to attract the other, and to keep both groups thriving on the digital marketplace.

AI is a collection of technologies that combine data, algorithms and computing power. Yet science is unable to agree even on a single definition of the notion 'intelligence' as such. AI often is not defined either. Rather, its purpose is described. A starting point to understand algorithms is to see them as virtual agents. Agents learn, adapt and even deploy themselves in dynamic and uncertain virtual environments. Such learning is apt to create a static and reliable environment of automated transactions. AI *seems* to entail the replication of human behaviour, through data analysis that models 'some aspect of the world'. But does it? AI employs data analysis models to map behavioural aspects of humans.[7] Inferences from these models are used to predict and anticipate possible future events.[8] The difference in applying AI rather than standard methods of data analysis is that AI does *not* analyse data as they were programmed initially. Rather, AI assembles data, learns from them to respond

5 B. Custers et al., *e-Sides, deliverable 2.2, Lists of Ethical, Legal, Societal and Economic Issues of Big Data Technologies. Ethical and Societal Implications of Data Sciences*, https://e-sides.eu/resources/deliverable-22-lists-of-ethical-legal-societal-and-economic-issues-of-big-data-technologies accessed 12 April 2019 (e-SIDES, 2017).

6 H. Feld, *The Case for the Digital Platform Act: Breakups, Starfish Problems, & Tech Regulation*, e-book, 2019.

7 UK Government Office for Science, *Artificial intelligence: opportunities and implications for the future of decision making*, 2016. OECD, *Algorithms and Collusion – Background Note by the Secretariat*, DAF/COMP (2017) 4 (OECD 2017).

8 The Society for the Study of Artificial Intelligence and Simulation of Behaviour, 'What Is Artificial Intelligence', *AISB Website* (no longer accessible); Government Office for Science, *Artificial Intelligence: Opportunities and Implications for the Future of Decision Making*, 9 November 2016; Information Commissioner's Office, UK, *Big Data, Artificial Intelligence, Machine Learning and Data Protection*, Report, v. 2.2, 20170904 (ICO 2017).

intelligently to new data, and adapt the output in accordance therewith. Thus AI is not ideal for linear analysis of data in the manner they have been processed or programmed. Conversely, algorithms are more dynamic, since they apply machine learning.[9]

Machine learning algorithms build a *mathematical model* based on sample data, known as *'training data'*.[10] Training data serve computer systems to make predictions or decisions, without being programmed specifically to perform the task. Machine learning focuses on prediction-based unknown properties learned from the training data. Conversely, data analysis focuses on the discovery of (previously) unknown properties in the data. The analytics process enables the processor to mine data for new insights and to find correlations between apparently disparate data sets through self-learning. Self-learning AI can be supervised or unsupervised. Supervised learning is based on algorithms that build and rely on labelled data sets. The algorithms are 'trained' to map from input to output, by the provision of data with 'correct' values already assigned to them. The first training phase creates models on which predictions can then be made in the second 'prediction' phase.[11] Unsupervised learning entails that the algorithms are 'left to themselves' to find regularities in input data without any instructions on what to look for.[12] It is the ability of the algorithms to change their output based on experience that gives machine learning its power.

For humans, it is practically impossible to deduct and contest in an adequate manner the veracity of a machine learning process and the subsequent outcome based thereon. This chapter contends that the deployment of AI on digital platforms could lead to potentially harmful situations for consumers given the circularity of algorithms and data. Policy makers struggle with formulating answers. In Europe, the focus has been on establishing that AI systems should be transparent, traceable and guarantee human oversight.[13] These principles form the basis of this chapter. Traceability of AI could contribute to another requirement for AI in the algorithmic society: veracity, or truthfulness of data.[14] Veracity and truthfulness of data are subject to the self-learning AI output.[15] In accepting the veracity of the data, humans

9 J. R. Koza, F. H. Bennett, D. Andre, and M. A. Keane 'Paraphrasing Arthur Samuel (1959), the Question Is: How Can Computers Learn to Solve Problems without Being Explicitly Programmed?' In *Automated Design of Both the Topology and Sizing of Analog Electrical Circuits Using Genetic Programming. Artificial Intelligence in Design*, Springer, 1996, 151–170. L. Bell, 'Machine Learning versus AI: What's the Difference?' *Wired*, 2 December 2016.

10 C. M. Bishop, *Pattern Recognition and Machine Learning*, Springer Verlag, 2006.

11 ICO 2017, p. 7.

12 E. Alpaydin, *Introduction to Machine Learning*, MIT Press, 2014.

13 European Commission, *White Paper on Artificial Intelligence – A European Approach to Excellence and Trust*, 19 February 2019, COM(2020) 65 final.

14 'The quality of being true, honest, or accurate', *Cambridge Dictionary*, Cambridge University Press, 2020.

15 J. Modrall, 'Big Data and Algorithms, Focusing the Discussion', Oxford University, *Business Law Blog*, 15 January 2018; D. Landau, 'Artificial Intelligence and Machine Learning: How Computers Learn', *iQ*, 17 August 2016, https://iq.intel.com/artificial-intelligence-and-machine-learning, now presented as 'A Data-Centric Portfolio for AI, Analytics and Cloud'; last accessed 14 March 2019.

require trust. Transparency is key to establishing trust. However, many algorithms are non-transparent and thus incapable of explanation to humans. Even if transparent algorithms would be capable of explanation to humans, then still the most effective machine learning process would defy human understanding. Hence the search for transparent algorithms is unlikely to provide insights into the underlying technology.[16] The quality of output using non-transparent AI is probably better, but it makes the position of the recipient worse, because there is no way for her to test the processes. Consequently, the Constitutional States may want to contain the potential harms of these technologies by applying private law principles.

This chapter's principal research question is how Constitutional States should deal with new forms of private power in the algorithmic society. In particular, the theorem is that regulatory private law can be revamped in the consumer rights' realm to serve as a tool to regulate AI and the possible adverse consequences for the weaker party on digital platforms. Rather than the top-down regulation of AI's consequences to protect human dignity, this chapter proposes considering a bottom-up approach of empowering consumers in the negotiations and the governance phases of mutual digital platform transactions. Following the main question, it must be seen how consumer rights can be applied to AI in a meaningful and effective manner. Could AI output be governed better if the trader must comply with certain consumer law principles such as contestability, traceability, veracity, and transparency?

One initial objection may query why we limit this chapter to consumer law. The answer is that consumers are affected directly when there is no room to negotiate or contest a transaction. Consumer rights are fundamental rights.[17] The Charter of Fundamental Rights of the EU (CFREU) dictates that the Union's policies 'shall ensure a high level of consumer protection'.[18] The high level of consumer protection is sustained by ensuring, inter alia, the consumers' economic interests in the Treaty on the Functioning of the European Union (TFEU).[19] The TFEU stipulates that the Union must promote consumers' rights to information. The TFEU stipulates that the Union must contribute to the attainment of a high-level baseline of consumer protection that also takes into account technological advances.[20] It is evident that in the algorithmic society, the EU will strive to control technologies if these potentially cause harm to the foundations of European private law. Responding adequately to the impact that AI deployment may have on private law norms and principles, a technology and private law approach to AI could,

16 W. Seymour, 'Detecting Bias: Does an Algorithm Have to Be Transparent in Order to Be Fair?', www.CEUR-WS.org, vol. 2103 (2017).

17 Art. 38 Charter of Fundamental Rights of the EU (CFREU).

18 Art. 38 Fundamental Rights Charter.

19 Article 169(1) and point (a) of Article 169(2) TFEU.

20 Article 114 (3) of the Treaty on the Functioning of the European Union (TFEU). This clause mentions that within their respective powers, the European Parliament and the Council will also seek to achieve a high level of consumer protection.

conversely, enforce European private law.[21] Although AI is a global phenomenon, it is challenging to formulate a transnational law approach, given the lack of global AI and consumer regulation.

The structure is as follows: Section 14.2 sets the stage: AI on digital platforms is discussed bottom-up in the context of EU personal data and internal market regulation, in particular revamped consumer law, online intermediary[22] and free-flow of data regulation. The focus is on contributing to the ongoing governance debate of how to secure a high level of consumer protection when AI impacts consumer transactions on digital platforms, along with what rights consumers should have if they want to contest or reject AI output. Section 14.2.1 explores why consumer law must supplement AI regulation to warrant effective redress. Section 14.2.2 alludes to principles of contract law. Section 14.2.3 juxtaposes consumer rights with the data strategy objectives. Section 14.2.4 discusses trustworthiness and transparency. Section 14.3 is designed to align consumer rights with AI. Section 14.3.1 reflects on the regulation of AI and consumer rights through GTC. Section 14.3.2 presents consumer law principles that could be regulated: contestability (Section 14.3.2.1), traceability and veracity (Section 14.3.2.2) and transparency (Section 14.3.2.3). Section 14.3.3 considers further harmonization of consumer law in the context of AI. Section 14.4 contains closing remarks and some recommendations.

14.2 AI ON DIGITAL PLATFORMS

14.2.1 *Consumers, Data Subjects and Redress*

Consumers may think they are protected against adverse consequences of AI under privacy regulations and personal data protection regulatory regimes. However, it remains to be seen whether personal data protection extends to AI. Privacy policies are not designed to protect consumers against adverse consequences of data generated through AI. In that sense, there is a significant conceptual difference between policies and GTC: privacy policies are unilateral statements for compliance purposes. The policies do not leave room for negotiation. Moreover, privacy policies contain fairly moot purpose limitations. The purpose limitations are formulated de facto as processing rights. The private consumers/data subjects consider their

[21] Reiner Schulze, 'European Private Law: Political Foundations and Current Challenges' and J. M. Smits, 'Plurality of Sources in European Private Law', in R. Brownsword, H.-W. Micklitz, L. Niglia, and S. Weatherill, *The Foundations of European Private Law*, Oxford, 2011, p. 303–306 and 327*ff*.

[22] The Modernization of Consumer Protection Directive and Regulation (EU) 2019/1150 of the European Parliament and of the Council of 20 June 2019 on promoting fairness and transparency for business users of online intermediation services *OJ L 186, 11* July 2019 (Online Intermediary Services Regulation). Regulation (EU) 2018/1807 of 14 November 2018 on a Framework for the Free Flow of Non-Personal Data in the European Union, *OJ* L 303/59, 28 November 2018, entry into force May 2019 (Free Flow of Non-Personal Data Regulation).

consent implied to data processing, whatever tech is employed. Hence, the traders might be apt to apply their policies to consumers who are subjected to AI and machine learning. The General Data Protection Regulation (GDPR) contains one qualification in the realm of AI:[23] a data subject has the right *to object* at any time against ADM including profiling. This obligation for data controllers is set off by the provision that controllers may employ ADM, provided they demonstrate compelling legitimate grounds for the processing which override the interests, rights and freedoms of the data subject.

Most of the traders' machine learning is fed by aggregated, large batches of pseudonymised or anonymised non-personal data.[24] There is no built-in yes/no button to express consent to be subjected to AI, and there is no such regulation on the horizon.[25] The data policies are less tailored than GTC to defining consumer rights for complex AI systems. Besides, it is likely that most private individuals do not read the digital privacy policies – nor the general contract terms and conditions (GTC) for that matter – prior to responding to AI output.[26] The provided questions reveal important private law concerns: 'What are my rights?' relates to justified questions as regards access rights and vested consumer rights, the right to take note of and save/print the conditions; void unfair user terms; and termination rights. Traders usually refer to the GTC that can be found on the site. There is no meaningful choice. That is even more the case in the continental tradition, where acceptance of GTC is explicit. In Anglo-American jurisdictions, the private individual is confronted with a pop-up window which must be scrolled through and accepted. Declining means aborting the transaction.

'How can I enforce my rights against the trader?' requires that the consumer who wishes to enforce her rights must be able to address the trader, either on the platform or through online dispute resolution mechanisms. Voidance or nullification are remedies when an agreement came about through settled European private law principles, such as coercion, error or deceit. Hence the consumer needs to know there is a remedy if the AI process contained errors or was faulty.[27]

23 Council Regulation (EU) 2016/679 on the on the protection of natural persons with regard to the processing of personal data and on the free movement of such data, and repealing Directive 95/46/EC, *OJ L* 119/1 (General Data Protection Regulation, or GDPR) contains the right to object and automated individual decision-making (articles 21–22 GDPR), subject to fairly complex exclusions that are explained in detail in the extensive considerations.

24 There is no legal basis under when there are no personal data involved; section 3, e.g., articles 16 (rectification), 17 (erasure), 18 (restriction on processing), and 20 (data portability) GDPR – the rights are often qualified, and the burden of proof is not clear. This makes the consumer's rights rather difficult to enforce.

25 H. U. Vrabec, *Uncontrollable Data Subject Rights and the Data-Driven Economy*, dissertation, University Leiden, 2019.

26 See *Eurobarometer Special 447 on Online Platforms* (2016).

27 This chapter does not discuss online dispute resolution.

14.2.2 *Principles of Contract Law*

In the algorithmic society, consumers still should have at least some recourse to a counterparty, whom they can ask for information during the consideration process. They must have redress when they do not understand or agree with transactional output that affects their contractual position without explanation. The right to correct steps in contract formation is moot, where the process is cast in stone. Once the consumers have succeeded in identifying the formal counterparty, they can apply remedies. Where does that leave them if the response to these remedies is also automated as a result of the trader's use of profiling and decision-making tools? This reiterates the question of whether human dignity is at stake, when the counterpart is not a human but a machine. The consumer becomes a string of codes and loses her feeling of uniqueness.[28] Furthermore, when distributed ledger technology is used, the chain of contracts is extended. There is the possibility that an earlier contractual link will be 'lost'. For example, there is a gap in the formation on the digital platform, because the contract formation requirements either were not fully met or were waived. Another example is where the consumer wants to partially rescind the transaction but the system does not cater for a partial breach. The impact of a broken upstream contractual link on a downstream contract in an AI-enabled transactional system is likely to raise novel contract law questions, too. An agreement may lack contractual force if there is uncertainty or if a downstream contractual link in the chain is dependent on the performance of anterior upstream agreements. An almost limitless range of possibilities will need to be addressed in software terms, in order to execute the platform transaction validly. When the formation steps are using automated decision-making processes that are not covered in the GTC governing the status of AI output, then this begs the question of how AI using distributed ledger technology could react to non-standard events or conditions, and if and how the chain of transactions is part of the consideration. The consumer could wind up in a vicious cycle, and her fundamental rights of a high consumer protection level could be at stake, more than was the case in the information society. Whereas e-Commerce, Distant Selling and, later, Services Directives imposed information duties on traders, the normative framework for the algorithmic society is based on rather different principles. Theories such as freedom of contract – which entails the exclusion of coercion – and error, when AI output contains flaws or defects may be unenforceable in practice. For the consumer to invoke lack of will theories, she needs to be able to establish where and how in the system the flaws or mistakes occurred.

[28] Spike Jonze, *Her* (2013). In this movie, the protagonist in an algorithmic society develops an intimate relationship with his operating system – that is, until he finds out the operating system communicates with millions of customers simultaneously.

14.2.3 Data Strategy

Does the data strategy stand in the way of consumer protection against AI? The focus of the EU's data strategy is on stimulating the potential of data for business, research and innovation purposes.[29] The old regulatory dilemma on how to balance a fair and competitive business environment with a high level of consumer rights is revived. In 2019–2020, the Commission announced various initiatives, including rules on (1) securing free flow of data within the Union,[30] (2) provisions on data access and transfer,[31] and (3) and enhanced data portability.[32] Prima facie, these topics exhibit different approaches to achieve a balance between business and consumer interests. More importantly, how does the political desire for trustworthy technology match with such diverse regulations? The answer is that it does not. The Free Flow of Non-Personal Data Regulation lays down data localization requirements, the availability of data to competent authorities and data porting for professional users.[33] It does not cover AI use. The Modernization of Consumer Protection Directive alludes to the requirement for traders to inform consumers about the default main parameters determining the ranking of offers presented to the consumer as a result of the search query and their relative importance as opposed to other parameters only.[34] The proviso contains a reference to 'processes, specific signals incorporated into algorithms or other adjustment or demotion mechanisms used in connection with the ranking are not required to disclose the detailed functioning of their ranking mechanisms, including algorithms'.[35] It does not appear that the Modernization of Consumer Protection Directive is going to protect consumers against adverse consequences of AI output. It also seems that the Trade Secrets Directive stands somewhat in the way of algorithmic transparency.

The provisions on data porting revert to information duties. Codes of Conduct must detail the information on data porting conditions (including technical and operational requirements) that traders should make available to their private individuals in a sufficiently detailed, clear and transparent manner before a contract is

[29] Directive (EU) 2019/1024 on open data and the re-use of public sector information, *OJ* L 172/56 (Open Data Directive); *Commission Communication*, 'Building a European Data Economy', COM (2017) 9 final.

[30] Free Flow of Non-Personal Data Regulation.

[31] Regulation 2017/1128/EU of the European Parliament and of the Council of 14 June 2017 on Cross-border Portability of Online Content Services in the Internal Market, [2017] *OJ* L 168/1 including corrigendum to regulation 2017/1128.

[32] GDPR, articles 13 and 20.

[33] The Free Flow of Non-Personal Data Regulation does not define 'non-personal data'. Cf. art. 3 of the Non-personal Data Regulation: '"Data" means data other than personal data as defined in point (1) of Article 4 of Regulation (EU) 2016/679'.

[34] Modernization of Consumer Protection Directive, recital (22).

[35] Directive (EU) 2016/943 of the European Parliament and of the Council of 8 June 2016 on the protection of undisclosed know-how and business information (trade secrets) against their unlawful acquisition, use and disclosure *OJ* L 157 (Trade Secrets Directive).

concluded.[36] In light of the limited scope of data portability regulation, there can be some doubt as to whether the high-level European data strategy is going to contribute to a human-centric development of AI.

14.2.4 Trustworthiness and Transparency

The next question is what regulatory requirements could emerge when AI will become ubiquitous in mutual transactions.[37] The Ethical Guidelines on AI in 2019 allude to seven key requirements for 'Trustworthy AI': (1) human agency and oversight; (2) technical robustness and safety; (3) privacy and data governance; (4) transparency, (5) diversity, non-discrimination and fairness; (6) environmental and societal well-being; and (7) accountability.[38] These non-binding guidelines address different topics, some of which fall outside the scope of private law principles. In this chapter, the focus is on transparency, accountability and other norms, notably traceability, contestability and veracity.[39] These notions are covered in the following discussion. First, it is established that opaqueness on technology use and lack of accountability could be perceived as being potentially harmful to consumers.[40] There are voices that claim that technology trustworthiness is essential for citizens and businesses that interact.[41] Is it up to Constitutional States to warrant and monitor technology trustworthiness, or should this be left to businesses? Does warranting technology trustworthiness not revive complex economic questions, such as how to deal with the possibility of adverse impact on competition or the stifling of innovation, when governments impose standardized technology norms to achieve a common level of technology trustworthiness – in the EU only? What if trust in AI is broken?

A possible denominator for trustworthiness may be transparency. Transparency is a key principle in different areas of EU law. A brief exploration of existing regulation reveals different tools to regulate transparency. Recent examples in 2019–2020 range from the Modernization of Consumer Protection Directive to the Online

36 Commission Communication DSM 2017, p. 2. The Commission mentions a number of activities, including online advertising platforms, marketplaces, search engines, social media and creative content outlets, application distribution platforms, communications services, payment systems and collaboration platforms.

37 *Commission Communication on Shaping Europe's Digital Future*, Brussels, 19.2.2020 COM (2020) 67 final; *White Chapter on Artificial Intelligence*, setting out options for a legislative framework for trustworthy AI, with a follow-up on safety, liability, fundamental rights and data (Commission Communication 2020).

38 Following two *Commission Communications* on AI supporting 'ethical, secure and cutting-edge AI made in Europe' (COM (2018)237 and COM (2018)795), a High-Level Expert Group on Artificial Intelligence was established: *Ethic Guidelines for Trustworthy AI*, 8 April 2019 (COM (2019)168; Ethic Guidelines AI 2019); https://ec.europa.eu/digital-single-market/en/high-level-expert-group-artificial-intelligence. The Guidelines seem to have been overridden by the White Paper AI 2020.

39 Ethic Guidelines AI 2019, p. 2.

40 e-Sides 2017, i.a., p. 85*ff*., and the attached lists.

41 Commission Communication AI 2018, para. 3.3.

Intermediary Services Regulation, the Ethical Guidelines on AI, the Open Data Directive and the 2020 White Paper on Artificial Intelligence.[42] All these instruments at least allude to the need for transparency in the algorithmic society. The Modernization of Consumer Protection Directive provides that more transparency requirements should be introduced. Would it be necessary to redefine transparency as a principle of private law in the algorithmic society? One could take this a step further: to achieve technology trustworthiness, should there be more focus on regulating *transparency* of AI and machine learning?[43] The Ethics Guidelines 2019 point at permission systems, fairness and explicability. From a private law perspective, especially permission systems could be considered to establish and safeguard trust. But reference is also made to the factual problem that consumers often do not take note of the provisions that drive the permission.

Explicability is not enshrined as a guiding principle. Nevertheless, transparency notions could be a stepping stone to obtaining explicability.[44] Accuracy may be a given. What matters is whether the consumer has the right and is enabled to contest an outcome that is presented as accurate.

14.3 CONSUMER RIGHTS, AI AND ADM

14.3.1 *Regulating AI through General Terms and Conditions*

There are two aspects regarding GTC that must be considered. First, contrary to permission systems, the general rule in private law remains that explicit acceptance of GTC by the consumer is not required, as long as the trader has made the terms available prior to or at the moment the contract is concluded. Contrary to jurisdictions that require parties to scroll through the terms, the European approach of accepting implied acceptance in practice leads to consumers' passiveness. Indeed, the system of implicit permission encourages consumers to not read GTC. Traders on digital platforms need to provide information on what technologies they use and how they are applied. Given the sheer importance of fundamental rights of human dignity and consumer rights when AI is applied, the question is whether consumers should be asked for explicit consent when the trader applies AI. It would be very simple for traders to implement consent buttons applying varied decision trees. But what is the use when humans must click through to complete a transaction? Take, for example, the system for obtaining cookies consent on digital platforms.[45] On the

42 White Paper AI 2020.

43 Ethic Guidelines AI 2019, p. 12–13: The Guidelines do not focus on consumers. Rather, the Guidelines address different stakeholders going in different directions.

44 P. Beddington, *Towards a Code of Ethics for Artificial Intelligence*, Springer International Publishing, 2017.

45 At the time of writing, the draft proposal Council Regulation concerning the respect for private life and the protection of personal data in electronic communications and repealing Directive 2002/58/EC COM 2017 final (draft Regulation on Privacy and Electronic Communications) was in limbo.

one hand, the traders (must) provide transparency on which technologies they employ. On the other hand, cookie walls prevent the consumer from making an informed decision, as they are coerced to accept the cookies. A recognizable issue with cookies in comparison with AI is that, often, it is the consumers who are unable to understand what the different technologies could mean for them personally. In the event the AI output matches their expectations or requirements, consumers are unlikely to protest prior consent given. Hence the real question is whether consumers should be offered a menu of choice beforehand, plus an option to accept or reject AI output or ADM. This example will be covered in the following discussion.

Second, where there is no negotiation or modification of the GTC, the consumer still will be protected by her right to either void or rescind black-, blue or grey-list contract provisions. Additionally, the EU Unfair Contract Terms Directive contains a blue list with voidable terms and conditions.[46] However, the black, grey and blue lists do not count for much. Rather, the GTC should contain clauses that oblige the trader to observe norms and principles such as traceability, contestability, transparency and veracity of the AI process. This begs the question of whether ethics guidelines and new principles could be translated into binding, positively formulated obligations or AI use. Rather than unilateral statements on data use, GTC could be subjected to comply with general principles and obligations.

The key for prospective regulation does not lie in art. 6 (1) Modernization of Consumer Protection Directive. Although this clause contains no less than twenty-one provisions on information requirements, including two new requirements on technical aspects, none of the requirements apply to providing the consumer information on the use of AI and ADM, let alone the contestability of the consumer transaction based thereon. Granted, there is an obligation for the trader to provide information on the scope of the services, but not on the specific use of AI technology. It is a very big step from the general information requirements to providing specific information on the application of AI and ADM in mutual transactions. When a consumer is subjected to AI processes, she should be advised in advance, not informed after the fact. A commentary to art. 6 clarifies that the traders must provide the information mentioned therein *prior* to the consumer accepting the contract terms (GTC).[47] The underlying thought is not new – to protect consumers, as weaker contractual parties, from concluding contracts that may be detrimental to them, and as a result of not having all the necessary information. Absent any relevant information, the consumer lags behind, especially in terms of not being informed adequately (1) that, (2) how and (3) for which purposes AI and machine learning is applied by the trader. The commentators generally feel that providing consumers with the relevant information prior to the conclusion of the contract is essential.

46 *Unfair Contract Terms Directive.*

47 J. Luzak and S. van der Hof, part II, chapter 2, in *Concise European Data Protection, E-Commerce and IT Law*, S. J. H. Gijrath, S. van der Hof, A. R. Lodder, G.-J. Zwenne, eds., 3rd edition, Kluwer Law International, 2018.

Knowing that the trader uses such technologies could be of utmost importance to the consumer. Even if she cannot oversee what the technological possibilities are, she should still get advance notice of the application of AI. Advance notice means a stand-still period during which she can make an informed decision. Going back to the cookie policy example, it is not onerous on the trader to offer the consumer a menu for choice beforehand. This would be especially relevant for the most used application of AI and ADM: profiling. The consumer should have the right to reject a profile scan that contains parameters she does not find relevant or which she perceives as being onerous on her. Granted, the trader will warn the consumer that she will not benefit from the best outcome, but that should be her decision. The consumer should have a say in this important and unpredictable process. She should be entitled to anticipating adverse consequences of AI for her.

The consumer must be able to trace and contest the AI output and ADM. The justification for such rights is discrimination, and lack of information on the essentials underlying the contract terms that come about through the private law principle of offer and acceptance. Granted, art. 9 Modernization of Consumer Protection Directive contains the generic right of withdrawal.[48] Contesting a consumer transaction based on AI is not necessary. The consumer can simply fill in a form to rescind the agreement. Regardless, the point of a consumer approach to AI use is not meant for the consumer to walk away. The consumer must have the right to know what procedures were used, what kind of outcome they produced, what is meant for the transaction and what she can do against it. As said, the consumer also must have a form of redress, not just against the trader but also against the developer of the AI software, the creator of the process, the third-party instructing the algorithms and/or the intermediary or supplier of the trader.

14.3.2 *Consumer Law Principles*

Which consumer law principles could be reignited in GTC that enable consumers to require the traders to be accountable for unfair processes or non-transparent output? This goes back to the main theorem. Transactions on digital platforms are governed by mutually agreed contract terms. It is still common practice that these are contained in GTC. Is there a regulatory gap that requires for Constitutional States to formulate new or bend existing conditions for traders using AI? The Bureau Européen des Unions de Consommateurs[49] proposes 'a set of transparency obligations to make sure consumers are informed when using AI-based products and services, particularly about the functioning of the algorithms involved and rights to object automated decisions'. The Modernization of Consumer Protection Directive is open for adjustment of consumer rights 'in the context of continuous

[48] Cf. the standard withdrawal form in Annex 1 to the Consumer Rights Directive.

[49] Bureau Européen des Unions de Consommateurs AISBL, *Automated Decision Making and Artificial Intelligence – A Consumer Perspective*, Position Chapter 20 June 2018 (BEUC 2018).

development of digital tools'. The Directive makes a clear-cut case for consumers catering for the adverse consequences of AI.[50] But it contains little concrete wording on AI use and consumers.[51] Embedding legal obligations for the trader in GTC could, potentially, be a very effective measure. There is one caveat, in that GTC often contain negatively formulated obligations.[52] Positively phrased obligations, such as the obligation to inform consumers that the trader employs AI, require further conceptual thinking. Another positively phrased obligation could be for the traders to explain the AI process and explain and justify the AI output.

14.3.2.1 Contestability

How unfair is it when consumers may be subject to decisions that are cast in stone (i.e., non-contestable)? An example is embedded contestability steps in smart consumer contracts. At their core, smart contracts are self-executing arrangements that the computer can make, verify, execute and enforce automatically under event-driven conditions set in advance. From an AI perspective, an almost limitless range of possibilities must be addressed in software terms. It is unlikely that these possibilities can be revealed step-by-step to the consumer. Consumers probably are unaware of the means of redress against AI output used in consumer transactions.[53] Applying a notion of contestability – not against the transaction but against the applied profiling methods or AI output – is no fad. If the system enables the consumer to test the correctness of the AI technology process and output, there must be a possibility of reconsidering the scope of the transaction. Otherwise, the sole remedy for the consumer could be a re-test of the AI process, which is a fake resolve. Indeed, the possibility of technological error or fraud underlines that a re-test is not enough. Traditional contract law remedies, such as termination for cause, could be explored. Furthermore, in connection with the information requirements, it would make sense to oblige traders to grant the consumer a single point of contact. This facilitates contesting the outcome with the trader or a third party, even if the automated processes are not monitored by the trader.[54]

14.3.2.2 Traceability, Veracity

Testing veracity requires reproducibility of the non-transparent machine learning process. Does a consumer have a justified interest in tracing the process steps of

50 Modernization of Consumer Protection Directive, recital (17).

51 Cf. Regulation (EU) 2017/2394 on cooperation between national authorities responsible for the enforcement of consumer protection laws and repealing Regulation (EC) No. 2006/2004 (OJ L 345, 27.12.2017, p. 1).

52 Cf. the Unfair Consumer Contract Terms Directive.

53 Modernization of Consumer Protection Directive, consideration (2).

54 Cf. the Online Intermediary Services Regulation where corrections can be made at the wholesale level.

machine learning, whether or not this has led to undesirable AI output? Something tells a lawyer that – no matter the output – as long as the AI output has an adverse impact on the consumer, it seems reasonable that the trader will have the burden of evidence that output is correct and, that, in order to be able to provide a meaningful correction request, the consumer should be provided with a minimum of necessary technical information that was used in the AI process. Traceability is closely connected with the requirement of accessibility to information, enshrined in the various legal instruments for digital platform regulation. As such, traceability is closely tied with the transparency norm.

It is likely that a trader using AI in a consumer transaction will escape from the onus on proving that the machine learning process, the AI output or the ADM is faulty. For the average consumer, it will be very difficult to provide evidence against the veracity of – both non-transparent *and* transparent – AI. The consumer is not the AI expert. The process of data analysis and machine learning does not rest in her hands. Besides, the trail of algorithmic decision steps probably is impossible to reconstruct. Hence, the consumer starts from a weaker position than the trader who applies AI. Granted, it was mentioned in Section 14.2.2 that it makes no practical sense for the consumer to ask for algorithmic transparency, should the consumer not agree with the output. The point is that at least the consumer should be given a chance to trace the process. Traceability – with the help of a third party who is able to audit the software trail – should be a requirement on the trader and a fundamental right for the consumer.

14.3.2.3 Transparency

Transparency is intended to solve information asymmetries with the consumer in the AI process. Transparency is tied closely with the information requirements laid down in the digital platforms and dating back to the Electronic Commerce Directive.[55] What is the consequence when information requirements are delisted because they have become technologically obsolete? Advocate General Pitruzzella proposed that the Court rule that an e-commerce platform such as Amazon could no longer be obliged to make a fax line available to consumers.[56] He also suggested that digital platforms must guarantee the choice of several different means of communication available for consumers and rapid contact

[55] Directive 2000/31/EC of the European Parliament and of the Council of 8 June 2000 on certain legal aspects of information society services, in particular electronic commerce, in the Internal Market [2000] OJ L 178/1 (Electronic Commerce Directive).

[56] Modernization of Consumer Protection Directive, recital (46); CJEU ECLI:EU:C:2019:576, Bundesverband der Verbraucherzentralen und Verbraucherverbände – Verbraucherzentrale Bundesverband e.V. v Amazon EU Sàrl, request for a preliminary ruling from the Bundesgerichtshof, 10 July 2019. The Court followed the non-binding opinion of the Advocate-General to revoke trader's obligations to provide certain additional information, such as a telephone or fax number.

and efficient communication.[57] By analogy, in the algorithmic society, transparency obligations on AI-driven platforms could prove to be a palpable solution for consumers. Providing transparency on the output also contributes to the consumer exercising some control over data use in the AI process, notwithstanding the argument that transparent algorithms cannot be explained to a private individual.

14.3.3 *Further Harmonization of Consumer Law in the Context of AI*

It should be considered whether the Unfair Commercial Practices Directive could be updated with terms that regulate AI.[58] At the high level, this Directive introduced the notion of 'good faith' to prevent imbalances in the rights and obligations of consumers on the one hand and sellers and suppliers on the other hand.[59] It should be borne in mind that consumer protection will become an even more important factor when the chain of consumer agreements with a trader becomes extended. Granted, the question of whether and how to apply AI requires further thinking on what types of AI and data use could constitute unfair contract terms. A case could be made of an earlier agreement voiding follow-up transactions, for example, because the initial contract formation requirements were not met as after AI deployment. But the impact of a voidable upstream contractual link on a downstream agreement in an AI-enabled or contract system is likely to raise different novel contract law questions, for instance, regarding third party liability.

In order to ensure that Member State authorities can impose effective, proportionate and dissuasive penalties in relation to widespread infringements of consumer law and to widespread infringements with an EU dimension that are subject to coordinated investigation and enforcement,[60] special fines could be introduced for the unfair application of AI.[61] Contractual remedies, including claims as a result of damages suffered from incorrect ADM, could be considered.

Prima facie, the Modernization of Consumer Protection Directive provides for the inclusion of transparency norms related to the parameters of ranking of prices and persons on digital platforms. However, the Directive does not contain an obligation to inform the consumer about the relative importance of ranking parameters and the reasons why and through what human process, if any, the input criteria were determined. This approach bodes well for the data strategy, but consumers

[57] Advocate General's Opinion in Case C-649/17 *Bundesverband der Verbraucherzentralen and Others* v. *Amazon EU*, CJEU, Press Release No. 22/19 Luxembourg, 28 February 2019.

[58] Directive 2005/29/EC of the European Parliament and of the Council of 11 May 2005 concerning unfair business-to-consumer commercial practices in the internal market (Unfair Commercial Practices Directive 2005), *OJ* 2005, L. 149.

[59] Unfair Contract Terms Directive, p. 29–34.

[60] Regulation (EU) 2017/2394.

[61] In order to ensure deterrence of the fines, Member States should set in their national law the maximum fine for such infringements at a level that is at least 4 per cent of the trader's annual turnover in the Member State or Member States concerned. Traders in certain cases can also be groups of companies.

could end up unhappy, for instance, if information about the underlying algorithms is not included in the transparency standard.

By way of an example, the Modernization of Consumer Protection Directive provides for a modest price transparency obligation at the retail level. It proposes a specific information requirement to inform consumers clearly when the price of a product or service presented to them is personalized on the basis of ADM. The purpose of this clause is to ensure that consumers can take into account the potential price risks in their purchasing decision.[62] But the proviso does not go as far as to determine how the consumer should identify these risks. Digital platforms are notoriously silent on price comparisons. Lacking guidance on risk identification results in a limited practical application of pricing transparency. What does not really help is that the Modernization of Consumer Protection Directive provides traders with a legal – if flimsy – basis for profiling and ADM.[63] This legal basis is, unfortunately, not supplemented by consumer rights that go beyond them receiving certain, non-specific information from the trader. The Modernization of Consumer Protection Directive, as it stands now, does not pass the test of a satisfactorily high threshold for consumer protection on AI-driven platforms.

14.4 CLOSING REMARKS

This chapter makes a case for a bottom-up approach to AI use in consumer transactions. The theorem was that the use of AI could well clash with the fundamental right of a high level of consumer protection. Looking at principles of contract law, there could be a regulatory gap when traders fail to be transparent on why and how they employ AI. Consumers also require a better understanding of AI processes and consequences of output, and should be allowed to contest the AI output.

Regulators alike could look at enhancing GTC provisions, to the extent that the individual does not bear the onus of evidence when contesting AI output. Consumers should have the right to ask for correction, modification and deletion of output directly from the traders. It should be borne in mind that the individual is contesting the way the output was produced, generated and used. The argument was made also that consumer rights could supplement the very limited personal data rights on AI.

When Constitutional States determine what requirements could be included in GTC by the trader, they could consider a list of the transparency principles. The list could include (1) informing the consumer prior to any contract being entered into that it is using AI; (2) clarifying for what purposes AI is used; (3) providing the consumer with information on the technology used; (4) granting the consumer

62 'Pricing that involves changing the price in a highly flexible and quick manner in response to market demands when it does not involve personalisation based on automated decision making.' Directive 2011/83/EU.

63 Modernization of Consumer Protection Directive, recital (45).

a meaningful, tailored and easy to use number of options in accepting or rejecting the use of AI and/or ADM, before it engages in such practice; (5) informing the consumer beforehand of possible adverse consequences for her if she refuses to submit to the AI; (6) how to require from the trader a rerun on contested AI output; (7) adhering to an industry-approved code of conduct on AI and making this code easily accessible for the consumer; (8) informing the consumer that online dispute resolution extends to contesting AI output and/or ADM; (9) informing the consumer that her rights under the GTC are without prejudice to other rights such under personal data regulation; (10) enabling the consumer – with one or more buttons – to say yes or no to any AI output, and giving her alternative choices; (11) enabling the consumer to contest the AI output or ADM outcome; (12) accepting liability for incorrect, discriminatory and wrongful output; (13) warranting the traceability of the technological processes used and allowing for an audit at reasonable cost and (14) explaining the obligations related to how consumer contracts are shared with a third party performing the AI process. These suggestions require being entitled to have a human, independent third party to monitor AI output, and the onus of evidence regarding the veracity of the output should be on the trader.

The fact that AI is aimed at casting algorithmic processes in stone to facilitate mutual transactions on digital platforms should not give traders a carte blanche, when society perceives a regulatory gap.

15

When the Algorithm Is Not Fully Reliable

The Collaboration between Technology and Humans in the Fight against Hate Speech

Federica Casarosa

15.1 INTRODUCTION

Our lives are increasingly inhabited by technological tools that help us with delivering our workload, connecting with our families and relatives, as well as enjoying leisure activities. Credit cards, smartphones, trains, and so on are all tools that we use every day without noticing that each of them may work only through their internal 'code'. Those objects embed software programmes, and each software is based on a set of algorithms. Thus we may affirm that most of (if not all) our experiences are filtered by algorithms each time we use such 'coded objects'.[1]

15.1.1 *A Preliminary Distinction: Algorithms and Soft Computing*

According to computer science, algorithms are automated decision-making processes to be followed in calculations or other problem-solving operations, especially by a computer.[2] Thus an algorithm is a detailed and numerically finite series of instructions which can be processed through a combination of software and hardware tools: Algorithms start from an initial input and reach a prescribed output, which is based on the subsequent set of commands that can involve several activities, such as calculation, data processing, and automated reasoning. The achievement of the solution depends upon the correct execution of the instructions.[3] However, it is

The contribution is based on the analysis developed within a DG Justice supported project e-NACT (GA no. 763875). The responsibility for errors and omissions remains with the author.

1 See Ben Wagner 'Algorithmic Regulation and the Global Default: Shifting Norms in Internet Technology' (2016) *Etikk i praksis: Nord J Appl Ethics* 5; Rob Kitchin and Martin Dodge *Code/Space Software and Everyday Life* (MIT Press, 2011).

2 See Jane Yakowitz Bambauer and Tal Zarsky 'The Algorithm Game' (2018) 94 *Notre Dame Law Review* 1.

3 The set of instructions can include different type of mathematical operations, ranging from linear equations to polynomial calculations, to matrix calculations, and so forth. Moreover, each instruction

important to note that, contrary to the common perception, algorithms are neither always efficient nor always effective.

Under the efficiency perspective, algorithms must be able to execute the instructions without exploiting an excessive amount of time and space. Although technological progress allowed for the development of increasingly more powerful computers, provided with more processors and a better memory ability, when algorithms execute instructions that produce great numbers which exceed the space available in memory of a computer, the ability of the algorithm itself to sort the problems is questioned.

As a consequence, under the effectiveness perspective, algorithms may not always reach the exact solution or the best possible solution, as they may include a level of approximation which may range from a second-best solution,[4] to a very low level of accuracy. In this case, computer scientists use the definition of 'soft computing' (i.e., the use of algorithms that are tolerant of imprecision, uncertainty, partial truth, and approximation), due to the fact that the problems that they are addressing may not be solved or may be solved only through an excessive time-consuming process.[5]

Accordingly, the use of these types of algorithms involves the possibility to provide solutions to hard problems, though these solutions, depending on the type of problems, may not always be the optimal ones. Given the ubiquitous use of algorithms processing our data and consequently affecting our personal decisions, it is important to understand in which occasions we may (or should) not fully trust the algorithm and add a human in the loop.[6]

15.1.2 *The Power of Algorithms*

According to Neyland,[7] we may distinguish between two types of power: one exercised *by* algorithms, and one exercised *across* algorithms. The first one is the traditional one, based on the ability of algorithms to influence and steer particular effects. The second one is based on the fact that 'algorithms are caught up within

can be another algorithm, which increases the level of complexity of the overall procedure. See Erika Giorgini 'Algorithms and Law' (2019) 5 *Italian Law Journal* 144.

4 A well-known example of this case is the Knapsack problem, where the goal is to select among a number of given items the ones that have the maximum total value. However, given that each item has a weight, the total weight that can be carried is no more than some fixed number X. So, the solution must consider weights of items as well as their value. Although in this case a recursive algorithm can find the best solution, when the number of items increases, the time spent to evaluate all the possible combinations increases exponentially, leading to suboptimal solutions.

5 See the definition at https://en.wikipedia.org/wiki/Soft_computing accessed 13 March 2020.

6 Council of Europe 'Algorithms and Human Rights – Study on the Human Rights Dimensions of Automated Data Processing Techniques and Possible Regulatory Implications' (2018) https://edoc.coe.int/en/internet/7589-algorithms-and-human-rights-study-on-the-human-rights-dimensions-of-automated-data-processing-techniques-and-possible-regulatory-implications.html accessed 13 March 2020.

7 Daniel Neyland, *The Everyday Life of an Algorithm* (Palgrave Macmillan, 2019).

a set of relations through which power is exercised'.[8] In this sense, it is possible to affirm the groups of individuals that at different stages play a role in the definition of the algorithm share a portion of power.

In practice, one may distinguish between two levels of analysis. Under the first one, for instance when we digit a query over a search engine, the search algorithm activates and identifies the best results related to the keywords inserted, providing a ranked list of results. These results are based on a set of variables that are dependent on the context of the keywords, but also on the trust of the source,[9] on the previous history of searches of the individual, and so forth. The list of results available will then steer the decisions of the individual and affect his/her interpretation of the information searched for. Such power should not be underestimated, because the algorithm has the power to restrict the options available (i.e., avoiding some content because evaluated as untruthful or irrelevant) or to make it more likely to select a specific option. If this can be qualified as the added value of algorithms able to improve the flaws of human reasoning, which include myopia, framing, loss aversion, and overconfidence,[10] then it also shows the power of the algorithm over individual decision-making.[11]

Under the second level of analysis, one may widen the view taking into account the criteria that are used to identify the search results, the online information that is indexed, the computer scientist that set those variables, the company that distributes the algorithm, the public or private company that uses the algorithm, and the individuals that may steer the selection of content. All these elements have intertwining relationships that show a more distributed allocation of power – and, as a consequence, a subsequent quest for a shared type of accountability and liability systems.

15.1.3 *The Use of Algorithms in Content Moderation*

In this chapter, the analysis will focus on those algorithms that are used for content detection and control over user-generated platforms, the so-called content moderation. Big Internet companies have always used filtering algorithms to detect and

8 Ibid. at 6.

9 As, for instance, the well-known algorithm used at the beginning by Google, namely Pagerank. See Larry Page et al. 'The PageRank Citation Ranking: Bringing Order to the Web' (1999) http://ilpubs.stanford.edu:8090/422/1/1999-66.pdf accessed 13 March 2020.

10 David Stevens 'In defence of "Toma": Algorithmic Enhancement of a Sense of Justice' in Mireille Hildebrandt and Keiran O'Hara (eds.) *Life and the Law in the Era of Data-Driven Agency* (Edward Elgar, 2010), analysing Mireille Hildebrandt, *Smart Technologies and the End(s) of Law: Novel Entanglements of Law and Technology* (Edward Elgar Publishing, 2015).

11 Kevin Slavin 'How Algorithms Shape Our World' (2011) www.ted.com/talks/kevin_slavin_how_algorithms_shape_our_world.html accessed 13 March 2020; Frank Pasquale 'The Algorithmic Self' (2015) *The Hedgehog Review*, Institute for Advanced Studies in Culture, University of Virginia. Note that this aspect is the premise of so-called surveillance capitalism as defined by Shoshana Zuboff in 'Big Other: Surveillance Capitalism and the Prospects of an Information Civilization' (2015) 30 *Journal of Information Technology* 75.

classify the enormous quantity of uploaded data daily. Automated content filtering is not a new concept on the Internet. Since the first years of Internet development, many tools have been deployed to analyse and filter content, and among them the most common and known are those adopted for spam detection or hash matching. For instance, spam detection tools identify content received in one's email address, distinguishing between clean emails and unwanted content on the basis of certain sharply defined criteria derived from previously observed keywords, patterns, or metadata.[12]

Nowadays, algorithms that are used for content moderation are widely diffuse, having the advantage of scalability. Such systems promise to make the process much easier, quicker, and cheaper than would be the case when using human labour.[13]

For instance, the LinkedIn network published the update of the algorithms used to select the best matches between employers and potential employees.[14] The first steps of the content moderation are worth describing: at the first step, the algorithms check and verify the compliance of the content published with the platform rules (leading to a potential downgrade of the visibility or complete ban in case of incompliance). Then, the algorithms evaluate the interactions that were triggered by the content posted (such as sharing, commenting, or reporting by other users). Finally, the algorithms weigh such interactions, deciding whether the post will be demoted for low quality (low interaction level) or disseminated further for its high quality.[15]

As the example of the LinkedIn algorithm clearly shows, the effectiveness of the algorithm depends on its ability to accurately analyse and classify content in its context and potential interactions. The capability to parse the meaning of a text is highly relevant for making important distinctions in ambiguous cases (e.g., when differentiating between contemptuous speech and irony).

For this task, the industry has now increasingly turned to machine learning to train their programmes to become more context sensitive. Although there are high expectations regarding the ability of content moderation tools, one should not underestimate the risks of overbroad censorship,[16] violation of the freedom of speech

[12] Thamarai Subramaniam, Hamid A. Jalab, and Alaa Y. Taqa 'Overview of Textual Anti-spam Filtering Techniques' (2010) 5 *International Journal of Physical Science* 1869.

[13] Christoph Krönke 'Artificial Intelligence and Social Media' in Thomas Wischmeyer and Timo Rademacher (eds.) *Regulating Artificial Intelligence* (Springer, 2019).

[14] For a description of the LinkedIn platform, see Jian Raymond Rui 'Objective Evaluation or Collective Self-Presentation: What People Expect of LinkedIn Recommendations' (2018) 89 *Computers in Human Behavior* 121.

[15] See the wider procedure described at https://engineering.linkedin.com/blog/2017/03/strategies-for-keeping-the-linkedin-feed-relevant accessed 13 March 2020.

[16] See, for instance, the wide debate regarding the effectiveness of filtering systems adopted at national level against child pornography. See Yaman Akdeniz *Internet Child Pornography and the Law – National and International Responses* (Routledge, 2016), and T. J. McIntyre and Colin Scott 'Internet Filtering – Rhetoric, Legitimacy, Accountability and Responsibility' in Roger Brownsword and Karen Yeung (eds.) *Regulating Technologies: Legal Futures, Regulatory Frames and Technological Fixes* (Bloomsbury Publishing, 2008).

principle, as well as biased decision-making against minorities and non-English speakers.[17] The risks are even more problematic in the case of hate speech, an area where the recent interventions of European institutions are pushing for more human and technological investments of IT companies, as detailed in the next section.

15.2 THE FIGHT AGAINST HATE SPEECH ONLINE

Hate speech is not a new phenomenon. Digital communication may be qualified only as a new arena for its dissemination. The features of social media pave the way to a wider reach of harmful content. 'Sharing' and 'liking' lead to a snowball effect, which allows the content to have a 'quick and global spread at no extra cost for the source'.[18] Moreover, users see in the pseudonymity allowed by social media an opportunity to share harmful content without bearing any consequence.[19] In recent years, there has been a significant increase in the availability of hate speech in the form of xenophobic, nationalist, Islamophobic, racist, and anti-Semitic content in online communication.[20] Thus the dissemination of hate speech online is perceived as a social emergency that may lead to individual, political, and social consequences.[21]

15.2.1 A *Definition of* Hate Speech

Hate speech is generally defined as speech 'designed to promote hatred on the basis of race, religion, ethnicity, national origin' or other specific group characteristics.[22]

[17] Natasha Duarte, Emma Llansó, and Anna Loup 'Mixed Messages? The Limits of Automated Social Media Content Analysis, Proceedings of the 1st Conference on Fairness, Accountability and Transparency' (2018) 81 *PMLR* 106.

[18] Katharina Kaesling 'Privatising Law Enforcement in Social Networks: A Comparative Model Analysis' (2018) *Erasmus Law Review* 151.

[19] Natalie Alkiviadou 'Hate Speech on Social Media Networks: Towards a Regulatory Framework?' (2019) 28 *Information & Communications Technology Law* 19.

[20] See Eurobarometer 'Special Eurobarometer 452 – Media Pluralism and Democracy Report' (2016) http://ec.europa.eu/information_society/newsroom/image/document/2016-47/sp452-summary_en_19666.pdf accessed 13 March 2020. See also Article 19 'Responding to "Hate Speech": Comparative Overview of Six EU Countries' (2018) www.article19.org/wp-content/uploads/2018/03/ECA-hate-speech-compilation-report_March-2018.pdf accessed 13 March 2020.

[21] See European Commission – Press Release 'A Europe That Protects: Commission Reinforces EU Response to Illegal Content Online' 1 March 2018 http://europa.eu/rapid/press-release_IP-18-1169_en.htm accessed 13 March 2020.

[22] Michel Rosenfeld 'Hate Speech in Constitutional Jurisprudence: A Comparative Analysis' (2002–2003) 24 *Cardozo L Rev* 1523; Alisdair A. Gillespie 'Hate and Harm: The Law on Hate Speech' in Andrej Savin and Jan Trzaskowski (eds.), *Research Handbook on EU Internet Law* (Edward Elgar, 2014); Natalie Alkiviadou 'Regulating Internet Hate: A Flying Pig?' (2016) 7 *Journal of Intellectual Property, Information Technology and E-Commerce Law* 3; Oreste Pollicino and Giovanni De Gregorio 'Hate Speech: una prospettiva di diritto comparato (2019) 4 *Giornale di Diritto Amministrativo* 421.

Although several international treaties and agreements do include hate speech regulation,[23] at the European level, such an agreed-upon framework is still lacking. The point of reference available until now is the Council Framework Decision 2008/913/JHA on Combatting Certain Forms and Expressions of Racism and Xenophobia by Means of Criminal Law.[24] As emerges from the title, the focus of the decision is the approximation of Member States' laws regarding certain offences involving xenophobia and racism, whereas it does not include any references to other types of motivation, such as gender or sexual orientation.

The Framework Decision 2008/913/JHA should have been implemented by Member States by November 2010. However, the implementation was less effective than expected: not all the Member States have adapted their legal framework to the European provisions.[25] Moreover, in the countries where the implementation occurred, the legislative intervention followed different approaches than the national approaches to hate speech, either through the inclusion of the offence within the criminal code or through the adoption of special legislation on the issue. The choice is not without effects, as the procedural provisions applicable to special legislation may be different to those applicable to offences included in the criminal code.

Given the limited effect of the hard law approach, the EU institutions moved to a soft law approach regarding hate speech (and, more generally, also illegal content).[26] Namely, EU institutions moved toward the use of forms of co-regulation where the Commission negotiates a set of rules with the private companies, under the assumption that the latter will have more incentives to comply with agreed-upon rules.[27]

As a matter of fact, on 31 May 2016, the Commission adopted a Code of Conduct on countering illegal hate speech online, signed by the biggest players in the online market: Facebook, Google, Microsoft, and Twitter.[28] The Code of Conduct requires

23 Note that the definitions of *hate speech* provided at international level focus on different facets of this concept, looking at content and at the manner of speech, but also at the effect and at the consequences of the speech. See the Rabat Plan of Action adopted by the United Nations in 2013, Annual report of the United Nations High Commissioner for Human Rights, A/HRC/22/17/Add.4.

24 Council Framework Decision on Combating Certain Forms and Expressions of Racism and Xenophobia by Means of Criminal Law, [2008] O.J. (L 328) 55 (Framework Decision 2008/913/JHA).

25 European Parliament 'Study on the Legal Framework on Hate Speech, Blasphemy and Its Interaction with Freedom of Expression' (2015) www.europarl.europa.eu/thinktank/en/document.html?reference=IPOL_STU%282015%29536460 accessed 13 March 2020.

26 See also the recent interventions on fake news and illegal content online, respectively the EU Code of Practice on Disinformation http://europa.eu/rapid/press-release_STATEMENT-19-2174_en.htm accessed 13 March 2020, and Commission Recommendation of 1.3.2018 on measures to effectively tackle illegal content online (C(2018) 1177 final https://ec.europa.eu/digital-single-market/en/news/commission-recommendation-measures-effectively-tackle-illegal-content-online accessed 13 March 2020.

27 Chris Marsden *Internet Co-regulation – European Law, Regulatory Governance, and Legitimacy in Cyberspace* (Cambridge University Press, 2011).

28 European Commission Press Release IP/16/1937 'European Commission and IT Companies Announce Code of Conduct on Illegal Online Hate Speech' (May 30, 2016); see also European Commission 'Countering Illegal Hate Speech Online #NoPlace4Hate' (2019) https://ec.europa.eu/

that the IT company signatories to the code adapt their internal procedures to guarantee that 'they review the majority of valid notifications for removal of illegal hate speech in less than 24 hours and remove or disable access to such content, if necessary'.[29] Moreover, according to the Code of Conduct, the IT companies should provide for a removal notification system which allows them to review the removal requests 'against their rules and community guidelines and, where necessary, national laws transposing the Framework Decision 2008/913/JHA'.

As is evident, the approach taken by the European Commission is more focused on the timely removal of the allegedly hate speech than on the procedural guarantees that such private enforcement mechanism should adopt in order not to unreasonably limit the freedom of speech of users. The most recent evaluation of the effects of the Code of conduct on hate speech shows an increased number of notifications that have been evaluated and eventually led to the removal of hate speech content within an ever-reduced time frame.[30]

In order to achieve such results, the signatory companies adopted a set of technological tools assessing and evaluating the content uploaded on their platforms. In particular, they finetuned their algorithms in order to detect potentially harmful content.[31] According to the figures provided by the IT companies regarding the flagged content, human labour alone may not achieve such task.[32] However, such algorithms may only flag content based on certain keywords, which are continuously updated, but they always lag behind the evolution of the language. And, most importantly, they may still misinterpret context-dependent wording.[33] Hate speech is a type of language that is highly context sensitive, as the same word may radically change its meaning if used at different places over time. Moreover, algorithms may be improved and trained in one language, but not in other languages which are less prominent in online communication. As a result, an algorithm that works only through the classifications of certain keywords cannot attain the level of complexity of human language and

newsroom/just/item-detail.cfm?item_id=54300 accessed 13 March 2020. Note that since 2018, five new companies joined the Code of Conduct: Instagram, Google+, Snapchat, Dailymotion and jeuxvideo.com. This brings the total number of companies that are part of the Code of Conduct to nine.

29 Ibid. at p. 2.

30 See the Commission Factsheet '5th evaluation of the Code of Conduct', June (2020) https://ec.europa.eu/info/sites/default/files/codeofconduct_2020_factsheet_12.pdf accessed 28 June 2021. In particular, the document highlights that 'on average 90% of the notifications are reviewed within 24 hours and 71% of the content is removed'.

31 See Sissi Cao 'Google's Artificial Intelligence Hate Speech Detector Has a "Black Tweet" Problem' (*Observer*, 13 August 2019) https://observer.com/2019/08/google-ai-hate-speech-detector-black-racial-bias-twitter-study/ accessed 13 March 2020.

32 See EU Commission 'Results of the Fourth Monitoring Exercise' https://ec.europa.eu/info/sites/info/files/code_of_conduct_factsheet_7_web.pdf accessed 13 March 2020. The Commission affirms that the testing evaluation provided for little more than 4,000 notifications in a period of 6 weeks, with a focus on only 39 organisations from 26 Member States.

33 Sean MacAvaney et al. 'Hate Speech Detection: Challenges and Solutions' (2019) 14(8) *PLOS One* 1.

runs the risk of producing unexpected false positives and negatives in the absence of context.[34]

15.2.2 *The Human Intervention in Hate Speech Detection and Removal*

One of the strategies able to reduce the risk of structural over-blocking is the inclusion of some human involvement in the identification and analysis of potential hate speech content.[35] Such human involvement can take different forms, either internal content checking or external content checking.[36]

In the first case, IT companies allocate to teams of employees the task of verifying the sensitive cases, where the algorithm was not able to single out if the content is contrary to community standards or not.[37] Given the high number of doubtful cases, the employees are subject to a stressful situation.[38] They are asked to evaluate in a very short time frame the potentially harmful content, in order to provide a decision regarding the opportunity to take the content down. This will then provide additional feedback to the algorithm, which will learn the lesson. In this framework, the algorithms automatically identify pieces of potentially harmful content, and the people tasked with confirming this barely have time to make a meaningful decision.[39]

The external content checking instead involves the 'trusted flaggers' – that is, an individual or entity which is considered to have particular expertise and

34 This is even more problematic in the case of image detection, as the recent case of the publication of the Led Zeppelin cover on Facebook was deemed contrary to community standards due to nudity and sexual images. See Rob Picheta 'Facebook Reverses Ban on Led Zeppelin Album Cover' (CNN, 21 June 2019) www.cnn.com/2019/06/21/tech/facebook-led-zeppelin-album-cover-scli-intl/index.html accessed 13 March 2020. For a wider analysis of the reasons to avoid the ubiquitous use of algorithms for decision-making, see Guido Noto la Diega 'Against the Dehumanisation of Decision-Making – Algorithmic Decisions at the Crossroads of Intellectual Property, Data Protection, and Freedom of Information' (2018) 9 JIPITEC 3.

35 Cambridge Consultants, 'The Use of AI in Content Moderation' (2019) www.ofcom.org.uk/__data/assets/pdf_file/0028/157249/cambridge-consultants-ai-content-moderation.pdf accessed 13 March 2020.

36 James Grimmelmann 'The Virtues of Moderation' (2015) 17 *Yale J.L. & Tech.* 42.

37 See the approach adopted by Facebook and Google in this regard: Issie Lapowsky 'Facebook Moves to Limit Toxic Content as Scandal Swirls' (Wired, 15 November 2018) www.wired.com/story/facebook-limits-hate-speech-toxic-content/ accessed 13 March 2020.; Sam Levin 'Google to Hire Thousands of Moderators after Outcry over YouTube Abuse Videos' (*The Guardian*, 5 December 2017), www.theguardian.com/technology/2017/dec/04/google-YouTube-hire-moderators-child-abuse-videos accessed 13 March 2020.

38 Nicolas P. Suzor *Lawless: The Secret Rules That Govern Our Digital Lives (and Why We Need New Digital Constitutions That Protect Our Rights)* (Cambridge University Press, 2019).

39 Sarah T. Roberts 'Commercial Content Moderation: Digital Laborers' Dirty Work' in S. U. Noble and B. Tynes (eds.) *The Intersectional Internet: Race, Sex, Class and Culture Online* (Peter Lang Publishing, 2016); Ben Wagner 'Liable, but Not in Control? Ensuring Meaningful Human Agency in Automated Decision-Making Systems' (2018) 11 *Policy & Internet* 104; Andrew Arsht and Daniel Etcovitch 'The Human Cost of Online Content Moderation' (2018) *Harvard Law Review* Online https://jolt.law.harvard.edu/digest/the-human-cost-of-online-content-moderation accessed 13 March 2020.

responsibilities for the purposes of tackling hate speech. Examples for such notifiers can range from individual or organised networks of private organisations, civil society organisations, and semi-public bodies, to public authorities.[40]

For instance, YouTube defines *trusted flaggers* as individual users, government agencies, and NGOs that have identified expertise, (already) flag content frequently with a high rate of accuracy, and are able to establish a direct connection with the platform. It is interesting to note that YouTube does not fully delegate the content detection to trusted notifiers but rather affirms that 'content flagged by Trusted Flaggers is not automatically removed or subject to any differential policy treatment – the same standards apply for flags received from other users. However, because of their high degree of accuracy, flags from Trusted Flaggers are prioritized for review by our teams'.[41]

15.3 THE OPEN QUESTIONS IN THE COLLABORATION BETWEEN ALGORITHMS AND HUMANS

The added value of the human intervention in the detection and removal of hate speech is evident; nonetheless, concerns may still emerge as regards such an involvement.

15.3.1 *Legal Rules versus Community Standards*

As hinted previously, both algorithms and humans involved in content detection and removal of hate speech evaluate content vis-à-vis the community standards adopted by each platform. Such distinction is clearly affirmed also in the YouTube trusted flaggers programme, where it is affirmed that 'the Trusted Flagger program exists exclusively for the reporting of possible Community Guideline violations. It is not a flow for reporting content that may violate local law. Requests based on local law can be filed through our content removal form'.

These standards, however, do not fully overlap with the legal definition provided by EU law, pursuant to the Framework Decision 2008/913/JHA.

Table 15.1 shows that the definitions provided by the IT companies widen the scope of the prohibition on hate speech to sex, gender, sexual orientation, disability or disease, age, veteran status, and so forth. This may be interpreted as the achievement of a higher level of protection. However, the width of the definition is not

40 Flagging is the mechanism provided by platforms to allow users to express concerns about potentially offensive content. This mechanism allows to reduce the volumes of content to be reviewed automatically. See Kate Klonick 'The New Governors: The People, Rules and Processes Governing Online Speech', 131 *Harvard Law Review* 1598, at 1626 (2018).

41 See 'YouTube Trusted Flagger Program' https://support.google.com/YouTube/answer/7554338?hl=en accessed 13 March 2020.

TABLE 15.1 *Hate speech as defined by several major IT companies*

Facebook definition[42]	YouTube definition[43]	Twitter definition[44]	Framework Decision 2008/913/JHA
What does Facebook consider to be hate speech? Content that attacks people based on their actual or perceived race, ethnicity, national origin, religion, sex, gender or gender identity, sexual orientation, disability or disease is not allowed. We do, however, allow clear attempts at humour or satire that might otherwise be considered a possible threat or attack. This includes content that many people may find to be in bad taste (example: jokes, stand-up comedy, popular song lyrics, etc.).	Hate speech refers to content that promotes violence against or has the primary purpose of inciting hatred against individuals or groups based on certain attributes, such as: - race or ethnic origin - religion - disability - gender - age - veteran status - sexual orientation/ gender identity.	*Hateful conduct*: You may not promote violence against or directly attack or threaten other people on the basis of race, ethnicity, national origin, sexual orientation, gender, gender identity, religious affiliation, age, disability, or serious disease. We also do not allow accounts whose primary purpose is inciting harm towards others on the basis of these categories.	All conduct publicly inciting to violence or hatred directed against a group of persons or a member of such a group defined by reference to race, colour, religion, descent or national or ethnic origin.

always coupled with a subsequent detailed definition of the selected grounds. For instance, the YouTube community standards list the previously mentioned set of attributes, providing some examples of hateful content. But the standard only sets two clusters of cases: encouragement towards violence against individuals or groups based on the attributes, such as threats, and the dehumanisation of individuals or groups (for instance, calling them subhuman, comparing them to animals, insects,

42 Facebook 'How Do I Report Inappropriate or Abusive Things on Facebook (Example: Nudity, Hate Speech, Threats)' www.facebook.com/help/212722115425932?helpref=uf_permalink accessed 13 March 2020.

43 Google 'Hate Speech Policy' https://support.google.com/YouTube/answer/2801939?hl=en accessed 13 March 2020.

44 Twitter 'Hateful Conduct Policy' https://help.twitter.com/en/rules-and-policies/hateful-conduct-policy accessed 13 March 2020.

pests, disease, or any other non-human entity).[45] The Facebook Community policy provides for a better example, as it includes a more detailed description of the increasing levels of severity attached to three tiers of hate speech content.[46] In each tier, keywords are provided to show the type of content that will be identified (by the algorithms) as potentially harmful.

As a result, the inclusion of such wide hate speech definitions within the Community Guidelines or Standards become de facto rules of behaviour for users of such services.[47] The IT companies are allowed to evaluate a wide range of potentially harmful content published on their platforms, though this content may not be illegal according to the Framework Decision 2008/914/JHA.

This has two consequences. First, there is an extended privatisation of enforcement as regards those conducts that are not covered by legal provisions with the risk of an excessive interference with the right to freedom of expression of users.[48] Algorithms deployed by IT companies will then have the power to draw the often-thin line between legitimate exercise of the right to free speech and hate speech.[49]

Second, the extended notion of harmful content provided by community rules imposes a wide obligation on platforms regarding the flow of communication. This may conflict with the liability regime adopted pursuant relevant EU law, namely the e-Commerce Directive, which imposes a three-tier distinction across intermediary liability and, most importantly, prohibits any general monitoring obligation over ISP pursuant art. 15.[50] As it will be addressed later, in the section on liability, striking the balance between sufficient incentives to block harmful content and over-blocking effects is crucial to safeguard the freedom of expression of users.

45 Article 19, 'YouTube Community Guidelines: Analysis against International Standards on Freedom of Expression' (2018) www.article19.org/resources/YouTube-community-guidelines-analysis-against-international-standards-on-freedom-of-expression/ accessed 13 March 2020.

46 Article 19, 'Facebook Community Standards: Analysis against International Standards on Freedom of Expression' (2018) www.article19.org/resources/facebook-community-standards-analysis-against-international-standards-on-freedom-of-expression/ accessed 13 March 2020.

47 Wolfang Benedek and Matthias C. Kettemann *Freedom of Expression and the Internet* (Council of Europe Publishing, 2013), 101. See the decision of Italian courts on this matter, as presented in F. Casarosa, 'Does Facebook get it always wrong? The decisions of Italian courts between hate speech and political pluralism', presented at Cyberspace conference, November 2020.

48 Council of Europe, Draft Recommendation CM/Rec (2017x)xx of the Committee of Ministers to Member States on the Roles and Responsibilities of Internet Intermediaries, MSI-NET (19 September 2017).

49 National and European courts are still struggling in identifying such boundary; see, for instance, the rich jurisprudence of the ECtHR, European Court of Human Rights Press Unit, Factsheet – Hate Speech (January 2020), www.echr.coe.int/Documents/FS_Hate_speech_ENG.pdf accessed 13 March 2020.

50 Note that this principle is also confirmed by the Council of Europe (n 48).

15.3.2 *Due Process Guarantees*

As a consequence of the previous analysis, the issue of procedural guarantees of users emerges.[51] A first question is related to the availability of internal mechanisms that allow users to be notified about potentially harmful content, to be heard, and to review or appeal against the decisions of IT companies. Although the strongest position safeguarding freedom of expression and fair trial principle would suggest that any restriction (i.e., any removal of potentially harmful content) should be subject to judicial intervention,[52] the number of decisions adopted on a daily basis by IT companies does not allow either the intervention of potential victims and offenders, or the judicial system. It should be noted that the Code of Conduct does not provide for any specific requirement in terms of judicial procedures, nor through alternative dispute resolution mechanisms, thus it is left to the IT companies to introduce an appeal mechanism.

Safeguards to limit the risk of removal of legal content are provided instead in the Commission Recommendation on Tackling Illegal Content Online,[53] which includes within the wider definition of illegal content also hate speech.[54] The Recommendation points to automated content detection and removal and underlines the need for counter-notice in case of removal of legal content. The procedures involve the exchange between the user and the platform, which should provide a reply: in case of evidence provided by the user that the content may not be qualified as illegal, the platform should restore the content that was removed without undue delay or allow for a re-upload by the user; whereas, in case of a negative decision, the platform should include reasons for said decision.

Among the solutions, the signatories to the Code of Conduct proposed Google provides for a review mechanism, allowing users to present an appeal against the decision to take down any uploaded content.[55] Then, the evaluation of the justifications provided by the user is processed internally and the final decision is sent afterward to the user, with limited or no explanation.

A different approach is adopted by Facebook. In September 2019, the social network announced the creation of an 'Oversight Board'.[56] The Board has the task of providing the appeals for selected cases that address potentially harmful content.

[51] Giancarlo Frosio 'Why Keep a Dog and Bark Yourself? From Intermediary Liability to Responsibility' (2018) 26 *Oxford Int'l J. of Law and Information Technology* 1.

[52] See, for instance, the suggestion made by UN Rapporteur Frank La Rue, in Report of the Special Rapporteur on the Promotion and Protection of the Right to Freedom of Opinion and Expression (2011) www2.ohchr.org/english/bodies/hrcouncil/docs/17session/A.HRC.17.27_en.pdf, p. 13 accessed 13 March 2020.

[53] Commission Recommendation 2018/334 on measures to effectively tackle illegal content online, C/2018/1177, OJ L 63, 6.3.2018, pp. 50–61

[54] Ibid., at 3.

[55] See Google 'Appeal Community Guidelines Actions' https://support.google.com/YouTube/answer/185111 accessed 13 March 2020.

[56] For a detailed description of the structure and role of the Oversight Board, see Facebook 'Establishing Structure and Governance for an Independent Oversight Board' (Facebook Newsroom, 17 September 2019) https://newsroom.fb.com/news/2019/09/oversight-board-structure/ accessed

Although the detailed regulation concerning the activities of the board is still to be drafted, it is clear that it will not be able to review all the content under appeal.[57] Although this approach has been praised by scholars, several questions remain open: the transparency in the selection of the people entrusted with the role of adjudication, the type of explanation for the decision taken, the risk of capture (in particular for the oversight board), and so on. And, at the moment, these questions are still unanswered.

15.3.3 *Selection of Trusted Flaggers*

As mentioned previously in Section 15.2.2., the intervention of trusted flaggers in content detection and removal became a crucial element in order to improve the results of said process. The selection process to identify and recruit trusted flaggers, however, is not always clear.

According to the Commission Recommendation, the platforms should 'publish clear and objective conditions' for determining which individuals or entities they consider as trusted flaggers. These conditions include expertise and trustworthiness, and also 'respect for the values on which the Union is founded as set out in Article 2 of the Treaty on European Union'.[58]

Such a level of transparency does not match with the practice: although the Commission Monitoring exercise provides for data regarding at least four IT companies, with a percentage of notifications received by users vis-à-vis trusted flaggers as regards hate speech,[59] apart from the previously noted YouTube programme, none of the other companies provide a procedure for becoming a trusted flagger. Nor is any guidance provided on whether the selection of trusted notifiers is a one-time accreditation process or rather an iterative process whether the privilege is monitored and can be withdrawn.[60]

13 March 2020, and Facebook 'Oversight Board Charter' (Facebook Newsroom, 19 September 2019) https://fbnewsroomus.files.wordpress.com/2019/09/oversight_board_charter.pdf accessed 13 March 2020.

57 The figures can clarify the challenge: the number of board members is currently set at 40 people, while the number of cases under appeal yearly by Facebook is 3.5 million (only related to hate speech), according to the 2019 Community Standards Enforcement Report https://transparency.facebook.com/community-standards-enforcement#hate-speech accessed 13 March 2020.

58 Commission (2018) Recommendation 2018/334 of 1 March 2018 on measures to effectively tackle illegal content online, C/2018/1177, OJ L 63, 6.3.2018, pp. 50–61.

59 See also the figures provided in Commission Factsheet, 'How the Code of Conduct Helped Countering Illegal Hate Speech Online', February (2019) https://ec.europa.eu/info/sites/info/files/hatespeech_infographic3_web.pdf accessed 13 March 2020. The Commission report affirms that 'The IT companies reported a considerable extension of their network of 'trusted flaggers' in Europe and are engaging on a regular basis with them to increase understanding of national specificities of hate speech. In the first year after the signature of the Code of conduct, Facebook reported to have taken 66 EU NGOs on board as trusted flaggers; and Twitter 40 NGOs in 21 EU countries.'

60 Sebastian Schwemer 'Trusted Notifiers and the Privatization of Online Enforcement' (2018) 35 *Computer Law & Security Review*.

This issue should not be underestimated, as the risk of rubberstamping the decisions of trusted flaggers may lead to over-compliance and excessive content takedown.[61]

15.3.4 *Liability Regime*

When IT companies deploy algorithms and recruit trusted flaggers in order to proactively detect and remove potentially harmful content, they may run the risk of losing their exemption of liability according to the e-Commerce Directive.[62] According to art. 14 of the Directive, hosting providers are exempted from liability when they meet the following conditions:

- Service providers provide only for the storage of information at the request of third parties;
- Service providers do not play an active role of such a kind as to give it knowledge of, or control over, that information.

According to the decision of the CJEU in *L'Oréal* v. *eBay*,[63] the Court of Justice clarified that whenever an online platform provides for the storage of content (in the specific case offers for sale), sets the terms of the service, and receives revenues from such service, this does not change the position of the hosting provider denying the exemptions from liability. In contrast, this may happen when the hosting provider 'has provided assistance which entail, in particular optimising the presentation of the offers for sale in question or promoting those offers'.

This indicates that the active role of the hosting provider is only to be found when it intervenes directly in user-generated content.[64] If the hosting provider adopts technical measures to detect and remove hate speech, does it fail its neutral position vis-à-vis the content?

The liability exemption may still apply only if two other conditions set by art. 14 e-Commerce Directive apply. Namely,

61 Note that evidence from the SCAN project highlights that removal rates differs between the reporting channels used to send the notification, with an average of 15 per cent higher, with the exceptional case of Google+, where all the notified cases were accepted by the company. See SCAN 'Diverging Responsiveness on Reports by Trusted Flaggers and General Users – 4th Evaluation of the EU Code of Conduct: SCAN Project Results' (2018) http://scan-project.eu/wp-content/uploads/2018/08/sCAN_monitoring1_fact_sheet_final.pdf accessed 13 March 2020.

62 Directive 2000/31/EC, of the European Parliament and of the Council of 8 June 2000 on Certain Legal Aspects of Information Society Services, in Particular Electronic Commerce, in the Internal Market, [2000] O.J. (L 178) 1, 16 (e-Commerce Directive). Note that the proposed Digital Services Act, COM(2020) 825 final, confirms that providers of intermediary services are not subject to general monitoring obligations.

63 Case 324/09 *L'Oréal SA and Others* v. *eBay International AG and Others* [2011] ECR I-06011.

64 Christina Angelopoulos et al. 'Study of Fundamental Rights Limitations for Online Enforcement through Self-Regulation' (2016) https://openaccess.leidenuniv.nl/handle/1887/45869 accessed 13 March 2020.

- hosting providers do not have actual knowledge of the illegal activity or information and, as regards claims for damages, are not aware of facts or circumstances from which the illegal activity or information is apparent; or
- upon obtaining such knowledge or awareness, they act expeditiously to remove or to disable access to the information.

It follows that proactive measures taken by the hosting provider may result in that platform obtaining knowledge or awareness of illegal activities or illegal information, which could thus lead to the loss of the liability exemption. However, if the hosting provider acts expeditiously to remove or to disable access to content upon obtaining such knowledge or awareness, it will continue to benefit from the liability exemption.

From a different perspective, it is possible that the development of technological tools may lead to a reverse effect as regards monitoring obligations applied over IT companies. According to art. 15 of the e-Commerce Directive, no general monitoring obligation may be imposed on hosting providers as regards illegal content. But in practice, algorithms may already deploy such tasks. Would this indirectly legitimise monitoring obligations applied by national authorities?

This is the question posed by an Austrian court to the CJEU as regards hate speech content published on the social platform Facebook.[65] The preliminary reference addressed the following case: in 2016, the former leader of the Austrian Green Party, Eva Glawischnig-Piesczek was the subject of a set of posts published on Facebook by a fake account. The posts included rude comments, in German, about the politician, along with her image.[66]

Although Facebook complied with the injunction of the First Instance court across the Austrian country, blocking access to the original image and comments, the social platform appealed against the decision. After the appeal decision, the case achieved the Oberste Gerichtshof (Austrian Supreme Court). Upon analysing the case, the Austrian Supreme Court affirmed that Facebook can be considered as an abettor to the unlawful comments; thus it may be required to take steps so as to repeat the publication of identical or similar wording. However, in this case, the injunction regarding such a pro-active role for Facebook could indirectly impose a monitoring role, which is in conflict not only with art. 15 of the e-Commerce Directive but also with the previous jurisprudence of the CJEU. Therefore, the Supreme Court decided to stay the proceedings and present a preliminary reference to the CJEU. The Court asked, in particular, whether art. 15(1) of the e-Commerce Directive precludes the national court to make an order requiring a hosting provider,

65 Case C-18/18, *Eva Glawischnig-Piesczek* v. *Facebook Ireland Limited* [2019] ECLI:EU:C:2019:821.

66 Ms Glawischnig-Piesczek requested Facebook to delete the image and the comments, but it failed to do so. Ms Glawischnig-Piesczek filed a lawsuit before the Wien first instance court, which eventually resulted in an injunction against Facebook, which obliged the social network not only to delete the image and the specific comments, but also to delete any future uploads of the image if it was accompanied by comments that were identical or similar in meaning to the original comments.

who has failed to expeditiously remove illegal information, not only to remove the specific information but also other information that is identical in wording.[67]

The CJEU decided the case in October 2019. The decision argued that as Facebook was aware of the existence of illegal content on its platform, it could not benefit from the exemption of liability applicable pursuant to art. 14 of the e-Commerce Directive. In this sense, the Court affirmed that, according to recital 45 of the e-Commerce Directive, national courts cannot be prevented from requiring a host provider to stop or prevent an infringement. The Court then followed the interpretation of the AG in the case,[68] affirming that no violation of the prohibition of monitoring obligation provided in art. 15(1) of the e-Commerce Directive occurs if a national court orders a platform to stop and prevent illegal activity if there is a genuine risk that the information deemed to be illegal can be easily reproduced. In these circumstances, it was legitimate for a Court to prevent the publication of 'information with an equivalent meaning'; otherwise the injunction would be simply circumvented.[69]

Regarding the scope of the monitoring activity allocated to the hosting provider, the CJEU acknowledged that the injunction cannot impose excessive obligations on an intermediary and cannot require an intermediary to carry out an independent assessment of equivalent content deemed illegal, so automated technologies could be exploited in order to automatically detect, select, and take down equivalent content.

The CJEU decision tries as much as possible to provide a balance between freedom of expression and freedom to conduct a business, but the wide interpretation of art. 15 of the e-Commerce Directive can have indirect negative effects, in particular when looking at the opportunity for social networks to monitor through technological tools the upload of identical or equivalent information.[70] This

67 Questions translated by the preliminary reference decision of the Oberste Gerichtshof, OGH, case number 6Ob116/17b.

68 In his opinion, A. G. Szpunar affirmed that an intermediary does not benefit from immunity and can 'be ordered to seek and identify the information equivalent to that characterised as illegal only among the information disseminated by the user who disseminated that illegal information. A court adjudicating on the removal of such equivalent information must ensure that the effects of its injunction are clear, precise and foreseeable. In doing so, it must weigh up the fundamental rights involved and take account of the principle of proportionality'.

69 The CJEU then defined information with an equivalent meaning as 'information conveying a message the content of which remains essentially unchanged and therefore diverges very little from the content which gave rise to the finding of illegality' (par. 39).

70 See Agnieszka Jabłonowska 'Monitoring Duties of Online Platform Operators Before the Court – Case C-18/18 Glawischnig-Piesczek' (6 October 2019) http://recent-ecl.blogspot.com/2019/10/monitoring-duties-of-platform-operators.html; Eleftherios Chelioudakis 'The *Glawischnig-Piesczek* v. *Facebook* Case: Knock, Knock. Who's There? Automated Filters Online' (12 November 2019) www.law.kuleuven.be/citip/blog/the-glawischnig-piesczek-v-facebook-case-knock-knock-whos-there-automated-filters-online/ accessed 13 March 2020; Marta Maroni and Elda Brogi '*Eva Glawischnig-Piesczek* v. *Facebook Ireland Limited*: A New Layer of Neutrality' (2019) https://cmpf.eui.eu/eva-glawischnig-piesczek-v-facebook-ireland-limited-a-new-layer-of-neutrality/ accessed 13 March 2020.

approach safeguards the incentives for hosting providers to verify the availability of harmful content without incurring additional levels of liability. However, the use of technical tools may pave the way to additional cases of false positives, as they may remove or block content that is lawfully used, such as journalistic reporting on a defamatory post – thus opening up again the problem of over-blocking.

15.4 CONCLUDING REMARKS

Presently, we are witnessing an intense debate about technological advancements in algorithms and their deployment in various domains and contexts. In this context, content moderation and communication governance on digital platforms have emerged as a prominent but increasingly contested field of application for automated decision-making systems. Major IT companies are shaping the communication ecosystem in large parts of the world, allowing people to connect in various ways across the globe, but also offering opportunities to upload harmful content. The rapid growth of hate speech content has triggered the intervention of national and supranational institutions in order to restrict such unlawful speech online. In order to overcome the differences emerging at the national level and enhance the opportunity to engage international IT companies, the EU Commission adopted a co-regulatory approach inviting the same table regulators and regulates, so as to defined shared rules.

This approach has the advantage of providing incentives for IT companies to comply with shared rules, as long as non-compliance with voluntary commitments does not lead to any liability or sanction. Thus the risk of over-blocking may be avoided or at least reduced. Nonetheless, considerable incentives to delete not only illegal but also legal content exist. The community guidelines and standards presented herein show that the definition of hate speech and harmful content is not uniform, and each platform may set the boundaries of such concepts differently. When algorithms apply criteria defined on the basis of such different concepts, they may unduly limit the freedom of speech of users, as they will lead to the removal of legal statements.

The Commission approach explicitly demands proactive monitoring: 'Online platforms should, in light of their central role and capabilities and their associated responsibilities, adopt effective proactive measures to detect and remove illegal content online and not only limit themselves to reacting to notices which they receive'. But this imposes de facto monitoring obligations which may be carried out through technical tools, which are far from being without flaws and bias.

From the technical point of view, the introduction of the human in the loop, such as in the cases of trusted flaggers or the Facebook Oversight board, does not reduce the questions of effectiveness, accessibility, and transparency of the mechanisms adopted. Both strategies, however, show that some space for stronger accountability mechanisms can be found, though the path to be pursued is still long.

16

Smart Contracts and Automation of Private Relationships

Pietro Sirena and Francesco Paolo Patti

16.1 INTRODUCTION

Technological advancements and cyberspace have forced us to reconsider the existing limitations of private autonomy. Within the field of contract law, according to regulatory strategies, the public dimension affects private interests in several ways. These include the application of mandatory rules and enforcement mechanisms capable of obtaining certain results and granting a sufficient level of effectiveness. This is particularly the case in European contract law, where the law pursues regulatory goals related to the establishment and the enhancement of a common European market.[1]

The digital dimension represents a severe challenge for European and national private law.[2] In order to address the implications of the new technologies on private law, recent studies were conducted inter alia on algorithmic decisions, digital platforms, the Internet of Things, artificial intelligence, data science, and blockchain technology. The broader picture seems to indicate that, in the light of the new technologies, the freedom to conduct business has often turned into power. Digital firms are no longer only market participants: rather, they are becoming market makers capable of exerting regulatory control over the terms on which others can sell goods and services.[3] In so doing, they are replacing the exercise of states' territorial sovereignty with functional sovereignty. This situation

[1] See generally Stefan Grundmann, 'The Structure of European Contract Law' (2001) 4 *Eur Rev Contr L* 505. On mandatory rules on consumer contracts, see Gerhard Wagner, 'Zwingendes Vertragsrecht' in Horst Eidenmüller et al., *Revision des Verbraucher-acquis* (Mohr Siebeck 2011) 1, 1–4.

[2] See especially Stefan Grundmann and Philipp Hacker, 'The Digital Dimension as a Challenge to European Contract Law' in Stefan Grundmann (ed.), *European Contract Law in the Digital Age* (Intersentia 2018) 3–45; Alberto De Franceschi and Reiner Schulze (eds.), 'Digital Revolution – New Challenges for the Law: Introduction' in *Digital Revolution – New Challenges for the Law* (C. H. Beck 2019) 1–15; Matthias Weller and Matthias Wendland (eds.), *Digital Single Market – Bausteine eines eines Digitalen Binnenmarkts* (Mohr Siebeck 2019).

[3] Alessandro Morelli and Oreste Pollicino, 'Metaphors, Judicial Frames and Fundamental Rights in Cyberspace' (2020) *Am J Comp L* 1, 26 (forthcoming).

raised concern in different areas of law and recently also in the field of competition law.[4]

As Lawrence Lessig pointed out, in the mid-1990s, cyberspace became a new target for libertarian utopianism where freedom from the state would reign.[5] According to this belief, the society of this space would be a fully self-ordering entity, cleansed of governors and free from political hacks. Lessig was not a believer of the described utopian view. He correctly pointed out the need to govern cyberspace, as he understood that left to itself, cyberspace would become a perfect tool of 'Control. Not necessarily control by government.'[6] These observations may be connected to the topic of private authorities who exercise power over other private entities with limited control by the state. The issue was tackled in a study by an Italian scholar which is now more than forty years old,[7] and more recently by several contributions on different areas of private law.[8] The emergence of private authorities was also affirmed in the context of global governance.[9] These studies were able to categorize forms and consequences of private authorities, to identify imbalances of power, envisage power-related rules of law, and question the legitimacy of private power. One of the main problems is that private authorities can be resistant to the application and enforcement of mandatory rules.

The present chapter aims to investigate whether and how blockchain technology platforms and smart contracts could be considered a modern form of private authority, which at least partially escapes the application of mandatory rules and traditional enforcement mechanisms.[10] Blockchain technology presents itself as democratic in nature, as it is based on an idea of radical decentralization.[11] This is in stark contrast to giant Big Tech corporations working over the internet in the fields of social networking, online search, online shopping, and so forth; with blockchain,

4 Viktoria H. S. E. Robertson, 'Excessive Data Collection: Privacy Considerations and Abuse of Dominance in the Era of Big Data' (2020) 57 *CML Rev* 161–190. On price discrimination based on big data, see Chiara Muraca and Mariateresa Maggiolino, 'Personalized Prices under EU Antitrust rules' (2019) *Eu Comp L Rev* 483.

5 Lawrence Lessig, *Code. Version* 2.0 (Basic Books 2006) 2: 'The space seemed to promise a kind of society that real space would never allow–freedom without anarchy, control without government, consensus without power.'

6 Lessig (n 5) 3. On whether cyberspace required new regulations, see also Frank H. Easterbrook, 'Cyberspace and the Law of the Horse' (1996) *U Chicago Leg Forum* 207–216.

7 C. Massimo Bianca, *Le autorità private* (Jovene 1977).

8 See Florian Möslein (ed.), *Private Macht* (Mohr Siebeck 2016); Kit Barker et al. (eds.), *Private Law and Power* (Hart Publishing 2017); Pietro Sirena and Andrea Zoppini (eds.), *I poteri privati e il diritto della regolazione* (Roma Tre Press 2018).

9 Rodney Bruce Hall and Thomas J Biersteker, *The Emergence of Private Authority in Global Governance* (Cambridge University Press 2009).

10 A relevant problem that is not tackled in the present essay is the liability of the blockchain-platforms' operators in cases of bugs or hacks. See Luigi Buonanno, 'Civil Liability in the Era of New Technology: The Influence of Blockchain' (16 September 2019). Bocconi Legal Studies Research Paper No. 3454532, September 2019, Available at SSRN: https://ssrn.com/abstract=3454532 (outlining a 'European strategy' to face the severe challenges).

11 See William Magnuson, *Blockchain Democracy. Technology, Law and the Rule of the Crowd* (Cambridge University Press 2020) 61–90.

technology users put their trust in a network of peers. Nevertheless, as happened with the internet, market powers could create monopolies or highly imbalanced legal relationships.[12] In this sense, contractual automation seems to play a key role in understanding the potentialities and the risks involved in the technology. In general terms, one of the main characteristics of a smart contract is its self-executing character, which should eliminate the possibility of a breach of contract. But smart contracts may also provide for effective self-help against breaches of traditional contracts. Finally, when implemented on blockchain platforms, smart contract relationships may also benefit from the application of innovative dispute resolution systems, which present themselves as entirely independent from state authorities.

16.2 SMART CONTRACTS: MAIN CHARACTERISTICS

In his well-recognized paper entitled 'Formalizing and Securing Relationships on Public Networks', Nick Szabo described how cryptography could make it possible to write computer software able to resemble contractual clauses and bind parties in a way that would almost eliminate the possibility of breaching an agreement.[13] Szabo's paper was just a first step, and nowadays basically every scholar interested in contract law may expound on the essentials of how a smart contract functions. Some jurisdictions, such as in Italy, have also enacted rules defining a smart contract.[14] The great interest is due to the growing adoption of Bitcoin and other blockchain-based systems, as for instance Ethereum.[15] The latter provides the necessary technology to carry out Szabo's ideas.

Smart contracts do not differ too greatly from natural language agreements with respect to the parties' aims or interests.[16] In reality, except where the decision to conclude the contract is taken by an 'artificial intelligent agent', they solely form a technological infrastructure that makes transactions cheaper and safer.[17] The main

[12] Ibid. 5.

[13] Nick Szabo, 'Formalizing and Securing Relationships on Public Networks' (1997) 2 (9) *First Monday*, at https://doi.org/10.5210/fm.v2i9.548.

[14] See article 8-ter Decreto legge 14 December 2018, n. 135 (converted in Legge 11 February 2019, n. 12): 'Si definisce "smart contract" un programma per elaboratore che opera su tecnologie basate su registri distribuiti e la cui esecuzione vincola automaticamente due o più parti sulla base di effetti predefiniti dalle stesse.' ('Smart contracts' are defined as computer programs that operate on distributed registers-based technologies and whose execution automatically binds two or more parties according to the effects predefined by said parties.) With respect to the Italian provision, see Andrea Stazi, *Automazione contrattuale e contratti intelligenti. Gli* smart contracts *nel diritto comparato* (Giappichelli 2019) 134–135.

[15] See Primavera De Filippi and Aaron Wright, *Blockchain and the Law. The Rule of Code* (Harvard University Press 2018) 74.

[16] See generally Eliza Mik, 'The Resilience of Contract Law in Light of Technological Change' in Michael Furmston (ed.), *The Future of the Law of Contract* (Routledge 2020) 112 (opposing all theories seeking to modify the principles of contract law due to the fact that a given transaction is mediated by technology).

[17] See Kevin Werbach and Nicholas Cornell, 'Contracts Ex Machina' (2017) 67 *Duke LJ* 313, 318 (declaring that 'Algorithmic enforcement allows contracts to be executed as quickly and cheaply as other computer code. Cost savings occur at every stage, from negotiation to enforcement, especially in replacing judicial enforcement with automated mechanisms').

quality of a smart contract relies on the automation of contractual relationships, as the performance is triggered by an algorithm in turn triggered by the fulfilment of certain events. In this sense, there is often talk of a distinction between the notions of 'smart contract' and 'smart legal contract' with the result that contractual automation in the majority of cases affects only its performance.[18] In contrast, the contract as such (i.e., the legal contract) is still a product of the meetings of the minds, through an offer and an acceptance.[19] In many cases, this induces parties to 'wrap' the smart contract in paper and to 'nest' it in a certain legal system.[20]

It is therefore often argued that 'smart contract' is a misnomer as the 'smart' part of the contract in reality affects only the performance.[21] In addition, smart contracts are not intelligent but rely on an 'If-Then' principle, which means, for instance, that a given performance will be executed only when the agreed-upon amount of money is sent to the system.[22] These critics seem to be correct, and this goes some way to demystifying the phenomenon,[23] which is sometimes described as a game-changer that will impact every contractual relationship.[24] Discussions are beginning to be held on automated legal drafting, through which contractual clauses are shaped on the basis of big data by machine learning tools and predictive technologies, but for now, they do not really affect the emerging technology of smart contracts on blockchain platforms.[25] The latter work is based on rather simple software protocols

[18] See Mateja Durovic and Fanciszek Lech, 'The Enforceability of Smart Contracts' (2019) 5 *Italian LJ* 493, 499.

[19] See especially Gregorio Gitti, 'Robotic Transactional Decisions' (2018) *Oss dir civ comm* 619, 622; Mateja Durovic and André Janssen, 'The Formation of Blockchain-Based Smart Contracts in the Light of Contract Law' (2018) 26 *Eur Rev Priv L* 753–771 ('neither on-chain nor off-chain smart contracts are really challenging the classic elements of English Common Law on formation of contracts – offer and acceptance, consideration, intention to create legal relations, and capacity').

[20] Jason G. Allen, 'Wrapped and Stacked: "Smart Contracts" and the Interaction of Natural and Formal Language' (2018) 14 *Eur Rev Contr L* 307–343.

[21] See Scott A. McKinney, Rachel Landy, and Rachel Wilka, 'Smart Contracts, Blockchain, and the Next Frontier of Transactional Law' (2018) 13 *Wash J L Tech & Arts* 313, 322 ('A smart contract, however, is not actually very "smart." Smart contracts do not (at least, as of the date of this Article) include artificial intelligence, in that a smart contract does not learn from its actions'); Jeffrey M. Lipshaw, 'The Persistence of Dumb Contracts' (2019) 2 *Stan J Blockchain L & Pol'y* 1. With specific regard to the well-known 'TheDAO' hack, see the critics of Adam J. Kolber, 'Not-So-Smart Blockchain Contracts and Artificial Responsibility' (2018) 21 *Stan Tech L Rev* 198. See also Blaise Carron and Valentin Botteron, 'How Smart Can a Contract Be?' in Daniel Kraus et al. (eds.), *Blockchains, Smart Contracts, Decentralised Autonomous Organisations and the Law* (Edward Elgar 2019) 101.

[22] See, e.g., Eliza Mik, 'Smart Contracts: Terminology, Technical Limitations and Real World Complexity' (2017) 9 *L Innovation & Tech* 269.

[23] See, in this regard, André Janssen, 'Demystifying Smart Contracts' in Corjo J. H. Jansen et al. (eds.), *Onderneming en Digitalisering* (Wolters Kluwer 2019) 15–29, at 22–23.

[24] See, e.g., the optimistic view of Jeff Lingwall and Ramya Mogallapu, 'Should Code Be Law: Smart Contracts, Blockchain, and Boilerplate' (2019) 88 *UMKC L Rev* 285.

[25] See, generally, Kathryn D. Betts and Kyle R. Jaep, 'The Dawn of Fully Automated Contract Drafting: Machine Learning Breathes New Life into a Decades Old Promise' (2017) 15 *Duke L & Tech Rev* 216; Lauren Henry Scholz, 'Algorithmic Contracts' (2017) 20 *Stan Tech L Rev* 128; Spencer Williams,

and other code-based systems, which are programmed ex ante without the intervention of artificial intelligence.[26]

Nevertheless, the importance of the 'self-executing' and 'self-enforcing' character of smart contracts should not be undermined. Most of the benefits arising from the new technology are in fact based on these two elements, which represent a source of innovation for general contract law. The 'self-executing' character should eliminate the occurrence of contractual breaches, whereas the 'self-enforcing' character makes it unnecessary to turn to the courts in order to obtain legal protection.[27] In addition, the code does not theoretically require interpretation, as it should not entail the need to explain ambiguous terms.[28] Currently, it is not clear whether smart contracts will diminish transaction costs, due to the complexity of digital solutions and the need to acquire the necessary knowledge.[29] For reasons that will be outlined, costs of implementation seem not to harm the potential spread of smart contracts, especially in the fields of consumer contracts and the Internet of Things.

16.3 SELF-EXECUTION AND SELF-ENFORCEMENT

As stated before, through the new technology one or more aspects of the contract's execution become automated, and having once entered into the contract, parties cannot prevent performance from being executed. Smart contracts use blockchain to ensure the transparency of the contractual relationship and to create trust in the capacity to execute the contract, which depends on the involved technology. As previously stated, the operation is based on 'If-Then' statements, which are one of the most basic building blocks of any computer program.

Undeniably, such a technology can easily govern the simple contractual relationship, in which the system has only to determine where a given amount of money has been paid in order to have something in return (e.g., a digital asset) or where the

'Predictive Contracting' (2019) *Colum Bus L Rev* 621. With respect to the differences between traditional contracts concluded through particular technological devices and contractual automation, which involves the use of AI, see Tom Allen and Robin Widdison, 'Can Computers Make Contracts' (1996) 9 *Harv J L & Tech* 25. On the philosophical implications, cf. Karen Yeung, 'Why Worry about Decision-Making by Machine?' in Karen Yeung and Martin Lodge (eds.), *Algorithmic Regulation* (Oxford University Press 2019) 21.

26 On the different technological steps that lead to a smart contract execution on a blockchain platform, see Michèle Finck, 'Grundlagen und Technologie von Smart Contracts' in Martin Fries and Boris P. Paal (eds.), *Smart Contracts* (Mohr Siebeck 2019) 1, 4–8. See also Valentina Gatteschi, Fabrizio Lamberti, and Claudio et al., 'Technology of Smart Contracts' in Larry A. DiMatteo et al. (eds.), *The Cambridge Handbook of Smart Contracts, Blockchain Technology and Digital Platforms* (Cambridge University Press 2019) 37.

27 See Finck (n 26) 9.

28 Cf. Michel Cannarsa, 'Interpretation of Contracts and Smart Contracts: Smart Interpretation or Interpretation of Smart Contracts?' (2018) 26 *Eur Rev Priv L* 773 (pointing out that computer language is deterministic (just one meaning and one result are conceivable), whereas natural language is open to more and potential different meanings).

29 Janssen (n 23) at 24–25.

performance is due when certain external conditions of the real world are met. Since a modification of the contractual terms of a smart contract implemented on a blockchain platform is hardly possible, execution appears certain and personal trust or confidence in the counterparty is not needed.[30] This has led to the claim that in certain situations, contracting parties will face the 'cost of inflexibility', as blockchain-based smart contracts are difficult to manipulate and therefore resistant to changes.[31] In fact, smart contracts are built on the assumption that there will not be modifications after the conclusion of the contract. As a result, if or when circumstances relevant to the smart contract change, a whole new contract would need to be written.

'Inflexibility' is often considered a weakness of smart contracts.[32] Supervening events and the change of circumstances may require parties to intervene in the contractual regulation and provide for some amendments.[33] Therefore, legal systems contain rules that may lead to a judicial adaptation of the contract, sometimes through a duty to renegotiate its content.[34] In this regard, smart contracts differ from traditional contracts, as they take an ex ante view instead of the common ex post judicial assessment view of law.[35]

In reality, this inflexibility does not constitute a weakness of smart contracts. Instead, it makes clear that self-execution and self-enforcement could bring substantial benefits only in certain legal relationships, where parties are interested in a simple and instantaneous exchange. Moreover, self-execution does not necessarily affect the entire agreement. Indemnity payouts, insurance triggers, and various other provisions of the contract could be automated and self-fulfilling, while other provisions may remain subject to an ordinary bargain and be expressed in natural language.[36] One can therefore correctly state that smart contracts automatically perform obligations which arise from legal contracts but not necessarily all the obligations. Finally, it should be observed that future contingencies that impact the contractual balance, as for instance an increase of the raw materials' price, could be assessed through lines of code, in order to rationally adapt the contractual performance.[37]

30 Rolf H. Weber, 'Smart Contracts: Do We Need New Legal Rules?' in De Franceschi and Schulze (n 2) 299, 302.

31 Enrico Seidel, Andreas Horsch, and Anja Eickstädt, 'Potentials and Limitations of Smart Contracts: A Primer from an Economic Point of View' (2020) 31 *Eur Bus L Rev* 169, 176–179.

32 Jeremy M. Sklaroff, 'Smart Contracts and the Cost of Inflexibility' (2017) 166 *U Penn L Rev* 263 (arguing that forms of flexibility – linguistic ambiguity and enforcement discretion – create important efficiencies in the contracting process). See also Finck (n 26) 11.

33 See generally Rodrigo A. Momberg Uribe, *The Effect of a Change of Circumstances on the Binding Force of Contracts Comparative Perspectives* (Intersentia 2011).

34 Ibid.

35 Eric Tjong Tjin Tai, 'Force Majeure and Excuses in Smart Contracts' (2018) 26 *Eur Rev Priv L* 787.

36 See McKinney, Landy, and Wilka (n 21) 325.

37 Ibid. at 338.

The latter issue makes clear that often the conditions for contractual performance relate to the real and non-digital world outside of blockchains. It is therefore necessary to create a link between the real world and the blockchain. Such a link is provided by the so-called oracles, which could be defined as interfaces through which information from the real world enters the 'digital world'. There are different types of oracles,[38] and some scholars argue that their operation harms the self-executing character of smart contracts, because the execution is eventually remitted to an external source.[39] Due to the technology involved, oracles do not seem to impact the automated execution of smart contracts. The main challenge with oracles is that contracting parties need to trust these outside sources of information, whether they come from a website or a sensor. As oracles are usually third-party services, they are not subject to the security blockchain consensus mechanisms. Moreover, mistakes or inaccuracies are not subject to rules that govern breach of contract between the two contracting parties.

In the light of the above, self-execution and self-enforcement assure an automated performance of the contract. Nevertheless, whether due to an incorrect intervention of an oracle, for a technological dysfunction, or for an error in the programming, things may go wrong and leave contracting parties not satisfied. In these cases, there could be an interest in unwinding the smart contract. According to a recent study,[40] this can be done in three ways. Needless to say, the parties can unwind the legal contract in the old-fashioned way by refunding what they have received from the other party, be it voluntarily or with judicial coercion. At any rate, it would be closer to the spirit of fully automated contracts, if the termination of the contract and its unwinding could also be recorded in the computer code itself and thus carried out automatically.[41] Finally, it is theoretically possible to provide for technical modifications of the smart contract in the blockchain. The three options, as also argued by the author,[42] are not easily feasible and there is the risk of losing the advantages related to self-execution. It is therefore of paramount importance to devote attention

[38] See, e.g., 'software oracles', which handle information data that originates from online sources, as temperature, prices of commodities and goods, flight or train delays, and so forth; 'hardware oracles', which take information directly from the physical world; 'inbound oracles', which provide data from the external world; 'outbound oracles', which have the ability to send data to the outside world; and 'consensus-based oracles', which get their data from human consensus and prediction markets (e.g., Augur, based on Ethereum).

[39] See Janssen (n 23) 23 (declaring that every oracle added to a smart contract decreases the self-enforcement level).

[40] Olaf Meyer, 'Stopping the Unstoppable: Termination and Unwinding of Smart Contracts' (2020) *EuCML* 17, at 20–24.

[41] See Larry A. DiMatteo and Cristina Poncibó, 'Quandary of Smart Contracts and Remedies: The Role of Contract Law and Self-Help Remedies' (2018) 26 *Eur Rev Priv L* 805 (observing: 'It is in the area of self-enforcement and remedies where the vision of smart contracts confronts the reality of contract law and business lawyering. Smart contracts need to be drafted by lawyers, focused on client interests and not technological prowess').

[42] Meyer (n 40) 24.

to the self-help and dispute resolution mechanisms developed on blockchain-platforms.[43]

16.4 AUTOMATED SELF-HELP

The functioning of smart contracts may also determine a new vast array of self-help tools (i.e., enforcement mechanisms that do not require the intervention of state power). The examples of self-help that have recently been discussed are related to Internet of Things technology.[44] The cases under discussion affect self-enforcement devices that automatically react in the presence of a contractual breach and put the creditor in a position of advantage with respect to that of the debtor. The latter, who is in breach, cannot exercise any legal defence vis-à-vis automated self-help based on algorithms. Scholars who addressed the issue stressed the dangers connected to a pure exercise of private power through technology.[45]

Among the most frequent examples, there is the lease contract, for which a smart contract could automatically send a withdrawal communication in case of a two-month delay in the payment of the lease instalment. If the lessee does not pay the due instalment within one month, the algorithm automatically locks the door and prevents the lessee from entering into the apartment. Another example is the 'starter interrupt device', which can be connected to a banking loan used to buy a vehicle. If the owner does not pay the instalments, the smart contract prevents the vehicle from starting. Similar examples are present in the field of utilities (gas, electricity, etc.).[46] If the customer does not pay for the service, the utilities are no longer available. In looking to general contractual remedies, the potentiality of such self-help instruments appears in reality almost unlimited. Automation could also affect the payment of damages or liquidated damages.

Self-help devices take advantage of technology and put in the creditors' hands an effective tool, which – at the same time – reduces the costs of enforcement and significantly enhances the effectiveness of contractual agreements. This is mainly due to the fact that recourse to a court is no longer necessary. Contractual

43 See Section 16.4.

44 Robin Matzke, 'Smart Contracts statt Zwangsvollstreckung? Zu den Chancen und Risiken der digitalisierten privaten Rechtsdurchsetzung' in Fries and Paal (n 26) 99, 103. See generally, on Internet of Things liability issues, Christiane Wendehorst, 'Consumer Contracts and the Internet of Things' in Reiner Schulze and Dirk Staudenmayer (eds.), *Digital Revolution: Challenges for Contract Law in Practice* (Hart Publishing 2016) 189; Francesco Mezzanotte, 'Risk Allocation and Liability Regimes in the IoT' in De Franceschi and Schulze (n 2) 169; specifically on consumer contracts, Katarzyna Kryla-Cudna, 'Consumer Contracts and the Internet of Things' in Vanessa Mak et al. (eds.), *Research Handbook in Data Science and Law* (Edward Elgar 2018) 83.

45 See Thomas Riehm, 'Smart Contracts und verbotene Eigenmacht' in Fries and Paal (n 26) 85; Florian Möslein, 'Legal Boundaries of Blockchain Technologies: Smart Contracts as Self-Help?' in De Franceschi and Schulze (n 2) 313.

46 With reference to the German legal system, see Christoph G. Paulus and Robin Matzke, 'Smart Contracts und Smart Meter – Versorgungssperre per Fernzugriff' (2018) *NJW* 1905.

automation may increase the awareness of the importance of fulfilling obligations in time. Moreover, the reduction of costs related to enforcement may lead to a decrease in prices for diligent contracting parties. At any rate, as correctly pointed out, the described 'technological enforcement' – although effective – does not necessarily respect the requirements set by the law.[47] In other words, even if smart contracts are technologically enforceable, they are not necessarily also legally enforceable.[48] In the examples outlined previously, it is possible to imagine a withdrawal from the contract without due notice or the payment of an exorbitant sum of money as damages.

How should the law react to possible deviations between the code and the law? It seems that a kind of principle of equivalent treatment should provide guidance to resolving cases:[49] limits that exist for the enforcement of traditional contracts should be extended to smart contracts. From a methodological point of view, practical difficulties in applying the law should not prevent an assessment of the (un)lawful character of certain self-help mechanisms. In cases where the law provides for mandatory proceedings or legal steps in order to enforce a right, the same should in principle apply to smart contracts.

Nevertheless, evaluation of the self-help mechanisms' lawfulness should not be too strict, and should essentially be aimed at protecting fundamental rights – for instance, the right to housing. The 'automated enforcement' relies on party autonomy and cannot be considered as an act of oppression exercised by a 'private power' per se. Therefore, apart from the protected rights, the assessment should also involve the characteristics of the contracting parties and the subject matter of the contract. In this regard, it was correctly pointed out that EU law provides for some boundaries of private autonomy in consumer contracts, which apply to smart contracts.[50]

For instance, the unfair terms directive[51] indicates that clauses, which exclude or hinder a consumer's right to take legal action, may create a significant imbalance in parties' rights and obligations.[52] The same is stated with respect to clauses irrevocably binding the consumer to terms with which she or he had no real opportunity of becoming acquainted before the conclusion of the contract.[53] According to

47 Möslein (n 45) 318.

48 See Max Raskin, 'The Law and Legality of Smart Contracts' (2017) 1 *Geo L Tech Rev* 305 (pointing out: 'The central problem in the final question of contract law is what happens when the outcomes of the smart contract diverge from the outcomes that the law demands'). With respect to blockchain technology, see also Roger Brownsword, 'Automated Transactions and the Law of Contract. When Codes Are Not Congruent' in Furmston (n 16) 94, 102 (declaring: 'If such technological enablement or disablement is at variance with what a court applying the law of contract would order, then we have a question of non-congruence').

49 Such a principle is discussed, in the context of contractual automation, by Brownsword, ibid. 102–110.

50 See Möslein (n 45) 323–324.

51 Council Directive 93/13/EEC of 5 April 1993 on unfair terms in consumer contracts [1993] OJ L 95/29.

52 Ibid., annex, terms referred to in article 3(3), let (q).

53 Ibid., let (i).

prevailing opinion, the scope of application of the unfair terms directive also covers smart contracts, even if the clauses are expressed through lines of code.[54]

Undeniably, smart contracts may pose difficulties to consumers when it comes to exercising a right against illicit behaviour on behalf of the business. At any rate, it would not be proper to consider the self-help systems directly unlawful. The enforcement of EU consumer law is also granted by public authorities,[55] which in the future may exercise control with respect to the adopted contractual automation processes and require modifications in the computer protocol of the businesses. If the self-help reacts to a breach of the consumer, it should not in principle be considered unfair. On the one hand, contractual automation may provide for lower charges, due to the savings in enforcement costs. On the other hand, it could augment the reliability of consumers by excluding opportunistic choices and making them immediately aware of the consequences of the breach. Finally – as will be seen – technological innovation must not be seen only as a menace for consumers, as it could also provide for an improvement in the application of consumer law and, therefore, an enhancement of its level of effectiveness.[56]

16.5 AUTOMATED APPLICATION OF MANDATORY RULES

A huge debate has affected the application of mandatory rules in the field of smart contracts. The risk that this innovative technology could be used as an instrument to fulfil unlawful activities, as the conclusion of immoral or criminal contracts, is often pointed out.[57] The mode of operation may render smart contracts and blockchain technology attractive to ill-intentioned people interested in engaging in illicit acts.

Among the mandatory rules that may be infringed by smart contracts, special attention is dedicated to consumer law.[58] The characteristics of smart contracts make them particularly compatible with the interests of individual businesses in business-to-consumer relationships, as blockchain technology can guarantee a high level of standardization and potentially be a vehicle for the conclusion of mass contracts. In terms of the application of mandatory consumer law to smart contracts, opinions differ significantly. According to one author, smart contracts will determine the end of consumer law, as they may systematically permit businesses to

54 See Janssen (n 23) 26 (arguing that the unfair terms directive does not per se require a textual form of the contractual terms in order to apply).

55 On the different enforcement mechanisms in the field of unfair terms, see generally Hans-Wolfgang Micklitz, 'Unfair Terms in Consumer Contracts' in Norbert Reich et al. (eds.), *European Consumer Law* (2nd ed., Intersentia 2014) 136; Peter Rott, 'Unfair Contract Terms' in Christian Twigg-Flesner (ed.), *Research Handbook on EU Consumer and Contract Law* (Edward Elgar 2016) 287, 293–296.

56 On the notion of effectiveness in EU consumer law, see generally Norbert Reich, 'The Principle of Effectiveness and EU Contract Law' in Jacobien Rutgers and Pietro Sirena (eds.), *Rules and Principles in European Contract Law* (Intersentia 2015) 45–68.

57 See generally De Filippi and Wright (n 15) at 86–88; Magnuson (n 11) 91–170.

58 See Tatiana Cutts, 'Smart Contracts and Consumers (2019) 122 *W Va L Rev* 389.

escape its application.[59] The claim has also been made that automated enforcement in the sector of consumer contracts amounts to an illusion, as mandatory rules prevent the use of automated enforcement mechanisms.[60]

Both opinions seem slightly overstated and do not capture the most interesting aspect related to smart consumer contracts. In fact, as has been recently discussed, technology and contractual automation may also be used as a tool to enforce consumer law and augment its level of effectiveness.[61] Many consumers are indeed not aware of their rights or, even if they are, find it difficult to enforce them, due to emerging costs and a lack of experience. In addition, most consumer contractual claims are of insignificant value.

In this regard, a very good example is given by the EU Regulation on Compensation of Long Delay of Flights.[62] The consumer has a right to get a fixed compensation, depending on the flight length, ranging from 125,00 to 600,00 euros. For the reasons outlined previously, what often happens is that consumers do not claim compensation; the compensation scheme thus lacks effectiveness. In the interest of consumers, reimbursement through a smart contract device has been proposed to automate the process.[63] The latter would work on the basis of a reliable system of external interfaces.[64] The proposal seems feasible and is gaining attention, especially in Germany, where the introduction of the smart compensation scheme in cases of cancellations or delays of flights has been discussed in Parliament.[65]

Two possible drawbacks are related to the described types of legislative intervention. Due to the wide distribution of the technology, which crosses national borders, the adoption of smart enforcement may produce strong distortions to international competition.[66] For instance, the imposition of a smart compensation model as the

59 Alexander Savelyev, 'Contract Law 2.0: "Smart" Contracts as the Beginning of the End of Classic Contract Law', Higher School of Economics Research Paper No. WP BRP 71/LAW/2016, available at SSRN: https://ssrn.com/abstract=2885241.

60 See Danielle D'Onfro, 'Smart Contracts and the Illusion of Automated Enforcement' (2020) 61 *Wash U J L & Pol'y* 173 (arguing that 'The volume of consumer protection laws, and their tendency to change over time, all but eliminates the prospect of coding smart contracts for perfect compliance ex-ante').

61 See Oscar Borgogno, 'Smart Contracts as the (New) Power of the Powerless? The Stakes for Consumers' (2018) 26 *Eur Rev Priv L* 885; Janssen (n 23) 26–29.

62 Regulation (EC) No 261/2004 of the European Parliament and of the Council of 11 February 2004 establishing common rules on compensation and assistance to passengers in the event of denied boarding and of cancellation or long delay of flights, and repealing Regulation (EEC) No 295/91 [2004] OJ L 46/1. On the latter, see generally Ricardo Pazos, 'The Right to a Compensation In Case Of Long Delay of Flights: A Proposal for a Future Reform' (2019) 27 *Eur Rev Priv L* 695(indicating i.a. the most relevant decisions of the European Court of Justice, which not seldom escape from the wording of the Regulation, especially with respect to long delays).

63 Borgogno (n 61) 897–898.

64 Ibid.

65 See for details Martin Fries, 'Schadensersatz ex machina' (2019) *NJW* 901; Anusch Alexander Tavakoli, 'Automatische Fluggast-Entschädigung durch smart contracts' (2020) *ZRP* 46.

66 See generally, on the regulatory challenges, Vincent Mignon, 'Blockchains – Perspectives and Challenges' in Kraus et al. (n 21) 1, 9.

one discussed in Germany for the delay or the cancellation of flights may lead to an increase in the costs for flight companies that operate predominantly in that country. In order not to harm the aims of the internal market, smart enforcement should thus be implemented on a European level.

Another danger of the proposed use of smart contract devices is 'over-enforcement'.[67] The latter may be detrimental because it could prevent businesses from running an activity in order to escape liability and sanctions. The described adoption of technology in cases of flight delays may determine a digitalization of enforcement that drastically drops the rate of unpaid compensations to almost zero. The outlined scenario is not necessarily convenient for consumers, as the additional costs sustained by flight companies would probably be passed on to all customers through an increase in prices. The level of technology required to automatically detect every single delay of an airplane, and grant compensation to the travellers would probably lead to an explosion in costs for companies. While this may increase efficiency in the sector, it is questionable whether such a burden would be bearable for the flight companies. That is not to say that this risk automatically means strict enforcement is inherently evil: enforcement of existing rules is of course a positive aspect. Nevertheless, the economic problems it may give rise to should lead to the consideration of enforcement through technological devices as an independent element that could in principle also require modifications of substantive law.[68] For instance, the technology could enable recognition of 'tailored' amounts of compensation depending on the seriousness of the delay.[69]

Many aspects seem uncertain, and it is not surprising that as things stand, smart enforcement mechanisms are not (yet) the core of legislative intervention.[70] In reality, the current regulatory approach appears quite the opposite. Legislators are not familiar with the new technologies and are tending towards lightening the obstacles set by mandatory rules to blockchain technology with the aim of not harming its evolution.[71] In many legal systems, contained 'regulatory sandboxes'

67 See generally Franz Hofmann, 'Smart Contracts und Overenforcement – Analytische Überlegungen zum Verhältnis von Rechtszuweisung und Rechtsdurchsetzung' in Fries and Paal (n 26) 125.

68 Ibid., at 130.

69 In the aforementioned context of compensation for flight delays or cancellation, the somewhat futuristic proposals for a 'personalization' of the legal treatment could be of interest: see, generally, Ariel Porat and Lior Jacob Strahilevitz, 'Personalizing Default Rules and Disclosure with Big Data' (2014) 112 *Mich L Rev* 1417; Omri Ben-Shahar and Ariel Porat, 'Personalizing Mandatory Rules in Contract Law' (2019) 86 *U Chi L Rev* 255. With respect to consumer law, see also Christopher G. Bradley, 'The Consumer Protection Ecosystem: Law, Norms, and Technology' (2019) 97 *Denv L Rev* 35.

70 See for an assessment Nico Kuhlmann, 'Smart Enforcement bei Smart Contracts' in Fries and Paal (n 26) 117.

71 Michèle Finck, 'Blockchains: Regulating the Unknown' (2018) 19 *German LJ* 665, 687 (arguing that there are very few blockchain experts, and most regulators have not yet familiarized themselves with the available knowledge on the matter). On the different regulatory techniques concerning blockchain technology, see also Karen Yeung, 'Regulation by Blockchain: The Emerging Battle for

were created,[72] in order to support companies exercising their activities in the fields of fintech and blockchain technology. In general terms, regulatory sandboxes enable companies to test their products with real customers in an environment that is not subject to the full application of legal rules. In this context, regulators typically provide guidance, with the aim of creating a collaborative relationship between the regulator and regulated companies. The regulatory sandbox can also be considered a form of principles-based regulation because it lifts some of the more specific regulatory burdens from sandbox participants by affording flexibility in satisfying the regulatory goals of the sandbox.[73] The described line of reasoning shows the willingness of legislators not to prevent technological progress and to help out domestic companies. The approach inevitably brings clashes when it comes to the protection of consumers' interests.[74]

16.6 SMART CONTRACTS AND DISPUTE RESOLUTION

Even if the claim 'code is law' or the expression 'lex cryptographica'[75] may appear exaggerated, it seems evident that developers of smart contracts and blockchain platforms are aiming to create an order without law and implement a private regulatory framework. Achieving such a goal requires shaping a model of dispute resolution capable of resolving conflicts in an efficient manner, without the intervention of national courts and state power.[76] The self-executing character of smart contracts may not prevent disputes occasionally arising between parties, connected for instance to defects in the product purchased or to the existence of an unlawful act. Moreover, the parties' agreement cannot always be encoded in 'if-then' statements and should be encompassed in non-deterministic notions and general clauses such as, for example, good faith and reasonableness. Unless artificial intelligence develops to the stage where a machine can substitute human reasoning in filling gaps of the contract or putting into effect general clauses,[77] contractual disputes may still arise. The way smart contracts operate could lead parties to abandon the digital

Supremacy between the Code of Law and Code as Law' (2019) 82 *Modern L Rev* 207; Roger Brownsword, 'Smart Contracts: Coding the Transaction, Decoding the Legal Debates' in Philipp Hacker et al. (eds.), *Regulating Blockchain. Techno-Social and Legal Challenges* (Oxford University Press 2019).

72 Hilary J. Allen, 'Regulatory Sandboxes' (2019) 87 *Geo Wash L Rev* 579, 592 (declaring that the United Kingdom adopted a regulatory sandbox for fintech in 2016, and Australia, Bahrain, Brunei, Canada, Hong Kong, Indonesia, Malaysia, Mauritius, the Netherlands, Singapore, Switzerland, Thailand, and the United Arab Emirates have followed suit in adopting some form of regulatory sandbox model). See also Dirk A. Zetzsche, Ross P. Buckley, Janos N. Barberis, and Douglas W. Arner, 'Regulating a Revolution: From Regulatory Sandboxes to Smart Regulation' (2017) 23 *Fordham J Corp & Fin L* 31.

73 Allen, ibid.

74 See Magnuson (n 11) 183–184.

75 The notion 'lex cryptographica' is adopted by De Filippi and Wright (n 15) 5.

76 See generally Pietro Ortolani, 'The Impact of Blockchain Technologies and Smart Contracts on Dispute Resolution: Arbitration and Court Litigation at the Crossroads' (2019) 24 *Unif L Rev* 430.

77 See Section 16.2.

world and resolve their disputes off-chain. The issue is of high importance, as the practical difficulties of solving possible disputes between the parties could obscure the advantages connected to contractual automation.[78]

On this, one of the starting points in the discussions about dispute resolution in the field of blockchain is the observation that nowadays regular courts are not well enough equipped to face the challenges arising from the execution of lines of code.[79] This claim could perhaps be correct at this stage, but it does not rule out courts acquiring the capacity to tackle such disputes in the future. In reality, a part of the industry is attempting to realize a well-organized and completely independent jurisdiction in the digital world through the intervention of particular types of oracles, which are usually called 'adjudicators' or 'jurors'.[80]

Whether such a dispute resolution model can work strictly depends on the coding of the smart contract. As seen before,[81] once a smart contract is running, in principle neither party can stop the protocol, reverse an already executed transaction, or otherwise amend the smart contract. Therefore, the power to interfere with the execution of the smart contract should be foreseen ex ante and be granted to a trusted third party. The latter is allowed to make determinations beyond the smart contracts' capabilities. It will feed the smart contract with information and, if necessary, influence its execution in order to reflect the trusted third parties' determination.[82]

Independence from the traditional judiciary is granted by 'routine escrow mechanisms'. Rather than paying the sale price directly to the seller, the latter is kept in escrow by a third party. If no disputes arise from the contract, the funds held in escrow will be unblocked in favour of the seller.[83] Nowadays, platforms adopt sophisticated systems based on 'multi-signature addresses', which do not really give exclusive control of the price to the third party involved as an adjudicator.[84] This

[78] Falco Kreis and Markus Kaulartz, 'Smart Contracts and Dispute Resolution – A Chance to Raise Efficiency?' (2019) 37 ASA *Bulletin* 336, 339 (affirming: 'If the parties revert to traditional means to resolve their dispute, the efficiency gained during the period of the contract performance will likely be significantly impaired').

[79] Markus Kaulartz, 'Smart Contract Dispute Resolution' in Fries and Paal (n 26) 73, 74–75.

[80] See, e.g., the 'Aragon Project' implemented on Ethereum is defined on the official website as 'a dispute resolution protocol formed by jurors to handle subjective disputes that cannot be resolved by smart contracts' (https://aragon.org/blog/aragon-court-is-live-on-mainnet). For other examples, cf. Amy Schmitz and Colin Rule, 'Online Dispute Resolution for Smart Contracts' (2019) *J Disp Resol* 103, 116–122.

[81] See Section 16.3.

[82] Kreis and Kaulartz (n 77) 341.

[83] See Ortolani (n 76) 433; Schmitz and Rule (n 80) 123.

[84] The system is described by Ortolani, ibid., 434, as follows: 'This device essentially works like a lock with two keyholes; it can only be opened if two keys are used. Two parties entering into a transaction can use this device to store coins (for example, the price for the sale of certain goods), until the obligations arising out of that transaction have been performed. Both parties are provided with a digital key to the address; if no dispute arises, they can use the two keys to unlock the coins, jointly determining their final destination (typically, the address of the seller). In case of a dispute, however, neither party can access the coins autonomously, but either of them can ask a private adjudicator to

should amount to an additional guarantee in favour of the contracting parties.[85] The outcome is a kind of advanced ODR system,[86] which is particularly suitable in the high-volume, low-value consumer complaints market.[87]

The autonomous dispute resolution system is not considered a modern form of the judiciary.[88] It is presented as a return to the ancient pre-Westphalian past, where jurisdiction did not usually emanate from state sovereignty but from a private service, largely based on the consent of the disputing parties. Nevertheless, given the development of the modern state judiciary, there are many problematic aspects related to dispute resolution on blockchain platforms. For instance, it has been pointed out that: the decision is granted by subjects who do not necessarily have a juridical knowledge (often selected through a special ranking based on the appreciation of users), the decision cannot be recognized by a state court as happens with an arbitral award, and that enforcement does not respect time limits and safeguards provided by regular enforcement proceedings.[89]

With respect to the aforementioned issues, the fear is that such advanced ODR systems based on rules which are autonomous from the ones of national legal systems may limit the importance of the latter in regulating private relationships.[90] On the other hand, some authors affirm that such procedures, under certain conditions, may become a new worldwide model of arbitration.[91]

Also, in this case, the advantages of the dispute resolution procedures are strictly connected to the self-enforcement character of the decision. The legitimacy of such proceedings must be carefully assessed; the outcome should not necessarily be considered unlawful. The parties voluntarily chose to be subject to the scrutiny of the adjudicator, and from a private law perspective, the situation does not differ significantly from the case of a third arbitrator that determines the contents of the contract. In addition, the scope of automated enforcement does not tackle the entire estate; the assets that are subject to the assignment decided by the adjudicator are made available by the parties on purpose. It is not yet clear how far such proceedings will spread or whether they could functionally substitute for state court proceedings.

review the facts of the case and determine which of the two disputants is entitled to the disputed funds.'

85 See also the proposals of Wulf A. Kaal and Craig Calcaterra, 'Crypto Transaction Dispute Resolution' (2017–2018) 73 *Bus Law* 109.

86 Schmitz and Rule (n 80) 114–124 (envisaging an 'ODR clause' to be implemented in the smart contracts).

87 See generally Richard Susskind, *Online Courts and the Future of Justice* (Oxford University Press 2019) 260–262.

88 Ortolani (n 76) 434.

89 Ortolani (n 76) 435–438.

90 See Christoph Althammer, 'Alternative Streitbeilegung im Internet', in Florian Faust and Hans-Bernd Schäfer (eds.), *Zivilrechtliche und rechtsökonomische Probleme des Internet und der künstlichen Intelligenz* (Mohr Siebeck 2019) 249, at 266–269.

91 See Gauthier Vannieuwenhuyse, 'Arbitration and New Technologies: Mutual Benefits' (2018) 35 *J Int'l Arb* 119.

Needless to say, in the absence of a specific recognition made by legal rules, these dispute resolution mechanisms are subject to the scrutiny of state courts.[92] Although it could be difficult in practice, the party who does not agree with a decision, which is not legally recognizable, may sue the competent state court in order to have the dispute solved.

16.7 CONCLUSION

The actual dangers caused by the creation of private powers on blockchain platforms are related to the technology that grants automation of the contractual relationship. On the one side, if rights and legal guarantees are excluded or limited the adoption of self-enforcement devices should of course be considered unlawful. On the other side, however, in principle every situation has to be carefully assessed, as the contracting parties have freely chosen to enter into a smart contract.

Problems may exist when smart contracts are used as a means of self-help imposed by one of the contracting parties. An automated application of remedies may harm the essential interests of the debtors. Nevertheless, automation does not seem to infringe debtor's rights if enforcement is compliant with deadlines and legal steps provided by the law. Moreover, some economic advantages arising from automation may produce positive effects for whole categories of users and self-enforcement could also become an efficient tool in the hands of the European legislator, in order to significantly augment the effectiveness of consumer protection.

In the light of the issues examined herein, if the technology wishes to augment user trust about the functioning of smart contracts and blockchain, it should not aim to abandon the law.[93] To be successful in the long run, innovative enforcement and dispute resolution models should respect and emulate legal guarantees. Smart contracts are not necessarily constructed with democratic oversight and governance, which are essential for a legitimate system of private law.[94] A widespread acceptance of new services requires that the main pillars on which legal systems are based should not be erased.

[92] Möslein (n 45).

[93] See Kevin Werbach, 'Trust, but Verify: Why the Blockchain Needs the Law' (2018) 33 *Berkeley Tech LJ* 487.

[94] See Mark Verstraete, 'The Stakes of Smart Contracts' (2019) 50 *Loy U Chi LJ* 743.

For EU product safety concerns, contact us at Calle de José Abascal, 56–1°,
28003 Madrid, Spain or eugpsr@cambridge.org.

www.ingramcontent.com/pod-product-compliance
Ingram Content Group UK Ltd.
Pitfield, Milton Keynes, MK11 3LW, UK
UKHW020400140625
459647UK00020B/2572
* 9 7 8 1 1 0 8 8 2 3 8 9 0 *